COMPLETE FAMILY
HISTORY BIOGRAPHIES
- PART ONE -

Maternal & Paternal

Thompson Family History Biographies, Vol. 10, Ed. 1

Genealogy of Thompson, Russell, Penman, Stoddart, Goodman, Brown, Carl, Hensel, Guise, Workman, Romberger, Updegrove, Reisch, Culp, Schneck, Batdorf, Steiner, Welker, Messerschmidt, Peters, DeHart, Swartz, Koval, Wert, Faber, Shoop, Wertz, Row, Rudy, Frantz, Gieseman, Duncan, Westphals, Kelling, Koppelmann, McCloud, Sarvis, Kankle, Layman, Klein, Raymond, Roush, Overlander, Warner, Gipe, Drust, Anderson, Arnold, Bordner, Emerich, Gaugler, Kelly, Shaffer, Keefer, Arnold(2), Bucher, Mantz, Lively, Culin, Kent, Roberts, et al from Southcentral England, Southeast Scotland, Ireland, East Finland, Central Sweden, South & Northeast Germany, and Northcentral Switzerland emigrated to Pennsylvania, New York, Virginia, and Louisiana; Mazo/Mason, Brown (2), Thompson (2), Shatteen, Morgan, Forsythe, Hampton, Washington, Robinson, Curry, Glover, Frazier et al of Nassau, Bahamas; Africa; Chatham, Jefferson & Washington Counties, GA; and Allendale, Barnwell & Beaufort Counties, SC; Romano, DiSimone, Vitale, Viviano, Carmona, Quintavalle, McCabe, Smith, O'Connor/Connor, Morrison of Sicilia, Italy and Ireland to New York, NY and reference to Barrett, Kilmartin/Gilmartin, Reilly (2), McLean, Brown, Boles, Nocton, DiStefano, Cutumachio, Tully, Kirrane, McGowan et al of Counties Cavan, Mayo & Sligo, Ireland; Palermo, Italy; New York, NY and PA: Wittle, Hummer, Kyle, Whitmoyer, Minick, Yaeger, Sheets, McKim, Stewart, Smith, McKinsey, Fry, Shover, Piper, Shannon, Swoveland, Acri (2), Curcio, Barbuscio Marsico, Buglio, Magnelli, DeStephano, Martino, Sammarco, et al of Ireland; Calabria, Sicily, Italy; Baden-Wurttomborg, Lower Saxony & Rhineland-Palatinate, Germany; and Cumberland, Dauphin, Franklin, Lancaster, Perry & York Counties, PA.

MARC D. THOMPSON

with S.W. Smith, Jack Butler, Mason M. Smith,
Alicia Craig, Jack Smiles & Neil McQueen

Photographs - Front Cover

William Duncan & Charlotte "Lottie" Layman
Sunbury, PA, circa 1905
Pres. by S M Duncan

Mer sott em sei Eegne net verlosse; Gott verlosst die Seine nicht.
(One should not abandon one's own; God does not abandon his own)
-Pennsylvania Dutch saying

ISBN: 978-1945376115

© 2017 Marc D. Thompson

Published by:

VirtuFit, Delray Beach, FL

info@marcdthompson.net

OTHER BOOKS BY AUTHOR

Client Genealogies

Anderson & Bordner Genealogy, © 2016

Armstrong Family History, © 2013

Batdorf & Welker Genealogy, © 2016

Biographies of our Paternal © 2015

Curry Family Biographies © 2016

Duncan & Kelling Genealogy, © 2016

Gaugler & Kelly Genealogy, © 2016

Goodman-Brown Genealogy, © 2016

Hensel & Workman Genelaogy, © 2016

Keefer & Booker Genealogy, © 2016

Layman & Raymond Genealogy, © 2016

Livezly & Kent Genealogy, © 2016

Mazo & Curry Family History, © 2010

McCloud & Searfoss Genealogy, © 2016

Mower Family History, Coming Soon

Overlander & Gipe Genealogy, © 2016

Peters & Swartz Genealogy, © 2016

Photographic Family History © 2016

Romano & O'Connor History, © 2012

Romano Family Biographies, © 2014

Row & Frantz Genealogy, © 2016

Thompson-Penman Genealogy, © 2016

Updegrove & Culp Genealogy, © 2016

Wert & Shoop Genealogy, © 2016

Wittle & Acri Family History, © 2011

Wittle Family Biographies, © 2017

Health & Fitness

Compendium of Virtual and..., © 2015

Fitness Book of Lists, © 2012, © 2016

Fitness for Eternal Moments, © 2016

Fitness for Virtual Training, © 2016

Fitness Quotes of Humorous Inspiration, © 2011, © 2016

Poems...Of Eternal Moments, © 2012

Virtual Personal Training, © 2013

Personal Genealogies

Anderson Family Bios, © 2014

Anderson, Keefer, Gaugler..., © 2014

Batdorf Family Bios, © 2014

Batdorf, Wert, Peters, Row..., © 2013

Bios of Paternal Family, © 2015, © 2016

Bios of Maternal Family, © 2017

Duncan Family Bios, © 2014

Duncan, Layman, McCloud..., © 2014

Thompson Family Bios, © 2015

Thompson Family History, © 2014

Thompson, Hensel, Goodman..., © 2013

DEDICATION

This volume is dedicated to all our family and friends, who selflessly donated information, time, effort, research and love to make this compilation possible.

Harper Thompson

The generations of living things pass in a short time,
And like runners hand on the torch of life.
-Lucretius

ACKNOWLEDGEMENTS

Thanks to my parents, my sisters, and my children for the knowledge and support. Thanks to my history teachers through high school and college and to Ray from Pennsylvania State Library for his early tutelage.

Thanks to my hundreds of cousins, near and far, who have donated their time as well as their long-toiled family histories and to every clerk, registrar, cemetery manager, LDS employee, ancestry.com staff and others who researched in places I couldn't visit.

Thanks the amazing literary talents of S.W. Smith, Jack Butler, Mason M. Smith, Alicia Craig, Jack Smiles, Neil McQueen and Gary Rosenberg. This book is truly the love of thousands.

La connaissance du passe est la cle pour ourvrir l'avenir.
(Knowledge of the past is the key to opening the future)
-Marc D Thompson

CONTENTS

FOREWORD

by Shirley M. Duncan

Why do people seek to learn about their family history? Decades ago, Marc asked me for information about our relatives. He was eager to start the journey into the past. As of today, I believe Marc has answered the question. He wanted to view our lives more fully.

Marc enjoys solving the multitude of mysteries regarding family histories and it is revealed in his family history volumes. While visiting Marc, he asked me to visit a local library to search for information regarding a family's ancestor. Fortunately, I found the information Marc needed.

Suddenly, I realized how searching for long ago addresses, pictures, and families is a wonderful way to reflect back to how and why things happened; in a way, making sense of it all! Marc truly knows how to present the past to each of us as we look toward the future. Allow his thirty years of research skill and efforts take you on a journey around the world!

Duncan family

There is a history in all men's lives.
-William Shakespeare

PROLOGUE

by Marc D Thompson

If I were given the opportunity to live in any era, I would most certainly pick the 1870s. The time was simple and the people were honest. Folks worked hard and took pride in their families, their homes and their reputations. When I look into the eyes of our ancestors from that time period, I feel a link; I would have fit nicely in their time.

The following are some housekeeping points to keep in mind as reading the narratives.

- In most cases, the Anglicized first and middle names were used; e.g., Johann Heinrich is John Henry and Orsala Francesca is Ursula Frances.

- The most commonly found surname was used, whether Anglicized or not.

- The female maiden name was used in most cases, except occasionally when with husband; e.g., photograph of family or double burial headstones.

- The majority of the collateral information was derived from the U.S. Census records and data from cousins' compilations.

- Place names were documented as precisely as possible, using the name of the place as it was at that time in history. For example, parts of Germany were once Prussia, parts of Lebanon County, Pennsylvania were once Lancaster County, Pennsylvania, etc.

- In some cases, the common name was used. Before Pennsylvania's statehood, although it was the Swedish Colony and later the Province of Pennsylvania, simply Pennsylvania was used. Lastly, to preserve privacy, all information on living persons has been removed or privatized.

- In the photo section, these abbreviations are used. r-right, l-left, c-center, w.-with, MNU-maiden name unknown, arrow-pictured under arrow

- I-signifies first ancestors of similar name and II, III designates later generation ancestor with same name, not necessarily father and son

Thompson family

Who we are cannot be separated from where we're from
-Malcolm Gladwell

INTRODUCTION

Genealogy is a lifelong duty. The day we were born or the day we bore children ourselves, we earned a responsibility of passing along our history. We are responsible for the knowledge of our parents and of our grandparents and all their wisdom.

Our duty, therefore, is our heritage—including the names and faces of our forefathers and mothers, the medical history and genetic backgrounds of their blood lines, the princes and the paupers, the photographs and historical places, the tragedies and the joys.

The ancient Scottish bards memorized their royal families, reciting the pedigrees of the Old Scot's Kings regardless of the complexity. The Irish kings would pass down their regal history orally. They would recite a list of names—their kin—noting outstanding events associated with the forbearers. West African families passed down stories from generation to generation.

On and on, the mnemonic Peruvians, the beads of New Zealand, the Indian Cera Kings, the extensive Chinese genealogies, the ancient Japanese string of names. Argument could be said that ALL families have the need for knowledge of their genealogy.

Genealogy was created in order for people to know the history of their lineage, to discover their origins, and to prove blood-lines and royalty. This volume was compiled in response to our deep desire to understand and discover their past. It shall stand as part of the legacy of our ancestry. Our ancestors had wisdom and understanding. They had goals, glories, and personalities.

Our forty-year journey has led to the numerous genealogy volumes and updates of previous volumes. Many genealogies tend to trace a descendant line or the paternal line (single ascendancy). Our purpose was to trace all ancestors with equal perseverance back in time. This is a monumental—if not near impossible—task. We have compiled a pedigree, beginning with our children and with the current emphasis on generations one through ten, although we have completed research as far back as generation 21. Additional collateral ancestral data have begun to be added as of 2015.

The mission of our genealogy books is four fold. First, to amass photographs—as a face can tell a thousand tales—as so much can be learned from them. The second goal is to document the medical background of our ancestors, so our children can lead a healthier life. The third goal is to continue to extend the lineage in order to link to as many relatives as possible. Our final goal leads us to the building of narratives from this amassed information, producing a readable experience of our ancestors and their lives.

Our ancestors are not mere names or dates—they have tales to tell, journeys to document, lives to discover. They have accomplishments and setbacks, which in turn help us with ours. As mentioned in Chapter Three, "Who we are cannot be separated from where we're from," this book therefore allows us to know precisely where we're from.

We are of course a nation of differences,
Those differences don't make us weak,
They're the sources of our strength…
The question is not when we came here,
But why our families came here
And what we did afterward.
-Jimmy Carter

CHAPTER 1
Generation One

Children travel from the heart to the heart

—Swedish proverb

Generation one comprises the folks born from about 1950 to 2000. The following are some of the meanings behind our children's names, our generation (generation one), followed by some very interesting family facts.

Philip Bordner probate

OUR CHILDREN

The following are the derivcations of some our children's names.

Adam: This is the Hebrew word for "man." It could be ultimately derived from Hebrew Adam meaning "to be red," referring to the ruddy color of human skin, or from Akkadian adamu meaning "to make." According to Genesis in the Old Testament Adam was created from the earth by God. There is a word play on Hebrew adamah meaning "earth." He and Eve were supposedly the first humans, living happily in the Garden of Eden until Adam ate a forbidden fruit given to him by Eve. As an English Christian name, Adam has been common since the Middle Ages, and it received a boost after the Protestant Reformation. A famous bearer was Scottish economist Adam Smith.

Andrew: English form of the Greek name Andreas, which was derived from andreios "manly, masculine," a derivative of aner "man." In the New Testament the apostle Andrew, the first disciple to join Jesus, is the brother of Simon Peter. According to tradition, he later preached in the Black Sea region, with some legends saying he was crucified on an X-shaped cross. Andrew, being a Greek name, was probably only a nickname or a translation of his real Hebrew name, which is not known. This name has been common throughout the Christian world, and it became very popular in the Middle Ages. Saint Andrew is regarded as the patron of Scotland, Russia, Greece and Romania. The name has been borne by three kings of Hungary, American president Andrew Jackson and, more recently, English composer Andrew Lloyd Webber.

Ashley: From an English surname which was originally derived from place names meaning "ash tree clearing," from Old English Aesc and Leah.

Until the 1960s it was more commonly given to boys in the United States, but it is now most often used on girls.

Connor: Anglicized form of the Gaelic name Conchobhar which means "dog lover" or "wolf lover." It has been in use in Ireland for centuries and was the name of several Irish kings. It was also borne by the legendary Ulster King Conchobar mac Nessa, known for his tragic desire for Deirdre.

Marie: French and Czech form of Maria. A notable bearer of this name was Marie Antoinette, a queen of France, and Marie Curie, a physicist and chemist who studied radioactivity with her husband Pierre. Latin form of Greek from Hebrew Mary. Maria is the usual form of the name in many European languages, as well as a secondary form in other languages such as English. In some countries, for example Germany, Poland and Italy, Maria is occasionally used as a masculine middle name. This was the name of two ruling queens of Portugal. It was also borne by the Habsburg queen Maria Theresa, whose inheritance of the domains of her father, the Holy Roman Emperor Charles VI, began the War of the Austrian Succession. The meaning is not known for certain, but there are several theories including "sea of bitterness," "rebelliousness," and "wished for child." However, it was most likely originally an Egyptian name, perhaps derived in part from my "beloved" or my "love."

Renae: French form of Renatus. A famous bearer was the French mathematician and rationalist philosopher René Descartes. Late Latin name meaning "born again."

Roman: From the Late Latin name Romanus which meant "Roman."
Sophia: Means "wisdom" in Greek. This was the name of an early, probably mythical, saint who died of grief after her three daughters were martyred.

Legends about her probably arose as a result of a medieval misunderstanding of the phrase Hagia.

Sophia: "Holy Wisdom," which was the name of a large basilica in Constantinople. This name was common among continental European royalty during the Middle Ages, and it was popularized in Britain by the German House of Hanover when they inherited the British throne in the 18th century. It was the name of characters in the novels Tom Jones by Henry Fielding and The Vicar of Wakefield by Oliver Goldsmith.

J. Daniel Angst Burial Church

I guess it hard not to agree,
You say it all depends on money,
And who's in your family tree.
-Supertramp

OUR NAMES

Here is a chart showing from whom our name – first, middle and last - derive from. Our namesakes!

Our Name	Given Name	Middle Name	Surname
Sophia Marie Thompson	*Sophia* Kelly, relative	*Mary* "Mamie" Duncan, g-grandma	John *Thomson*, ancestor
Connor Adam Thompson	Mary O'*Connor*, grandmother	*Adam* Frantz, ancestor	John *Thomson*, ancestor
AndrewRoman Thompson	*Andrew* Hensel, great-grandfather	Paul *Roman*o, grandfather	John *Thomson*, ancestor
Ashley Renae Thompson	*Asher* Prail Row, relative	Michelle *Renae*, mother	John *Thomson*, ancestor
Marc Duncan Thompson	*Mark* Twain, author/ *Marcellus* Culp, rel.	Shirley *Duncan*, mother	John *Thomson*, ancestor
Jill Elaine/Duncan Thompson	*Jill* St. John, actress	*Elaine* Keefer, rel./ Shirley *Duncan*, mot.	John *Thomson*, ancestor
Tory Ann/Saint Thompson	*Tory* Ann Fretz, tennis pro	*Tory Ann* Fretz, pro/ *Saint*, mother	John *Thomson*, ancestor
Gerald Gilbert Thompson	*Gerald* Shultz, relative	*Gilbert* Row, relative	John *Thomson*, ancestor
Harper Bruce Thompson	*Harper* Hensel, relative	Robert *Bruce* Thompson, grandpa	John *Thomson*, ancestor
Myrtle Adeline Batdorf	*Myrtle*, unknown	*Adeline* Wert, grandmother	Johannes *Baddorf*, ancestor
Shirley Mary Duncan	*Shirley* Temple, actress	*Mary* "Mamie" Duncan, mother	Georg *Dankert*, ancestor
Irvin Wilfred Duncan	Irvin, unknown	*Wil*liam, father & *Fred*erick, grandpa	Georg *Dankert*, ancestor
Mamie Lucetta Anderson	*Mary* Bordner, ancestor	*Lucetta* Anderson, grandmother	William *Enderson*, ancestor

TORY ST. SHANNON

Tory: Diminutive of Victoria. Means "victory" in Latin, being borne by the Roman goddess of victory. It is also a feminine form of Victorius. This name was borne by a 4th-century saint and martyr from North Africa. Though in use elsewhere in Europe, the name was very rare in the English-speaking world until the 19th century, when Queen Victoria began her long rule of Britain. She was named after her mother, who was of German royalty. Many geographic areas are named after the queen, including an Australian state and a Canadian city.

Ann: French form of Anna. In the 13th-century it was imported to England, where it was also commonly spelled Ann. The name was borne by a 17th-century English queen and also by the second wife of Henry VIII, Anne Boleyn, the mother of Queen Elizabeth I. This is also the name of the heroine in Anne of Green Gables by Canadian author L. M. Montgomery.

JILL D. THOMPSON

Jill: Medieval English feminine form of Julian. This spelling has been in use since the 13th century, though it was not declared a distinct name from Julian until the 17th century.

Elaine: From an Old French form of Helen. It appears in Arthurian legend; in Thomas Malory's 15th-century compilation Le Morte d'Arthur, Elaine was the daughter of Pelleas, the lover of Lancelot, and the mother of Galahad. It was not commonly used as an English given name until after the appearance of Tennyson's Arthurian Epic Idylls of the King.

MELVALEAN C. THOMPSON

Melvalean Thompson wrote: I am named for my uncle Melvin, but as a child my mother called me Mel for a nickname. I remember nothing of my birth city Savannah as we moved to Philadelphia when I was an infant. I lived with my mom, step-father and siblings. We had a gas stove and my mother prepared delicious meals that we usually ate in the kitchen.

We had electricity and well water and never used kerosene or candles, but we camped very often as a family. What I remember most about my mom was her smile and she taught us how to properly discipline our children. Mom did all the cooking, cleaning, etc. and she taught me to cook and bake. She also taught me to sew and crochet. I was extremely close to mom and my one brother Oliver. Mom worked at home and my step-dad was a counselor at a local high school.

My mom's mother was Cressie Jo but I never knew my grandparents because we had moved from Georgia. I kept in touch with my family, distant and near. I graduated high school, running track as a sport, and also self-taught auto mechanics. We received our mail in a mailbox and we had a dog named Sheba. I was a middle child and remember watching my baby sister and sweeping the steps as a chore. I never received an allowance. After high school I went to culinary school. I got my first job and then I had Tiffany; she was followed by Tyler and Sophia. My children are my most important part of life. I hope people will remember me

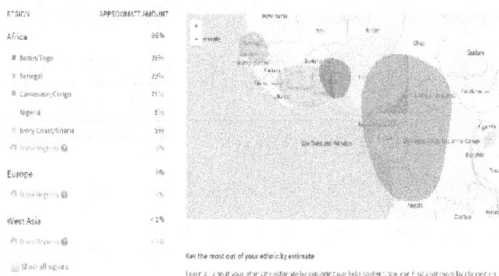

for my honesty, integrity, sense of humor and knowledge. [Mel and Marc D. Thompson, April 2002]

MARC D. THOMPSON

Marc: Form of Marcus. Saint Mark was the author of the second Gospel in the New Testament. He is the patron saint of Venice, where he is supposedly buried. Though in use during the Middle Ages, Mark was not common in the English speaking world until the 19th century, when it began to be used alongside the classical form Marcus. In the Celtic legend of Tristan and Isolde, this was the name of a king of Cornwall.

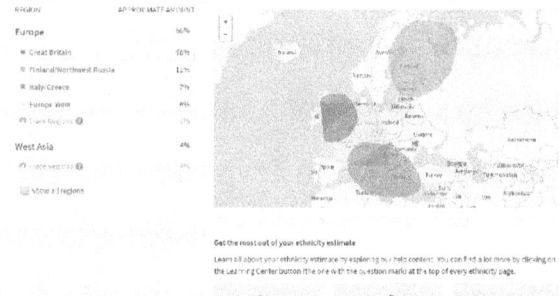

It was also borne by the American author Mark Twain—real name Samuel Clemens—the author of Tom Sawyer and Huckleberry Finn. He actually took his pen name from a call used by riverboat workers on the Mississippi River to indicate a depth of two fathoms. This is also the usual English spelling of the name of the 1st-century BC Roman triumvir Marcus Antonius.

Marc in other languages

American	English	French	German	Scottish	Swedish
Mark	Marcus	Marc	Markus	Marcas	Marcus
Duncan	Duncan	Forte	Dankert	Donnchad	Dankert
Thompson	Thomson	De Thomas	Thomsohn	Thomson	Tomasson

Duncan: Anglicized form of the Gaelic name Donnchadh meaning "brown warrior," derived from Gaelic donn "brown" and cath "warrior." This was the name of two kings of Scotland, including the one who was featured in Shakespeare's play Macbeth. Originally German Dunkart, a North German nickname from Middle Low German dunker meaning "dark," "conceited," or "unclear."

Marc's Favorite Teams

The Best!				
Football	Miami Dolphins	Dallas Cowboys	Denver Broncos	Seattle Seahawks
Basketball	Philadelphia 76ers	Dallas Mavericks	Denver Nuggets	Portland Trailblazers
Baseball	Philadelphia Phillies	Texas Rangers	Colorado Rockies	Seattle Mariners
Hockey	Florida Panthers	Dallas Stars	Colorado Avalanche	San Jose Sharks
College	PSU Lions	Texas Longhorns	Air Force Falcons	Washington Huskies
Honorable Mention				
Miami Hurricanes	Florida Gators	FAU Owls	Texas State Bobcats	SMU Mustangs

INTERESTING FACTS

Through the research of the TFH, we have discovered that we are related to some famous and infamous folks, and even found that there are some areas of the world named for our distant families.

We are direct-line descendants of William Duke of Jülich-Cleves-Berg and Maria of Austria, Duchess of Jülich-Cleves-Berg, Countess Clothilde de Valois de Reni and Jacques de Sellaire, Von Zeller of Castle Zellerstein of Zurich, John Thomson of Haddington, Johann La Hentzelle of Lorraine, General John Benfield of Normandy, Henri Banage de Beauval of Rouen, Alexander Thompson of Schuylkill, the Guerne family of Eschert, the Bager family of Wiesbaden, the Emmerich family of Delkenheim, the Batdorf family of Darmstadt, the Gaukel family of Miltenberg and the Lotz family of the Palatinate.

We are direct-line descendants of soldiers who sacrificed for our freedom: Civil War servicemen Andrew G. Hensel and Daniel Updegrove, and possibly Elijah Anderson and Thomas E. Batdorf. War of 1812 servicemen Adam Frantz, Andrew W. Hensel and Joseph Workman, and possible William Row and John Gipe.

Revolutionary War servicemen Andrew Messerschmidt, Andrew Miller, Frank Row, Henry Bucher, Jacob Lehman, Jacob Livezey, Jacob Philip Bordner, Jacob Rudy, John Adam Guise, John Balthaser Romberger, John Casper Hensel, John Conrad Bucher, John Daniel Angst, John Faber, John George Herrold, John George Schupp, John Henry Reiman, John Jacob Loyman John Miller, John Peter Braun (British), John Peter Shaffer, Jonas Rudy, Michael Garman, Michael Leyman, Nicholas Mantz, Peter Keefer, Valentine Welker, and William Anderson.

Our children's maternal lines include WWII servicemen Ed Mazo, Percy Forsythe and Robert Forsythe; WWI serviceman Raymond Barbush; and Civil War servicemen Cyrus Shannon, Jacob Wittle, John Shover, John Minnick, and Sebastian Shover.

Emma Livezly Keefer

We are collateral descendants of Presidents Dwight D. Eisenhower and William McKinley; Pennsylvania politicians Samuel Pennypacker, John Morton, and Jonas Row; Civil War Brigadier General Galushia Pennypacker; entertainers Marlon Brando, Les Brown, and Ray W. Brown; religious leaders Conrad Weiser and Michael Enderline; and famed Melba Dodge, Jesse Runkle, Enrico Caruso, and Galla Curci. Lastly, Taylor Wittel lists relations to James Madison, Zachary Taylor, Jefferson Davis, and Gene Autry.

Our ancestors' names have been immortalized at these locations: the Bager Homestead, Abbottstown, Pennsylvania; the Chris Miller Homestead, North Lebanon Township, Pennsylvania; the Benfield homestead, Berks Co., Pennsylvania; the Livesey Homestead, Philadelphia, Pennsylvania; the Wirth Homestead, Dauphin Co., Pennsylvania; the Keefer Homestead in Berks, Pennsylvania; the Morton Homestead in Chester, Pennsylvania; the Herrold Homestead in Northumberland, Pennsylvania; and the Jacob Lehman Homestead in Hanover, Pennsylvania. Additionally, these place names were named after our forbearers: Bordnersville, Kelly Crossroads, Livesey Street, Herrold's Island, Keefer's Station, Deibler's Gap, Deibler's Dam, and Shoemakertown, all in Pennsylvania.

The approximate percentages of relatives' birthplaces are: 45% born in Pennsylvania, 17% Germany, 14% Scotland, 9% Italy, 4% Georgia, 4% South Carolina, 4% Ireland, 2% New York, and 1% Africa, Virginia, Florida, Switzerland, England, Bohemia, France, Sweden, Finland, and the West Indies.

At the moment, our paternal line breaks down to about 11/16 German, 3/16 Britain, 1/16 French, 1/16 Swiss. Our maternal line breaks down to about 10/16 German, 4/16 Britain, 1/16 French, 1/16 Swiss/Scandinavian. Our children's maternal lines break down to 7/16 Italian, 4/16 African, 2/16 Irish, 2/16 German, 1/16 West Indian/Britain.

This and the following Family History narratives are our heritage. With this information we can be proud of ourselves and our past, and aim toward bright futures and better lives. If our duty is neglected, as each generation passes, so will our family history.

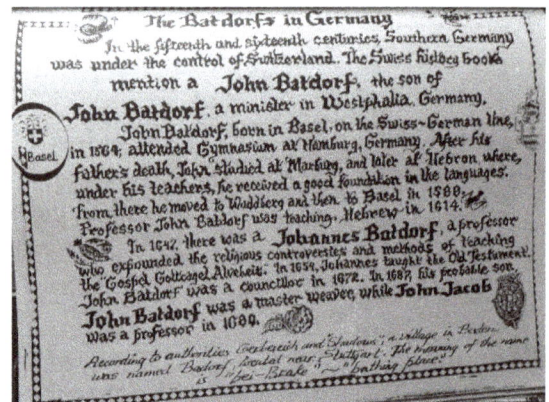

We have a desire and we have a bond. We have a desire to know from whence we came. We want to know our history, our origins. We want to know what our ancestors did, how they persevered and how the spark of life made its way from Geoffrey Livesay, born over 600 years ago, to our latest cousin, born just this winter 2015.

Fame is the inheritance not of the dead, but of the living.
It is we who look back with lofty pride to the great names of antiquity.
-William Hazlitt

Here are some interesting TFH factoids.

3 Ancestors who died at sea: N. Benesch, G. Reith & G. Shoemaker
3 Ancestors named Ashley or Renae
5 Number of birth states
8 Ancestors named Gerald or Gilbert
8 Most different lines with same surname: Miller, Mueller, etc.
10 Generations, FTM lines only (numerous)
11 Number of birth countries
14 Youngest age having child, female: Anna Maria Hamm & Anna Barbara Knerr
17 Youngest age having child, male, John George Werner
17 Number of children, one couple, Mary Louisa Peters/ Thomas Edward Batdorf
18 Youngest age at death, female: Emma Keefer
21 Generations, FTM & additional lines (Livesay)
22 Number of children, one man, Isabelle Penman & Mary Bast/Alexander Thompson
24 Ancestors named Sophia or Marie
24 Most letters in name, male: Howard Andrew Carson Hensel
27 Most letters in name, female: Amelia Dorothy Elizabeth Bager
30 Youngest age at death, male: William Duncan
34 Ancestors named Andrew or Roman 34 Media records, collateral lines
50 Oldest age having child, female: Veronica Schmidt
50 Most variations for single surname: Batdorf, Bodorff, Batterff, Pottorf, etc.
57 Ancestors named Connor or Adam
59.6 Average lifespan, all lines
63.2 Average lifespan, Thompson lines
68 Oldest age having child, male: Alexander Thompson
94 Oldest age at death: Sarah Faber, Anna Bleymeyer & Michael Goodman
256 Ancestors named Shirley or Mary
412 Media records, Thompson lines
491 Media records, all lines
569 Direct-line ancestors, Thompson lines
776 Place names, Thompson lines
870 Direct-line ancestors, all lines
923 Sources used, Thompson lines
983 Total surnames, Thompson line
1,328 Sources used, all lines
1,371 Place names, all lines
1,230 Total surnames, all lines
4,675 Sources checked, Thompson lines
5,801 Relatives, Thompson lines
5,825 Sources checked, all lines
8,569 Relatives, all lines
1410 Earliest birth, unrecorded lines, Geoffrey Livesay
1689 Earliest birth, recorded lines, John Wendel George Traut

CHAPTER 2
Generation Two

Generations pass like leaves fall from our family tree.
Each season new life blossoms and grows benefiting from
the strength and experience of those who went before.
—Heidi Swapp

Our parents are including in the second generation, comprising those born in Pennsylvania from about 1930 to 1950. To place ourselves in our parent's generations, one must understand the occurrences of the time just preceding their births.

Here are the derivations of their names and a brief summary of Pennsylvania's happening from 1910 to 1930, leading into our paremnt's brith periods.

Shirley Duncan

THE THOMPSON FAMILY

As this family is still living, most information is private. Please enjoy this historical text.

1910s.

Pennsylvania Railroad began service to New York City. Rayon was 1st commercially produced by Marcus Hook in Pennsylvania. In Philadelphia John Wanamaker's The Grand Depot department store was replaced by a 250-foot tall, 12-story edifice known as Wanamaker's. Bellevue Park, first planned neighborhood in central PA, was built. The Philadelphia Athletics, forerunners of the Oakland A's, won the World Series, beating the New York Giants of the National League, today's SF Giants. Rotary Club, First Service Club in Harrisburg, opened. The football team of PA's Carlisle Indian School, with running back Jim Thorpe, defeated the Army team, with Dwight D. Eisenhower as linebacker, 27-6. Engraver George T. Morgan is believed to have produced five Liberty Head V nickels at the Philadelphia Mint with a 1913 stamped date. Leopold Stokowski was hired as the music director of the Philadelphia Orchestra. Harrisburg Riverwalk construction begun. Perry Como, singer, was born in Canonsburg.

The first drive-in automobile service station, built by Gulf Refining Co., opened in Pittsburgh. In Pennsylvania a fire at the Red Ash colliery ignited a coal mine. As of 2009 it was still burning and was the oldest of 36 ongoing mine fires. The transit company reorganized as "Harrisburg Railways." Harrisburg City Beautiful continues, raises money with bonds and City library opened. Geisinger Health Systems was founded in PA. Great Migration brings many black workers to Harrisburg's steel mills.

The Mercer Museum in Doylestown was completed by Henry Chapman Mercer, archeologist and collector. Bethlehem Steel takes over Pennsylvania Steel Company in Steelton. A munitions factory explosion at Eddystone, killing 133 workers. Bernstein, artist, helped found the Philadelphia Ten, a female art group. John G. Johnson, Philadelphia lawyer, died and left his home a collection of Renaissance art to the city. Outbreak of Spanish Influenza. A TNT explosion in chemical factory in Oakdale, killed 200. A race riot in Chester left three blacks and two whites dead. Milton Hershey endowed the Milton Hershey School with $60 million in stock. The influenza epidemic killed 11,000 people in Philadelphia. Penn-Harris Hotel constructed in Harrisburg. African-American YMCA branch established.

1920s

The first radio broadcast of presidential elections in the United States were made by radio. Westinghouse had built radio station KDKA on its factory roof in Pittsburgh and was among the first to broadcast returns from the Harding-Cox presidential election. 8MK, the first US station owned by a newspaper, also broadcast the election returns. The 1st Thanksgiving Parade was held in Philadelphia. The last trolleys were acquired. Electricity begins to become available for most households. Religious services were first broadcast on radio. Police in Sunbury issued an edict requiring women to wear skirts at least four inches below the knee. The first radio broadcast of a baseball game took place in Pittsburgh. Baldwin Locomotive Works in Philadelphia built Engine 2472. The Philadelphia Phillies beat the Chicago Cubs 26-23. John Wanamaker, US merchant who founded a chain of stores in Philadelphia, died.

Mennonites from Canada and Pennsylvania fled persecution and settled near Chihuahua, Mexico. The 18-story Philadelphia Inquirer building was completed as home for the Philadelphia Inquirer newspaper. First radio station begins to broadcast. Decline in trolley ridership began on both sides of the river. Dr. Albert C. Barnes built a mansion to house his collection of French art masterpieces in Merion. The Pottsville Maroons beat the Chicago Cardinals for the NFL championship, but lost it on a technicality. Gene Tunney defeated Jack Dempsey for the World Heavyweight Boxing championship in Philadelphia. Market Street Bridge widened from two lanes to four and part of the Capitol complex, State Street Bridge, built, in Harrisburg. The 1st armored commercial car hold-up in US took place in Pittsburgh. The Great Depression begins.

GERALD G. THOMPSON

Gerald: From a Germanic name meaning "rule of the spear," from the elements ger "spear" and wald "rule." The Normans brought this name to Britain. Though it died out in England during the Middle Ages, it remained common in Ireland. It was revived in the English-speaking world in 19th century.

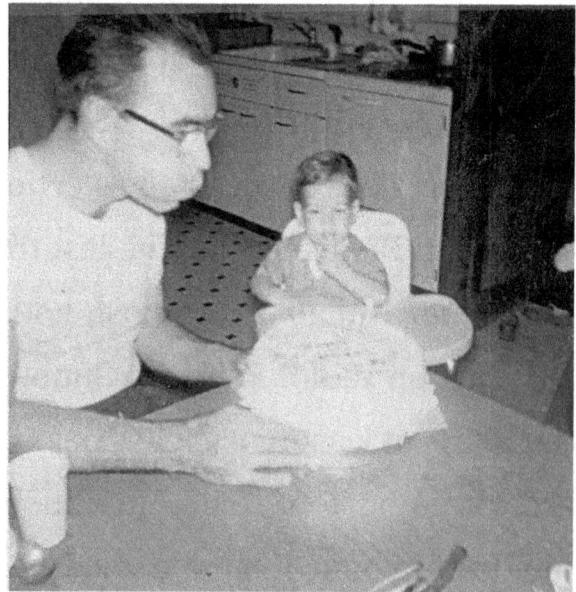

Gilbert: Means "bright pledge," derived from the Germanic elements gisil "pledge, hostage" and beraht "bright." The Normans introduced this name to England, where it was common during the Middle Ages. It was borne by a 12thcentury British saint, the founder of the religious order known as the Gilbertines.

Gerald Gilbert Thompson was counted in the census in 1940 in Tower City, Schuylkill County, Pennsylvania. Political Party: (Democrat) He was affiliated with the Catholic religion. He had a medical condition of Blood type O+, arthritis, hypertension, cataracts. He was named after Cousins Gerald L. Shultz.

Gerald G. Thompson writes: I left home at seventeen for service, felt very alone, and misunderstanding about war. When I returned my first regular job was making 50-cents a day delivering on a milk truck. Eventually I worked as an electrician for forty years. I belonged to IBEW, American Legion, Moose lodge, Knights of Columbus, and 998 Color Guard, Dauphin County VHC. I listened to all types of music except Heavy Metal. The first President I recall voting for was Ike [who turns out to be a relative] and at 22, I married and had three children. Our biggest problem was financial but we enjoyed holidays and birthdays together. The best times were when we had our friends around. We didn't travel but occasionally work took me to New York, New Jersey and Delaware. My firmest rule was that my kids had to be in by 9 pm each night and I always tried to teach them survival, independence, faith and truth. I believe that Faith will overcome all. I think the biggest advance in my lifetime has been computers and the thing that disturbed me the most was war. I consider my two best achievements seeing my children in adulthood and teaching others in the trades. My biggest influences were my father, an honest hard-working man, and JCV Lahr, who stressed always doing the best you can. Volunteering at the Honor Guard has made the largest and longest lasting impression on me. I believe in friendship, honor, truth, your word and love, especially when you don't expect it. The best piece of advice I can give is money is not the most important part of life, health is! [Gerald G. Thompson & Marc D. Thompson, May 1990].

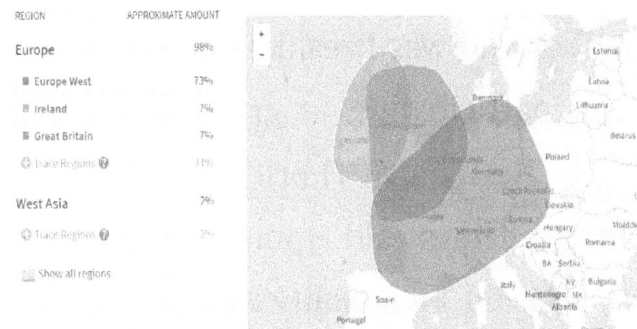

REGION	APPROXIMATE AMOUNT
Europe	98%
Europe West	73%
Ireland	7%
Great Britain	7%
Trace Regions	11%
West Asia	2%
Trace Regions	2%
Show all regions	

Gerald was born in Lykens, Pennsylvania, and grew up with two brothers, Bob and Eugene. He graduated from William Penn High School in 1953. While in high school, he was highly involved in the electrical shop class and a member of the stage crew for the theatre productions. After high school, Gerald enlisted in the Air Force and completed his three-year contract, during which he inspected and repaired motors. He was stationed at Lake Geneva in New York. After military service, Gerald worked for the US Postal Service and then went on to enroll in the IBEW electrical apprenticeship program. He later married and had three children, Tory, Jill and Marc. Although they did not travel much, he remembered a trip that they took to Atlantic City. When asked what was so memorable about it he replied, "It was memorable because we were all together as a family." Gerald worked as a master electrician most of his life, inspecting houses. He also worked as an instructor of an electrical class at Cumberland Perry County Vo-Tech. Gerald became involved in the American Legion in 1972. As his membership continued over the years, he eventually became the President of the color guard for Post 998, located on Derry Street in Harrisburg. He is also a charter member and was President of the Dauphin County Honor Guard for many years, participating in graveside services for departed service members. [Meet a Resident at Thornwald Home, By Brent Winder, Director of Lifestyle Services, Thornwald Home; Author, 1990]

Gerald Personality Analysis: Gerald is a friendly and conservative man; he is warm hearted and enjoys social events. In particular he enjoys social events where the act of socializing is formal and planned in advance. He is a versatile man and can get along with a wide variety of different types of people as he enjoys lively and conversations. This versatility is born of sensitivity; rather than be subject to the critical nature of others he has developed ways of adapting to different types of company and social

settings. It is clear that his energy patterns have changed over the years and today, where he may lack the natural vitality that he enjoyed in previous years he still maintains stamina through determination and tenacity and is lively, natural and curious. Although he can appear to be at ease and in balance Gerald is often tense, an offshoot of his once competitive nature. He would benefit greatly from finding an activity that he enjoys in a natural fashion and that gives him pleasure such that he can relax on a regular basis. Gerald is an alert man, his mind is constantly active and in search of mental stimulus. He enjoys problem solving and is capable of rational and abstract thinking. He has a great desire for knowledge and was always happy to share his findings on those subjects closest to his heart. The writing reflects a relatively complex person who may be easy to socialize with but is not that easy to get to know in a deep way. Gerald may be a defiant and opinionated person but is always accommodating and ready to help those he loves. Looking at the individual words it is clear that dates and places are of particular importance to Gerald. Not only is the date of the letter is placed in the center middle but interestingly the historical date is written in a full and clear manner highlighting his interest in history. He seems to have mixed feelings towards Germany as the word is initially written in a full manner and then in a lean and narrow way. The most uncomplicated and full word in the whole letter is the word 'DAD'. It is written with the most time and care of any word and I can only surmise that this is an aspect of life that he finds most fulfilling. Progression between 1955 and 2008: The biggest difference in the two samples is the pressure. The signature written in 1955 has a great deal more pressure than the text that was written in

2008. This means that naturally he had more energy and drive in 1955 than 2008. As he become older it appears that he enjoyed spending more in his own company. This is evident from the fact that in the text the words are much more clearly spaced. There is also a greater variability in the spacing between letters which would indicate a more flexible attitude towards close relationships also. Where the stroke in the signature is pasty and distinct, the script in the text is sharp. Again this is quite a natural progression; as a young man he enjoyed the more material aspects of life and as he became older he then became more cerebral and tended to analyses things from afar more than actually becoming involved. There is also a notable difference in the style although this cannot be conclusive without seeing a signature from 2008. The style in the text is much more simplified; for example, there are no knots within the loops. Although the text is a mix of print and cursive it is plain to see that it is less elaborate and more simplified. As Gerald became older perhaps he saw the merits in a less complicated and more open and communicative way of living.

Give me your tired, your poor,
Your huddled masses yearning to breathe free,
The wretched refuse of your teeming shore.
Send these, the homeless, tempest-tossed, to me:
I lift my lamp beside the golden door.
-Emma Lazarus

SHIRLEY M. DUNCAN

Shirley: From a surname which was originally derived from a place name meaning "bright clearing" in Old English. This is the name of the main character in Charlotte Bronte's semi-autobiographical novel Shirley. The child actress Shirley Temple helped to popularize this name.

Mary: Usual English form of Maria, the Latin form of the New Testament Greek names and, which were from Hebrew Miryam, a name borne by the sister of Moses in the Old Testament. The meaning is not known for certain, but there are several theories including "sea of bitterness," "rebelliousness," and "wished-for child." However, it was most likely originally an Egyptian name, perhaps derived in part from "my beloved" or "my love." This is the name of several New Testament characters, most importantly Mary, the virgin mother of Jesus, and Mary Magdalene. Due to the Virgin Mary this name has been very popular

REGION	APPROXIMATE AMOUNT
Europe	96%
Ireland	24%
Scandinavia	20%
Great Britain	16%
Europe West	14%
Italy/Greece	9%
Europe East	7%
Trace Regions	6%
West Asia	4%
Trace Regions	4%
Show all regions	

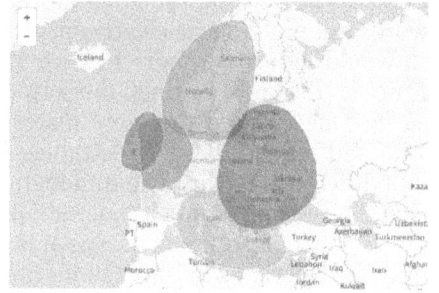

in the Christian world, though at certain times and in some cultures it has been considered too holy for everyday use. In England it has been used since the 12th century, and it has been among the most common feminine names since the 16th century. The Latinized form Mariais also used in English as well as in several other languages. This name has been borne by two queens of England, as well as a Queen of Scotland—Mary Queen of Scots. Another notable bearer was Mary Shelley, the author of Frankenstein. A famous fictional character by this name is Mary Poppins, from the children's books by P. L. Travers.

Shirley Mary Duncan was counted in the census in 1940 in Hummel's Wharf, Snyder County, Pennsylvania. Political Party: Independent. She was named after Actress Shirley Temple and her mother Mary Anderson. She had a medical condition of Blood type A+, astigmatism, Parkinson's.

Shirley Personality Analysis: Shirley is a woman of consistent, reliable energy. She is able to work steadily and in an organized fashion towards a goal. Her practical and realistic outlook enables her to perceive reality accurately; she is able look at situations and appraise them in a realistic manner such that a reasonable and attainable schedule can be drawn up. Her logical and lively mind would have been and perhaps is highly valued by an employer. Shirley is able to adjust her manner in an appropriate way relative to the circumstances and the parties involved with the intention of reaching an agreeable outcome. Her natural refrain is one of quick minded curiosity and nervous energy however she does not always come across as such and can hide her high energy levels behind a reserved, conservative exterior. She is very interested in culture, literature and to a lesser extent the arts. She is quite open and even opinionated about how she feels regarding such matters and enjoys conversation that revolves around these subjects. Such is her practical nature that she may have found a way of engaging with her cultural interests in a meaningful way such as writing about the topics that interested her or photographing them. Shirley has an enormous amount of mental energy, her mind is incredibly busy and as a result she is meticulous both professionally and around

the home. Her sharp mind gives her great abilities in concentration and also a brilliant memory especially for anything in the written form such as recitals. Academia may well have played a large part in her life. Her mind moves so quickly that it is difficult for her not to become muddled and as a result stressed out. She would benefit enormously from learning when she is about to become over loaded and taking a step back from her activities and relaxing a little. At those times when her mind is overloaded she can, at times, crowd people. Shirley wastes nothing; everything around her she can put to good use. Where others might see Shirley as frugal for her it is a normal way of living; there may have been times when it was necessary to use everything at hand. Naturally she hates to throw anything of use (such as food) away and is quick to admonish others for doing so. Shirley Duncan is an original character with a very sharp mind. She is able to help others and express herself in a very genuine fashion. She administers warmth and affection for those she cares for and also some harsh words for those that she feels could use a little improvement. She is deeply interested in culture and can even be described as culturally acquisitive; as she keenly seeks to gather information about those historical and cultural topics that she connects with. Looking at the individual words that stand out, it is clear that 'restaurant' is written in a different way to the rest of the text. It is written with heavier pressure and the t bar is heavier and more elongated. I can only suppose that this is a facet of life that she enjoys very much and may also have some professional link to. The word 'telephone' is also written in strong and elevated fashion; perhaps she likes to talk on the phone a great deal. The word 'love' on the last line of the third sample leans extensively towards the right and jumps up a huge amount from the line; both changes are reflective of genuine expression.

PATERNAL LINEAGE TEST RESULTS FOR

Your DNA test results show that you belong to haplogroup I1, (formerly I1a) The Stonemasons.

PATERNAL HAPLOGROUP
I1
THE STONEMASONS

This map shows the likely migration pathways of your ancient ancestors, The Stonemasons (haplogroup I1). Your ancestors may have crafted tools and ornaments from stone, and probably lived in present day Scandinavia. To use your test results to build your family tree, visit dna.ancestry.com and learn about other participants with genetic profiles similar to your own.

ancestry | DNA

YOUR HAPLOTYPE

Location	19a	19b	385a	385b	388	389I	389II	390	391	392	393	426	437	438	439	441	442	444	445	446	447	448	449
Value	14	-	13	14	14	12	28	22	10	11	13	11	16	10	11	17	17	13	11	15	22	20	27
Location	452	454	455	456	458	459a	459b	460	461	462	463	464a	464b	464c	464d	464e	464f	GGAAT1 B07	YCAIIa	YCAIIb	Y-GATA-A10	635	Y-GATA-H4
Value	31	11	8	18	15	8	9	12	12	12	24	12	14	15	15				11	19	21	15	23	10

Let me in, let me in,

Immigration man

Can I cross the line and pray

Can I stay another day

-Crosby & Nash

THE MAZO FAMILY

The baby boy who would become Eddie Mazo was born to Mack Mason and Sarah Thompson of Jefferson County, Georgia, on September 7, 1912. Edward was born their fifth child, joining a family that already included two older brothers and two older sisters, Jesse, John, Annie Lee, and Maria. After Edward's birth, siblings Mack, Robert, and Melvin were born to the Masons.

Mack and Sarah Mason named their son Edward Mason after Mack's father, Edward "Ned" Mason. The senior Edward held a special position in the family based on the fact that he represented the last generation of this Mason family to be born a slave. He had had been freed as a young man by Abraham Lincoln's Emancipation Proclamation and guaranteed equality of rights by the 13th, 14th, and 15th Amendments to the U.S. Constitution.

Unfortunately, as soon as Georgia was readmitted to the Union in 1871—the last previously Confederate state to be accepted—Federal troops started pulling out. With the direct threat reduced, former Confederates and their offspring began trying every political trick they could to keep the black Georgians from achieving equality with the whites. By 1916, every black person in Georgia had come to understand the wide gap between what the Federal Government promised and what the state and local governments delivered. Just before Edward Mason's birth, the State of Georgia had gone so far as to issue an official State charter for the rebirth of the Ku Klux Klan, which had been closed down and wiped out by the Federal troops.

To be sure, black people were organizing and working for change—more than a million and a half left the south and moved to the industrial cities of the Northeast and Midwest. The NAACP had been formed in New York in 1909, and was heavily pushing court cases to end lynchings and overturn the Jim Crow laws that legalized racial segregation. They were having some successes, but progress was slow and the families that stayed in Georgia still had lives to live as best they could.

Mack Mason worked hard to provide for his family, sometimes as a farm laborer or a stable hand, and sometimes as a sharecropper farmer. But even for a hard-working man, jobs were not always available for a laborer in rural Georgia. Mack and his family often had to follow opportunity from place to place. When Edward Mason was born, Mack was working as a day laborer at a saw mill in Louisville, Georgia. Day laborers only work when there is a need for them—there was no assurance of working every day.

Circumstances following Edward's birth suggest that Sarah may have had a hard time with the birth, or may have suffered an illness afterwards. As already mentioned Edward was his mother's fifth child in nine years. The strain of so many children, combined with having to shift house and worry about money, may have been too heavy a load. Whatever the reason, the family apparently needed some relief—and the solution that they found would change Edward's life forever. They decided to send Edward to live with his Aunt Ida in her home in Atlanta, Georgia.

When Edward Mason came to her, Ida Jones, a recent widow, was a clothing presser for a department store. She was also already acting as a temporary surrogate mother for a niece named Jeraline Banks. Ida shared a house with three other adult women. Two of them worked outside the house, but one lady stayed at home and made her money by taking in laundry. Also, Jeraline was eleven years old when Edward came so she could act as playmate and sometimes as babysitter for him. She could always call the older woman for help if she needed it. This allowed Ida to work without worrying too much about having an adult close at hand if needed.

The arrangement between Mack and Sarah Mason and Aunt Ida was probably intended to be a temporary one—just a break meant to give Edward's folks a little rest and some breathing room. But month ran into month, and then year ran into year, and it turned out that Edward Mason lived with his Aunt Ida until he was fifteen years old. By then, Ida was referring to him as her son. During these years with Aunt Ida, Edward got most of his schooling, made friends, and first started noticing girls. It was also during these years with Ida that Edward met a man named Mazo, a war hero, who family stories say made a great impression on young Edward and whom he came to greatly admire. Motivated by this admiration—and maybe also by some resentment towards a family that he felt had abandoned him—Edward took it on himself to change his name to Eddie Mazo.

By 1930, the times in Georgia and America had changed—and not for the better. The Jim Crow problems and the Great Depression had roared in, making life much tougher than it had been. Bread lines popped up around Atlanta, and men who had worked all their lives found themselves hoping for a handout. Like tens of thousands of other people, Aunt Ida—who was also getting older—lost her job with the department store. Her younger brother, Wallis Oliver, a recent widower, came to live with them. He, at least, was still working—also as a clothing presser. But even for people who still had jobs, wages were low, money was scarce, and living was difficult.

In April of that year, perhaps to alleviate some of the hardship on Ida, Eddie left his Aunt's house and went to live with the family of Jeraline Banks in Birmingham, Alabama. Henry Banks, Jeraline's father, and Gary Smith, Jeraline's new husband, still had jobs with a freight company. They loaded and unloaded trucks and worked in the warehouse.

The Banks family took Eddie in and called him their adopted son. Since Eddie worked in similar industries for much of his later life, it is likely they also got Eddie at least part-time work with them at some point. But one thing did not change. When the census taker came to the house that year, Eddie was listed as Edward Mazo. And that is how he always introduced himself.

Even though he never lived with his parents, it is likely that Eddie had at least occasional contact with some of his family. When he was in his early twenties, he moved to Savannah, Georgia, where most of the Masons were living at the time. He found a job there working with trucks for the State of Georgia. A few years later, he changed his job direction and found work as a cook.

In Savannah, Edward met and married a woman named Florence, and they soon had a daughter named Constance. The marriage very quickly appeared to be in trouble and continued up and down for some years. In November of 1945, with World War II all but over, the U.S. Army was still recruiting men for the huge job of bringing the boys home and returning U.S. installations to peacetime mode. Eddie enlisted in the Army Air Corps and spent nearly two years in Hawaii. It seems likely that at least part of his motivation was the chance to get away from his troubled marriage.

After he came home from the military, Eddie reunited briefly with Florence, but by the mid-fifties, the marriage was over. Eddie also had a daughter named Sarah with another woman, and he continued to live in Savannah, Georgia, for most of the remainder of his life. It is here in Savannah where Eddie would meet Delores Ann Curry.

Delores was born on February 24, 1948, in Savannah, Georgia, the child of Robert Joseph Forsyth and Cressie Jo Curry. Both of Delores's parents were also natives of Savannah, and Delores grew up and went to school there.

When Delores was in her late teens, she met Eddie and they had a daughter, Melvalean Curry, and a son, both born in the 1960s. Eddie was often not home and Delores had to raise the children with bare necessities. Opportunities for a single black woman with a family in the South were nearly nonexistent. Racism was still rampant and economic viability was low. Delores left Eddie shortly thereafter, moving to Philadelphia, Pennsylvania, and remarrying. She lived out her life in Philadelphia, and died there on December 16, 2000, at the age of 52.

In his last few years, Eddie had moved to Plains, Georgia, where he died on December 20, 1997. Eddie's World War II service in the Army Air Corps earned him the right of burial in a National Cemetery, and he was buried with honors in Section I, Row 682, of the Andersonville National Historic Site in Macon County, Georgia. This famous cemetery began during the Civil War as the final resting place for Union soldiers who perished while POWs at the nearby Confederate Camp Sumter, better known as Andersonville Prison Camp. Eddie and Delores's daughter, Melvalean Curry Thompson, is the family's direct ancestor.

The history of the American Negro
is the history of this strife,
He simply wishes to make it possible for a man
to be both a Negro and an American...
-W.E.B. Du Bois

THE ROMANO FAMILY

As this family is still living, the information is private. Please enjoy this historical text. The name Romano is literally the old Latin word for Roman. While this strongly suggests that the original family member to bear the name came from Rome, it leaves open the possible timelines for the arrival of this family line in Sicily. They may have come with the invading Roman army 22 centuries ago, or the earliest known Romano of this family may have been the immigrant ancestor, arriving in the late 1700s.

The Romano ancestors lived at one point or another over the roughly 165 years of history that we attempt to track in Sicily, including

- Palermo, where the first three generations appear to have lived
- Alia, where the immigrant ancestor, Pietro Romano, was born
- Bronte, where Annetta Carmona was born
- Messina, where Annetta Carmona Romano's family died in the 1908 Earthquake
- Lercara Friddi, the town in which the Romanos lived by the late 1800s and from which they immigrated to the United States in 1914

Sitting very close to the half way point on the road running between Palermo and Agrigento, Lercara Friddi began life as a trading post in the late 1500s. The road from Palermo used to stop at Lercara Friddi. The connection to Agrigento was built during Pietro Paolo Romano's childhood.

"May you live in interesting times!" was said to be a favorite curse among the ancient Chinese. Modern Americans, with their nearly constant search for new ways to avoid boredom, often don't understand how interesting times could be a curse. But nobody ever had to explain that curse to a Sicilian. By the time that our earliest known ancestors appear in the records of the island, Sicilians had been suffering through interesting times for more than 2500 years.

To understand the character and the lives of the Sicilian ancestors, it is necessary to understand the elements that created and shaped those characters and those lives. It is necessary to understand a little of what created the place called Sicily.

Known originally as Trinacria because of its triangular shape, Sicily, with nearly 10,000 square miles of territory, it is the largest island in the Mediterranean Sea. The name Mediterranean is taken from the Latin word mediterraneus meaning, "middle of the Earth". The ancient Greeks called it Mesogeios, meaning "interior or inland." To the ancient Greeks and Romans, the Mediterranean Sea was the center of the Earth as they knew it.

The island sits just off of the southwestern tip of Italy, with less than two miles of sea, known as the Straits of Messina, separating it from mainland Italy. Note that while the northeastern tip of Sicily practically kisses mainland Italy, the southernmost point of the island is only about 100 miles from the African coast. Indeed, parts of the African country of Tunisia are farther north than the southern tip of Sicily.

To the north and northwest are Spain and France, and Italy sits to the due north. In the northeast and east lie Greece, Yugoslavia, Bulgaria, Turkey and Syria, Lebanon, and Israel; and in the southeast Egypt and Jordan, while in the south and southwest we find Libya, Tunisia, Algeria and Morocco. If the Mediterranean was the center of the ancient world, Sicily was very nearly at the dead center of that sea. It was, in simple fact, the gateway to the Mediterranean. Any society or culture venturing out into the Mediterranean seeking trade, conquest, or simply adventure would, sooner or later, encounter the island – and most of them did.

Nearly everyone who came to early Sicily really liked what they saw: a heavily forested, mountainous island with highly fertile coastal plains. The forests to provide timber for building ships, ten thousand years' worth of weathered volcanic ash to create fertile soil and short, moderate winters to provide a long growing season created a jewel to be desired and coveted by nearly all passers-by. And coveted it was, by virtually every adventuring society in the Mediterranean and in Europe as a whole. As a result, Sicily is known to modern historians as the most conquered island in the world.

Recorded Sicilian history begins with the colonization of the island by the ancient Greeks starting about 800 - 750 BC. But Greek mythology indicates that the Greeks knew about Sicily much earlier than that. For example, Homer's epic, Odyssey, has Sicily as the home of the mighty Cyclops and of the sea monsters Scylla and Charybdis.

According to the Greek historian Thucydides, when the Greeks arrived in Sicily they found three distinct groups of people living on the island, the Sicani, the Elymians and the Sicels.

The Sicani were apparently the earliest group of inhabitants on the island. Modern archaeology has shown them to be the likely descendants of cave dwellers who painted on the walls of caves in the Monte Pellegrino area near Palermo. The paintings have been dated to about 8,000 B.C. and show strong similarities to cave paintings found in Spain. This has led some scholars to theorize that the earliest Sicani came from the Iberian Peninsula.

The Elymians are thought by some scholars to have originated in the lands bordering the Aegean Sea. The ancient Greeks claimed that they were descendants of the Trojans. Their true origins are uncertain. They settled in the extreme northwest corner of Sicily, displacing the Sicani in that area and forcing them further south and inland. Despite retaining a separate language, over time, they seem to have largely blended culturally with the Sicani.

The Sicels, or Siculi, after whom the island was eventually named were the latest settlers, arriving around 1200 BC. They spoke an Indo-European language and came from the Italian mainland. The Siculi, like the Elymians before them, displaced the Sicani, eventually settling the eastern end of the island.

There seems to have been a lot of cultural blending of these three groups, probably through intermarriage. Archeology shows almost no difference in the later settlement sites. Undoubtedly, the genes of all of these tribes can be found among the modern Sicilians.

The list of peoples that invaded and eventually took over Sicily reads like a Who's Who of the warlike peoples of Europe and Africa. The Phoenicians (known in the Judeo-Christian Bible as the Canaanites) arrived around 800 BC, then came the Greeks (abt 750-260 BC), the Carthaginians (311-241 BC) Romans (241 BC – 440 AD), Vandals (440-476 AD), Ostrogoths (476 – 535 AD), Byzantines (535 – 831 AD), Saracens (Arabs 831 – 1072 AD), Normans (1072 – 1266 AD), Angevins (early French, 1266 – 1282 AD), Spanish (1296 – 1713 (includes Aragonese), Bourbons, and finally, the Italians.

All of these conquerors left at least some impression on Sicily and its culture. But there are a few of the invaders who deserve further mention:

The Phoenicians - Their superior sea-going skills had made the greatest traders of their day and their trade routes took them to all parts of the Mediterranean and beyond. Sicily was an ideal location for establishing trading centers and the Phoenicians established several trading colonies in western Sicily, including towns that became the current cities of Marsala and Palermo. These colonies were established to promote trade and they made little to no effort to conquer their Sicilian neighbors. During this same period, however, the Phoenicians established the city-state of Carthage on the nearby African coast. The descendants of the Phoenicians and their wars with the Greeks and Romans would make their city-state world famous. And they would include Sicily in their wars and adventures for centuries.

The Greeks, unlike the Phoenicians, did not come to trade - the Greeks came to colonize and occupy new lands. In 750 BC, the Greeks were a series of city-states that some time cooperated and sometimes made war on one another. Greeks came from most of the larger Greek City-States to grab choice sites in Sicily. They settled first in eastern Sicily and spreading across the Island. Within a century, the Sicani, Elymians, and Siculi had been thoroughly Hellenized. While substantial numbers of Sicilians were undoubtedly treated as slaves, others prospered under the Greeks. Despite frequent wars with Carthage, the Greeks ruled most of Sicily for the next 3-4 centuries. Sicily became renowned as the most beautiful part of Magna Graecia (Greater Greece) and was said to have more Greek temples and more Greeks than Greece itself. The city-state of Syracuse, on the Island's southeast coast, was reputed to be the most beautiful city in all of Greece.

The Romans - had adopted much of the Greek culture themselves, felt that they could deal with the Greeks. But when the Carthaginians took Messina, the Romans decided that they could not afford having a force that powerful or that adventurous so close to their domain. So they made a temporary treaty with the Greeks in Syracuse and made war on Carthage. It took them nearly 60 years, but by 212 BC, Rome had all of Sicily as its first

Province. They found that they liked owning another country and they held the island for the next 600 years.

Rome granted Roman citizenship to the inhabitants of a few of the larger cities, but overall Roman occupation cost the average Sicilian a lifetime of poverty and hard work. As a province of Rome, Sicily had to pay taxes of one tenth of its wheat and barley. Tributes were also levied on wine, olives, fruit, vegetables, and even on pasturage. On top of the taxes, the crops that the people were allowed to keep could only be sold to Rome. Cato, a Roman politician and soldier wrote that Sicily was the "Republic's granary, the nurse at whose breast the Roman people is fed." To keep the breadbasket of Rome fulfilling its role, the Romans instituted what turned out to be perhaps the worst curse that they laid on the Sicilians - the latifundia (from the Latin for "spacious farm/estate"). Roman latifundia were parceled out to powerful Romans, retiring soldiers, and, in later centuries, to the church and its ecclesiastical arms. They were usually huge estates and they were closest thing that the ancient world had to modern industrialized agriculture. Lacking the technology of the modern world, the latifundia required slave labor. They enslaved the Sicilians, of course, and when that proved inadequate, they imported thousands of slaves from their wars and conquests elsewhere. This resulted in numerous slave revolts over the centuries and in the crucifixion of thousands of Sicilian rebels. The latifundia also required large expanses of land. When the Romans arrived, the island was largely wooded. But over the centuries the forests of Sicily fell to the latifundia and to provide the wood for fleets of Rome and for wooden buildings for the city itself. Today only a few spotty forests exist on the island.

The Saracens - In 827 AD, they were replaced by the Saracens –Arab Muslims from North Africa. The Saracens ruled Sicily for just over 200 years, but they had a major impact on the island that was long lasting and overwhelmingly positive in economic terms. They removed taxes detrimental to agriculture, added an excellent irrigation system, and introduced oranges, lemons, pistachios, and sugar cane into Sicily's agriculture. The Muslims kept their religion predominant, but there was no harsh persecution of the Christians and no attempt to prevent the practice of the religion.

The Bourbons (French nobles who had taken the crown of Spain through marriage.). The Bourbons took control of Sicily in 1734, and they ruled the Island at the time that the earliest known Romano ancestor was born. They were harsh rulers who used the latifundia and the feudal system to keep the people down and in poverty. Revolutions against them were frequent and it was the excessive force used to put down an 1820 Revolt that led to the creation and spread throughout the island of secret anti-government societies – the largest of which was the Carbonari. Some historians believe that the Mafia also came out of these secret societies. The Bourbons were still ruling Sicily when Pietro Paolo Romano – the ancestor who brought the family to America - was born.

The Italians – There had long been efforts by both mainland Italians and Sicilian sympathizers to join Sicily to Italy. In 1861 a mercenary freebooter named Giuseppe Garibaldi, who had been active in the efforts to unite mainland Italy, landed at Palermo and began an invasion that led directly to Sicily being annexed into Italy. The majority of Sicilians did not accept annexation easily, but in the end they succumbed to their final conquest – they became Italian.

As a result of their history, Sicily never developed self-rule or any real sense of nationalism – it never existed as an independent country. Greece created most of the major cities as City-States, each responsible only to and for itself.

It took 1500 years for the populace to unite and seek self-government. And when they did, it was too little, too late.

The Sicilians suffered oppression at the hands of a foreign – and frequently absentee king/dictator and his locally appointed officials. Governmental justice was so often non-existent or so unfair in its administration that the Sicilians essentially rejected the concept. As a result, the working class, or peasantry, developed a strong distrust of the government and of the wealthy, both foreigners and Sicilians alike.

They held the right of justice or, more frequently, vengeance to themselves. They often refused to speak to or go through governmental agencies – the rule of Omertà was in effect long before the Mafia was fully organized. Secret societies, some aimed at liberation from foreign powers and others at criminal profit, grew out of this resentment and refusal to work with foreign kings.

So did the belief that the only people to be trusted were family and friends that one knew personally. The Sicilians most often chose to depend on the people "within the sound of the bells" – the people who could hear the bells from their local church. Everyone else was a stranger. This continued to be reflected among the Sicilian immigrants - in the Little Italy section of New York; each block tended to be populated by people from a specific Sicilian village or town.

THE WITTLE FAMILY

As this family is still living, the information is private. Please go to Chapter 3 for the next generations, including the Germanand Italian ancestors.

Jacob Wittle

Il sangue non e acqua.
(Blood is thicker than water)

Tutte le strade conducono a Roma.
(All Roads Lead to Rome)
-Italian sayings

CHAPTER 3
Generation Three

Who we are cannot be separated from where we're from
—Malcom Gladwell

Our 4-sets of grandparents comprise the Third Generation and is the starting point for the biographies included in this volume. They were born in early twentieth century in Pennsylvania, Georgia and Italy.

Five sisters of James Anderson

HARPER B. THOMPSON
& MYRTLE A. BATDORF

Harper Thompson was born on September 28, 1907 in Sheridan, Schuylkill County, Pennsylvania to Abel & Gussie Thompson. Harper was counted in the census in 1910 in Porter, Schuylkill County, Pennsylvania. He was counted in the census in 1920 in Porter, Schuylkill County, Pennsylvania. He was employed as a Boxer about Abt. 1929. He lived in Emmaus, Lehigh County, Pennsylvania in 1930. He was employed as a Lineman, Telephone Co in 1930. He and Myrtle were married on June 15, 1935 in St. John's Lutheran, Berrysburg, Dauphin County, Pennsylvania. He was counted in the census in 1940 in Tower City, Schuylkill County, Pennsylvania. He was employed as a Lineman, Bell Telephone Co in 1940. He died on July 23, 1981 in Polyclinic Hospital, Harrisburg, Dauphin County, Pennsylvania. His funeral was in 1981 in Jesse H Geigle, 2100 Linglestown Road, Harrisburg, Dauphin County, Pennsylvania. He was buried in 1981 in Woodlawn Memorial Gardens, Harrisburg, Dauphin County, Pennsylvania.

Myrtle Batdorf was born on January 5, 1918 in Big Run, Dauphin County, Pennsylvania to James & Beulah Batdorf. Myrtle was baptized on October 11, 1918 in Evangelical Lutheran Circuit, Lykens, Dauphin County, Pennsylvania. She was counted in the census in 1920 in Washington,

Dauphin County, Pennsylvania. She was counted in the census in 1930 in Lykens, Dauphin County, Pennsylvania. She was counted in the census in 1940 in Tower City, Schuylkill County, Pennsylvania. Her religious affiliation was Lakeside Lutheran Church. She died on May 8, 1983 in Polyclinic Hospital, Harrisburg, Dauphin County, Pennsylvania. Her funeral was in 1983 in Jesse H Geigle, 2100 Linglestown Rd., Harrisburg, Dauphin County, Pennsylvania. She was buried on May 11, 1983 in Woodlawn Memorial Gardens, Harrisburg, Dauphin County, Pennsylvania. Her estate was probated in May 1983 in Harrisburg, Dauphin County, Pennsylvania.

As they began raising their three sons, Harper and Myrtle began their life renting a home for $9 in 1940 at 335 Main Street, Tower City, Pennsylvania. That is the equivalent of about $150 today.

Gerald G. Thompson writes: My mother Myrtle was a good home maker and my father Harper was quietly powerful. My mother Myrtle was 5'9" tall with brown hair and hazel eyes. She was a housewife and lived in Dauphin County, Pennsylvania and was a Lutheran and a Democrat. She taught all three of us boys to cook and bake. We took turns doing the dishes, and she always made sure we were clean and dressed for school. She was an out-spoken, sometimes loud, when correcting our errs. She was the "mother hen" and she made sure we had the necessities, for they did not have a lot, but love and praise took care of the rest. Dad was very tall and had been a boxer until mom made him work for Postal Service. He was also a lineman I recall and had very large hands. He provided as best he could for our family of five. As a child, we had a dog named Domino and we got our first TV about 1952, that mom said was for part of our education. For what I can remember, up to the early 1940's we lived in Tower City. We moved to East Lane in Middletown in 1942. Six years later relocated to 416 Clinton Street, then to 5th and Radnor Streets and finally to Green Street, all in Harrisburg. We also we spent time with aunt Lydia and uncles Abel and Wilbur. We were closer to the Batdorf family and we usually had cats and dogs as pets. As a child, I was nicknamed Jerry and wanted to simply grow up as a good person. We lived in multi-level home with coal and gas stoves and outside toilets. Although we had electricity, we used kerosene and candles. Initially we had a water pump, but later when we moved to Harrisburg, we had city water. However, we did all bath in one tub to conserve water usage. As a child, we were expected to wash and dry dishes, set table and help in garden. My mother and grandma taught us to cook. When I was a teen, I earned money working on a milk truck, as a paperboy and in food stores. Sundays always meant going to Evangelical Lutheran church and dinner at Grandmas. We also went there for holiday cookouts. We'd have food, games and cookies on special days, even Labor Day and Halloween. In High School we liked the football games between William Penn and John Harris High Schools. At dances they played Big Band and Slow songs, and we said "No way" as a slang term all the time. After graduating with Electrical Training I bought my first car, a Used Terraplane Hudson for $50 in 1955. I learned to drive when I was 18 and we went on vacation to the seashore, maybe once or twice. My family is known for their stubbornness and I learned from my parents to take care of family and then take care of neighbors. [Gerald G. Thompson and Marc D. Thompson, May 1990]

Harper Bruce Thompson was counted in the census in 1910 in Porter, Schuylkill County, Pennsylvania. He was educated at School in 1920. He was counted in the census in 1920 in Porter, Schuylkill County, Pennsylvania. He was employed as a Boxer about 1929. He was employed as a Lineman, Telephone Co in 1930. He lived in Emmaus, Lehigh County, Pennsylvania in 1930. He was counted in the census in 1930 in Emmaus, Lehigh County, Pennsylvania (w/uncle James Knittle). He was employed as a Laborer in 1935. He was employed as a Lineman, Bell Telephone Co in 1940. He was counted in the census in 1940 in Tower City, Porter Township, Schuylkill County, Pennsylvania. He lived in Tower City, Porter Township, Pennsylvania in 1940 (335 Main Street). He lived in Harrisburg, Dauphin County, Pennsylvania in 1972. His Social Security Number was 205-05-3254. He lived in Harrisburg, Dauphin County, Pennsylvania in 1981 (2600 Green Street). He lived in Beaufort Farms, Camp Curtain, Estherton, Fort Hunter, Harrisburg, Hecktown, Lucknow, Rockville, Uptown, Windsor farms, all Dauphin County, Pennsylvania in 1981. He was buried in 1981 in Harrisburg, Dauphin County, Pennsylvania (Woodlawn Memorial Gardens). His funeral took place in 1981 in Harrisburg, Dauphin County, Pennsylvania (Jesse H Geigle, 2100 Linglestown Road). His funeral took place in 1981 in Harrisburg, Dauphin County, Pennsylvania (Lakeside Lutheran Church). He was employed as a Retired mail handler, Harrisburg Post office in 1981 in

Harrisburg, Dauphin County, Pennsylvania. He had medical conditions, cardiac arrest due to clot in brain, cataracts, heart disease, and hernia. His cause of death was cardiorespiratory arrest w/subdural hematoma. He was named after Cousin named Harper and his grandfather Robert Bruce Thompson. He was affiliated with the Lutheran < Methodist religion. Political Party: (Republican)

Harper Personality Analysis: Harper was very persistent, had a fluid mind and was a generous person. Blunt and honest. He had the jealousy stroke in his writing as well. Had a fear of losing one particular person. He had the ability to be diplomatic, and could deliver bad news in a pleasing way. Very emotionally expressive. Would have been a good salesman. Had the ability to put himself in others shoes. Understanding their needs. Harper Personality Analysis II: Upon initial introduction to Harper many would have found him to be a gruff, opinionated and curt individual, however after some conversation he opens up and turns out to be a communicable and likeable individual. Indeed, Harper had no set, tried and tested way of communicating and socializing with others. Where some may have seen him as volatile and ill-tempered others would have known him to be funny, fluid and good humored! Harper was found it very difficult to maintain continuous direction in his life. He may have taken to boxing as a way of countering the frustration that he felt in everyday life born on an inability to maintain consistency in his relationships. Any merits he enjoyed in this sport were won from his skill and tenacity and not from vitality and stamina. His fighting style would have been quite guarded until the opportunity presented itself and then he would have been quick, practical and opportunistic: sharp, upper body jabs! Harper Thompson was a very ambitious man and was quite hard on himself when things were not going as planned. He worked hard and was tenacious but his lack of harmony made it quite difficult for him to catch a break. Another factor that may have hampered him on the road to fortune was his lack of resistance to shortcuts. If Harper saw a way to cut corners and make a quick profit from doing something that might have been slightly out with convention, he would not be able to hold himself back. From the way that the surname is written, in relation to the first name, it is clear that he enjoyed very much thinking about and spending time with his family as they gave him a feeling of relaxation, humor and altruism. From this early acceptance he found himself with enough flexibility and open mindedness to be in possession of an easy charisma; he was confident and amenable. Cheerful and articulate he had the gift of storytelling and would often add, to his tales many colorful and elaborate details.

Harper Thompson, 73, died Thursday at Polyclinic Hospital. He was a member of Lakeside Lutheran Church. A former Postal Service employee, Mr. Thompson is survived by his wife Myrtle, and 3 sons Eugene, Gerald and Robert, and 10 grandchildren and 2 great grandchildren. Services will be held...and so on reads the obituary. And that's all it says. But what about the man, the husband, the father, the brother, grandfather and friend? That's the person you and I have known. A tall, rugged-looking man who sometimes cried at movies, who was sensitive to others, and friendly. I only knew Harper for two years, but I won't forget him. Every Sunday when he and Myrtle were in church, I could depend on hearing Harper's deep baritone, 'Hi ya Gregg!' as the tall man walked by and shook my hand. I remember, too, the man in the hospital who got teary-eyed talking about his sons, 'good sons' he would say; who nearly beamed when Myrtle was near. And who cried when he received communion. You have memories, too. Some fonder than others, I suspect. Some of joy and fun. Others, perhaps, of father angry with erring boys. Of a husband maybe working too hard or worried about bills. Others of Harper's broad smile and great laugh. Of dad playing with his 'boys. You remember, too. That's Harper. For him we grieve. For him we weep. Because we loved him and will miss him. Like Jesus and Lazarus. A good friend. Dead. So he mourned. But the question came "Could not the one who opened the eyes of the blind kept this man from dying?" That's our question too, I think, if we really face up to our grief. "Why couldn't God keep Harper alive and well?" Though death comes to each of us, the timing could usually do better. So we not only weep but we are somewhat angry as well: with hospitals, doctors and a God who didn't seem to help. Yet in the midst of our grief and anger comes a word, a story, of life and hope that overcome death and sorrow. "I am the resurrection and the life - unbind him and let him go." Lazarus was raised - a sign to John's church that resurrection is not only for the end-time but happens now - in the midst of life and death, joy and sorrow - new life, restored life comes into our world. As we may loosen and let go of the bonds of death and the past. Harper, unlike Lazarus, will not rise and walk among us. Lazarus was for John's church and for us a sign that life overcomes death. We have the sign. Yet not only that. For Jesus' own death and resurrection stand before us - cross and empty tomb - not only as sign but as gift and power. For we, like Harper, who are baptized have taken part in that death and resurrection - washed in it, enlivened through it, "I am the resurrection and the life" said Jesus. Yet he wept and grieved as we do. But death and grief are not final. God has the last word and the last laugh. We are resurrection and life in the midst of Sorrow and death. For God is with us, inseparable from us and Harper. We remember him. And we untie him, to let him go. For us there is life now. There is more to give and to receive. There is time for joy and laughter. We remember Harper. But we also hope - as the communion of saints and in the resurrection of the dead - for nothing, not even death, can separate him or us from God's love in Christ Jesus. I am the resurrection and the life. [Funeral of Harper Thompson, Pastor Gregory Harbaugh, John 11:17-44, July 1981]

Myrtle Adeline Batdorf was baptized on October 11, 1918 in Lykens, Dauphin County, Pennsylvania (Evangelical Lutheran Circuit). She was counted in the census in 1920 in Washington, Dauphin County, Pennsylvania. She was counted in the census in 1930 in Lykens, Dauphin County, Pennsylvania. She was educated at School in 1930. She was counted in the census in 1940 in Tower City, Schuylkill County, Pennsylvania. She was employed as a Housewife in 1940. She signed her will on March 30, 1979 in Harrisburg, Dauphin County, Pennsylvania. She was employed as a Housewife in 1983. She lived in Harrisburg, Dauphin County, Pennsylvania in 1983 (2660A Green Street). She was affiliated with the Lakeside Lutheran Church religion in 1983 in Harrisburg, Dauphin County, Pennsylvania. She lived in Beaufort Farms, Camp Curtain, Estherton, Fort Hunter, Harrisburg, Hecktown, Lucknow, Rockville, Uptown, Windsor farms, all Dauphin County, Pennsylvania in 1983. Her funeral took place in 1983 in Harrisburg, Dauphin County, Pennsylvania (Jesse H Geigle, 2100 Linglestown Road). Her Social Security Number was 165-26-7303. Her estate was probated May 1983 in Harrisburg, Dauphin County, Pennsylvania. She was buried on May 11, 1983 in Harrisburg, Dauphin County, Pennsylvania (Woodlawn Memorial Gardens).

She was named after Grandmother Adeline Row. She had medical condition of Arthritis, cataracts, diabetes, and heart disease. Her height was 5 foot, 9 inches. Her cause of death was cardiorespiratory arrest w/ASHD w/pacemaker. She was affiliated with the Lutheran < Evangelical United Brethren (Methodist) religion. Political Party: (Democrat). As they began raising their three sons, Harper and Myrtle began their life renting a home for $9 in 1940 at 335 Main Street, Tower City, Pennsylvania. That is the equivalent of about $150 today.

Myrtle Personality Analysis: Myrtle was a strong-minded lady who made her way through life with definite poise and purpose. She had a confidence that was derived in part from the fact that it did not take her long to grasp the essentials other people's motivations and where a particular situation was heading. She also drew confidence from her abilities to work relentlessly on tasks through to their completion. Although she was conservative and formal she was not averse to change and as part of her ambitious nature she may have embraced it on the provision that it was a change in the right direction. The material aspects of her life did play a large role and she would have had solace in the knowledge that her family were moving up in the world. In an indirect (perhaps even behind the scenes) way she would have been quite uncompromising on decisions that carried weight towards, or away from progress in monetary matters. Myrtle's nervous energy made her very guarded towards giving away too much information (in certain company she was very careful with regard to how she presented herself). It also spurred her on in thought and action and at times put her into 'go-getter' mode. Historical thoughts of her complicated family life were countered by her energy and ambition and her determination to out-do her ancestors. Although witty and trustful and jovial in a social context Myrtle was a private person who was reluctant to invite people in her world. Judging from the way that she wrote her surname this distance side to her character was picked up in her younger years during family life. Reminiscing on the harder aspects of these times created sudden dips in her mood. To the world at large Myrtle was a diplomatic, protective and conservative lady who was a wonderful housewife. Her good taste would have been evident from the way that her home was presented but because her thoughts were so private perhaps few would have realized that she also was a highly original character with a lively imagination and innate artistic ability.

Myrtle Thompson's death came as a big surprise to me. I'm sure that was true for many of you--especially her family. I was called by Vaughn Miller on Monday morning. The family had asked if I would take care of the funeral services. I said I would and asked who died. 'Myrtle Thompson', he said. The name didn't ring a bell. I thought for a while. 'You took care of her husband's funeral.' Thompson. Harper. Myrtle. I was stunned. I sat down. I had visited her Friday and she was fine. We had a good talk. She had been thinking a lot about her mom, her sons and Harper, with Mother's Day coming up and all. She shared some stories--and told me her doctor said she was fine but she wanted to lose some weight. She hugged me when I left with the bags she had kept for the Food Pantry. Then on Sunday, I saw Myrtle in church. I was stunned on Monday morning. I liked Myrtle. I will miss her. So will you. A sad Mother's Day for you--Beulah, Gerry, Gene and Bob--for your families, for friends. A sad day--period. We begin to think of the 'what ifs' or the 'might have beens.' I know I do. I think: I might have visited Myrtle more often, to talk. She worried a lot. I might have helped. You probably do the same. Perhaps you are somewhat angry--with yourself; with God for taking her; with Myrtle for leaving so suddenly--and on Mother's Day, no less. Martha was angry with Jesus when Lazarus died. They had called him when their brother became ill. But he had delayed, taken too long. Lazarus died. His friend Jesus--the healer and wonder-worker--had failed him. And Jesus wept. But Martha was angry. Listen to their dialog with some different tones: 'Jesus, where've you been? If you wouldn't have taken so long, Lazarus wouldn't have died. So, why don't you ask God to do something now.' Jesus replied, 'Martha, you know Lazarus will rise again.' 'Of course I know that--on the last day.' But I'm talking about now! Perhaps not. Perhaps Martha was soft and pious in her sorrow. She went out to meet him though. She was aggressive. Perhaps seeking. I suspect angry. And Jesus accepted the confrontation with care and comfort and strength: 'I am the resurrection and the life; whoever believes in me will live and never die.' Yet Myrtle is dead. We know that. The story of her life for us has come to a sudden close. All we have left are the memories. Yet, a sudden unexpected death was just like Myrtle. I mean, it fits the story. The time I've known Myrtle she's been loving, but tough. Caring but straight forward and painfully honest. She said what she thought and meant it. I always knew where I stood with Myrtle. And she told me stories of how she handled I 'her boys' and how she always told Harper, "You let people use you too much." "I won't put up with that!" Fiercely independent and self-assertive. Even abrupt. But caring--sort of the 'thundering, velvet hand' of Dan Fogleberg's song. Myrtle loved her family deeply. And you loved her and remember her. So, we come together wondering, perhaps, 'where were you Lord?' Sad, angry, hurt. Yet, we recognize that all of us will die, all of our stories, our biographies will end. Lazarus died. But Jesus called him back 'that you may come to believe', he told his disciples. Jesus added a few chapters. And hanged the message. Like the disciples, we look at death as the last reality, the lost fight-of-life, the end. Even when we think in terms of the dead person's soul going to heaven, we have to face the reality that Myrtle is no longer with us--no more talking, or laughing or yelling or threats or love will come from Myrtle. We see death as the end of the story. But the story of Lazarus is a sign for us that the story is not over--'whoever believes in me will never die! That's the promise of Jesus--the one who died and who now lives. Lazarus would die again. Jesus is risen and returned to the Father--forever. I am the way, the truth and the life. No one comes to the Father except by me'. Risen. To give us hope--for life, for living. Yes, Myrtle is dead. But we are not. We remember her life, and we will tell stories about her, and we will live with hope that new chapters will yet be added by our Lord who brings life from death. We are alive--to go from here back to our world--home, school, work, play. Having faced death, we can laugh--the laughter of hope and faith in the Lord of life. The laughter of the living. And I remember well that Myrtle really knew how to laugh. I am the resurrection and the life. Whoever believes in me will never die. Amen. [Funeral for Myrtle Thompson, Pastor Gregory Harbaugh, John 11:1-43, May 1983]

IRVIN W. DUNCAN
& MAMIE L. ANDERSON

Irvin Wilfred Duncan was born one day before Thanksgiving on November 27, 1901 in Sunbury, Northumberland County, Pennsylvania to William and Lottie Duncan. Irvin was counted in the census in 1910 in Sunbury, Northumberland County, Pennsylvania. He was counted in the census in 1920 in Sunbury, Northumberland County, Pennsylvania. He and Mamie were married on June 7, 1926 in Sunbury, Northumberland County, Pennsylvania. He was counted in the census in 1940 in Hummel's Wharf, Snyder, Pennsylvania. He was employed as a Proprietor of Retail produce in 1940 in Hummel's Wharf, Snyder, Pennsylvania. He died on April 8, 1978 in Geisinger Medical Center, Mahoning, Montour County, Pennsylvania. His funeral was on April 11, 1978 in M. Quay Olley Funeral Home, 539 Race St., Sunbury, Northumberland County, Pennsylvania. He was buried on April 11, 1978 in Pomfret Manor Cemetery, Sunbury, Northumberland County, Pennsylvania.

Mamie Anderson was born on April 11, 1908 in Mother's home, Sunbury, Northumberland County, Pennsylvania to William and Emma Anderson. Mamie was counted in the census in 1910 in Sunbury, Northumberland County, Pennsylvania. She was counted in the census in 1920 in Monroe, Snyder County, Pennsylvania. She was employed as a Silk Mill about Abt. 1935. She was counted in the census in 1940 in Hummel's

Wharf, Snyder, Pennsylvania. She died on April 3, 1989 in Derry, Montour County, Pennsylvania. Her funeral was in 1989 in VL Seebold, 601 N High St, Selinsgrove, Snyder County, Pennsylvania. She was buried on April 5, 1989 in Pomfret Manor Cemetery, Sunbury, Northumberland County, Pennsylvania. Her estate was probated on February 5, 1990 in Montour County, Pennsylvania.

As they began raising their five of seven surviving children, Irvin and Mamie began their life renting a home for $15 in 1940 at 41 Main Street, Hummel's Wharf, Pennsylvania. That is the equivalent of about $250 today.

Irvin Wilfred Duncan lived in Pennsylvania in 1901 (Susquehanna Ave.). He lived in Sunbury, Northumberland County, Pennsylvania in 1901 (Susquehanna Ave.). He lived in Pennsylvania in 1910 (Produce Store, 63 8th St.). He was educated at School in 1910. He was counted in the census in 1910 in Sunbury, Northumberland County, Pennsylvania. He lived in Sunbury, Northumberland County, Pennsylvania in 1910 (Produce Store, 63 8th St.). He lived in Sunbury, Northumberland County, Pennsylvania in 1920 (920 Susquehanna Ave.). He was educated at School in 1920. He lived in Pennsylvania in 1920 (920 Susquehanna Ave.). He was counted in the census in 1920 in Sunbury, Northumberland County, Pennsylvania. He was counted in the census in 1930. He lived in Hummel's Wharf, Snyder County, Pennsylvania in 1940 (41 Main St.). He lived in Hummel's Wharf, Snyder County, Pennsylvania in 1940 (41 Main St.). He was employed as a Proprietor of retail produce in 1940 in Hummel's Wharf, Snyder County, Pennsylvania. He was counted in the census in 1940 in Hummel's Wharf, Snyder County, Pennsylvania. He was employed as an Owner about 1940 in Hummel's

Wharf, Sunbury, Pennsylvania. He lived in Sunbury, Northumberland County, Pennsylvania in 1963. He lived in Pennsylvania in 1963. His Social Security Number was 209-24-9584. He lived in Blue Hill, Dogtown, Jackson, Kantz, Kratzerville, Penn Avon, Salem, Selinsgrove, and Verdilla, all Snyder, Pennsylvania. He lived in Selinsgrove, Snyder County, Pennsylvania 17870 in 1978 (RD 2). He was employed as a Fruit and Produce in 1978. He lived in Selinsgrove, Snyder County, Pennsylvania 17870 in 1978 (RD 2). He lived in Blue Hill, Dogtown, Jackson, Kantz, Kratzerville, Penn Avon, Salem, Selinsgrove, and Verdilla, all Snyder, Pennsylvania in 1978. His funeral took place on April 11, 1978 in Sunbury, Northumberland County, Pennsylvania (M. Quay Olley [Olley-Gotlob] Funeral Home, 539 Race St.). He was buried on April 11, 1978 in Sunbury, Northumberland County, Pennsylvania (Pomfret Manor Cemetery). His funeral took place on April 11, 1978 in Pennsylvania (M. Quay Olley [Olley-Gotlob] Funeral Home, 539 Race St.). Political Party: Republican. His cause of death was squamous cell carcinoma of lung w/pulmonary edema w/ASCVD. He was affiliated with the Methodist < Lutheran religion. He had a medical condition of lung cancer due to pulmonary edema and arteriosclerosis. Member: in Hummel's Wharf, Snyder County, Pennsylvania (Hummel's Wharf Fire County, Financial and recording Sec., Rescue Hose Co Sby.)

Irvin Personality Analysis: Irvin was a balanced and conservative man. He was both practical and dutiful and would have no doubt have been regarded as an upstanding member (if not a pillar) of the community. He was reserved, well turned out and had good taste. Socially he was talkative, engaging and ambitious for status. Irvin was able to work to a very high standard. When starting out on a project it was easy for him to be easily put off by the obstacles ahead of him, however he was tenacious enough to hold on and communicative enough to see seek advice on a project in order for it to be completed. Although appearing conservative there was humorous, earthy and fun side to Irvin. He really enjoyed life and liked to indulge in the more enjoyable aspects of life: behind the veil of restraint and conservatism there lies the desire to enjoy and indulge. Irvin was a private man but in the context of a well-defined goal in a professional environment he was a valuable team player as he communicative and responsive. Irvin had just enough of the competitive instinct but this was tempered as he was able to see the benefits of compromise and conciliation. With his energy, concentration, ambition and desire to fit in and be seen as successful he would have made a huge asset to any employer. When working in a familiar environment he was generally confident. Occasionally this confidence could bubble over and lead to a little flamboyance and indeed he expected to be rewarded for his efforts and was not averse to receiving a bonus now and again. In his personal life it was difficult for Irvin to make and maintain close personal ties. Although he may have had a very strict father it was important for him to talk about the history of his family and it gave him great pleasure and a sense of relaxation to do so. He was quite hard on himself and often did not give himself full credit for his achievements. This touch of lacking in self-esteem manifested in occasions where he was momentarily over the top. Generally, Irvin was a very well balanced individual. To the outer world he could across as rather too clean cut and indeed he did have a love of concealment; there was a side to him that was rather impenetrable. He had the enviable skill of being able to talk fluently and charismatically whilst being able to screen his thoughts and pick put out and word well those thoughts that were the most suitable for the person and moment at hand.

Mary "Mamie" Lucetta Anderson was counted in the census in 1910 in Sunbury, Northumberland County, Pennsylvania. She was counted in the census in 1920 in Monroe, Snyder County, Pennsylvania. She was educated at School in 1920. She was counted in the census in 1930. She was employed as a Domestic cook about 1930. She was employed as a Silk Mill about 1935. She was counted in the census in 1940 in Hummel's Wharf, Snyder County, Pennsylvania. She lived in Pennsylvania 1969-1970. Her Social Security Number was 170-26-9870. Her funeral took place in 1989 in Selinsgrove, Snyder County, Pennsylvania (VL Seebold, 601 N High Street). She lived in Danville, Montour County, Pennsylvania in 1989 (RD 2, Box 574). She was buried on April 5, 1989 in Sunbury, Northumberland County, Pennsylvania (Pomfret Manor Cemetery). Her estate was probated on February 5, 1990 in Montour County, Pennsylvania. She had a medical condition of lung cancer metastasis, hypertension, lung cancer, and stroke. Her cause of death was Carcinoma of lung w/ metastasis. She was named after Grandmother Lucetta Gaugler. Political Party: (Democrat). She was affiliated with the Lutheran religion.

Mamie Personality Analysis: When looking at the handwriting of Mamie Anderson the recurring factor is her mind. It was as though she lived her life through her intellect. When she was focused and committed to a task (which she was inclined to be) she would become very single minded about its completion. She would work in a steady, tireless fashion towards this end. Her work would have played a central part in her overall life. She made a fantastic employee, as she was precise and accurate to the point of being pedantic. She was also a very reliable person and was able to ensure that her output was highly consistent. A very interesting facet of her hand-writing is the light pressure which combined with the sharpness, elaborations and distinct stroke (light pressure on the way up, heavy on the down stroke) reveals the trait extraordinary manual skill. This distinct stroke is very rare these days and reflects an ability to harmonize work and rest, those who write in this way have an innate ability to know how to balance hard work and recreation. If there were any emotional upsets in her life they would have been short lived and rare. Mamie had a degree of inner harmony as she was very much in control of her life and had sharp perception and common sense to the point of knowing (even controlling) what was ahead. Mamie had a brilliant memory. This should be as no surprise as she was alert and also possessed of a high degree of mental acuity. She may also have had strong interests in spiritual matters and must have held herself with a degree of dignity and decorum often expressing more interest in the more intellectual and refined side of life rather than the material. She lived by a strict moral code and was critical of those that could not see the value of having such principles. However, she would never waste too much energy on arguing or coming up against others as her main priority was always her day to day labors and to that end she would fit in without a struggle. Much of Mamie's life was not understood or appreciated by others because quite simply, she was not of a habit to advertise her thoughts. Although most people did not realize it, she was a highly original, principled and interesting character who was happy to give up her time and energy to help others without expectation of reciprocation or recognition.

Robert M. Anderson writes:
I recall Uncle Irvin and his family. Aunt Mamie used to cook often and Irvin was always out selling produce or at the firehouse. I remember cousin Shirley as a young girl at the homestead in Hummel's Wharf where I used to run around with her brother Raymond. Ray and I used to swipe cigars from their father Irvin's produce stand. I sure Ray still remembers how we hid in the bushes and smoked them. In those days there were few cars on Route 11/15 and not many places of business, mostly open fields and woods. We went down to Monroe Elementary School across the street and ran around town. [Uncle Robert M. Anderson and Marc D. Thompson, January 1998]

MACK MASON
& SARAH A. THOMPSON

The morning of September 25, 1880, came into Washington County, Georgia, cool and clear, with wide blue skies and light breezes. "Shirt-sleeve weather," the locals called it. It was so like all the other late September days in that part of Georgia it was only made memorable for Edward "Ned" Mason and his wife, Ranie, by the arrival of their newest son, Mack Mason.

Ned and Ranie had married young, and children had followed quickly and regularly, so that even though Ned and Ranie were only 33 and 27, respectively, Mack was their seventh child and their fifth son. Waiting to meet the new baby boy were older brothers George, Jim, Plum, and Austin, and sisters Jane and Dicey. And Mack would not be Ned and Ranie's last child—he would himself become older brother to two brothers, Alonzo and Oliver, and two sisters, Janice and Ella. Ned Mason and Ranie Brown had been born as slaves on the plantations of Washington County, Georgia. They had been freed by the Civil War and the Emancipation Proclamation. Mack and his brothers and sisters were the first generation to be born free.

As a slave, Mack Mason's father had been a farmhand and he continued to do that work for wages as a free man. But times were hard and pay was poor—everyone had to do what they could to help the family. This meant that education often took a backseat to financial need, and Mack only got through the fifth grade before he went to help, as had each of his brothers in their turn.

Mack Mason was born into a strange time in the lives of Georgia's freed slaves. For almost twenty years, African Americans in Georgia had been enjoying relatively mild political and racial relations with their white neighbors—which is what they had hoped for when emancipation had come.

To be sure, this favorable climate did not spring from good will on the part of former slave owners and Confederates who had started the Civil War in an effort to keep their slaves. Indeed, as soon as possible after the close of the Civil War, the former slave owners and Confederate veterans had regained control of the Georgia Legislature. They had then immediately passed harsh laws intended to remove the black man's recently granted right to vote and to physically and socially segregate black and white Georgians.

The U.S. Congress, though, totally controlled by Union men and in no mood to tolerate bad acts by former Confederates, brought out the hobnailed boots and kicked the white supremacists' plans to pieces. A series of new Federal laws intended to suppress the white supremacists' actions forced the former Confederates to backpedal. As a result, nearly all of the recently passed racist laws in the eleven former Confederate states were repealed by 1868. In addition, the 13th, 14th, and 15th Amendments to the U.S. Constitution were ratified with the intent of guaranteeing the former slaves and their descendants all of the rights due the white majority.

The effect of the Congressional actions was strong and immediate. Between 1867 and 1872, sixty-nine African Americans served as delegates to the Georgia State Constitutional Convention or as members of the Georgia State Legislature. Jefferson Franklin Long, a tailor from Bibb County, sat in the U.S. Congress from December 1870 to March 1871. Former slaves and slave owners shopped in the same stores, used the same banks, and walked on the same sidewalks.

With all of this forced change, Georgia was still a potentially dangerous place for the African American. A wrong word or even a particular glance at the wrong place or time could easily get a black man killed. Between 1880 and 1930, more than 450 men were lynched in Georgia, and prosecutions for those killings were rare.

But the years of Mack Mason's early childhood were times when, if they were a little careful, former slaves and their children could begin to feel, if not the full winds, surely the breezes of freedom. Mack, as a young boy going out to work, had little reason to suspect that, by his sixteenth birthday, events would create a very strong turn for the worse.

Having the Federal Government slap them down did not alter the segregationists' goal one iota. They still tested the waters on a regular basis by passing segregationist laws where they thought they might get away with it. In early 1872, Georgia schools were segregated. Then some cities and towns began mandating separate black and white cemeteries. But the real troubles began in 1883, when the U.S. Supreme Court ruled that, while the Federal Government could govern discrimination by other governmental bodies, the Constitution gave it no power over discrimination by individual citizens.

Former slave states saw this as a signal to start trying to expand the envelope on segregation. New restrictive laws were passed in the different states and some survived. Then in 1890, Louisiana passed a law requiring that railroads provide separate cars for blacks and whites. Determined to fight the law, a concerned group of prominent black, Creole, and white residents of New Orleans formed a Committee of Citizens with the stated purpose of attempting to repeal the law. The best thing, they decided, would be to create a case that would test the law in the courts. In 1892, one of the group—a mixed race man named Homer Plessy—bought a first-class ticket, boarded a "whites only" car, and found himself a seat. Mr. Plessy was immediately asked to move to the "blacks only" car, which he refused to do. He was arrested on the spot and the Committee of Citizens had their case.

The case, which was known as *Plessy vs Ferguson,* spent the next four years winding its way through the local and state courts. Finally, in 1896, it came before the United States Supreme Court. As the Court convened for oral arguments on April 13, 1896, there was little to suggest that the ultimate outcome of *Plessy vs Ferguson* was going to be far worse for African Americans than anyone could have imagined.

Simply stated, the majority of the Supreme Court ruled that there was nothing in the Constitution, including the new 13th, 14th, and 15th Amendments, that prohibited the forced separation of the black and white races in public facilities. The Constitution, according to the Court, required that all citizens be protected equally, but that as long as the separate facilities provided to African Americans were equal to those provided to whites, no inherent violation of the U.S. Constitution would occur.

As each of the governments of the former slave states immediately perceived, the *Plessy* decision essentially legitimized the state laws establishing racial segregation in the South. All the various states had to do to totally exclude their black citizens from public places was to claim that separate and equal facilities had been provided for them. For the next sixty years, "Separate but Equal" would be the catchphrase that white supremacists would use to repress and separate black people from the mainstream white society.

But in 1896, the average American—black or white—did not typically follow the workings of the Supreme Court, and few of them saw what was on the horizon. Oblivious to exactly what was coming, Mack Mason, went on with the process of shifting from boyhood to being a man.

Mack was a fully grown young man out of his parent's house and living on his own when he met and courted a pretty nineteen-year-old named Sarah Shatteen Thompson, commonly called Sallie. His courtship was ultimately successful, and Mack and Sallie were married on December 15, 1902, in Washington County, Georgia.

Sallie Thompson had been born in June of 1883 in Washington County, Georgia, to parents Peter Thompson and Ann M. Shatteen. Sadly, Sallie's mother died when she was only five years old. Sallie's father had to work, so she went to live with her grandmother, Sallie Shatteen, for whom she was named. She was still living with her grandmother when she married Mack Mason.

By the time of their marriage, many of the harsh segregation laws that the white supremacists had been pushing had been put in place. The collection of repressive laws that forced separation between whites and African Americans in nearly every element of life became known as "Jim Crow." The name was taken from a character in a mid-1800s minstrel show in which white men would dress up in blackface and outlandish costumes and sing and dance to "colored" music. History does not record when or how the name became associated with the pattern of segregationist laws, but everyone soon knew what it meant.

And what Jim Crow meant for black people was all bad. By 1910, ten of the eleven former Confederate states had passed new constitutions or amendments to existing constitutions that used a combination of poll taxes, literacy and comprehension tests, along with residency and record-keeping requirements, to effectively disenfranchise most blacks and tens of thousands of poor whites. Suddenly, black men who had been voting for nearly 30 years were suddenly told that they were no longer qualified to vote.

The deliberate and unapologetic nature of these acts is shown by a law passed in Oklahoma. Seeing that their new anti-black laws were also causing thousands of poor whites to lose their voting rights, Oklahoma passed an incredibly cynical amendment to their new law stating that anyone who had voted, or whose ancestor had voted, prior to 1866, would be exempt from the restrictive elements of the new law. Since only white men voted prior to 1866, this amendment made all white men exempt from the literacy test and the other new requirements.

In Washington, D.C., Woodrow Wilson, the first Southern-born President since the Civil War, had apparently decided to become the "Racist-in-Chief." The Federal Government had been integrated pretty much since the Civil War. Wilson changed that by firing all black department heads, demoting a number of black military officers to noncommissioned officers, and, where black employees were not fired, segregating departments into black and white offices.

In the various states, all public facilities were suddenly made separate. From the iconic water fountains, to buses, street cars, restaurants, bathrooms, city and county parks, doctor's offices, and on and on, henceforth, some were for blacks, some for whites—none were for both.

Blacks and whites could not marry, could not share hospital rooms, could not play baseball together, could not be in the same insanc asylums, and could not be buried in the same cemeteries. The goal seemed to be to make the black people invisible to white society—and it seemed to be working. The progress made during the years since the Civil War had been turned on its head. Anyone violating one of these laws could easily end up in jail . . . or worse. This was the world in which Mack and Sallie Mason began their married lives.

Mack Mason was a hard-working man who did what was necessary to provide for his family. While growing up, his only training had been in farm labor, and early in his marriage he usually worked as a farmhand. Farm work often came and went with the season, requiring the family to sometimes move to follow the work. In the years after their marriage, Mack, Sallie, and the family moved to Louisville, Jefferson County, Georgia, where they lived for many years.

Mack worked as a stable hand on a farm for a while, and then later worked for a sawmill in the same area. After the sawmill, Mack got a chance to farm for himself as a sharecropper. The farm was in Wadley, Jefferson County, Georgia, and he rented it by agreeing to share the profits of the crops that he raised. It was during these years in Washington and Jefferson Counties that Mack and Sallie's seven children were born: Jesse, John, Annie Lee, Maria, Eddie, Robert, and Melvin. Eddie—the progenitor of this line— would eventually honor his brother, Melvin, using his name as the base for his daughter's name, Melvalean.

Sometime between Melvin Mason's birth and April of 1930, Mack and Sallie moved the family to Savannah, Georgia, where Mack and Sallie lived out the remainder of their lives. Mack worked for some years in a fertilizer plant, and later got a job as a woodcutter in a pulpwood mill. It would be the job that he finally retired from.

Sallie Thompson Mason, a dedicated wife, mother, and support for her husband, came down with cancer and succumbed to it in Savannah on March 21, 1938. She and Mack had been married for 35 years. Sallie was buried in the Lincoln Cemetery, Chatham County, Georgia. Mack lived on in Savannah for another 24 years. He never remarried. He retired in the early 1940s, and lived with his daughter Annie Lee after that. Mack died in her house on September 18, 1962.

Mack had been born during the relatively brief period following the Civil War when it appeared that African Americans in Georgia were going get at least most of the rights guaranteed them by the U.S. Constitution. He went on to live the bulk of his life under the heavy weight of the Jim Crow laws that stole that promise away from them. But before he died, he got to see the beginnings of change: the rise of leaders like Martin Luther King and the passage of the first laws that would start the pendulum swinging back toward a greater freedom again.

Mack and Sallie's fifth child, Eddie Mason, is the direct ancestor of this family line. Eddie was born at a hard time for Sallie and the family. As a result, he spent most of his life being raised by willing relatives. During this period, he met an Army man named Mazo whom he came to greatly admire. [See the previous narrative fore details]

ROBERT J. W. FORSYTH
& CRESSIE JO CURRY

Wednesday, the fifteenth of September, 1926—the day that Robert Joseph Washington Forsyth was born as the second child of Percy Campbell Forsythe and Nina Washington—dawned hot and muggy in the city of Savannah, Georgia. Despite the fact that the first day of fall was only nine days away, summer was tenaciously refusing to surrender its hold, and the citizens of the city had resigned themselves to another day of sweating in the sweltering heat. To Robert, of course, it made little difference. It was his day and his time.

Unfortunately, it was a difficult time in Georgia. Soaring manufacturing and production were making the early 1920s boom times for much of America, but not for all. In the South, and especially in Georgia, earlier economic good times had been built on the back of a strong cotton industry. And by the time that Robert J. was born, overproduction, foreign competition, new man-made fabrics, a long drought—and worst of all, the boll-weevil—had seriously devastated Georgia's cotton-based economy.

Then in October of 1929, when Robert J. was only three years old, the financial collapse that became known as the Great Depression began and times got very hard for the entire world. Life was especially harsh for blacks, many of whom were part of Georgia's sharecropping farming culture. Unable to earn a living, many were forced off their land entirely by declining crop prices. Some took to the road, heading north into major urban areas and industrial centers. But many found themselves forced into Georgia's towns and cities, where they often competed with locals for menial jobs.

Fortunately, Savannah, as one of America's premier seaports, fared better than most of Georgia. Some businesses, such as the paper pulp and food- and sugar-processing industries that had begun prior to the Depression, were able to not only survive, but to thrive. No working man was going to get rich, but there were jobs to be had. This was the environment in which Robert J. Forsythe spent his first fifteen years

Robert's father, Percy, was one of those men who benefited from the Port of Savannah. He worked as a cook on a steamship of the Steamship of Savannah Company that hauled cargo and passengers from the Port of New York to Boston and then on to Savannah, Georgia. The ship then made the same trip in reverse with a new cargo and passenger load. The job was steady, and it probably paid better than many jobs that were available locally. But it was also a job that often left Nina and Robert at home alone for weeks at a time.

Savannah's port facilities also played a prominent role in World War II. When the war that would soon become World War II started in Europe in 1939, the U.S. started sending supplies overseas to help England. To help do this, they contracted ships belonging to the Savannah Steamship Company. Beginning in September 1941, Percy Forsythe's ship ended passenger service began carrying only cargoes considered important to the U.S. war effort. At the same time, the shipyard at the Port of Savannah began gearing up and was soon one of the nation's most active Atlantic shipyards for the construction of Liberty Ship transports for the U.S. war effort.

At nine minutes after nine, on the evening of 19 January, 1942, Percy Forsythe's ship, the *City of Atlanta,* was about eight miles off Cape Hatteras, North Carolina, en route to Savannah, when it was torpedoed by a German submarine. The ship was badly damaged and quickly rolled over and sank before any lifeboats could be launched. Percy and forty-two other sailors died in the attack.

The death of his father at the hands of the German submarine seems to have had a major and very specific effect on sixteen-year-old Robert J. Forsythe: ten months later, Robert went to the U.S. Navy recruiting station and enlisted. He almost certainly had to lie about his age to do so.

Because of his race and his age, Robert was assigned to the Messman Branch of the Navy—which was soon retitled as the Steward Branch. At the beginning of 1942, whites were not allowed to serve in the Steward Branch, and the entire Branch was made up of black and Filipino sailors. The Steward Branch was responsible for feeding everyone on the ship, but after Robert's training and satisfaction of a required period of service, he was rated as a Stewards Mate 1st Class. Men in this specialty were essentially waiters for the officer's mess (dining room).

This should not be taken to mean that Robert had no other duties or that he never faced the dangers of war. Stewards were actually the first African Americans to see action in World War II because following Pearl Harbor the Navy was more or less in regular contact with the enemy. And every man on a ship had a battle station when the action started. Indeed, it was after several Stewards had been recognized for extreme bravery in battle that the Navy realized that it was missing a bet and dropped its ban on African Americans serving in fields outside the Steward Branch.

Following three years of service in World War II, Robert was discharged on 15 November, 1945. Undoubtedly, he, like most African Americans returning from the war, hoped to find that his service would warrant better treatment than he had experienced growing up. If so, he was destined to be disappointed.

Racially, Savannah had always had something of split personality. During the early days of slavery, the white population had shown an unusually liberal disposition toward slaves. Slaves had been allowed to have their own public church, which could be attended by slaves from all over the city—something unheard in other slave states. After the abolition of slavery, white Savannah prided itself on having a more "genteel" relationship with the black population. In truth, Savannah never had the same level of violence between blacks and whites that was found in other Georgia cities. And certainly, as the war ended in the 1940s, Savannah's business leaders wanted to show a more cosmopolitan face to the growing numbers of foreign tourists that had begun coming into America through her port. They wanted the world believe in the idea of the city's genteel view of race relations.

But while less violent and less obvious than other Georgia cities, Jim Crow still lived in Savannah's streets. Returning black servicemen often found themselves either denied the right to vote outright, or having so many roadblocks placed in their paths it amounted to the same thing. They still had to use separate facilities from whites. Black schools still had insufficient resources, and in most places blacks were still forced to sit in the back of the bus. It was a bitter disappointment; but a man had to live and had to work to do so, and Robert Forsythe got on with it as best he could.

It was during this period of readjustment that Robert met a young woman named Lucretia "Cressie" Jo Curry, and romance ensued. Cressie Jo was also a native of Savannah, having been born there on March 5, 1929, as the first child of Frederick Curry and his young wife, Elizabeth Brown.

Despite being their first child, little Cressie Jo always found herself surrounded by numerous older children. Her father, a hardworking and responsible man, had taken the responsibility for looking after all seven of his new wife's minor siblings when both of her parents died suddenly and unexpectedly.

Frederick Curry supported this crowd, along with his own increasing family, by working as a laborer in a fertilizer plant and later as a "blocker" for a shipping company, where he ran a cotton compressor—a machine for compacting the large raw cotton bales into smaller, rectangular sizes to allow more of them to fit into the available space on a cargo ship.

As each of Elizabeth Brown Curry's siblings got older, they moved out on their own or to live with one another. But while the aunts and uncles were growing up and moving out, the Curry family was having children of their own. By the time Cressie Jo was ten years old, all of the Browns were out of the house, and they had been replaced by her own sister, Nancy, and her brothers, Frederick, Jr., Frank, and Sam.

Cressie Jo was in her late teens when she met Robert Forsythe, and was only nineteen years old when they married in Savannah, Georgia, on April 17, 1948. Robert Forsythe was twenty-one years old. Robert and Cressie Jo's daughter, Delores Ann Curry, was born that same year.

As it turned out, Robert and Cressie Jo's marriage was rather short-lived. Robert had a hard time adjusting back into the City he had left as a teenager, and had encountered some hard times following his term in the Navy. And he had apparently fallen in with some reckless friends.

In January of 1949, less than a year after his marriage to Cressie Jo, Robert Forsythe was arrested and convicted of five counts of burglary. He was sentenced to spend a minimum of five years and a maximum of twenty years in the State penitentiary, and on February 9, 1949, he entered prison. It no doubt broke Cressie Jo's heart, but the long prison term also quickly resulted in the termination of Robert and Cressie Jo's brief marriage.

Shortly after the dissolution of her marriage to Robert Forsythe, Cressie Jo had children with Edward Mazo, her future son-in-law. It was an on-again, off-again relationship, with Edward and Cressie Jo living together, parting, and coming together again for several years before parting yet again.

Over the years, Cressie Jo and Edward Mazo had several children, including four daughters: Eddie Mae, Rainey, Gobbie Denise, and Selena; and five sons: Kenneth, James, Mark, Emmanuel, and Eddie. Everyone were born in Savannah, Georgia.

In the end, Edward Mazo finally left for good. This time, Cressie Jo's older sons were of an age to get work and help support the family, and she never remarried. Life in Savannah got better for African Americans: civil rights laws were passed by Congress and locally a very strong and effective civil rights movement was proving successful at moving local laws and attitudes in a better direction.

Cressie Jo spent most of her life in Savannah, Georgia, raising her children and watching them begin their own families. In 1965, she went to Philadelphia, Pennsylvania, where she had relatives, and lived there for about a year before returning to Savannah. In her last years—when her children were all grown and gone— Cressie Jo went to live with her son Kenneth in Hinesville, Georgia.

On December 10, 1998, Cressie Jo died in the Liberty Regional Medical Center in Hinesville, Liberty County, Georgia. She was buried in the Midway Congregational Church Cemetery in Hinesville.

As for Robert Forsythe, when he was released from prison he left Georgia permanently, seeking an opportunity for a new life. Apparently, he found that opportunity in Seattle, Washington, where he settled and lived out the remainder of his life. Robert Forsythe died there on November 22,

1999, and was buried in the Tahoma National Cemetery in Kent, King County, Washington, with military honors, in recognition of his World War II service. Cressie Jo Curry and Robert Forsythe's child, Delores Curry, is the direct ancestor of this family line.

PAUL P. ROMANO
& KATHLEEN MCCABE

Paolo Pietro (known as Paul Peter) Romano, son of Pietro Giuseppe Romano and Annetta Pierina Camilla Carmona was born on 31 January 1911 in Lercara, Palermo, Sicily, Italy, died on 6 October 1981 in Queens, Queens, New York, and was buried on 9 October 1981 in St. Michaels, Elmhurst. Paul married Kathleen Elizabeth McCabe, daughter of Owen McCabe and Mary Smith, on 21 August 1933 in Manhattan, New York, New York. Kathleen was born on 14 July 1905 in Manhattan, New York, New York and died on 1 October 1997 in Cumberland County, Pennsylvania. Paul Romano and Kathleen McCabe had three children.

Paul Romano was 3 years old when he stepped onto American soil. Unlike some of his older brothers and sisters, he would have had virtually no significant memories of his homeland – he would grow up thinking of himself as an American. But the America – and, more specifically, the New York that he grew up in was a very different place than it is today.

The horse was just beginning to give way to the automobile and a rash of construction between 1900 and 1915 was improving living conditions by simply providing a greater selection in living space. The cramped quasi-ghettos that faced immigrants a decade earlier were certainly not gone, but housing was improving greatly. That, along with concerted efforts on the part of New York health authorities had led to a decrease in deaths from contagious diseases. But a decrease is not a disappearance – in 1914, the year that Paul Romano arrived in Manhattan, Manhattan alone had 224 cases of typhoid, resulting in 38 deaths.

Television journalist Tom Brokaw named the generation that included Paul Romano and Kathleen McCabe as "The Greatest Generation." He gave them that label because of what they lived through and how they went on to shape America.

When they were small children, the ports, and sometimes the streets, of New York were full of American soldiers – the doughboys on their way "Over There" to save Europe from the Hun in World War I. And then, from 1918-1920, the great flu pandemic struck – more than 25,000,000 people died worldwide. New York, then a city of around six million people, lost 20,000 to 24,000 residents to the flu.

As young adults, they lived through the time of the bread lines and soup kitchens of the Great Depression. More than 20% of men of working age were out of work. It was the time when wages of $1.50-$3.00 per WEEK were common – and men were glad to work for that. It was the decade that turned men into hoboes who traveled the country looking for work to feed themselves and, often their families.

In the 1940s, as their own family was starting to grow, they watched family and friends enlist in the military and go off to serve in World War II. Paul Romano's brother Anthony Romano. He had enlisted in the Army in March of 1941, ahead of America's entry into the war. Following the war, the Romanos participated in the expansion that created the most prosperous middle class – indeed, the most prosperous country in the world. It is also interesting to consider the vast multitude of changes in the world that they saw during their lifetimes.

Paul Romano appears to have worked much of his life in the moving business – household moving. In 1930, the U. S. Census report shows him as a shipping clerking for a moving van business. In 1981, when he died, his death certificate described him as a driver for Duken Van Lines.

ALBERT E. WITTLE
& MILDRED I. STEWART

Albert Elmer Wittle was born on August 14, 1904 in Harrisburg, Pennsylvania. He was one of eight children born to John and Mary Wittle. Albert was more than likely born at home as this was the common birthing practice in 1904. At the time of Albert's birth tuberculous, typhoid and Spanish influenza were in the epidemic stages in Harrisburg. Control of these diseases was hampered by the lack of a proper sanitation system in the city. Raw sewage ran down many of the unpaved streets, thereby polluting the Susquehanna River.

There was a need for major changes in the city. Several of Harrisburg's residents became involved in the City Beautiful Movement to improve the quality of life for Harrisburg residents. The first phase of the City Beautiful was completed when Albert was about eleven years old. Harrisburg transformed from an industrial city covered in mud and filth to a beautiful city with paved streets, a modern sanitary system, clean water, city hall and a covered sewer interceptor along the river. The Harrisburg park system was enlarged by creating Riverfront Park, Reservoir Park, Wildwood Park and the Italian Lake. Albert and his siblings probably played and picnicked in one or all of these parks after their completion.

Around this same time the first wave of what is historically called the Great Migration started. African-Americans from southern states migrated to Harrisburg and the surrounding areas in search of employment. The First World War had just begun and many of the steel and factory workers had gone off to fight. This was the perfect opportunity for many African-

Americans and poor whites to move from the economically oppressed South to the North where they could get jobs in the Harrisburg railroad industry and steel mills.

In one year the African-American population of Philadelphia and surrounding cities more than doubled; from approximately 62,000 in 1914 to over 134,000 in 1915. For most of the immigrants, life was harder than they were led to believe by the employment recruiters and black newspapers. They were excluded from most of the labor unions, given the lowest paying and most dangerous jobs. They had to compete with European migrants for housing in overcrowded rundown shanty housing. All of this led to racial unrest, which resulted in a race riot in nearby Chester where three blacks and two whites were killed. This happened when Albert was 13 and then another riot in Philadelphia just a year later.

Oh, the things Albert must have seen and heard about at such a young age. By the time Albert was sixteen years old he had seen many things; the beginning and end of the First World War. The Philadelphia Athletics, forerunners of the Oakland A's, won the World Series in 1910, 1911 and 1913. Chocolate candy mogul, Milton Hershey founded a school for orphaned boys in Hershey, PA. The first black YMCA was established in 1919. He saw the takeover of Pennsylvania Steel by the Bethlehem Steel Company in nearby Steelton and the construction of the Penn-Harris Hotel.

Motel T automobiles were now in mass production, making them more affordable to the middle-class. Perhaps Albert's family was one of the first in his neighborhood to purchase an automobile. His father worked as a locomotive engineer for the Pennsylvania Railroad, surely one of the better paying jobs in the area. The first drive-in gas station, in the country, was built by Gulf Refining Co. in Pittsburg in 1913.

Before the gas station, pumps were located curbside of local businesses such as grocery stores and hardware stores. At these locations multiple cars lining up to refuel caused traffic congestion. In addition to the historical events Albert saw, he also witnessed the birth of his younger sisters, Mary born in 1908 and Leona born in 1913; and the birth of his younger brother, George born in 1911. Albert had four older siblings, Stella, Ross, Alvin and Irvin.

Come the 1920's most homes in Harrisburg had electricity. The popular, at home, entertainment was the radio. When Albert was 18 the first radio station licensed in Harrisburg was WBAK. It was run by the Pennsylvania State Police. Other stations followed; WABB in 1923, WHBG in early 1925 and WPRC started broadcasting in October, 1925. WPRC later changed its call letters to WKBO. As of 2010 it was still operating and owned by Open Heart Ministries, broadcasting Christian contemporary music. Most of the first radio programs were religious services. During the 1920's and even through the 1940's WKBO was broadcast from the Penn-Harris Hotel. The antenna tower was located on the roof of the hotel. The radio often broadcast live events in the hotel ballroom featuring local bands.

The first radio broadcast was made by Pittsburgh station KDKA on Nov.2, 1920. It was Election Day and radio's first announcer, Leo Rosenberg, sent the news that Warren Harding had won the election over James Cox to about 1,000 listeners. The first baseball game to be broadcast was in 1921 by the same radio station. Albert and his family probably spent many hours around the radio listening to Graham McNamee announce every World Series game between 1923 and 1934.

When Albert turned 21, Gene Tunney defeated Jack Dempsey for the World Heavyweight Boxing championship in Philadelphia. No doubt he, his brothers and father listened to the fight on the radio or maybe they drove the Model T to Philadelphia to watch the fight in person. City Beautiful projects were moving forward at this time also. The expansion of the Market Street Bridge from two to four lanes made commuting over the Susquehanna River a lot easier. The construction of the new Capital Complex and its entrance, the State Street Bridge, began when Albert was 21.

Sadly, his father, John, passed away the next year, on May 12, 1927. He was buried in the East Harrisburg Cemetery. Albert may have moved into his parent's home to take care of his mother, as he was still single at this time. A 1930 census registered him at a residence on Susquehanna St. in Harrisburg; the same given for his father at the time of his death.

A few years later the global economic downturn of the Great Depression started with the collapse of Wall Street on Oct. 29, 1929. Most of the world experienced the downturn with unemployment at 25% in the U.S. and up to 33% unemployment in other countries. Albert's mother, Mary, passed away, March 17, 1934, before the major effects of the depression hit the Harrisburg area.

The worst conditions could be felt in single industry towns. Harrisburg however had a greater distribution of political and financial leadership that allowed them to consider a wide range of strategies to weather the storm. Even so, the city did not have enough resources to keep businesses open and residents employed through the end of the depression in 1939/1940.

Beginning in late 1935 the federal work relief program Works Progress Administration (WPA) began employing men to work on various Pennsylvania road projects. At the peak of the program in November of 1938, it employed 143,000 men. This may be where Albert began his career as a truck driver. He later worked for the City Highway Department as a truck driver.

Mildred Irene Stewart was born on Oct. 21, 1920 in Harrisburg, PA. She was one of seven children born to Johnny and Kathleen Annie Stewart. When she was about 10, the family moved to Wormleysburg, Johnny's hometown. Mildred and Albert were married on Feb. 16, 1943 in Enola, Cumberland County, PA. She was 22 and Albert was 38.

There are a few possibilities as to how Mildred and Albert met. One possibility is that Albert met her when he was working on roads in Cumberland County, PA with the WPA. Or maybe Mildred also worked for the WPA and they met at work. A third possibility could be that the Wittle and Stewart families were already acquainted. Johnny was an auto mechanic working at various garages around the area. Perhaps he worked on John's prized Model T or other automobiles and they struck up a friendship and introduced their children. Regardless of how they met, they fell madly in love and were married in Enola.

They had seven children. All but one child, David, are still living. David passed away in 1970 at the age of 15. Albert passed away on Dec. 25, 1970, when he was 66 years old. He was buried in the East Harrisburg Cemetery. After Albert's death, Mildred remarried. She passed away on Feb. 8, 1985 at the Sunbury Hospital from cardiac arrest due to a blood clot in the heart. She was 64 years old. She was buried in the East Harrisburg Cemetery; we assume next to Albert. At the time of her death she was retired from the PA Department of Transportation. Albert and Mildred's son John carries on the family lineage.

AMEL A. ACRI
& SYLVIA F. BARBUSH

Amel Angelo (Emilio Angiolo) Acri was baptized on July 9, 1904 in J.C. Thompson, Sacred Heart of Jesus, Harrisburg, Dauphin County, Pennsylvania. He was counted in the census in 1910 in Harrisburg, Dauphin County, Pennsylvania. He was educated at School in 1910. He was employed as a Bricklayer helper at local Steel Company in 1920. He was counted in the census in 1920 in Harrisburg, Dauphin County, Pennsylvania. He was counted in the census in 1930. He lived in 7131 Somerset Rd., Harrisburg, Dauphin County, Pennsylvania in 1963.

Amel was affiliated with the St. Catherine Laboure Catholic Church religion in 1963. His funeral took place in 1963 in Daily Funeral, 650 S. 28th St., Harrisburg, Dauphin County, Pennsylvania. He was buried on March 1, 1963 in Holy Cross Cemetery, Harrisburg, Dauphin County, Pennsylvania. He was employed as a Maintenance Supervisor in Dauphin County in 1992. His cause of death was Pulmonary embolism w/acute pancreatitis and post-operative cholodocholithisis. Member: in Holy Name Society, St. Michaels Lodge and Sons of Italy He had a medical condition of cardiac arrest due to blood clot in lung, gall stones, pancreatitis. He was employed as a Steelworker for the local Steel Company. He was employed as a Grocer.

Sylvia Frances (Silvia Francesca) Barbush lived in Via Nanca, Castiglione, Cosenza, Italy in 1908. She immigrated in 1928. She was counted in the census in 1930 in Harrisburg, Dauphin County, Pennsylvania. Her estate was probated in 1992 in Dauphin County, Pennsylvania. She lived in 375 Claremont Dr., Carlisle, Pennsylvania17013 in 1992.

Sylvia was affiliated with the St. Catherine Laboure Catholic Church religion in 1992. She was employed as a Homemaker in 1992. Her funeral took place in 1992 in Neill Funeral Home, 3501 Derry St., Harrisburg, Dauphin County, Pennsylvania. She was buried on March 4, 1992 in Holy Cross Cemetery, Harrisburg, Dauphin County, Pennsylvania. She had a medical condition of pneumonia, cataracts, glaucoma, stroke, hypertension. Her cause of death was Pneumonia. Sylvia was named for her father, "Francesco" Acri. Sylvia and Amel had the following children: Charles Acri, Frank Acri, Teresa F Acri, and Mary Frances Acri.

CHAPTER 4
Generation Four

We need to haunt the house of history
and listen anew to the ancestors' wisdom
—Maya Angelou

Our Fourth Generation includes our Great-grandparents, of the late 1880's.

Church for burial of Gipe's, York, PA

ABEL R. THOMPSON
& GUSSIE MAE HENSEL

Abel Robert Thompson came into this world on the eve of another cold Pennsylvania winter. He was born just after Thanksgiving, November 28, 1880, to proud parents, Robert Bruce Thompson and Lydia Ann Goodman both Pennsylvania natives living in Sheridan at the time. Carrying on the family tradition of honoring their ancestors, Abel bore the middle name Robert, his father's name. Abel's family had a long and important history in the area where he was born and grew up. The town of Sheridan was laid by his grandfather, Alexander Thompson, on his former lands. Grandfather Alexander was the first to sell coal from the area, later known as the York Farm Colliery, and Alexander was the owner of Thompson's Mill.

Just two days after the celebration of St. Valentine's Day, February 16, 1885, an adorable baby girl was born to Howard Andrew Carson Hensel and Clara Matilda Updegrove. She was baptized Augusta Mae on Easter Sunday of the same year, in Dauphin County, Pennsylvania. Gussie, as she was fondly known, grew up during the staunch age of Victorianism. She was able to attend school only until the fifth grade.

Being the oldest of eleven children, her formal education was cut short when it became necessary for Gussie to begin assisting in the household duties and the care of her siblings. With so many mouths to feed in the family, it was later necessary for her to become an additional bread winner—

as a teen, she was employed as a domestic servant. However, it wouldn't be long before she would move on to married life. Both, according to the 1900 census return, were literate, able to read and write.

When Gussie met Abel, he was working as a general laborer. He was a tall, handsome man with dark hair, grey eyes, and a lean physique from the efforts of his occupation. Gussie never had eyes for any other man. She was a lovely June bride dressed in flowing white when the two married on June 15, 1904, in Schuylkill County, Pennsylvania. The new couple was soon expecting their first child. However, their joy turned tragic when their baby daughter, Virginia, died not long after she was born. A son, Wilbur Clark, came along in 1906, and a second son, Harper Bruce, was born in September of 1907.

Now with two children, Abel sought to better his financial position. His uncle, the Honorable Alexander F. Thompson, had been a member of the Dauphin County bar and served as a state senate member. These political connections may have led to Abel's position as a probationer with the local courts.

By 1910, the couple had been married for six years and was well settled in Porter Township. Schuylkill County would soon be celebrating its centennial and nearby Pottsville was a growing mini-metropolis with ample educational opportunities for neighboring children. Abel had decided to return to the family roots and had been working as a coal miner for eight years. Perhaps the coal miners' strike of 1902, which ended with shorter work days and 10% pay increases after President Theodore Roosevelt's successful arbitration, played a role in Abel taking up mining.

Soon, he and Gussie had saved enough to purchase their own home. They were even able to rent space in the household to a small family. Gussie was expecting their fourth child, Abel Franklin, who would be born in October 1910. Their daughter, Lydia Mae, would follow as a Valentine's present, in February four years later.

With a growing family, Abel sensed the increased responsibility that came with it. His job as a miner was fraught with peril—it was all too often he heard of explosions, cave-ins, or exposure to deadly mine gasses. These dangers were impressed upon him by the 1892 explosion at York Farm Colliery—when he was eleven years old—that killed fifteen men. The Molly Maguires, a society of activists who fought to improve the dangerous working conditions in the mines, had actively campaigned for better working conditions, but positive changes were still some time off.

Violent clashes between organized workers and mine bosses continued throughout Abel's life, from the hanging of twenty Pennsylvania coal miners believed to be members of the Molly Maguires in the 1870s and the Lattimer Massacre in nearby Hazleton in 1897, to the infamous Ludlow Massacre and ensuing Colorado Coalfield War, in which hundreds died in that very year of 1914. Realizing both the apparent and unseen dangers of his profession, Abel took no chances in providing for his family should some ill-fated event occur. He filed his will at the local courthouse in Porter on July 2, 1914.

Abel was obviously pondering the future when he filed his will. Perhaps it was a general sense of foreboding, or maybe he had the feeling that something just wasn't quite right. One of the unseen dangers of a coal miner's life was black lung, always a concern for both current and former miners. Or perhaps it was his plans for an adventurous trip to Colorado. Whatever the case, he was wise to plan well.

Abel heard of the mining booms taking place in Colorado. Family stories say that he left Pennsylvania in search of copper in Colorado. Although copper mines were scarce in Colorado, swindlers like the notorious W. C. Calhoun were not. Abel could have met or heard about Calhoun and the copper mine stocks he was selling. Wanting to provide for his wife and new children, Abel may have left for Colorado to check on his investments; or maybe it was the adventurous spirit instilled in Abel by his grandfather, Alexander, who left Scotland to come to the New World. Upon his arrival in Colorado, Abel found that his stocks were potentially fraudulent and took up employment in one of the many booming gold or silver mines of the time. Gussie, a resourceful woman, was left at home to care for their children.

Abel's trip to Colorado left him feeling rather unwell and he had a strong yearning to return home to familiar soil. Shortly thereafter, he became a victim of the influenza pandemic, and after contracting pneumonia, he died on October 15, 1918. He was just 37 years of age. The leaves had begun to fall, and the Pennsylvanian mountains were awash with beauty and color. The family gathered for Abel's burial services on a windswept October day. They said their final goodbyes as he was returned to the soil so near to where his life had begun. His mortal remains were laid to rest in Greenwood Cemetery in Tower City, Pennsylvania.

Abel died leaving Gussie with four small children all under the age of twelve. Rather than choosing to remarry, Gussie decided to brave the world on her own. Luckily, the family home had already been paid for so she and the children had a secure roof over their heads. Gussie's lack of education left her with few options for income, but this did not hinder her in finding a way to earn much needed funds. With her agile hands, she found plenty of work as a seamstress. This allowed her to remain at home and tend to her children while also supporting the family financially. The boys were still attending school and too young to contribute to the family income, but they managed to persevere and remain together as a family through this trying period of their lives.

In just a decade, Gussie was a financially stable widow living in a community among many other widows. It was a coming new age of amazing technologies. Advances in aviation allowed the imagination to take flight by following the travels and tragedies of Amelia Earhart and Charles Lindbergh. The Jazz age was in full swing, and for a few hard-earned pennies, one could enter the strange and wonderful world of The Wizard of Oz, a moving picture show. Gussie was likely amazed at seeing so many things she never could have dreamed of at the turn of the century.

Still the family prevailed as a whole. Gussie was fortunate to be keeping house for her children well away from the Midwestern Dust Bowl and they were lucky enough to be among those who still had jobs at the beginning of the Great Depression. The boys were working as coal miners and Lydia had begun her long-term job as a looper at a hosiery factory. Even for those in a household with multiple incomes, the nation's financial situation dictated frugality in all things. By 1930, Gussie owned a home valued at $3,500, and they no longer farmed.

Gerald G. Thompson writes: My father's parents were Gussie and Abel from Tower City. Grandpa Abel, a coal miner, died well before I was born and we spent little time at Gussie's. She was a homemaker and I do remember listening to her piano player. [Gerald G. Thompson and Marc D. Thompson, May 1990] Abel was a very smart person with an analytical mind. He had a great interest in philosophical matters. His forward slant shows he was outgoing and emotionally expressive and very honest.

Radio was gaining popularity as an economic American pastime. Like many other families who owned a radio set, Gussie and her children probably spent the evenings listening to their favorite broadcast programs. A pleasant accompaniment would have been a fresh-baked plate of the newly invented Toll House chocolate chip cookies and fresh milk all around.

Several years later, Gussie and Lydia were still living on Main Street in Sheridan. It was a middle-class neighborhood populated mostly by miners and mill workers. Gussie was surely proud to own her home at a value of $680, which would be equal to about $12,000 today. She took care of the house while Lydia worked at the stocking mill. Being the highest paid looper in the area, Lydia earned $550 a year to support them both. It was a modest lifestyle when a loaf of bread cost about eight cents, a quart of milk averaged eleven cents, and eggs were nearly 27 cents a dozen. With a little more than $10 a month to live on, economizing was a continuing necessity.

While the radio was one of the main leisure activities available, it was also the main means of getting the news. When Germany invaded France and Italy declared war on Britain and France, it no doubt caused them much concern. It was the beginning of a period of unrest that would last for many years. The loss and devastation of WWII may have been the catalyst for Gussie to face her own eventual mortality. She filed her last will and testament at the local courthouse on May 27, 1950, not long after her 65th birthday, at which point she would have started drawing on her Social Security benefits, another innovation of the 20th century.

Victor Hensel writes: I remember my aunt Gussie. Her husband died before I was born but I remember going to Gussie's house, her daughter Lydia was always there. Her son harper was a line-man for the Telephone Company. Our family was always invited into her front room, usually going in the side entrance. I can see aunt Gussie saying, "Here comes Junior and his family." In the front room, I remember the "Piano Organ." Aunt Gussie would take out albums showing us pictures of the Hensel and Thompson family. I can still see the coal and wood stove being used, nor only for heating, but also for cooking. When we went there we had to use the outhouse but later I remember going upstairs to an indoor bathroom. Talking of the second floor, I recall hearing a story that bats lived in the second story. As for Gussie's parents, my grandparents, I was about six when Howard and Clara passed. I have hardly any remembrances of them. I do remember their homestead in Tower City, PA. I have seen pictures of it and remember the inside of the house, it was small but warm, homey and organized. [Uncle Victor Hensel and Marc D. Thompson, August 1998]

It would be several more decades before the reading of Gussie's will would come to pass. During that time, she continued to live with and keep house for Lydia, who never married. She continued to find comfort in Lydia's countenance, which reminded her of the dear husband so many years gone. Living through these years, she would see many changes in youth morality, racial discrimination, and in the political face of America. She would experience the loss of her son Wilbur Clark, who left behind a widow, Elva May.

Gussie, an aging widow with a childhood rooted in the Victorian age, took these changes in stride. She occupied her time in charitable efforts as a member of the Women's Society of Christian Service. Finding a commonality amongst other Methodist ladies of similar age and like mind, she spent her days in Bible study fellowship, sharing the gospel with others, aiding the poor, visiting the aged, and assisting those of general misfortune. When she was not on her missions as benefactor, she practiced her faith at the Lykens United Methodist Church or the Wesley United Methodist Church in Tower City. It was a faith that Gussie continued to practice until her passing in March of 1973.

Gussie Hensel Thompson departed this world at the grand and respectable age of eighty-eight years. Her heart and circulatory system failing, she experienced a brain hemorrhage and breathed her last breath peacefully at home on March 27, 1973. It was a chilly day when her loved ones attended her funeral services at the Dean O. Snyder Mortuary in Tower City.

There to pay respects were her sons Abel Franklin and wife, Almeda Ellen; Harper Bruce and wife, Myrtle Adeline; and of course, her faithful daughter, Lydia Mae. She was laid to rest next to her beloved Abel in Tower City's historic Greenwood Cemetery. Buried amongst many family and friends, their place of committal is a peaceful memorial garden overlooking a meandering branch of the great Schuylkill River. Abel and Gussie's third child, Harper, was the direct ancestor of the Thompson line.

Abel Robert Thompson was counted in the census in 1900 in Porter, Schuylkill County, Pennsylvania (w/brother Oliver). He lived in Sheridan, Schuylkill County, Pennsylvania in 1900 (Wiconisco St.). He was employed as a Day laborer from 1900-1904. He lived in Porter Township, Schuylkill County, Pennsylvania in 1904. He was employed as a probationer from 1907-1908. He was employed as a Miner, Coal mines in 1910. He was counted in the census in 1910 in Porter, Schuylkill County, Pennsylvania. He signed his will on July 2, 1914 in Porter Township, Schuylkill County, Pennsylvania (No 1, Vol 22, page 283). He was employed as a Miner about 1915 in Colorado. He lived in Tower City, Schuylkill County, Pennsylvania in 1918. His funeral took place in 1918 in Tower City, Schuylkill County, Pennsylvania (John F Dreisingacer). He was employed as a miner at PR CSJ County, West Brookside in 1918 in Tower City, Schuylkill County, Pennsylvania. He was employed as a Miner in 1918. He signed his will on October 15, 1918 in Schuylkill County, Pennsylvania (22, 283). He was buried on October 19, 1918 in Tower City, Schuylkill County, Pennsylvania (Greenwood Cemetery). His estate was probated between February-November 1919 in Porter Township, Schuylkill County, Pennsylvania. He was named after Father, Robert Thompson. He was affiliated with the Methodist religion. His height tall, build medium, eyes gray, and hair dark. His cause of death was Pneumonia w/influenza.

Abel Personality Analysis: Analytical mind, investigative. Perfectionist, extremely emotional, great highs and lows. Talkative. Great interest in intellectual pursuits. Organizational skills.

89

Desire for responsibility. Open to learning about other religions. Good balance between the Spiritual and physical aspects of life. Abel Detailed Personality Analysis: Abel was a robust and larger than life character who had a great deal of energy. He was an extroverted and talkative man with a quick and bold sense of humor. If one were to have been in the same room as him, it is unlikely that you would have failed to notice him. If one were to have spent an evening in his company it would not have been an evening one would likely forget in a hurry. Abel was an interesting and original character. He was at once curious about others and a fascinating character himself. Such was his charisma that people would be automatically drawn to him for his speaking and storytelling abilities. He had a brilliant ability to draw people in, introduce others and integrate people. At times Abel was not entirely open, he would sometimes not tell others what was on his mind and, whilst including some of the facts, omit the parts that he feels would compromise his position. In his own way Abel was a creative man. He used his charisma and humor in order to safe guard his mobility, he was rebellious and consequentially enjoyed his freedom to the point that he would do anything to maintain it. Abel may well have had a degree of moral flexibility but he was also empathetic and was willing to help others whenever he could. Although hard working and tenacious, he was also quite flexible and sometimes impressionable himself. To the outsider it may have appeared that Abel never had a bad day because he tended to gloss over those matters that had the potential to make him appear weak however there is a degree of stress and tension in his writing. When it came to financial matters Abel enjoyed money, he liked making it and spending it. He may have been bold, acquisitive and tenacious in these matters but he was also generous and giving to his close friends and family. Abel may have been somewhat of a leader in his community, his larger than life persona would have drawn in many a follower. Still more people may have been drawn to him for the strength that he exuded and his versatility; Abel was a clever man who could solve life's problems in many ways including but not limited to brute force, cunning and humor.

Augusta "Gussie" Mae Hensel was baptized on April 5, 1885 in Dauphin County, Pennsylvania. She was educated at School in 1900. She was counted in the census in 1900 in Tower City, Schuylkill County, Pennsylvania. She was employed as a Domestic in 1904. She lived in in 1904. She was counted in the census in 1910 in Porter Township, Schuylkill County, Pennsylvania. She was employed as a Seamstress in 1920 in Porter Township, Schuylkill County, Pennsylvania. She lived in Sheridan, Schuylkill County, Pennsylvania in 1920 (329 Main St.). She was counted in the census in 1920 in Porter Township, Schuylkill County, Pennsylvania. She was counted in the census in 1930 in Porter, Schuylkill County, Pennsylvania. She lived in Sheridan, Schuylkill County, Pennsylvania in 1930 (329 Main St., Highway Route 199). She was employed as a Housewife in 1935. She was employed as a Housewife in 1940. She lived in Sheridan, Schuylkill County, Pennsylvania in 1940 (34 Main Street). She was counted in the census in 1940 in Sheridan, Schuylkill County, Pennsylvania. She signed her will on May 27, 1950 in Sheridan, Schuylkill County, Pennsylvania. She lived in Orwin, Porter, Reinerton, Rush, Sheridan, Tower City, all Schuylkill County,

Pennsylvania in 1973. She lived in Tower City, Schuylkill County, Pennsylvania in 1973 (329 West Grand Ave.). Her Social Security Number was 173-46-1535. Her funeral took place in 1973 in Tower City, Schuylkill County, Pennsylvania (Dean O Snyder, 304 E Grand Ave.). Her funeral took place in 1973 in Lykens, Dauphin County, Pennsylvania (Lykens United Methodist). She was employed as a Housewife in 1973. She lived in Schuylkill County, Pennsylvania in 1973. She was affiliated with the Wesley United Methodist religion in 1973. She was buried on March 30, 1973 in Tower City, Schuylkill County, Pennsylvania (Greenwood Cemetery). She signed her will on May 27, 1973 in Schuylkill County, Pennsylvania (No 3, Vol 145, page 578). She was affiliated with the Methodist religion. Her cause of death was medullary paralysis w/thrombosis w/cerebral hemorrhage and arteriosclerosis. Member: Member of Women's Society of Christian Service.

Gussie Personality Analysis: They all liked to argue, particularly Gussie, she could be aggressive in her approach, possibly sharp tongued as well. She has a large jealousy stroke in her capital letter T, she had an interest in philosophical and spiritual pursuits. Interested in other religions. She needed time spent alone to recharge her batteries so to speak. She was extremely emotionally expressive. Could have been an actress. Her slant shows she had emotional highs and lows to deal with. Could be resentful at times. Gussie Personality Analysis II: Gussie had highly original writing and was therefore a very original character. She was a positive person and believed that life was designed to go up: constant progress! Such was her natural ability to find joy in the small matters of everyday life that she was quite excitable and enthused in her working and private life. Gussie may have had a cheerful and happy go lucky disposition most of the time however when things were not going her way or an opinion was not to her liking she was happy to contravene and was capable of mustering a solid argument when required. Although there is a degree of disorganization in the writing, such was the force of her work ethic and harmony in life that she had a keen awareness of what she wanted and was savvy and practical enough and worked hard enough that she usually achieved what she was going for. Gussie had an incredibly sharp intellect and it was very easy for her to see people in a highly accurate way. She was also a very expressive and spontaneous person and these traits combined may have resulted in her being, occasionally, quite critical. Such comments were said on the spur of the moment and may have led to regret, on her part, later on. The writing is quite cerebral with overtones of literary interest. Gussie was an original character with quite individualistic thoughts that she might have put to paper at some stage in the form of a diary or other such writings. The long lead in strokes suggest that Gussie thought a great deal about the past and may have been unnecessarily hard on herself. From the way that the surname is written one can conclude that her parents instilled in her strict conservative views that were not quite suitable for her. Gussie was a head strong, positive and good humored person. She had an analytical mind and worked hard. She was forward looking and was a force to be reckoned with: she had little tolerance for those that tried to hold others back through their words.

J. EDWARD BATDORF
& BEULAH I. WERT

Having been born in Loyalton, Dauphin County, Pennsylvania, in 1885, James Edward Batdorf had little control over his fate. In an area where nearly all employment was tied directly or indirectly to the world's largest deposits of anthracite coal, he became a coal miner. Loyalton is an unincorporated community within Washington Township and it's likely that James went to one of the nine one-room schoolhouses in Washington Township, and dropped out after the equivalent of eighth grade to go to work. According to a 1900 Bureau of Mines report, 363 collieries in the anthracite region employed 143,826 workers, one-fourth of them boys under the age of sixteen.

Though deep-mining anthracite coal was tough and dangerous work—anthracite mine accidents in Eastern Pennsylvania in 1900 killed 411, injured 1,057, and made 230 widows and 525 orphans—it also offered substantial pay. A certified miner could earn twice the national average 1910 pay of $750 a year, equivalent of about $19,000 today. To be certified, a miner had to pass a test in English, buy his own tools and equipment, and hire his own laborers or, as they were called, butties.

Anthracite is the highest grade of coal in the earth. Anthracite burns cleaner, hotter, and four times longer than bituminous and is virtually smoke free, while bituminous combustion emits a sooty black smoke. The anthracite coal mined in Eastern Pennsylvania fueled iron blast furnaces for the production of high-grade steel, drove railroads, and heated homes. The U.S.

Navy especially coveted anthracite. The heat gave warships speed and the lack of smoke gave them stealth.

At 5'6" and about 145 pounds as an adult, James Batdorf was an ideal size for deep mining work. He was a family man, good friend, and a public servant. Just following the New Year of 1906, when he was nineteen, he went to the state capital of Harrisburg to be a pallbearer for a family friend of his sister Frances's finance Samuel Lutz. In August of that year James attended the marriage of his sister and Lutz in his parents' home, where he still lived. Pastor Brown of the Evangelical Church performed the wedding of Frances and Samuel and they departed immediately to honeymoon in Atlantic City.

James and Frances were two of seventeen children born to Thomas

Edward Batdorf and Mary Louisa Peters, both of whom were born in Dauphin County, Pennsylvania. Thomas, who shared the middle name Edward with his son, was the descendant of Batdorfs who were among the Palatines, so called because they emigrated from Palatinate, a region in southwestern Germany. Due to economic devastation and religious persecution following the Thirty Years War that occurred from 1618 to 1638 in Central Europe, many of these German left for America. Those immigrants spoke a German dialect that became the Pennsylvania Dutch language still spoken today by the Amish.

Four of Thomas and Mary's children—Alvin, George, Kirby, and Norman— died in childhood. The other twelve—Verna, Stella, Cora, Harvey, Joseph, Frances, Oscar, James, Adam, Mary Ellen, William, and John—lived into adulthood. James and Beulah, according to the 1900 census return, were literate, able to read and write.

In 1908, James, twenty-three, married Beulah Wert, nineteen. Though James, as his father had, went by his middle name Edward in his day-to-day life, when he was mentioned in local newspapers, such as when he ran as a Republican for inspector of elections in 1917, he was always James. James and Beulah settled in Washington Township to live next to her parents— John Wert, born in neighboring Northumberland County, and Adeline Row, born in Dauphin County.

In the 1910 census the Werts and Batdorfs lived right next door to one another. At age 32, James was listed as short height and medium build, with brown eyes and mixed gray hair. The 1920 census shows both families moved to State Road in Washington Township, and again James and Beulah lived next door to her parents' home, which was described as a farm. The 1920 census also shows John and Adeline had a grandson, John Schiffer, living with them. As James and Beulah had five of their eventual six children by then—Alvin Leroy, Margaret Irene, Mildred Catherine, Harry Franklin and Myrtle Adeline—it's likely they moved to a bigger home. Romaine came later.

James and Beulah were counted in the 1930 and the 1940 census, having moved to Lykens Borough, adjacent to Washington Township. By 1930, although they did not own a radio, the Batdorfs owned a home valued at $4,500, no longer living on farmland. A decade later the family owned a home valued at only $600, equivalent of nearly $10,000 today.

Beulah was born in 1889 in Elizabethville, just five miles southwest of Loyalton, where James was born. Both towns are in the Lykens Valley between the Mahantango and Berry ranges of the Appalachian Mountain range, an idyllic setting of rolling pastures and quaint towns set off by green mountains turning red and gold in the fall and gradually climbing to 1,500 to 2,000 feet. Beulah was the fifth of six siblings of John and Adeline Row Wert, coming after Caroline, Harriet, a third child about whom little is known, and Florence.

Beulah was the fifth child, followed by her sister Margaret. Beulah's work ethic was as strong as her husband's. She did most of the child rearing, kept the house, worked the family's garden, and was also a skilled dressmaker. In 1950, at the age of sixty-one, she was working hanging wallpaper.

Mildred Moon writes: The Batdorf Family of Lykens, Pennsylvania. Daughter Mildred was born Mildred Catherine Batdorf on January 29, 1911 the daughter of Beulah Wert and James "Edward" Batdorf. She was the sister of my grandmother Myrtle, Alvin, Margaret, Harry, Ruth and Romaine. Mildred and Myrtle were born and raised in Big Run, Pennsylvania. Their mother Beulah was the daughter of John and Adeline Wert of Big Run. The Wert family farmed and "were hard-working people." James Edward was the son of Thomas and Mary Batdorf, also of Big Run. Their "grandmother Batdorf was a housewife and grandfather Batdorf was a farmer and worked in the mines." Myrtle and Mildred "lived in a two-story house and ate in the kitchen." Their home was heated by coal and they did not have a fireplace. The family did not always have electricity, as candles, kerosene and coal were used. The home had a cellar and water was retrieved from a well. Mail was delivered by rural route and they "had a cat named Blacky." Mildred was the fourth child born and Myrtle was the youngest of the seven children. As a child, their major chore, among others, was doing the dishes. Their mother did the cooking and ironing and she taught them to sew, crochet, knit and embroider. Mildred learned to drive a car from a neighborhood boy and her husband Randall Moon taught her to cook. Mildred and Myrtle's father, Edward Batdorf, was a miner and Mildred worked to help contribute to the family income. She was fourteen years old when she secured her first job. The family had a garden and they "dug the ground and got it ready to plant. They grew potatoes, lettuce, celery, onions, tomatoes, peppers, cabbage and a lot more." They had cherry and peach trees. Their mother did canning and raised chickens and the family often ate beef, pork and chicken. Her parents and siblings did all the work, hiring no one to help with the house, garden or animals. "Saturday was the day that you got a rest for the weekend and Sunday we got ready for church." The family attended a little church in Loyalton. For Christmas they would wake up early to see the tree and they received clothes as gifts. On July Fourth, "my brother had a birthday and we had games that we played." In general, however, sibling's birthdays were just another day. For her birthday, Mildred received clothes made by her mother. The family did not entertain often but they did go to family picnics. She kept in touch with distant family and visited relatives often. In the summer, "we sat under a nice shade tree to keep cool" and in the winter kept warm with long johns. Mildred recalls one extreme winter storm when the snow reached up over the fences. For recreation, the children played jump rope, ball and cards. Mildred's best friend was Hilda Buffington and they often played games for fun. Mildred did not learn to swim and the family never went on vacation. Growing up, there was no place to shop so the family ordered items from "men who came around and the next day he came with it." They never went to the city to shop but there was a small country store. Lykens was the largest town nearby and Mildred used to take the train to visit her grandmother in Elizabethville. My father "got a car when I was ten years old. It was a Ford model T." Mildred attended a little red one-room schoolhouse in Big Run. It was only two houses away and she usually walked to school alone. Mildred was closest to her mother and she admired her father most. When young, Mildred "hoped to be a good housekeeper." Her family supported and encouraged her and they influenced her and helped her develop skills. When asked if she would choose the same career path, she said, "No. I would choose for a better life." "I met my husband in Lykens. I was engaged on Easter and married on October 1, 1926." Mildred was married a dentist in Hagerstown and her children were born in...[remainder missing]. [Mildred Batdorf Moon and Marc D. Thompson, January 1999]

Growing industries, railroads, and WWI kept the demand for coal high during the 1910s and 1920s—thus James and Beulah thrived. About 1922, the family bought its first automobile, a Ford Model T. They found plenty of recreation in the Lykens Valley with home-based card parties, church picnics, hiking clubs, and colliery competitions with baseball and tug of war games. Visiting family and friends was a pastime. The area was well connected by rail and in 1911, when James's brother Harvey visited his parents at Elizabethville, it was a news item in the Harrisburg Patriot's Nearby Towns section. A card party held by a Beatrice Batdorf at Lykens was also news.

They likely did not have electricity for the first twenty-five years of their marriage, because as late as 1936, 75 percent of Pennsylvania farms were not electrified. So they used candles and lanterns for nighttime light, heated with coal, and fetched water from a well. The family kept a garden—really a small truck farm— growing potatoes, lettuce, celery, onions, tomatoes, peppers, and cabbages, cherry and peach trees, and raising chickens, cows, and hogs. The children were expected to help with chores, and by the age of fourteen or so, they were getting their first jobs and contributing to the family's expenses.

Baseball and bowling were popular pastimes. Lykens and Elizabethville both had teams in the Twin County baseball league. A man named Batdorf, no first name given, was one of the top bowlers in the Allison

Hill league. An F. Batdorf played basketball for the Wiconisco High School team in the early 1920s. It is not known if James was a ballplayer or bowler, but it's likely he participated in colliery games

When the anthracite industry waned in the 1930s due to the Depression, James continued working as a road construction laborer with the Work Progress Administration and later for Lykens Borough, and was still working when he died in 1954 at age sixty-nine. Beulah survived him by twenty-nine years, living to her late nineties, the oldest age reached by any female ancestor in this line. They are buried side by side at Calvary United Methodist in Wiconisco. Myrtle, the direct ancestor of the Thompson line, grew up and went to school in the very small town of Big Run.

Gerald G. Thompson writes: On my mother's side, my grandma was Beulah and she was a homemaker and my grandpa was James Batdorf, a miner, from Lykens. They were extremely down to earth folks. I always looked forward to our Sunday dinner at Grandma's house, where I learned patience and truthfulness. I remember dinners at Beulah's being regular and long, getting treats and listening to her bible stories. [Gerald G. Thompson and Marc D. Thompson, May 1990]

James Edward Batdorf was baptized on June 6, 1886 in Dauphin County, Pennsylvania (Oakdale Evangelical Circuit). He was counted in the census in 1900 in Washington, Dauphin County, Pennsylvania. He was employed as a Day laborer in 1900. He was employed as a Miner in 1908. He was employed as a Miner, Coalmine in 1910. He was counted in the census in 1910 in Washington, Dauphin County, Pennsylvania. He lived in Loyalton, Dauphin County, Pennsylvania in 1918. He was employed as a Miner, Susquehanna Colliery Co in 1918 in Dauphin County, Pennsylvania. He lived in Loyalton, Dauphin County, Pennsylvania in 1918. He was counted in the census in 1920 in Washington, Dauphin County, Pennsylvania. He lived in Washington Township, Dauphin County, Pennsylvania in 1920 (State Road 199). He was employed as a Miner, Coal mine in 1920. He was employed as a Miner, Lykens Coal Co about 1925 in Dauphin County, Pennsylvania. He lived in Lykens, Dauphin County, Pennsylvania in 1930 (480 North Street). He was counted in the census in 1930 in Lykens, Dauphin County, Pennsylvania. He was employed as a Laborer, Coal washery in 1930. He owned $4500 in 1930. He was employed as a Laborer in 1935. He was counted in the census in 1940 in Lykens, Dauphin County, Pennsylvania. He was employed as a Laborer at a Road Construction Yard in 1940 in Lykens, Dauphin County, Pennsylvania. He lived in Lykens, Dauphin County, Pennsylvania in 1942 (542 North Street). He was employed as a WPA worker in 1942 in Harrisburg, Dauphin County, Pennsylvania. His Social Security Number was 205-09-5145. He was affiliated with the Loyalton EUB Church religion in 1954 in Loyalton, Dauphin County, Pennsylvania. He lived in Lykens, Dauphin County, Pennsylvania in 1954 (542 North St.). His funeral took place in 1954 in Lykens, Dauphin County, Pennsylvania (John R. Shultz Funeral Home, 406 Market St.). His funeral took place in 1954 in Lykens, Dauphin County, Pennsylvania (Reiff? Helt?, 523 W. Main St.). He was employed as a Labor in 1954 in Lykens, Dauphin County, Pennsylvania. His estate was probated in 1954. He was buried on August 23, 1954 in Wiconisco, Dauphin County, Pennsylvania (Calvary United Methodist Cemetery). His weight was 143 pounds. His cause of death was Coronary occlusion w/hypertension w/diabetes mellitus. His height was 5 foot, 6 inches. He was affiliated with the Evangelical United Brethren (Methodist) < Reformed religion. He was named after Father Thomas Edward Batdorf. He was listed as short height, medium build, brown eyes, and mixed gray hair [1917].

James Personality Analysis: Early life: James was a warm-hearted person. He enjoyed the good life, had dreams of material wealth and had a good sense of humor. His relaxed nature made it easy for him to keep and make friends. He had a strange mix of having a deep interest in cultural matters and also a high level of social intelligence; he was both extroverted and cultured. In this period of his life James was a flexible individual who welcomed change. This skill of adapting was not limited to vocation and location he was also a pragmatic individual who was able to be friendly and conservative at different points. Such was his adaptability that at times he could be easily coerced into a course of action and could easily lose himself in the more liberal aspects of life. James was an extremely empathetic person. He had an open, honest and friendly nature. He was highly sympathetic and was always willing to give of his time and energy to help others. Such was his sociable nature it was easy for him to become emotionally involved in the concerns of others. It is my guess that he would use his fun loving, generous and humorous nature to lift other people spirits in a conscious effort to see them through their harder times. Such was James's enthusiastic spirit that he was unrealistically ambitious when he was younger. At that stage in his life he over assessed his abilities and undertook projects or workloads that were larger than he could ever have possibly completed. Had he set his sights a little lower and set an easier pace he would not have been so easily dis-heartened and would therefore have achieved more. However, this aspect of James was part of the warm, funny and larger than life persona that he was living at that time in his life and was probably viewed a little quirk or eccentricity of his. James was a fluid man; his early life was one of free flowing expression and friendship. He gave a great deal to other people in the way of kind words, stories, support and encouragement. As much as he gave he also sought, greatly valued and to an extent depended upon the support of others. Later life: There are some marked differences between the writing produced by James when he was 32 and the writing he produced when he was 59. The writing in the first sample is wider and fuller indicating that, as one might expect, in his earlier life James was more relaxed and active. As is natural, when he was younger he was constantly searching for something but as he became the years passed on his exuberance and desire to give vivid and colorful descriptions diminished. As he became older and more experienced his approach to work also changed. The writing has variable pressure and a convex baseline in 1917 but by 1945 all this has changed and at this point the writing is more regular; by then it had developed a straight baseline and the pressure was even. This change is definitely the result of nearly 30 years in the workforce. In his early days he was unable to assess his own abilities and although he began projects with much gusto he would be easily dis-heartened at the first glitch. At this time, he also had trouble managing his energy levels and would become easily tired. By the age of 59 these problems had been ironed out and he had the 'know how' to gauge a project with accuracy and manage his own expectations and energy effectively. Whilst the writing in 1917 has a fairly poetic quality (full, elaborate and detailed) the writing in 1945 has a more competitive (angular), practical (less legible) and stressed (narrow) nature. Life was hard back then and I imagine especially hard for those who spent their working lives in mineshafts. The more compressed nature of the writing reflects the adaptive skill of James. The fact that he worked for so long and so hard and lived to the ripe age of 68, which was very old for those days can only mean that he was a survivor, he had to smarten up and harden up just in order to keep his head above water. The fact that in 1945 he now took the time to elaborate on his middle name and write it out in full could only mean that he had more confidence and pride in himself, which was no doubt well earned.

Beulah Irene Wert was baptized on May 18, 1890 in Berrysburg, Dauphin County, Pennsylvania (St. Johns (Hill) Lutheran). She was counted in the census in 1900 in Washington, Dauphin County, Pennsylvania. She was educated at School in 1900. She was counted in the census in 1910 in Washington, Dauphin County, Pennsylvania. She was counted in the census in 1920 in Washington, Dauphin County, Pennsylvania. She was employed as a Dressmaker in 1920 in Washington, Dauphin County, Pennsylvania. She was counted in the census in 1930 in Lykens, Dauphin County, Pennsylvania. She was employed as a Housewife in 1935. She was counted in the census in 1940 in Lykens, Dauphin County, Pennsylvania. She was employed as a Wallpaperer about 1950. She lived in Harrisburg, Dauphin County, Pennsylvania in 1956. She lived in Dauphin County, Pennsylvania in 1983.

She was affiliated with the St. Christopher Evangelical Lutheran Church religion in 1983 in Lykens, Dauphin County, Pennsylvania. She lived in Selinsgrove, Snyder County, Pennsylvania in 1983 (800 Broad Street). She lived in Big Run, Coaldale, Erdman, Germantown, Loyalton, Lykens, and Specktown, all Dauphin County, Pennsylvania in 1983. Her Social Security Number was 162-22-1417. Her funeral took place in 1983 in Lykens, Dauphin County, Pennsylvania (Schultz Funeral Home, 406 Market St.). She was employed as a Seamstress (Clothing) in 1983. She was buried on June 14, 1983 in Wiconisco, Dauphin County, Pennsylvania (Calvary United Methodist Cemetery). Her cause of death was acute congestive cardiac failure w/poss. brain stem CVA and ASCVD. She was affiliated with the Evangelical United Brethren (Methodist) < Lutheran religion. She was named after Cousin Beulah May Rowe.

Beulah Personality Analysis: Beulah was a friendly and a harmonious person. She enjoyed life and had found professions that suited her visual and aesthetic interests and abilities. Due to her settled nature and balanced emotions she seemed to drift easily into vocations that suited her. She most likely never gave any thought as to why it was she was able to find herself in the right place at the right time but most likely this aspect of her life was due to her enthused but relaxed, casually expectant energy. Her abilities in her working life were the direct result of her open communication style (on professional matters), ability to concentrate for long periods of time and natural feel for what would work visually and crucially, what would not. Beulah was a highly ambitious woman although she may not have advertised this. She had a strong work ethic and was always very conscious of deadlines. Although she was happy in her working life, she could be quite distant in her personal life and would enjoy spending time alone perhaps reading or indulging in other visual, creative activities. She was also prone to having periods where her mood could dip, often quite suddenly. I have noticed this trait (characterized by a sudden dip towards the end of lines or signatures) is present in every Batdorf signature I have seen and therefore I have to conclude that it is a learned behavior. On certain topics such as history, politics and art Beulah was openly expressive and found it easy to form and discuss her opinions. However, due to an early home life that was slightly complex and restrictive it was difficult for her to express how she felt emotionally and she would often gloss over (often with the use of humor) the parts of her personal life that she was less at ease with. Any bottling up of feelings and expression were manifested through her ambition and work drive and homemaking skills. Beulah was an earthy and warm woman, who was friendly and loved life. She may well have had an expressive and vivacious nature but at the same time she was a difficult person to really get to know well. As a consequence of her natural visual abilities she threw herself into her work and must have been an outstanding asset for her employers of the time.

WILLIAM DUNCAN
& CHARLOTTE V. LAYMAN

William Duncan, the eldest son of Fredrick and Catherine Duncan, was born in just after New Years of 1876 in Sunbury, Pennsylvania. He was baptized that same year at the Zion Evangelical Lutheran Church and bore the name of his German grandfather, Wilhelm, anglicized as William. The building that housed the church was built in 1803 with the help of another similar but decidedly different religion, the German Reformed Church. The two denominations shared the building and its 65-acre grounds for almost 100 years. It would later be known as the Stone Valley Church.

William grew up in Sunbury with his two older sisters, Melinda and Sallie, and was followed by three more siblings, Gerty, Lilly, and Charley. Being the oldest boy, William probably preferred to follow his father as a laborer, but settled into the blacksmith trade. William was working as a blacksmith's apprentice when he met Charlotte Virginia Layman, called Lottie by her family and friends. The two were married in 1899—he was 23 and she was twenty. Both, according to the 1900 census return, were literate, able to read and write.

The following year, William started his own blacksmith business, but the business was short-lived as the Industrial Age made small blacksmithing enterprises all but obsolete. By the late 1800s, the railroads had linked the country and hardware was manufactured at plants and sold in hardware stores. In 1901, William was a laborer, possibly in the rail yards, providing for his wife and new son, Irvin Wilfred Duncan, born one day before Thanksgiving November 27, 1901. William would need to use the adventurous spirit instilled in him by his father, Fredrick, who left Germany to come to the New World to make ends meet.

Lottie was the second of fourteen children born to Joseph Layman and Rebecca Overlander Layman. Lottie was born on May 12, 1879 in Brogueville, York County, Pennsylvania. At that time in history, Brogueville was largely a lush agricultural area of mainly wheat and tobacco. It is speculated that Joseph may have been a farmer of one or both of these crops. Being the second of fourteen children, Lottie was undoubtedly depended upon to look after her younger siblings and probably worked on the family farm as well. These experiences at such a young age almost certainly taught her confidence and self-reliance.

A devastating flood of 1884 effected the Layman family greatly. A rainstorm started on the night of June 25 and lasted until about three a.m. the next morning. A record twelve inches of rain fell in just over seven hours. The devastation was realized the next morning when the Codorus Creek, usually about 85 feet wide, was now one-quarter of a mile wide. Bridges and train tracks were washed away, debris from up the stream—buildings, farming implements, furniture, dead and living animals—were seen in the passing waters. The cost of repairs to the county exceeded $700,000 with $91,000 just in temporary bridges. In today's terms that would equal approximately a Billion Dollars. In addition, an earthquake rocked York

County only two months later in August and shortly thereafter Joseph pulled up stakes in Brogueville and moved to Sunbury, Pennsylvania.

After their marriage, William worked for a short period as a machinist, probably for the railroad. Unfortunately, pulmonary tuberculosis would take William from the family in September 1906, at the young age of thirty. Lottie was left to care for her son, now age five. Shortly after William's death, Lottie married William H. McNutt, a gentleman five years her junior and, after that marriage dissolved, Lottie remarried another William—William Grant Willard—in 1920. William Willard had nine children with his first wife, Elizabeth, who died in 1916; he brought five of these children into his marriage with Lottie.

The blending of the two families did not go well and Irvin was ostracized by his step-brothers and step-sisters. They were married for thirteen years. He was eighteen at the time of the marriage and probably moved out on his own. However, Lottie and Irvin's relationship went unrivaled and Irvin remained the main man in her life.

By 1930, the Willards owned a home valued at $5,000, no longer living on farmland, and had a radio to entertain throughout the evenings. That home value is the equivalent of about $70,000 today. In 1933, the third William passed away. After the death of her third husband, Lottie went to live with Irvin and his wife, Mamie. Lottie passed away in 1936 at their home in Monroe, Snyder County, Pennsylvania. William and Lottie's only child, Irvin, was the direct ancestor of the Thompson line.

Shirley M. Duncan writes: I know little of my Duncan grandparents. Grandpa William died before I was born. Although Lottie died just months after I was born, she was a lady ahead of her time.

She was a strong, independent woman, a good mother and wife. She remarried after my grandpa died but she divorced him because he had hit my father when he was a child. She finally remarried a third time, to William Willard. Our family was very impoverished. [Shirley M. Duncan and Marc D. Thompson, December 1995]

William Duncan was baptized on September 29, 1876 in Pennsylvania (Zion Evangelical Lutheran). He was counted in the census in 1880 in Sunbury, Northumberland County, Pennsylvania. He lived in Pennsylvania in 1899. He was employed as a Blacksmith helper in 1899. He lived in Sunbury, Northumberland County, Pennsylvania in 1899. He lived in Pennsylvania in 1900 (929 Railroad Ave.). He was employed as a Blacksmith in 1900. He lived in Sunbury, Northumberland County, Pennsylvania in 1900 (929 Railroad Ave.). He was counted in the census in 1900 in Sunbury, Northumberland County, Pennsylvania. He was employed as a Laborer in 1901. He lived in Pennsylvania in 1901 (918 Susquehanna Ave.). He lived in Sunbury, Northumberland County, Pennsylvania in 1901 (918 Susquehanna Ave.). His funeral took place in 1906 in Pennsylvania (J. Hartman). He lived in Pennsylvania in 1906 (920 Susquehanna Ave.). His funeral took place in 1906 in Sunbury, Northumberland County, Pennsylvania (J. Hartman). He lived in Sunbury, Northumberland County, Pennsylvania in 1906 (920 Susquehanna Ave.). He was employed as a Machinist in 1906. He signed his will on July 24, 1906 in Sunbury, Northumberland County, Pennsylvania (No 424). He was buried on September 14, 1906 in Sunbury, Northumberland County, Pennsylvania (Pomfret Manor Cemetery, 130B). His estate was probated on September 17, 1906 in Pennsylvania. His estate was probated on September 17, 1906 in Sunbury, Northumberland County, Pennsylvania. His cause of death was pulmonary tuberculosis. He was affiliated with the Evangelical Lutheran religion. He was employed as a Railroad. He was named after Grandfather William Dankert.

William Personality Analysis: William had a great deal of energy available to him and this enabled him to cope with the everyday business of doing a physical day's work. Vitality levels were enough for him to accomplish whatever he wanted to do, however his restlessness and constant search for new stimuli made it difficult for him to definitely commit to any one profession or prolonged task. It was this component of persistence that he lacked; the draw of the new and the interesting was quite simply too much for him to resist and consequently he had multiple purposes in life. William's lack of staying power and excitability may have meant that he lacked long-term goals but it also gave him tremendous flexibility and he willingly adapted to new people, novel experiences and occupations. In working life, he was proud, competitive and forthright with his opinions. Socially William had a strange mix of characteristics. He was a social man; a great story teller who was able to add detail for effect and tell tales with some flamboyance. He loved company was relaxed and humorous but was also a private man who would 'keep the sunny side out' always maintaining, or at least appearing to maintain, an optimistic outlook. It was important for him to spend time alone and he enjoyed his own company. William was a creature of temperament and may have occasionally come into conflict with other people as he could be quite vocal, opinionated and unwilling to back down from an argument once a conflict was underway. Occasionally his competitive spirit may have over extended itself and where he may have been previously bold he could become verbally brutal and insensitive. On the whole though he was a humored and encouraging person who would take the time to listen to the opinions of other people. He had a lively and original mind and was drawn towards visual stimuli enjoying nature and human contact to the fullest extent.

Charlotte "Lottie" Virginia Layman lived in Pennsylvania in 1899. She lived in Sunbury, Northumberland County, Pennsylvania in 1899. She was counted in the census in 1900 in Sunbury, Northumberland County, Pennsylvania. She was listed as "own income" in 1900. She lived in Sunbury, Northumberland County, Pennsylvania in 1910 (63 8th St.). She lived in Pennsylvania in 1910 (63 8th St.). She was counted in the census in 1910 in Sunbury, Northumberland County, Pennsylvania. She was counted in the census in 1920 in Sunbury, Northumberland County, Pennsylvania (w/Willard). She lived in Sunbury, Northumberland County, Pennsylvania from 1920-1930 (920 Susquehanna Ave.). She lived in Pennsylvania from 1920-1930 (920 Susquehanna Ave.). She was counted in the census in 1930 in Sunbury, Northumberland County, Pennsylvania (w/Willard). Her funeral took place in 1936 in Selinsgrove, Snyder County, Pennsylvania (F.K. Sutton). She was employed as a Retired in 1936. She was buried on March 3, 1936 in Sunbury, Northumberland County, Pennsylvania (Pomfret Manor Cemetery). Her cause of death was cerebral hemorrhage w/interstitial nephritis. She signed her will (Intestate). She was named after Great-grandmother Charlotte Geib. She was affiliated with the Methodist religion.

Lottie Personality Analysis: Lottie was a highly organized, intelligent and conservative lady who was happy to give of her time in order to encourage others. Throughout her life her main point of reference was society; she always had a particular set of rules in place when consciously determining her behavior. As a result, she lived life in a highly controlled and cautious way. The availability of energy would vary a great deal in this writer's life. When starting a task or a project, at the beginning things would seem to be too much for her and she would become overwhelmed. With perseverance and organization, she did learn to overcome and work through these temporary feelings of confusion to a successful end. Although she was highly controlled and she concealed much of her life she had a congenial attitude towards other people and would be happy to be involved and to contribute to any discussions that were underway. She could harbor strong sentiments of either love or distain but was not always able to openly communicate these emotions as she was almost always afraid of creating the wrong impression. Lottie was a bit of an escapist and would often retreat into pleasant pastimes (perhaps she had a deep appreciation of history to a cultural level) rather than face unpleasant realities. She did tend to bottle up her feelings and as a result has a degree of unexpressed anger in her writing. Lottie was, at times, conflicted between a desire to get out there and enjoy with abandon and a frustration derived from her desire to live up to the idea that she had of other's expectations. She had cultural leanings and was keen to learn. As a way of expressing her desire (but inability) to live life to the fullest she was happy to share and even promote her cultural knowledge. Lottie learned to be conservative from her upbringing. Her family were often distant and the mood in her household might have seemed stable, but there was much that was unexpressed and unexplained to her. Lottie found a great deal of joy and (some) release in the more conservative and visual endeavors of the time.

WILLIAM M. ANDERSON
& EMMA L. KEEFER

William Morris Anderson and Emma Louisa Keefer married in 1902 and were husband and wife for more than sixty years. They spent their entire lives within 50 miles of their birthplaces, and upon their deaths came to rest together in a local cemetery. It made perfect sense to them that they would never move from the area as both of them came from families with very deep local roots. Their parents had all been born nearby, as had six of their eight grandparents.

Neither William nor Emma was highly educated, but they were physically strong, tireless, and determined to make a good life for themselves and for their children. Both, according to the 1900 census return, were literate, able to read and write. They never felt entitled to "something for nothing." They were never wealthy in terms of possessions, but because they had worked for everything they had, they valued it all the more.

They took for granted that their commitment to each other was meant to last a lifetime. They were a devoted couple until Emma's death, at the age of eighty, in 1963. When William passed away eight years later, he was buried with Emma in Orchard Hill Cemetery in Shamokin Dam, Snyder County, Pennsylvania.

For his whole life, William made his living through the sweat of his brow and the effort of his strong arms. Emma worked hard too in a silk mill even before she was out of her teen years, as a housekeeper for pay in other people's homes, and—like nearly all the women she knew—as a mother and a wife. In an era when large families were the norm, Emma's growing brood of eight children was not unusual, except for one remarkable fact: her eight children included three sets of twins!

The Pennsylvania in which William and Emma lived their lives was known as the "most foreign" of the former American colonies. Unlike its neighboring colonies, Pennsylvania was founded by the Dutch not by the English. As a result of this history, it became a magnet for immigrants from German-speaking regions of Europe. More than 70 percent of immigrants to Pennsylvania before 1790 had been German, and German influence was still pervasive in rural areas such as Snyder, Northumberland, and Schuylkill counties.

Among the strong values the German immigrants had brought with them was their belief in education. As a result, Pennsylvania was one of the first states to pass a public education law. The Pennsylvania State Constitution of 1790 required free public education for children whose families could not afford to pay for schooling. However, despite the good intentions of the law, the development of public schools was slow, and it was only when William was fifteen years old—in 1895—that the state authorized every county to establish public high schools. Chances are that William and

Emma's education ended before high school age, when they became old enough to begin to earn a living.

William was born on June 11, 1880, in McKees Half Falls in southeastern Pennsylvania's Snyder County. He was the son of James M. Anderson and Lucetta Gaugler, both of whom had been born in Snyder County. William had one older brother, Charles, and he was followed by Theodore, Thomas, Amy, Josephine, and Catherine. William bore the name of his great and great-great-grandfathers, both named William Anderson, who immigrated to America and began the Anderson legacy.

Emma came along two years later on the final day of March 1882, in the town of Ashland, two counties to the east in Schuylkill County. Her parents were James Pollock Keefer, who was born in Northumberland County, Pennsylvania, and Emma Louisa Livezly, born in Schuylkill County. Emma was named for her own mother, who died four days after baby Emma's birth.

Curiously, Emma's paternal grandmother, Margaret Matilda Keefer, is the only relative who seems to have been present at Emma's baptism, which took place at the local Zion Evangelical Lutheran Church. After her mother Emma's death at age eighteen and her father's death ten years later, young Emma relocated to her paternal grandparents' home—The Keefers—in Sunbury, Pennsylvania until she met and wed William.

By the time they were out of their teens, William had temporarily moved one county to the east and Emma had moved one county to the west. It was there, in Northumberland County, where they met and married. William grew to 5 foot 7 inches tall, an average height for a man in those days, and he was strong and sturdy with a medium build. His dark hair and blue eyes must have been attractive to Emma, and his strong work ethic would have suggested that he make be a good life partner.

At the time of their marriage on July 19, 1902, William was employed as a woodworker and Emma was a winder in a local silk mill. William later joined Emma in the local Northumberland County textile industry working as a laborer in a Sunbury dye works. By the turn of the century, synthetic dyes had largely replaced natural dyes. A dye works, in which raw threads and fabrics were colored, would have been a hot, backbreaking place to work.

Within a few years, though, the Andersons had moved their growing family across the Susquehanna River into Snyder County, a rural region of rolling hills and flat creek valleys, nearly all in farms or forests. In those days, most local residents made their living as farmers through harvesting and milling the hardwoods and softwoods of the forests, or on the railroad.

At one time or another during his life, William tried his hand at every one of the region's primary economic enterprises. He had been a woodworker in Northumberland County, then he went to work for the railroad, and within a few more years he would become a one of the nation's several million small farmers.

In those decades, the Pennsylvania Railroad was a powerful wealthy enterprise. Laying track throughout the state to serve the state's coal mines and moving goods and passengers, it had an overstated influence in Pennsylvania State politics. Highly skilled railroad workers—such as locomotive engineers—were well-paid but common laborers who worked in dangerous exhausting jobs for very low wages. For a few years, William was one of these hard-working, poorly paid men.

During the 1920s, he tried his hand at farming, but it was a difficult time in America to be a farmer. America had suffered recession and depression in the aftermath of World War I, and though urban America had recovered, rural America suffered economically through the 1920s. Small farmers throughout America made do with very little money, though they were able to cushion themselves by raising most of their own food. When the Great Depression slammed rural America, however, the life of the small farmer became untenable and William had to find another line of work.

The New Deal's Works Progress Administration put millions of men to work as laborers in all parts of the nation. William was one of them, doing whatever he needed to do in order to care for his family. In addition to frequent jobs as a housekeeper, Emma kept busy as the mother of their eight children. The Andersons' first child, William Clemens, was born the year after their marriage. Next came Florence Violet.

Starting in 1908, Emma bore three sets of twins in a row. Charles Benton and Mamie Lucetta were born in 1908. This birth took place in the Andersons' house not in a hospital, which was typical for rural America in the early 1900s. It is likely that Emma's other births took place at home, too. Harvey Melvin and Harry Nevan were born next, with Donald Morris and David George completing the family. Remarkably, in those days before modern medicine, all eight children survived to adulthood.

By 1930, they were the only remaining couple of this generation not to own home or a radio. They rented on what would be the last couple to be engaged in farming, the others of the generations owning homes and working for businesses outside of agriculture and mining. A decade later, they were renting a home for $10, approximately equal to $160 today.

During their lifetimes, from the 1880s to the 1960s, William and Emma witnessed astonishing technological advances in their world. At the turn of the century, people's transportation choices had been limited to walking or riding steam-powered railroads and horse-drawn wagons. But in 1908, Henry Ford introduced the Model T—reliable, serviceable, and relatively affordable.

A typical assembly-line worker could earn enough to buy a Model T in four months. It would take longer for a farmer to earn enough to purchase an automobile or truck, but by the end of the 1920, even rural areas were connected by paved roads, with automobiles buzzing back and forth. We don't know when William and Emma first "got wheels," but it must have been an exciting day for the whole family!

The typical rural house in the 1880s lacked heating, electric lighting, and indoor plumbing. In fact, in 1925, of the 6.3 million farms in America, barely 200,000 had electric service. Beginning with the New Deal's Rural Electrification Act, the federal government began working with local authorities to bring electricity to rural areas like southeastern Pennsylvania. It is not known when William and Emma were first able to flip a switch and turn on a simple lightbulb, or when they were able to make a telephone call, or turn a tap, or flush a toilet, but by the end of their lives, the lack of these amenities was a distant memory.

William and Emma both lived to see their eighties, Emma passing in April 1963 and William in May of 1969. They are buried in the Orchard Hill cemetery in Shamokin Dam. William and Emma's fourth child, Mamie—one of the sets of twins born in 1908—was the direct ancestor of the Thompson line.

William Morris Anderson was baptized on June 11, 1880 in McKees Half Falls, Chapman, Snyder County, Pennsylvania. He was counted in the census in 1900 in Sunbury, Northumberland County, Pennsylvania. He was employed as a Day laborer in 1900. He lived in Pennsylvania in 1900 (Front St.). He lived in Sunbury, Northumberland County, Pennsylvania in 1900 (Front St.). He was employed as a Woodworker in 1902. He lived in Sunbury, Northumberland County, Pennsylvania in 1902. He lived in Pennsylvania in 1902. He was employed as a Laborer, at the Dye works in 1910. He was counted in the census in 1910 in Sunbury, Northumberland County, Pennsylvania. He lived in Sunbury, Northumberland County, Pennsylvania in 1910 (1129 Railroad Ave.). He lived in Pennsylvania in 1910 (1129 Railroad Ave.). He lived in Shamokin Dam, Snyder County, Pennsylvania in 1917. He lived in Shamokin Dam, Snyder County, Pennsylvania in 1917. He was employed as a laborer at the Dye Works, Sunbury in 1917. He had medium height, medium build, blue eyes, and dark hair in 1917. He was counted in the census in 1920 in Monroe, Snyder County, Pennsylvania. He was employed as a Laborer, Railroad in 1920. He was counted in the census in 1930 in Buffalo, Union County, Pennsylvania. He was employed as a Farmer, general farming in 1930. He was employed as a Laborer, WPA in 1940. He was counted in the census in 1940 in Hummel's Wharf, Snyder County, Pennsylvania. He lived in Selinsgrove, Snyder County, Pennsylvania in 1942 (315 E. Walnut St.). He lived in Selinsgrove, Snyder County, Pennsylvania in 1942 (315 E. Walnut St.). He lived in Williamsport, Pennsylvania in 1950. He lived in Williamsport, Pennsylvania in 1950. He was employed as a Custodian, Selinsgrove High School about 1950 in Pennsylvania. He lived in

Selinsgrove, Snyder County, Pennsylvania from 1963-1969 (310 W. Snyder St.). He lived in Selinsgrove, Snyder County, Pennsylvania from 1963-1969 (310 W. Snyder St.). He lived in Selinsgrove, Snyder County, Pennsylvania in 1969 (RD 2). He lived in Blue Hill, Dogtown, Jackson, Kantz, Kratzerville, Penn Avon, Salem, Selinsgrove, and Verdilla, all Snyder, Pennsylvania in 1969. His Social Security Number was 205-03-1604. His funeral took place in 1969 in Selinsgrove, Snyder County, Pennsylvania. He lived in Selinsgrove, Snyder County, Pennsylvania in 1969 (RD 2). He lived in Blue Hill, Dogtown, Jackson, Kantz, Kratzerville, Penn Avon, Salem, Selinsgrove, and Verdilla, all Snyder, Pennsylvania in 1969. He was buried on May 14, 1969 in Shamokin Dam, Snyder County, Pennsylvania (Orchard Hill (West Side) Cemetery). He was affiliated with the Methodist religion. He was named after Great-grandfathers William Anderson and William Kelly. His cause of death was Gastrointestinal bleeding w/possible cancer of stomach and arteriosclerosis.

William Personality Analysis: William was a good worker, he was persistent and goal orientated. He also possessed tremendous willpower and was positive in the sense that he was always working towards completion of a task. Such was his practical and analytical nature he would have been good at seeing quicker and more efficient ways of completing a designated task. What he had in efficiency and analytical ability he lacked in pliability and flexibility; he was frequently tense preferring to forsake the smooth, easy going way of life for the quick advantages gained from more contentious methods of negotiation and progression. William was a highly intelligent man; he had a great memory and when he was not clouded my emotion, clear reasoning. To a large extent he lived in his mind, that is not to say that he was a dreamer because he backed up his ideas and thinking with action. His energy levels were linked to his moods and were therefore variable. When he upbeat and working hard he was proud of what he achieved, however when his energy lagged and he felt that he was falling behind in his work he could become quite downbeat. William had abundant social skills. He was curious, talkative and articulate (he was able to give charismatic and vivid descriptions). His natural ambition and work drive might well have served to evolve these social skills into business and leadership skills. There were however some factors that hampered his development: he was quite short term in his strategies and thinking and would often overreact to objection and criticism and become confrontational. When he came up against these obstacles his reaction, at least in his early years, would be to head off and start again in a new direction rather than persist on existing projects with alternative methods. When he liked and trusted an individual William would go out of his way to help them; for those he admired he could be very giving with his personal time and energy. His mind was a very busy place and his thought processes were often tainted by emotions, perhaps it is for this reason that he grew to appreciate the beauty of human kindness so much. The style of the two samples (1902 and 1945) are largely the same but there are some differences worthy of remark. The second sample is clearly more regular (and therefore legible) especially in the middle zone; latterly he had much more of a calm confidence about him and was a great deal more organized and less stressed out attitude towards life (although he was still a competitive and hardworking). There is also a great deal more rhythm in the second sample indicating that as he became older he was able to gain a greater command on the direction of his life and anticipate forthcoming events with greater accuracy. Furthermore, the baseline becomes more even indicating that his moods were on a more even keel in 1945 as compared to 23 years earlier. There is some relief when comparing the second signature to the first, particularly in reference to the surname. Where the surname in the first signature is very narrow, irregular, flooded and contains some retracing over a mistake, the surname in the second signature is clearer, has rhythm, is regular and even has an extended right tend on the last letter. It is as if William, by the age of 65, had made his peace with his family and held them in much higher esteem ('Anderson' is larger and wider in the second sample) than he did when he was a young man of 22.

Emma Louise Keefer was baptized on June 2, 1882 in Pennsylvania (Zion Evangelical Lutheran, Emma's grandmother, Matilda Keefer, was present at baptism, but her parents were not). She was counted in the census in 1900 in Sunbury, Northumberland County, Pennsylvania. She was employed as a Winder, Silk Mill in 1900. She lived in Pennsylvania in 1902. She lived in Sunbury, Northumberland County, Pennsylvania in 1902. She was counted in the census in 1910 in Sunbury, Northumberland County, Pennsylvania. She was employed as a Housework in 1920. She was counted in the census in 1920 in Monroe, Snyder County, Pennsylvania. She was counted in the census in 1930 in Buffalo, Union County, Pennsylvania. She was counted in the census in 1940 in Hummel's Wharf, Snyder County, Pennsylvania. Her funeral took place in 1963 in Selinsgrove, Snyder County, Pennsylvania (RC Montgomery). She was affiliated with the Evangelical United Brethren (Methodist) Church religion in 1963 in Northumberland County, Pennsylvania. She lived in Selinsgrove, Snyder County, Pennsylvania in 1963 (310 W. Snyder St.). She lived in Selinsgrove, Snyder County, Pennsylvania in 1963 (310 W. Snyder St.). She was buried on April 9, 1963 in Shamokin Dam, Snyder County, Pennsylvania (Orchard Hill (West Side) Cemetery). She was named after her mother Emma Louise, who died four days after her birth. Her cause of death was Myocardial infarction w/chronic myocardial failure and senility. She was affiliated with the Evangelical United Brethren (Methodist) religion.

EDWARD MASON
& RANIE BROWN

Edward "Ned" Mason was born into slavery on a plantation in Washington County, Georgia, in the year 1847. He was the first child of the young couple Alfred and Hannah Mason, who had both been born into slavery themselves, probably on the same plantation where Edward was born.

Unless Edward was born during the night, Alfred would not have met his new son until he returned to his quarters after finishing his day's work. But female slaves were typically given two or three days off after childbirth, so Hannah would have had little time to welcome Edward into his new world.

Edward was followed the next year his by the birth of his brother Noah. A five-year break between the birth of Noah and the next son, Thomas, in 1853, suggests the likelihood that Alfred and Hannah lost a child or two to stillbirth or death in early childhood. But after Thomas, Edward got a new brother or sister every year or two for the next seventeen years. There was his brother James, sister Linda, brothers Andrew, Jacob, George, and Jefferson, sister Josephine, brother Alfred, and lastly, brother Cleveland, born in 1870.

As mentioned earlier, Edward and his family were part of a Washington County, Georgia, plantation. But hearing of a "plantation," we should not be too quick to visualize the estates of white-columned mansions surrounded by miles of cotton fields that were presented to us in films such as *Gone With the Wind*. According to the 1850 U.S. Census, 1,342 white families lived in Washington County that year. An addendum to that census, known as the Slave Schedule, reported that 607 of those families—46% of the white families—owned a total of 5,809 slaves. This gave Washington County a much higher rate of slave ownership than the average for the state as a whole, at 37%. There were, however, very few of the movie-style grand plantations with their hundreds of slaves. Several plantations did hold 80 or more slaves, but the average slaveholder owned between one and eight slaves. It is far more likely, therefore, that the plantation on which the Masons lived and worked was more like a large working farm.

Customs and requirements for slave behavior and treatment varied from plantation to plantation, but in Georgia many slaves were able to live in family units, spending their limited time away from the masters' fields together. Georgia slave families also frequently cultivated their own gardens, and some were even allowed to raise livestock or supplement their families' diets by hunting and fishing. Some were permitted to gather wild berries during their off-time and sell them for money, which they were allowed to keep. They were typically given Sundays off to pursue these activities. There was a payoff to the slave owner too, of course—in the form of reduced costs for feeding his slaves.

Eventually, Christianity came to serve as a pillar of slave life in Georgia. Unlike their masters, slaves drew from Christianity the message of black equality and empowerment. In the early nineteenth century, African American preachers played a significant role in spreading the Gospel in the quarters.

Regardless of the liberalness or harshness of plantation culture, one thing was pretty much constant on each plantation: every slave there was expected to work. As a very small child, Edward would have had a relatively simple life. He would have been tended to by one of older children—if there were any—or maybe by an elderly slave woman who could no longer do her usual work. The small children would have been free to play and sleep.

However, by the time Edward was seven or eight, he would have been assigned tasks that he could be expected to complete, such as pulling weeds around the house or walking down the rows of tobacco plants picking caterpillars off the leaves and stalks. When he was a couple of years older, he might have been put to churning butter and fetching eggs from the chicken pens. Unless he got assigned to a particular job, such as caring for the animals, this progression toward heavier work would have continued until his middle to late teens, when he would have gone to the fields with the other men.

Edward Mason was sixteen years old when Abraham Lincoln's Emancipation Proclamation went into effect in January of 1863. Legally, he was free as of that moment, and with so many of the white slave masters away in the Civil War, some slaves did take the chance and begin to slip away looking for opportunities to make it on their own. Most blacks, however, remained enslaved for another year or more until Sherman's march to the sea reached its goal in Savannah and the Union Army was able to put some teeth into the Proclamation. Edward was eighteen when the Civil War ended in 1865, and slavery finally collapsed everywhere across the Confederacy. He was finally and forever free—though there were times during the coming years when it may not have felt like such a great gift.

Jobs were scarce and times were hard in those first years. Much of Georgia's wealth had been destroyed by the war and the collapse of slavery. Most of the former slave owners still had land, but without their slaves, making it profitable again was difficult. This often made life hard for both the former slave owner and former slave alike. The lack of jobs and the fear of starvation made it fairly common in those first hard years for freedmen to go back to their old plantations and work the same fields they had worked as slaves.

But there were major differences now. From the end of the Civil War until 1877, the State of Georgia was under the control of the U.S. military. Troops and Union officials overseeing the civilian leadership ensured that the new laws guaranteeing the rights of the freedmen were not violated—or that they were violated less frequently. The military also set up a court of sorts where disputes between blacks and whites could be settled fairly. These courts had arrest powers, and they also dealt swiftly with any violence or retaliation done to the freedmen by their former owners.

For the first time in his life, Edward Mason had a choice as to what he would do with his life. Under the circumstances, he initially elected to continue to work at what he knew, so he went back to the fields. But now it was his choice, and he worked as a hired hand for wages. The wages were small in those first days, but he also found that his time was now his own, and when he was not working he got to decide how to spend it. And on the third day of July in 1867, Edward spent his time doing something that neither he nor anyone else had ever thought that he would be able to do. He registered as an eligible voter in Washington County, Georgia. For the remainder of his life, Edward would be one of the deciders of how he would be governed.

At about the same time he became a voter, Edward Mason met a young neighbor girl named Ranie Brown, a freed slave like himself. Edward went on to court Ranie, and the two were married about 1869. Ranie was only eighteen when she married Edward Mason.

Ranie Brown had been born in Washington County, Georgia, in December of 1852. She was the first child of George and Mary A. Brown. Ranie's father, George, had become a sharecropper farmer within a few years of the collapse of slavery, and he and Mary built a life on the farm. Ranie was their first daughter, but she was soon joined by his sisters Rachel and Mary, and brothers Samuel, Simon, and Remus.

Ranie was barely thirteen when slavery ended, and her life on the plantation would have been very different from Edward's simply because she was freed before she became old enough for the heavy field or house work. That does not, of course, mean that she got away with not working. Like the boys, the girls were assigned tasks as soon as they were deemed old enough to perform them. Ranie would have been old enough to watch the younger children, help clean the slave master's house, churn butter, or help pick pests off the crops. Her heaviest work came later when she married Edward Mason and became the mother of twelve children.

Edward worked hard and was soon able to get his own farm on a sharecropping contract. There, his and Ranie's own family grew quickly. Their first son, George W. Brown, was born by the end of their first year of marriage, and over the next eighteen years they had ten additional children: James Mason in 1872, Aggie in 1872, Jane in 1875, Dicey in 1876, Austin in 1878, Mack in 1880, Alonzo in 1882, Janice in 1885, Ella in 1886, and Oliver in 1888.

Sometime between 1888 and 1900, Edward "Ned" Mason died in Washington County, Georgia. Some might think him lucky—he had lived to see the ending of slavery in America, he had managed his own business for his own benefit and that of his children, and he had expressed his opinion on how he should be governed through his vote. And in the end, his journey ended before the tragedy of the Jim Crow era began.

After Edward's death, Ranie Brown Mason lived on in Washington County with her children. And Ranie did live long enough to see the beginning of the Jim Crow era bring a major erosion of the freedoms won by Civil War and Emancipation. She had to watch as stores, banks, and other businesses went from being open to everyone to being for whites only. Ranie had to watch the black man lose the right to vote after forty years of voting. And she had to watch her sons walk carefully around white women, where a simple glance taken wrong could end in a lynching. It wasn't as bad as slavery, but it no longer really felt like freedom, either.

Ranie Brown Mason died in Washington County, Georgia, sometime between 1910 and 1920. Edward and Ranie's son, Mack Mason, became the direct ancestor of this family line.

PETER THOMPSON
& ANNE M. SHATTEEN

February of 1860 was cold in Jefferson County, Georgia, especially in the slave quarters where fires were used only on the coldest nights. It was not a particularly good place or time to be born, but here he was anyway, Peter Thompson—first and only child of his father and Polly Thompson—taking his first breath. The women who helped with the birth had gone to their cabins or to work, and her husband had also just been called to work, as usual. Polly, though, had been allowed a few days lying-in time to get the baby off to a good start. She hugged the baby to her chest and tucked the blanket in around them as best she could. As she drifted back to sleep, she wondered briefly what life would have in store for her son. But not in her wildest dreams could she have imagined the turbulent times into which he had just been born.

Totally unknown to the Thompsons, within days of Peter's birth, Illinois lawyer and politician Abraham Lincoln would make a speech in New York City at a private college called The Cooper Union. His goal was to introduce himself to New York as a candidate for Republican nomination for President of the United States. He spoke of his opposition to slavery and to its spread into new territories and states that would be created from America's expansion into the West.

The speech would achieve his goal beyond all expectations. The *New York Times* and the *New York Tribune* both published the speech, and the *Tribune* hailed it as "one of the happiest and most convincing political arguments ever made in this City . . . No man ever made such an impression on his first appeal to a New-York audience." To top it off, just prior to the speech Lincoln had visited the photography shop of Matthew Brady and sat for a few photos. Four days after the speech, one of these photographs of Lincoln appeared on the cover of *Harper's Weekly* magazine.

Two months later, Lincoln won the nomination as the Republican candidate for President, and six months after that he was elected President of the United States. Lincoln later remarked that Matthew Brady and his day at The Cooper Union had made him President.

Back in Georgia, slaves on the plantations had still heard almost nothing about Lincoln. But soon the talk among the whites was about little else than Lincoln and his enmity towards slavery. Indeed, prior to the election, several of the slave states had vowed to secede if he was elected. By the time of Peter Thompson's first birthday, slave owners across the South were in an uproar, and nearly every slave had heard of Abraham Lincoln. Seven states, including Georgia, had seceded from the United States, and four more would soon follow.

Surviving records show that Georgia originally hoped for a peaceful and legal separation from the Union. But when South Carolina attacked Fort Sumter, on April 12, 1861, that possibility was lost and conflict was made inevitable. Georgia's governor called for volunteers six days later and the Civil War was on. Peter Thompson was fourteen months old.

Slave life during the Civil War varied widely according to location and the financial condition of the slave owner. The war did not come directly—in the form of Union soldiers—to Washington County and Jefferson Counties until well into 1863. But long before that, very early in the war, Georgians and, consequently, their slaves were being adversely impacted. With the trains blocked, most of the foodstuffs that had come into Georgia were stopped almost immediately. And with Union ships blocking all of the Georgia ports, cotton that would have provided income was stacking up on the wharves, unable to get to market.

On the other hand, slavery broke down somewhat during the war. With most of the white men gone off to war and women running the plantations and businesses, slaves used the absence of white males to secure better working and living conditions. And as Union forces made their way into the interior of the state, many slaves ran away to seek their freedom with the advancing Northern troops.

Peter was aware of none of this, of course. No doubt, short rations made for some hungry times. And his parents had some hard choices to make about whether to stay on the plantation or risk running away toward the Union troops—especially after the Emancipation Proclamation officially made them free in the eyes of the Union forces. But Peter was only two years old when the Emancipation Proclamation was issued, and for him it was all just childhood.

When Union General William T. Sherman made his famous march from Atlanta across Georgia to the sea at Savannah in November and December of 1864, the early trickle of slave runaways became a flood. Thousands of former slaves abandoned their white former owners and followed Sherman's army to actual—as well as official—freedom. Sherman's own path to the sea took him directly through Washington County, Georgia.

On January 16, 1865, General Sherman issued Special Field Order No. 15, a temporary plan that granted each freed family forty acres of tillable land and one of the many mules that had been confiscated in his march across Georgia.

No records exist to tell us if the Thompson family were recipients of land under Special Order No. 15, but for one brief, shining year in one small part of Georgia, the fabled promise of forty acres and a mule for each family of freed slaves was actually true. Unfortunately, about a year later—after Abraham Lincoln's assassination and Vice President Andrew Johnson's becoming President—Johnson terminated Special Order No. 15, and returned all of the land to the original owners.

The Civil War ended when Peter was still only five years old. Freedom of all slaves was now official throughout the land and the United States had installed a military government over Georgia and all of the other Confederate States to protect the rights of the newly freed. Special courts were established to handle disputes or legal issues between the freedmen and the whites and to assist the former slaves in getting established. For the first time, Peter's family lived in a house that they could think of as their own. As with most freedmen, Peter's family went on doing the same kind of farm work they had done as enslaved workers, but now they worked for wages. As soon as he was old enough to handle the work, Peter also went to the fields to help the family.

Both of Peter's parents appear to have died before 1880, and his siblings scattered to their own lives. By age nineteen, Peter was again living in Washington County and was out on his own. He was still working as a farm laborer, but now he was renting his own house with the help of two boarders. Among Peter's neighbors was the Shatteen family, whose daughter Anne soon caught his eye.

Anne M. Shatteen was born about 1866, in Washington County, Georgia, the second child of Mason Shatteen and Sallie Morgan. Anne's parents had been born and raised in slavery, but slavery had finally collapsed under the Civil War and Federal law. Anne, her older sister Linnie (born in

1862), her brother James (born in 1867), and sister Lillian (1868), were all born after slavery ended and grew up on a farm obtained by their father as a free sharecropper. They grew up in the turmoil, hardships, and conflicts of the aftermath of slavery, and never knew the harsh reality of enslavement.

With her parents' consent, Peter Thompson married fifteen-year-old Anne on May 19, 1881, in Washington County, Georgia. The young couple soon set up house in the same neighborhood where they had been living. After two years together, in June of 1883, daughter, Sarah A. Thompson, was born.

Sometime between Sarah's birth and 1900, Anne Shatteen Thompson died. The records that might have told us more about Anne Shatteen's life, or that might have told us exactly how and when she died, simply do not exist for that part of Georgia in that period.

We do know that Anne's widowed husband, Peter, had to continue to work to make a living, and so her daughter, Sarah, went to live with Anne's mother. The 1900 census report shows Peter Thompson back in Jefferson County, Georgia, living with Polly Thompson. His daughter, Sarah, was living with her grandmother, Sallie Shatteen, back in the old neighborhood in Washington County.

After several years as a widower, Peter married again and had other children. He died in Jefferson County, Georgia, between 1930 and 1940. Sarah A. Thompson is the direct ancestor of this family line.

PERCY C. FORSYTHE
& NINA WASHINGTON

Until wealthy foreigners recognized the joy of escaping the snow and ice of winter to sit on the beach of a tropical island, the majority of common people of the Bahama Islands lived in some level of poverty. Since their discovery by the Europeans in the 1600s, many schemes had been brought to the islands in an effort to create an economy that would benefit everyone. Most of them failed and the people stayed poor.

During the early- to mid-1800s, wrecking—salvaging cargos and sometimes passengers from ships that had wrecked on the rocky reefs in the shallow waters around the islands—was a lucrative activity. Then Britain found out that some islanders were going beyond simple salvage and were taking active action to trick ships onto the rocks. The government began regulating the practice and eventually outlawed it all together.

There was a truly wonderful flurry of wealth during the American Civil War while the Confederates used the Bahamian island of New Providence as their base of operations for the blockade-running fleet. But to the islanders' great dissatisfaction, the end of the Civil War also ended the good economic times and triggered what would be the beginning of a fifty-year economic depression.

As fortune would have it, Percy Campbell Forsythe was born on New Providence in St. Agnes Parish on the outskirts of Nassau, the island's largest town. Percy was the first child of Samuel James Forsythe and his young wife, Amelia Deane. He was born on 10 June, 1879, in the fourteenth year of the economic depression engulfing the Bahamas.

Samuel Forsythe was a hotel worker in Nassau, but pay was low and the family was poor. This probably contributed to the hard times that Samuel and Amelia had with their children—in the next few years after Percy's birth, first a daughter and then a son were born, but both died before their first birthday. Finally, in 1885, another son, Samuel James Forsythe, Jr., was born and survived.

Percy grew up in a society where about 85% of the population was black. This was partially the result of Americans with pro-slave English ideals and the large number of slaves that were brought to the Bahamas with the doomed hope of keeping the plantation economy and lifestyle alive.

Others of the majority black population were the descendants of freshly captured Africans who were taken off slaver ships when Britain outlawed the slave trade in 1807. Britain required their navy to stop the slavers and confiscate the human cargoes, which they did with great vigor. The British Navy did not, however, feel obligated to haul the freed Africans all the way back to Africa. Instead, thousands of freed Africans were off-loaded onto the various islands of the British West Indies with a modicum of supplies and with the expectation that they should make do as best they could. In 1834, Britain freed all slaves everywhere in their Empire and the black majority of the West Indies were suddenly all free to seek their fortunes and grow into whatever they could be.

It is no surprise that the white business and land owners comprised the upper social class. But it is surprising that the middle class was made up primarily of light-skinned blacks and the lower class was made up of darker-skinned people. And for a long time, it was not possible for a darker-skinned person to climb out of the lower class and into one of the higher classes—it simply wasn't allowed. It wasn't the same form of harsh discrimination faced by African Americans in America under the Jim Crow laws, but in some ways it was worse. A black American, if he was careful, could improve his own economic and social position within the black community despite white discrimination. In the Bahamas during the Percy's early years, it was almost impossible for a dark-skinned islander to do the same. Under these circumstances, it is easy to see why Percy and his brother, Samuel James, decided to emigrate to America for better opportunities.

According to his own testimony on a petition for U.S. citizenship, Percy Campbell Forsythe stated that he left the Bahamas for America in about 1898. Some records suggest that Percy may have gone first to Nova Scotia, Canada, for a while before moving to Manhattan, New York, but it appears that Samuel James went straight to Manhattan. One thing seems clear: Percy was fascinated by steamships from early on. Shortly after entering America, he found a job with a steamship company, and once he reached a position he liked, he never left.

By 1914, Percy was working in a steamer sailing up and down the east coast of the United States, hauling cargo and passengers between New York and Savannah, Georgia. Percy worked in the kitchens of the ships starting as a pantry man and, over the years, he worked his way up to one of the head cook positions.

At some point—undoubtedly during one of his layovers in Savannah— Percy Forsythe met a young woman named Lula Bachelor, a Savannah native. They apparently got along well, and when his ship turned north toward New York again, she went with him. Percy Campbell Forsythe and Lula Bachelor were married on 27 September, 1915, in Manhattan, New York.

For the next several years, Lula held down the fort at their home in Manhattan while Percy sailed the seas, away from home for days and sometimes weeks at a time. In the early 1920s, he sailed on a ship called the *Cristobal*, making runs from New York to Haiti and back. Later, Percy rejoined the Ocean Steamship Company of Savannah and was soon back on the old route between New York and Savannah, Georgia. Unfortunately, Lula Bachelor Forsythe died unexpectedly a few years later in Manhattan.

Percy Campbell Forsythe continued his work on the New York to Savannah run and some years later met and married Nina Washington, another girl from Savannah. Percy and Nina had two children: Nina Forsythe, born February 24, 1925, and Robert J. Forsythe, born September 15, 1926. Marriage and family were enough to induce Percy to shift his home base from New York City to Savannah, where he could live with the family between sailings. But it was not enough to get him to give up his career on the steamships.

Nina Washington was born October 31, 1908, in Daufuskie, Beaufort County, South Carolina, the daughter of Joseph Washington and Mary Robinson. Nina was less than a year old when the family moved from South Carolina to Savannah, Georgia, where Nina grew up.

Whether he died or left, Nina's father soon disappeared from her life. But her mother, Mary, was an enterprising lady and kept the family housed and fed by running a boarding house and lunch room—she prepared more food for lunch than was needed for her boarders and sold it to the local public. Her older brother Albert, who continued to live at home until his marriage, was a blacksmith who also helped meet expenses for the family.

Nina worked as a cook's helper after she went out on her on, but she also followed in her mother's footsteps and took in boarders. That is probably how she met Percy Campbell Forsythe. With time off between sailings—while the ship was being refueled and new cargo was being loaded—he would have needed a place to stay. The combination of interest and proximity came together, and marriage occurred.

Having regularly spent time in Savannah during his employment with a company named Ocean Shipping of Savannah, Percy quickly settled into his new life there. In July of 1941, possibly with an eye toward retirement and living out his life in his adopted country, Percy filed a petition with the United States District Court at Savannah to become an American citizen.

A little over four months later, the Japanese bombed Pearl Harbor and everybody's world shifted a bit. Shortly after the United States declared war on Japan, and recognizing an immediate need for the ability to move men and materials sooner than a new Naval fleet could be created, the United States essentially drafted all major U.S. shipping into the Merchant Marine. Percy's job did not really change, except that now passenger service was sharply curtailed and priority was giving to hauling strategic materials that would best support America's war effort.

It was a necessary step, but one that turned out to be an unfortunate one for Percy Campbell Forsythe. On 19 January, 1942, his ship, the *City of Atlanta* was in the middle of a run from New York to Savannah. The ship was unarmed and had no military escorts. It was just off the coast of North Carolina, running closer to the coast than usual in an effort to reduce the likelihood of attack by German submarines. The tactic did not succeed.

Just after 9:00 p.m., the *City of Atlanta* was hit by one torpedo from the German U-Boat U-123. The torpedo was a surface runner and struck the *City of Atlanta* at the waterline. The ship quickly took on water and began to list onto its side, making it very difficult for the crew of eight officers and 38 crewmen to abandon ship. The vessel rolled completely over and went down in about ten minutes, long before any of the four lifeboats could be launched.

Percy Campbell Forsythe and all but three of his shipmates were killed. When help finally arrived about six hours later, only one officer and two men were found clinging to wreckage. The officer later died of his injuries.

Needless to say, Percy's death impacted the family greatly. Ten months after his death, Percy's son, Robert, ran off and lied about his age to join the U.S. Navy. And sadly, Nina Washington Forsythe survived her husband, Percy, by only two and a half years. She died in a Savannah, Georgia, hospital on August 5, 1944. The line continues through Robert J. Forsythe, the son of Percy and Nina Forsythe.

FREDERICK CURRY
& ELIZABETH BROWN

Frederick Curry was born on George Washington's birthday—February 22—in 1907. It was an unusually cold winter day in Savannah, Chatham County, Georgia, where winter days were usually fairly mild.

The ninth child of Duncan Curry and Elizabeth Alston, Frederick was born into an already large and active family, with three older brothers and five older sisters: William was born first, followed by Elizabeth, Ira, Hilda (who died in infancy), Rosa Leola, Solomon, and Edmonia. And Frederick was not the last child—brothers Frampton and Charles came along after Frederick, rounding out the siblings to an even ten.

Frederick's father, Duncan, supported this large brood by doing heavy labor, first for the railroads and later on the docks at Savannah's harbor. With a little help from the older children, the family just got by.

But financial hardships were the least of the troubles for most black Georgians in those days. Those years of the early 1900s were tough, tense times for the black people of Georgia. It was Frederick's bad luck to have been born into some of the harshest of all the Jim Crow segregation years.

In September of 1906, just months before Frederick was born, three of Atlanta's evening newspapers ran featured stories of alleged rapes by black men. Whites in Atlanta went on a "revenge" spree. When the dust settled after several days of violence and bloodshed—later known as the Atlanta Race Riot—twenty-five blacks and one white were confirmed dead. Several dozens more had been injured, and sources suggested that the casualty count was actually much higher.

Six years later, in 1912, in Forsyth County, a black teenager confessed to the rape and murder of a white girl. After a week of inflammatory reporting by three county newspapers, local whites rioted against local blacks. Three black men were hanged the first night, which was followed by a campaign of terror by night riders. Black-owned houses were dynamited and black churches were burned. More than ninety percent of the black population were told, "leave or die." In the end, it was a successful use of terror to drive more than one-thousand blacks completely out of their homes and out of the county. To this day, Forsyth County is still one of the whitest counties in Georgia.

The City of Savannah was not a place where such large-scale and violent racial drama took place during those years—the first reported Savannah race riot did not happen until 1963 during the protests to end segregation. Instead, during the first half of the twentieth century, Savannah was a place where both races lived through a kind of stylized behavioral dance that was beginning to play out all over the South. The whites taught their children how to carry themselves and how to act toward blacks, to keep "the coloreds in their place" while trying to stop short of inciting a violent reaction. Black people simultaneously taught their children how to avoid eye contact, and to say "yes sir" and "no ma'am" to all whites, even those younger than themselves. They taught the children to play the part that the whites wanted to see while living their own lives the best they could.

This uncomfortable existence went on in the midst of Jim Crow segregation, and the lack of major racial conflagrations allowed Savannah to present itself to the world as a more cosmopolitan city—one that did not really have a "colored problem." But every black person living there knew how strongly racism still thrived and how it was still taking large, if less obvious, bites out of black lives. And the threat of violence, while not always obvious, was constantly there.

In June of 1914, the lives of the Curry family suddenly and unexpectedly got even harder, both emotionally and financially. Just four months after Frederick's seventh birthday, his father, Duncan Curry, died. The older children stepped up and initially took on most of the burden of earning the family living. Two of the girls worked in a local match factory and the older boys found jobs as laborers. When Frederick got old enough, he did his part by going to work as a laborer in a fertilizer plant.

It was while working in this job that Frederick met and took a liking to the girl next door. Frederick and seventeen-year-old Elizabeth Brown hit it off and Frederick was soon courting her in earnest. Elizabeth accepted his interest and, later, his proposal. Frederick and Elizabeth were married in September of 1928.

Elizabeth Brown was born in June of 1911 in Allendale, Barnwell County, South Carolina. She was the daughter of Joseph Brown and Nancy Frazier, and the first of what would eventually become that couple's ten children. Like Elizabeth, her parents had grown up in Allendale and had made a life for their new family there.

But for much of his life, Joseph Brown earned his living as a farm laborer, and times were getting difficult for farmers in Georgia. Much of South Georgia still had cotton as their major cash crop, but then in 1915, the boll weevil hit the area, devastating crops. From there, things just got worse for the farmer—competition from new made-made fabrics, overproduction by farmers trying to make up earlier losses, and the continuing effects of the boll weevil hit the price of cotton hard. By the mid-1920s, workers like Joseph Brown were finding it hard to earn a steady living. Eventually, Joseph

Brown gave up on his home town and moved his family to Savannah, seeking better economic opportunities.

Unfortunately, his timing was terrible. A little over a year after Frederick and Elizabeth Brown's marriage, the beginning of the Great Depression hit the entire country, and like millions of other Americans—both black and white—Joseph Brown found himself out of work again. By 1930, both Joseph and Nancy Brown were out of work and living next door to their new son-in-law and seven of their minor children. Frederick still had that one hugely valuable thing that year—a job.

Frederick Curry proved himself a hardworking and responsible man when he took on the task of supporting his new wife's minor siblings. He supported this crowd, along with his own increasing family, by working as a laborer in Savannah's Virginia-Carolina Chemical Company, a fertilizer plant.

The economy remained poor throughout the 1930s and real recovery did not start until the beginning of World War II. There were small pockets of improvement, though, and these small changes allowed Elizabeth Brown Curry's siblings to begin their move out of the Curry household. Some went to new marriages, some moved out on their own, and some went in together and lived with one another until the economy recovered.

By 1940, Frederick and Elizabeth were back to having only their own family living in the household. This was a good thing for the Curry's because while the aunts and uncles were growing up and moving out, the Curry family was just plain growing on its own. Frederick and Elizabeth's first child, daughter Lucretia Jo Curry, was born on March 5, 1929, but she did not stay an only child for very long. Sister Nancy was born in 1931, and brother Frederick Curry, Jr., followed on August 18, 1936.

Frederick's job with the Virginia-Carolina Chemical Company had protected his family against the very worst of the Depression—though wages and perks dropped with the economy. With the Japanese attack on Pearl Harbor and America's entry into World War II, the Virginia-Carolina Chemical Company began to expand into new fields. It went through a few corporate name changes, but operations kept growing and expanding into many divisions in several states. For Frederick, this more or less assured him of indefinite full-time employment. Toward the end of the 1930s he had been moved into a job as a tractor operator for the company's plant in Savannah. It turned out to be a position that he was to keep for the rest of his working days.

Like all families, the Curry's had their successes and their failures. After WWII, they just settled down and got on with life. They watched their children grow up and go out to seek their new lives as adults.

Neither Frederick nor Elizabeth Curry lived long lives. But in their lifetimes they had seen some subtle changes in the humiliating behavioral dance that black people were forced to perform during their long segregation. And near the end of their lives, they got to see the beginning of the end for segregation—the 1963 street protests in Savannah where black men did not step off the sidewalk to let white people pass; where black men came before the whites, not with their hats in hand or with downward cast eyes, but with their heads up. They saw black people come into the streets, not asking for favors, but demanding their rightful place in the American story. Perhaps it was enough to allow them to them see the beginning of a new future.

Frederick Curry died in Savannah on November 13, 1964, at the age of 57 years. He was buried in Laurel Grove Cemetery in Savannah, Georgia. Elizabeth Brown Curry outlived her husband by about 11 months, and died on October 16, 1965, in Savannah, Chatham County, Georgia. She was also buried in Laurel Grove Cemetery in Savannah. Frederick Curry and Elizabeth Brown's first child, Lucretia Jo Curry, is the direct line ancestor of this family line.

PIETRO G. ROMANO
& ANNETTA P.C. CARMONA

Pietro Giuseppe Romano, son of Ireneo Romano and Felice Vitale, was born between 18 July 1858 and 1861 in Alia, Palermo, Sicily, Italy and died sometime after 1930. Pietro married Annetta Pierina Camilla Carmona, daughter of Angelo Carmone and Marianne Quintavalle on 3 August 1905 in Lercara Friddi (see marriage license on page 47). Annetta was born 18 June 1878 in Bronte, Catania, Sicily, Italy and died on 25 August 1936 in Manhattan, New York, New York. Marianne Quintavalle, mother of Annetta Pierina, died in the great Messina earthquake.

Children of this union were Rosalia Francesca Maddalena Romano (adopted the name Lillian in America) was born on 14 October 1899 in Lercara-Friddi, Sicily, Italy and died on 30 June 1963 in New York, New York at age 63; Iolanda Margherita Romano (used Yolanda in America) was born on 26 July 1902 in Lercara, Palermo, Sicily, Italy and died on 21 June 1986 in New York, New York at age 83; Ireneo Romano was born in 1905 in Lercara, Palermo, Sicily, Italy and died in 1941 in New York at age 36. Ireneo married Constance Taylor; Angelo Romano was born in 1908 in Lercara, Palermo, Sicily, Italy and died in 1985 in Delray Beach, Florida at age 77.

Angelo married Yolanda Tripoda. Yolanda was born on 24 October 1915 and died in November 1985 in Delray Beach, Florida at age 70; Paul Peter (Paolo Pietro) Romano to follow; Antonino Lindoro Romano (Anthony, Tony) was born in 1 July 1914 in Lercara, Palermo, Sicily, Italy and died 3 May 1991 in New York at age 77; Livia Romano was born on 20

December 1917 in New York and died on 4 September 1994 in Ulster County, New York at age 76. Livia married Anthony Peter Marchese.

Alia, the town where Pietro was born, perches 750 meters above sea level on the slopes of the southern hills of the Province of Palermo. It was founded in 1615 by Pietro Celesti, Marquis of Santa Croce, on the site of an ancient Spanish landed estate named Lalia which he had passed down to him through marriage.

Sitting along the ancient road between the city of Palermo and the city of Syracuse, Alia is located in one of Sicily's ancient places. There are ruins of at least two very early Muslim settlements nearby and archeological digs have uncovered coins, amphoras and other materials from throughout the Roman period. And the Gurfa Caves, dug into the cliffs above the town, show evidence of human occupation as early as 5000 BC.

Between 1848 and 1860, a desire for a unified Italy had grown and spread. In 1859, King Ferdinand of the Kingdom of the Two Sicilies died, leaving his inexperienced son, Francis as King. At the same time, a revolutionary general named Giuseppe led numerous expeditions and battles toward the goal of unification. After the annexation of the Grand Duchy of Tuscany, the Duchies of Modena and Parma and the Romagna to Piedmont in March 1860, Garibaldi and the Italian nationalists set their sights on the Kingdom of the Two Sicilies, which comprised all of southern Italy and Sicily, as the next step in their planned unification of Italy.

Garibaldi, aided by the English Navy, which kept the Bourbon King's ship's off of Garibaldi's back, landed in Sicily in May of 1860 with 1,000 volunteers. Soon after landing, he announced that he was assuming the dictatorship of Sicily in the name of the Victor Emanuel, the King of Sardinia. He began an assault on

Palermo on May 27th, 1860. The people rose up on both sides, with many volunteers joining Garibaldi while large numbers of peasants fought against him. Where supported, Garibaldi cheerfully accepted volunteers into his army. Where opposed, he brutally and bloodily repressed the peasant rebellions.

By September, Sicily had been largely taken, and Garibaldi turned his attention on Naples. In October, the Kingdom of the Two Sicilies ceased to exist. Garibaldi turned his conquests over to King Victor Emanuel. In March 1861, the Kingdom of Italy was formally established.

The battle was also far less costly in terms of death and destruction than it might have been had not the English bribed many of the King's senior officers to surrender without fighting. The battles for unification occurred primarily around the major cities where the King's troops were stationed. In the smaller towns and villages, the battle only came where partisan guerillas brought it.

Lying about 40 miles southeast of Palermo, Lercara Friddi sits on the slopes of Pizzo Lanzone, the 2nd highest peak (2,165 feet above sea level) of the hilly region between the Platani and Torto rivers. Only the nearby Colle Mare is higher. Like much of Sicily, the area has been occupied since ancient times. Recent archeological research found a prehistoric Sicani site just outside the present town.

Lercara Friddi itself had its earliest beginnings as a trading post along the royal road between Palermo and Agrigento. In 1605, Spanish nobleman D. Baldassare Gomez de Amescua, acquired the fief through his marriage to Francesca Lercara and organized a proper village that over the centuries led directly to the present town.

It seems likely that the Romanos moved to Lercara, a town about 11 miles from Pietro Giuseppe Romano's birthplace in Alia and about 40 miles southeast of Palermo, long before the first record proves their residence there in 1905. It is also very unlikely that they were the first Romanos there. In modern times, Romano has become one of the most common names in Lercara Friddi.

As a side note, the Romanos had two notable neighbors in Lercara. One was shoemaker named Francesco Sinatra who was born in the town in 1857. Francesco moved his family to America in 1900, and it was there that his grandson, Frank Sinatra became a famous singer and actor. The second neighbor of interest was Salvatore Lucania, born in Lercara in 1897. His family migrated to America in 1907, where Salvatore changed his name, became known as Lucky Luciano, and founded La Cosa Nostra.

According to a prominent Italian editor, Lercara was located in "the core territory of the Mafia." The town lies about 12 miles from Corleone, and it was no simple whim that made Mario Puzo choose Corleone for his title character in his book, The Godfather. According to the Organized Crime element of the Federal Bureau of Investigation, Corleone sent more gangsters to America than any other place in Sicily.

By the time of Pietro Romano's birth, Lercara Friddi itself had already become a primary center of organized livestock theft in Sicily. This might be thought of as the 19th century equivalent of a hot car ring. The livestock theft ring traded in hot horses and mules, which were stolen throughout the island and then sold to the mining companies around Lercara Friddi. The leaders of this group were Giuseppe Anzalone and Antonino Petta, both sons of prominent land owning families in the area.

Interaction with the Mafia was probably not a daily thing, but there is no way that a successful businessman could have survived without at least some kind of interaction or arrangement with the local capos.

Romano family tradition is that Pietro Giuseppe Romano became wealthy as owner of sulfur mines near Lercara Friddi. This is totally possible, as there were literally hundreds of mines in the region. And there was at least one sulfur mine known as the Romano mine - the Romano mine was a partnership between a Romano family and an English company. It was a very large modern mine that utilized the latest technologies and the best mining practices. Steam engines powered the elevators that took the workers up and down the shafts, the small cars that moved the sulfur to the surface and the pumps that ventilated the mine.

As a result, the mine produced huge amounts of sulfur and during the best years, great profits. It has been impossible, however, to prove any connection between the Romano family connected to that mine and the family of Pietro Romano. The Romano Mine family appears to have lived on the Italian mainland, and while there is an excellent chance that he is related, I do not believe that he was directly connected to the family of Pietro G. Romano.

The same unstable plate tectonics that give Sicily its volcanoes and its earthquakes also deposited among the hills of the southern end of Palermo and northern end Girgenti Provinces with huge, and easily accessible, sulfur deposits. These deposits would play a major role in the social and economic development of Lercara Friddi – indeed, of Sicily, itself – for centuries.

It was perhaps both Sicily's luck and its misfortune that sulfur has turned out to be one of the most useful elements on earth. Originally called brimstone and believed by some cultures to be the fuel of the hell's fires, sulfur was not recognized or named as a separate element until 1770.

That did not, of course, keep the ancients from using it to aid in the smelter of copper or in the manufacture of bronze, or from finding a myriad of other uses for the stuff. The Egyptians used sulfur compounds to bleach fabric as early as 2000 B.C., and a few hundred years later, sulfur was crucial to the creation of certain colored pigments. The ancient Greeks used sulfur as a disinfectant, and the Romans used it in pharmaceutical applications, and when the Chinese developed gunpowder in the 13th century, sulfur was an essential component.

In Sicily, there is substantial evidence that the original settlers in the region (Sicani, Sicels, Elymians) discovered sulfur deposits near Lercara very early and that they were exporting it to Greece and northern Africa by around 900 BC. But it was the increased demand for gun powder beginning in the late 17th century and the increased need created by the Industrial Revolution in England in the late 18th century that brought prosperity to Lercara and to Sicily. By 1800, Sicily had become the global supplier of sulfur, most of it sold through exclusive contracts with England.

Profits from the sulfur trade encouraged the development of more and more mines until the area around Lercara contained literally hundreds of sulfur mines. Large numbers of men and boys found employment in the mines. It was during this time that Lercara Friddi prospered and blossomed. It was not uncommon for newspapers of the day to refer to the town as piccolo Palermo, or little Palermo.

Over the next 100 years the demand for sulfur rose and fell many times – and with it the price. And when the price of sulfur rose and fell, so did the fortunes of those who depended upon it, from the mine owners to the workers who went down into the mines. When large new sulfur deposits were discovered in America, sulfur mining began a long, very slow slide down into extinction.

The driver saw the rider approaching his string from the side trail and flicked his stick against the shoulder of his lead donkey to keep him moving along. He nodded politely as his donkeys pulled abreast of the rider who had pulled his mule to a stop to let them pass. He did not recognize the man, but he had the look of a boss.

The rider waited patiently as he watched the pack train of donkeys loaded with smelted sulfur pass. Why not? It could well be sulfur from his nearby mine, and, if so, it had to get to the station to be hauled to the port. He waited a moment for the dust to settle and then kicked the mule into motion and rode on toward the mine.

As he rode, he briefly remembered how green and fresh these hills looked when he first saw them as a boy at his father's side. Now, so many mines had been opened in the region that it was sometimes difficult to tell where one ended and the next began. Oh well, silly to complain, even if only to himself; the sulfur had been good to him and his family.

Rounding a small hill of mine tailings – the piles of mined earth leftover after the sulfur had been smelted out – he was struck by the heavy fumes of burning sulfur. He quickly directed the mule onto another path that would allow him to approach the mine from a windward direction.
He could easily picture the scene that was producing the terrible fumes. Sulfur came out of the mine in large blocks and was piled onto a grill over the flames of a furnace. This causes the blocks to split and the sulfur, which melts at a mere 116 degrees, to stream down into waiting molds. Invariably, some of the sulfur went into the flames, making the fumes nearly unbearable. Back

when he had first come to the mines, as a much younger man, he had thought he might become less sensitive to the fumes.

Arriving at the mine, he quickly moved to the entrance. Rather than the cage used in more prosperous mines, this one had a simple flat board on which he stood as he was slowly lowered into the darkness. As he descended, he noticed that the pervasive smell of sulfur being replaced by purer air. Finally, the descent halted and he stepped off the platform into a great vault from which several narrow, dark, grooved passages lead in different directions. Gleams of light and a thin smoke could be seen down some of these tunnels and he ducked and went down one low tunnel toward the light. The tunnel opened into another large chamber where groups of nearly nude men lit up by flickering candles and little lamps were loading a line of little trucks with ore. A little further along one of the little passages, he saw men boring and blasting. As the borers drove home their drills, they groaned as though in agony. The little boys who help bear the sulfur to the little trucks also groaned as they move along.

The mine owner knows that the groans are more drama that actual physical suffering, but it still adds a strange effect of misery and anguish that to the effect of the scene. And he knows that the workers are, in fact, suffering. The prices for sulfur have dropped yet again and these men are getting somewhere between forty and sixty cents for an eight-hour shift in the mine – the boys get no more than ten to fifteen cents for the same shift. Even at that, it could be worse – if prices continue to fall, it may be impossible to keep the mines open.

Shaken awake in the predawn darkness, he waited for the tremors to subside and made his way to the door. No sign of fire in the sky, so it was probably an earthquake and not the old volcano; he would look for smoke when the sun came up, just to be sure. He lit a lamp and went back to his bedroom. His wife was already up and dressed. Together, they quickly moved through the house checking the children and the house itself. No serious damage – just frightened children and a few cups rattled off a cupboard. He and his wife breathed easier and relaxed a little; they knew from the strength of the tremors, though, that it was almost certain that somewhere on people were probably dying.

It took a full day for the news of Messina to arrive in Lercara, and nearly a week longer to be sure of her family's fate. They were gone, all of them; lost to the terror of the earthquake that shook a city into fragments.

At 5:21 in the morning of 28 December 1908, the deadliest earthquake to ever hit Europe occurred in the straits of Messina between Sicily and Calabria on the Italian mainland. For a moment, it sounded like a heavy peal of thunder, and then the earth began to move. For about 35 seconds, tremors great and small rolled through Messina. For 35 seconds, the city's buildings, many of them built a hundred or more years earlier, shook and moved in ways the builders never imagined that they ever would; and the buildings began to fall.

Moments later, the tsunami, a wall of water estimated at 20-30 feet high hit the coast and rolled over the lower part of the city. Because it formed in the Straits, the big wave rolled back and forth between Calabria and Sicily, striking Messina several times. When it finally withdrew, it had taken the lighthouses, most of the port facilities, large amounts of debris, and dead people with it. Higher in the city, above the line covered by the rolling sea, fires broke out and roared through the tons of wooden debris from the collapsed buildings.

Damaged railroads and downed telegraph lines hampered initial relief efforts. Initial rescue attempts came from survivors and from the sea, in the form of the crew of a civilian British ship that had managed to survive the tidal waves and keep itself from being thrown onto the rocks. These crewmen saved several children from the third floor of building that had lost its face by having the children lower string and then pull up and secure a rope. Two seamen then scrambled up the rope and helped the children to safety. The two men were then able to help more people trapped on even higher floors.

And then the aftershocks began, hundreds of them, continuing over the next several days. Buildings that had survived the initial quake fell to the aftershocks, injuring or killing rescuers looking for survivors in the rubble of the city. At the same time, a steady rain fell on Messina, forcing the dazed and injured survivors, dressed in nightclothes or whatever they could grab, to take shelter in caves, grottoes, and impromptu shanties built out of materials salvaged from the rubble of their former homes.

Rescuers searching the rubble for trapped survivors. Over ninety percent of the buildings in Messina, including all 87 churches, were destroyed. Searchers clearing rubble found trapped survivors up to 18 days after the earthquake.

Survivors awaiting transportation out of Messina – disease and conditions were a great concern and everyone knew that rebuilding would be a long, slow process. Most survivors were moved to the Italian mainland near Naples, but some went to other countries.

Months after the earthquake, survivors who stubbornly insisted staying near their old homes were living in tents or in shanties cobbled together from wood and materials recovered from the rubble.

Nations from all over the world sent help. Among the earliest to arrive were the American Battleships, the Connecticut, Illinois, Culgoa and Yankton. The ships were part of an American fleet – known as the Great White Fleet – which President Roosevelt had sent on a round the world tour as a show of American naval power. The fleet was in Egypt, for the traversal of the Suez Canal when word of the earthquake arrived. The ships named above were dispatched to Messina immediately. The crew of the Illinois recovered the bodies of the American consul and his wife, entombed in the ruins. The officers and crews of the other ships went into rescue and recovery mode.

The United States Navy provided hundreds of thousands of meals, medical personnel, cots, and blankets. When it was realized much more assistance was required in the face of the nearly total devastation, the Navy came forward with an extensive building program to provide critically needed housing. The houses built by American sailors became known as 'the American village.' The operation lasted for weeks and elicited genuine appreciation from Italian officials who had to create a somewhat delicate temporary relinquishment of national sovereignty to an American base in Italy.

The new Messina that eventually was rebuilt was a modern city, built to survive the earthquakes typical for the region. But the rebuilding was a long, long process. Fifty years after the earthquake, some people were still living in temporary shelters built in the days after that terrible event.

The specific details for the Romano family's decision to emigrate when they did are not known. The pressures were many, but it probably boiled down to simple economics. America had taken over domination of the global sulfur markets, reducing its selling price. And heavy emigration, particularly from western Sicily, had reduced the available labor force, pushing up the cost of production. For smaller mine operators, the squeeze simply became too much.

In the 10 years prior to our Romano family's emigration, more than 40 other Lercara Friddi Romano's had immigrated to America. Literally hundreds of other Lercara residents had taken the same trip. There would have been a great deal of news and substantial money coming back into the community from America, making it seem a more reasonable alternative to what was going on in Sicily.

"Papa," his oldest daughter said as they road through the streets of Palermo, "where are the chimneys? There are no chimneys!"
He glanced up at the building they were passing before chuckling. His children had rarely seen the city – and the younger children had never seen it "I had forgotten, but you are right! Most of the houses in Palermo, big or small, don't have fires. It is almost time for dinner - we will visit the Fiera Vecchia and introduce you to the economical kitchens."

The late afternoon sun was still shining brightly on the buildings facing the sun, but shadows were already forming in the narrow alleys as the stopped the buggy on one side of the square to wander about the market on foot. They stepped into instant bedlam of hurrying people, of dazzling light of the sun on white walls contrasted by the darkness of shadowed alleyways leading off the main square and of open shops not yet lit for the evening. And the noise was constant everywhere – the dull buzz of people conducting business pierced regularly by the competing calls of vendors: "Water here," "Olives", "Artichokes," "Fish!" "Look, children," the man said, waving his arm to encompass the square. "Here you can find in one spot elements of every part of Sicily."

Men, women and children by the score are everywhere, some eating where they stand, some taking food home. Small pails of gleaming charcoal bear upon their heads kettles of boiling artichokes. Steam and aroma from the cooking meats and vegetables; the smoke of lamps, candles and torches and burning fat and grease in the frying pans; escaping gases from the ranges in the "economical kitchens," from the charcoal fires, and from the coal stoves; the innumerable smells of fresh vegetables, meat, fish, both salt and fresh, cut flowers and goats, with an additional tang of cheap wine, gushing from big casks into pails and bottles in the open shops, mingle in a composite odor by no means as un-pleasant as might be thought.

The whole scene is a delight to the eye. Here is a good sized wine shop, its front entirely open, showing two rows of casks and an imposing array of copper bright as the sun; yonder a vegetable store completely covered with onions suspended in long strings, bunches and wreaths, decorated fancifully with green leaves and little rosettes. Beside us a tiny restaurant, its front all gas-range, yawns enticingly, while opposite glows the fiery eye of an artichoke man's tiny charcoal fire among the rustling strings of bulbs over the door.

Vendors of fried entrails and stomachs squat beside their frying pans and baskets, perforated ladles in their hands, exactly like our frankfurter men; while water-men with their highly colored stands full of clinking glasses swing along, bellowing cheerfully.

A man with a stand like the American quick lunch counters stood behind a narrow smoking counter full of hidden fire, bearing a frying pan on top. On his left a bowl of strong shredded cheese faced other dishes of butter and rolls. He was a very popular caterer, too, because as we watched him, a number of customers came up and placed an order. The proprietor, with a deft turn of his hand, split a roll, covered it liberally with a thick rich layer of shredded cheese, placed a few scraps of meat that he was cooking below and, deluging the whole with a spoon full or two of boiling grease served up the tit-bit to his eager customer.

They wandered about the market for more than an hour before the father led them to a small café where they took their meal. As they boarded the carriage and traveled to their hotel, he thought to himself that no matter what wonders they saw on the long trip or in America itself, they would not forget the hour in the Old Market.

Over the next few days while they waited to go aboard their ship, they saw the whole of Palermo. They saw the cathedrals and visited the theaters. They walked the docks, watching the hustle bustle of porters scurrying about with supplies and baggage, the scores of small gaudily painted boats of every color darting about like schools of surface dwelling tropical fish and the row of great black trans-Atlantic steamers awaiting the boarding of their passengers. They visited the great gardens with their golden orange and lemon trees and their beautiful fountains. And at night they sat on the veranda of their hotel overlooking the Marina, or walked the footpath of the Marina itself, listening to the gentle lap of the sea and enjoying the cooling sea airs. Then, finally it seemed, the day came; it was time to leave.

On 21 July 1914, the Romano family departed Palermo, Sicily, bound for the Port of New York on board the S. S. Martha Washington. The Martha Washington was a relatively new ship, as ships went in those days. She had been built in the shipyards of Glasgow, Scotland and launched in 1907. By the time that the Romanos boarded her, she had been making regular voyages from Trieste, Italy to Patras, Palermo and New York for eight years.

The ship was 460 feet long and had accommodations for 60 1st class, 130 2nd class, and 2000 3rd class passengers. The differences in these classes of accommodation were stark, as was the difference in their costs. First Class staterooms had all modern improvements and were located outside (to allow viewing of the sea through portholes) and amidships. First class passengers had access to the First Class Dining Room, which was well ventilated and was furnished with small tables, and where all first class passengers dined at one sitting. First class status also accorded the passenger access to the lounge and music room and to the Promenade Deck.

The Second Class passengers were accorded many of the same types of accommodations as First Class, but on a substantially less elegant scale. Their cabins were all well ventilated and neatly furnished, and rooms could be secured for two or four persons.

In these "modern" steam ships, Third Class accommodations had improved immensely over those of just a few years earlier, but none of them could be called commodious or luxurious in any way. There were large multi-berth dormitory like rooms for single men and similar rooms for single women. For married couples or passengers traveling with children, there were two, four or six berth cabins. The private 3rd class cabins were rather small, with a built in sink and berths in the form of bunk beds.

Oddly enough, the Romanos voyage was the last for the S. S. Martha Washington. World War I broke out while they were en route and the officers and crew decided to keep the ship in the New York harbor after debarking all of the passengers. A short time later, the U.S. government interned the ship, eventually taking it over and converting it to a U.S. Troop transport for the duration of World War I. Three years after the war, the ship was sold back into passenger service and once again worked in the Mediterranean waters, now renamed the Tel Aviv.

New York – Arrival in the New Land

Like most of this generation of Italian immigrants, the Romanos took their first steps onto U.S. soil in a place at the legendary intake center at Ellis Island. They were far from alone – in the 30 years between 1880 and 1920, more than 4 million Italians had come to the United States.

Ellis Island, approaching from the harbor where the passenger ships anchored. Jacob Riis, a turn of the century writer who studied and wrote widely on the immigrant's experience in America described Ellis Island this way in his book Children of the Tenement. Even though he wrote of immigrants arriving a full decade ahead of the Romano family, little had changed by 1914:

"Ellis Island is the nations' gateway to the promised land. In a single day it has handled seven thousand immigrants. "How much you got?" shouts the inspector at the head of the long file moving up from the quay between iron rails, and, remembering, in the same breath shrieks out, "Quanto monèta?" with a gesture that brings up from the depths of Pietro's pocket a pitiful handful of paper money. Before he has half of it out, the interpreter has him by the wrist, and with a quick movement shakes the bills out upon the desk as a dice-thrower "chucks" the ivories. Ten, twenty, forty lire. He shakes his head. Not much, but-he glances at the ship's manifest-is he going to friends? "Si, si! signor," says Pietro, eagerly. The inspector stuffs the money back in the man's pocket, shoves him on, and yells, "Wie viel geld?" at a hapless German next in line.

Newcomers were numbered, sorted, and sent through a series of inspections, where they were checked for physical and mental fitness and for their ability to find work in the U.S. The consequences of failing an eye exam, or of seeming too frail for manual labor, could be devastating; one member of a family could be sent back to Italy, perhaps never to see his or her loved ones again, because of a hint of trachoma or a careless inspector. Although less than 2 percent of Italians were turned away, fear of such a separation led some immigrants to rename Ellis Island L'Isola dell Lagrime—the Island of Tears.

Even for those who made their way successfully through the battery of inspections, Ellis Island was generally not a pleasant experience. The regulations were confusing, the crowds disorienting, the officials rushed, and the hubbub of countless competing languages must have been jarring to the nerves. The moment of departure, when successful immigrants boarded ferries for New York City or destinations further west, came as a tremendous relief. "

The Romanos, of course, came to America better prepared financially than most immigrants from Sicily. A review of the S. S. Martha Washington's passenger manifest reveals that the majority of the Romanos' fellow passengers reported between the required minimum of $50 and $100. Pietro Romano reported that he was arriving with $600 in cash - worth about $19,000 in today's money. But the rest of the experience would probably not have been much different for them.

On the day that the Romanos debarked into Ellis Island, Germany declared war on France, opening what would become World War I. The front pages of the newspapers blared stories of these world events and of an on-going Wall Street financial crisis. While these crises would eventually touch millions of American lives, in August of 1914, they were of less importance to the Romanos than finding a place to live.

The largest portion of the turn of the century Italian immigrants moving into New York City elected to settle in the numbered streets of Little Italy; later immigrants went there or moved into east Harlem. In both neighborhoods, they clumped together, with each block housing its own village from the old country. This new living environment was something of a shock to the new immigrants. People who in Italy may well have slept in small cramped houses, routinely spent most of their waking hours outdoors, socializing, working, shopping, eating. For these people, the tiny apartments in Little Italy provided a closed, claustrophobic existence - and immense hardship.

The Romanos appear to have largely avoided this experience. By 1920, the family was living in lower Midtown, on East 42nd Street, Manhattan. None the less, nearly all of their neighbors were Italians, with a Portuguese family thrown in here and there.

It is interesting to note that on the second page of the S. S. Martha Washington's manifest the family claims that they are going to New York to join Pietro Romano's brother-in- law, Luigi Mavaro. Luigi Mavaro is said to live at 92 Lexington Avenue, New York, New York. A quick check of passenger lists shows that Luigi Marvaro, of Lercara Friddi, Sicily, arrived in New York on 17 January aboard the S.S. Principe di Piemonte. On the passenger manifest, Luigi Mavaro reported that his closes living relative back in Sicily was his wife Rosa Ferrara, who lived in Lercara Friddi.

By 1920, Luigi Mavaro and family are living at 1488 Fifth Avenue, Manhattan. Luigi's occupation is reported as "Regulator" of pianos. It is almost certainly not a coincidence that his "brother-in-law", Pietro Romano is working in a piano factory that same year. It is unknown as to how Luigi Mavaro would fit the relationship of brother-in-law, but it is clear that he is a man from the old hometown back in Sicily and that Pietro Romano knew him well.

Pietro Romano was working as a laborer in a piano factory and the oldest daughters, Lillian and Yolanda, were working as dress beaders – they sewed decorative beads onto dresses. This may have felt like something of a comedown for the family, and especially for Pietro Romano, from the days when he owned the sulfur mine and employed others to work for him.

In 1920, the Romano family lived at 241 East 42nd Street, a couple of blocks east of Grand Central Station. In 1925, the New York City Directory reported Anna Romano as still living at 241 East 42nd Street, but now as a widow. By 17 April 1930, when the 1930 U. S. Census was taken for their neighborhood, the Romano family had moved from 241 East 42nd to 179 East 96th Street. Pietro Romano, father of the family, was not with them and Anna Carmona Romano was again reported as a widow. Details of exactly what became of Pietro Romano are unavailable from independent sources.

The census suggests that he died, but there is no death certificate in Manhattan for him. Family stories say that Pietro Romano was actually deported for attempting to kill his wife. In the end, both stories may be true. Pietro Romano may have returned to Sicily and died there by 1925.

By April of 1930, the Romano family had moved to 179 East 96th street, a few blocks east of Central Park. In 1930, Anna Carmona Romano was reported as head of house with no other occupation. The two older girls, Lily and Yolanda were still working as dress beaders. Kenny (Ireneo) had taken a position as a chauffeur for a private family, Angelo was a shipping clerk for Silverman's Store, and Paul was a shipping clerk for a moving company.

Beginning in the late 1920s, all of the Romano sons began the process of becoming naturalized citizens. By 1940, all of them had filed the final Petition of Citizenship. You can see copies of these petitions in the section "Some Romano Family Records' later in this document.

JOHN E. WITTLE
& MARY E. MINNICH

John Elmer Wittle was counted in the census in 1870 in Lower Paxton, Dauphin County, Pennsylvania. He was educated at School between 1870-1880. He was counted in the census in 1880 in Lancaster, Lancaster County, Pennsylvania, living with Annie Killian. He lived in 122 Strawberry Avenue, Harrisburg, Dauphin County, Pennsylvania between 1882-1900. He was employed as a Hostler between 1887-1900. He lived in 117 Broad, Harrisburg, Dauphin County, Pennsylvania between 1887-1900. He lived in 1336 Penn, Harrisburg, Dauphin County, Pennsylvania between 1887-1900.

John was employed as a Fireman between 1887-1900. He was employed as a Fireman in 1893. He lived in 127 Verbeke St., Harrisburg, Dauphin County, Pennsylvania in 1900. He was counted in the census in 1900 in Harrisburg, Dauphin County, Pennsylvania. He was employed as a RR Fireman in 1900. He was counted in the census in 1910 in Susquehanna, Dauphin County, Pennsylvania. He was employed as a Locomotive Engineer in 1910. He lived in 2610 Verbeke St., Harrisburg, Dauphin County, Pennsylvania in 1910. He lived in 1622 Wallace St., Harrisburg, Dauphin County, Pennsylvania in 1920. He was employed as Railroad an Engineer in 1920. He was counted in the census in 1920 in Harrisburg, Dauphin County, Pennsylvania. He was employed as an Engineer for the Pennsylvania Railroad in 1927. His funeral took place in 1927 in Hawkins Funeral, 1207 N. 3rd St., Harrisburg, Dauphin County, Pennsylvania. He was buried on May 16, 1927 in East Harrisburg Cemetery, Harrisburg, Dauphin County,

Pennsylvania. His cause of death was Acute myocarditis. John was named for his grandfather "John" Wittle.

Mary Elizabeth Minnich was counted in the census in 1880 in Harrisburg, Dauphin County, Pennsylvania. She was educated at school in 1880. She lived in Harrisburg, Dauphin County, Pennsylvania in 1893. She was counted in the census in 1900 in Harrisburg, Dauphin County, Pennsylvania. She was counted in the census in 1910 in Susquehanna, Dauphin County, Pennsylvania. She was counted in the census in 1920 in Harrisburg, Dauphin County, Pennsylvania. She lived in Harrisburg, Dauphin County, Pennsylvania in 1930. She lived in H1418 Susquehanna St., Harrisburg, Dauphin County, Pennsylvania in 1930. She was counted in the census in 1930 in Harrisburg, Dauphin County, Pennsylvania.

Mary lived in 1427 Susquehanna St., Harrisburg, Dauphin County, Pennsylvania in 1934. Her funeral took place in 1934 in Harry Pierce, North Third, Harrisburg, Dauphin County, Pennsylvania. She was employed as a Home in 1934. She was buried on March 20, 1934 in East Harrisburg Cemetery, Harrisburg, Dauphin County, Pennsylvania. Her cause of death was Acute cardiac dilatation w/chronic myocarditis with decompensation. Mary Elizabeth was named for her grandmother "Mary Elizabeth" McKim. Mary and John had the following children: Stella Wittle, Ross Henry Wittle, Alvin John Wittle, Irvin H Wittle, Albert Elmer Wittle, Elizabeth "Mary" Wittle, George Wittle and Leona C Wittle.

JOHN M.L. STEWART
& CATHERINE A. SHOVER

John "Johnny" Martin Louis Stewart lived in 2nd Street, Wormleysburg, Cumberland, Pennsylvania in 1898. He was counted in the census in 1900 in East Pennsboro, Cumberland County, Pennsylvania. He was counted in the census in 1910 in East Pennsboro, Cumberland County, Pennsylvania. He was educated at School in 1910. He lived in 1222 N Front St., Harrisburg, Dauphin County, Pennsylvania in 1918. He was employed as a Steamboat Engineer for the Harrisburg Light Heat and Power in 1918. He was counted in the census in 1920.

Johnny lived in 528 North 3rd St., Wormleysburg, Cumberland County, Pennsylvania in 1930. He lived in Wormleysburg, Cumberland County, Pennsylvania in 1930. He was employed as a Mechanic at Kimmel's Garage in 1930. He was counted in the census in 1930 in Wormleysburg, Cumberland County, Pennsylvania. He was employed as a Mechanic at an Auto shop in 1930. He was employed as a Mechanic at Philip Bloom in 1936. He lived in 1618 1/2 Fulton, Harrisburg, Dauphin County, Pennsylvania in 1936. He lived in 30 St. extension, Penbrook, Pennsylvania in 1950. He had a medical condition of Height Med, Build Medium, Eyes Gray, Hair D. Brown. His cause of death was Cardiac arrest.

Catherine Ann "Kathleen Annie" Shover was educated at School in 1910. She was counted in the census in 1910 in Harrisburg, Dauphin County, Pennsylvania. She was counted in the census in 1920. She was counted in the census in 1930 in Wormleysburg, Cumberland County, Pennsylvania. She lived in 1225 N. Front St., Harrisburg, Dauphin County, Pennsylvania in 1937.

Catherine was affiliated with the Harrisburg, Dauphin County, Pennsylvania religion in 1965. She lived in Beaufort Farm, Camp Curtain, Estherton, Fort Hunter, Harrisburg, Heckton, Lucknow, Rockville, Uptown, Windsor Farm, all Dauphin County, Pennsylvania in 1981. She lived in 2340 Logan St., Harrisburg, Dauphin County, Pennsylvania17110 in 1981. She lived in Dauphin County, Pennsylvania in 1981. She was employed as a Pennsylvania State Clerk in 1981. Her funeral took place in 1981 in John E Neuemeyer, 1334 N. 2nd St., Harrisburg, Dauphin County, Pennsylvania. She was buried on October 27, 1981 in East Harrisburg Cemetery, Harrisburg, Dauphin County, Pennsylvania. She was adopted in Believed adopted. Her cause of death was Congestive heart failure w/myocardial infarction. It seems probable that Catherine's biological mother was Bessie Shannon and her adoptive mother was Mary Potteiger. Catherine and John had the following children: Mildred Irene Stewart, Robert L Stewart, Doris Stewart, James L Stewart, John C Stewart, Audrey M Stewart and Sarah "Sadie" M Stewart.

FRANK ACRI
& THERESA CURCIO

Frank (Francesco) Acri immigrated to Italy to New York, NY in April 1884. He lived in New York, NY about 1890. He was ordained in 1891 in Laborer. He lived in Etna, Allegheny County, Pennsylvania in 1891. Frank may have immigrated more than once to the United States: He immigrated to Italy to New York, NY on the ship Rugia, possibly as a stowaway on March 26, 1894. He immigrated to Italy to New York, NY in 1896. He immigrated to Italy to New York, NY on the ship Ems on February 23, 1899. He immigrated to Italy to New York, NY o the ship Aller on August 8, 1899.

Frank was employed as a Boarder, Unemployed in 1900. He was counted in the census in 1900 in 1st Ward Steelton, Dauphin County, Pennsylvania. He lived in Steelton, Dauphin County, Pennsylvania in 1902. He was employed as a Steelworker in Steelton in 1902. He was naturalized on October 8, 1902 in Pennsylvania. He was employed as a Laborer at the Central Iron and Steel about 1905. He lived in 113 Dock St., Harrisburg, Dauphin County, Pennsylvania in 1909. His funeral took place in 1909 by Speere, 130 South Second Street, Harrisburg, Dauphin County, Pennsylvania. He was employed as a Grocer in 1909. He was buried on March 9, 1909 in Mt. Calvary, Harrisburg, Dauphin County, Pennsylvania. His estate was probated on October 10, 1911 in Dauphin County, Pennsylvania. His cause of death was Cancer liver, exhaustion w/hepatitis. He was affiliated with the St. Mary's, Sharpsburg, Allegheny County, Pennsylvania religion. Frank Acri may have immigrated as stowaway more than once. There may have been two Frank Acris of same age in Steelton, PA.

Although Frank died in 1909, he is in 1910 census and has a passport application in 1913.

Theresa (Teresa) Curcio lived in Etna, Allegheny County, Pennsylvania in 1891. She immigrated on June 5, 1893, Italy to New York, NY on the ship Charles Martel. She was employed as a Farmer in 1901. She immigrated on June 13, 1901, Italy to New York, NY on the ship Isola Di Levanzo. She was employed as a Merchant, Owner of Groceries in 1910. She was counted in the census in 1910 in Harrisburg, Dauphin County, Pennsylvania.

Theresa lived in 113 Dock St., Harrisburg, Dauphin County, Pennsylvania in June 1916. She lived in 221 Schuylkill St., Harrisburg, Dauphin County, Pennsylvania in 1920. She was counted in the census in 1920 in Harrisburg, Dauphin County, Pennsylvania. She was employed as a Grocer between 1920-1930. She lived in 2547 N 4th, Harrisburg, Dauphin County, Pennsylvania in 1930. She was counted in the census in 1930 in Pittsburgh, Allegheny County, Pennsylvania. She lived in 113 Dock, Harrisburg, Pennsylvania between 1936-1942. She was employed as a Grocer between 1939-1946. She signed her will in 1950 in Harrisburg, Dauphin County, Pennsylvania. She was employed as a Housewife in 1951. She lived in 1937 N. 3rd St., Harrisburg, Dauphin County, Pennsylvania in 1951. She was affiliated with the Our Lady of the Blessed Sacrament, Harrisburg, Dauphin, Pennsylvania religion in 1951. Her funeral took place in 1951 in Jos. A. Wiedeman Funeral Home, 357 South Third Street, Steelton, Dauphin County, Pennsylvania. She was buried on October 31, 1951 in Mt. Calvary, Harrisburg, Dauphin County, Pennsylvania. Her estate was probated on November 13, 1951 in Harrisburg, Dauphin County, Pennsylvania. Her cause of death was Myocardial infarction w/ coronary occlusion and coronary artery disease. Theresa and Frank had the following children: Charles H Acri,

Mary Angelina Acri, Michael Acri, Sarah "Sadie" Ernestine Acri, James A Acri, Amel Angelo Acri, John Acri, Alfred Acri and Ella G Acri.

RAYMOND F. BARBUSH
& MARIA A. DESTEPHANO

Raymond Frank (Raimondo Francesco) Barbush lived in Via Nanca, Castiglione, Cosenza, Italy in 1880. He immigrated on November 12, 1894. He was counted in the census in 1900 in Hazel, Luzerne County, Pennsylvania. He was naturalized on May 21, 1906 in Wilkes-Barre, Pennsylvania. He was employed as a Farmer in 1908. He lived in Via Nanca, Castiglione, Cosenza, Italy in 1908. He immigrated in 1909, Hamburg to USA. He was counted in the census in 1910 in Hazelton, Luzerne County, Pennsylvania. He served in the WWI military about 1919. He was counted in the census in 1920. He immigrated on January 6, 1921 on the Regina d'Italia.

Raymond was employed as a Barber in 1930. He lived in 910 North 4th, Harrisburg, Dauphin County, Pennsylvania in 1930. He lived in Barbershop, 1016 Market St., Harrisburg, Dauphin County, Pennsylvania in 1930. He was counted in the census in 1930 in Harrisburg, Dauphin County, Pennsylvania. He lived in 910 6th St., Harrisburg, Dauphin County, Pennsylvania between 1930-1942. His funeral took place in 1945 in GH Sourbier, Harrisburg, Dauphin County, Pennsylvania. He lived in 34 N. 19th St., Harrisburg, Dauphin County, Pennsylvania in 1945. He was employed as a Bar owner in 1945. He was buried on September 20, 1945 in Holy Cross Cemetery, Harrisburg, Dauphin County, Pennsylvania. His cause of death was Coronary occlusion w/hypertension cardiovascular disease. He had a medical condition of Height 5'6", Weight 147, White, Brown eyes, Gray-Black hair, dark complexion, wears glasses and moustache.

Maria "Sadie" Assunta DeStephano was employed as a Homemaker about 1900. She was employed as a Farmer in 1908. She was buried in 1918. Maria was named for her grandmother "Maria" Acri. Maria and Raymond had the following children: Sylvia Frances and Frances Barbush.

CHAPTER 5
Generation Five

All the flowers of all the tomorrows are in the seeds of today
—Indian Proverb

Our Fifth Generation includes our 2G-grandparents, of the mid 1880's.

William Willard, Lottie Layman's third husband

ROBERT B. THOMPSON
& LYDIA A. GOODMAN

Named for his grandfather, Robert Bruce Thompson was delivered into this earthly world on September 24, 1847. The family gathered expectantly at their home on York Farm in Pottsville, Schuylkill County, Pennsylvania. The happy expectant parents, Alexander Thompson and Isabelle Stoddart Penman Thompson, eagerly awaited his arrival along with Robert's seven older brothers and sisters, George, Robert, David, William, Elizabeth, Janette, and Alexander. Robert was not the last child to be born to these parents—his younger siblings, Isabelle and James, would later follow.

Robert's early years were spent growing up on York Farm, where his father raised crops. His family was also known to sell coal from the site, which would later become the famous York Farm Colliery. But his carefree childhood existence would soon see many changes. In 1851, at only four years old, Robert would mourn the loss of his mother. It was the same year that Pottsville became the Schuylkill County seat.

Three years later, the family would move to a 110-acre farm in the sparsely settled Porter Township area. The farm grew smaller as Robert grew older and the town of Sheridan grew around him. Robert would gain a stepmother when his father took Mary Bast as his new wife. Over the next several years, Robert would be joined by an additional twelve half-siblings as well. He was still living at home and working as a laborer in 1870.

Almost nine years after Robert was born, the Goodman family was expecting the birth of a child. Lydia Ann Goodman arrived on February 20, 1856, and was baptized the very same day. She was the tenth child born to Michael Goodman and his wife, Mary Magdalene Brown, of Clarks Valley, Dauphin County, Pennsylvania. Lydia grew up on a farm as well. Her youth was uneventful as her older brothers and sisters married and left the nest one by one. By 1870, her brother George was the only sibling remaining at home. According to the census returns, Robert and Lydia were literate, able to read and write.

Lydia herself left the parental nest to marry Robert in 1873. She was a delicate young bride at just seventeen years of age. Her sisters Susan and Magdalena were probably on hand to give marital advice to the blushing bride as sisters Sarah and Anna helped Lydia into a crisp white dress accentuated with lace and bows. Dainty earrings adorned her lobes and her soft dark curls framed a face that showed both trepidation and bright expectation.

Robert was fashionably dressed in a debonair suit. One could easily imagine the slight smile that played upon his lips as Lydia's brothers, William and John, took him aside for hearty congratulations. Clean shaven, dark hair slightly parted to the side, he faced his new bride with delight. Their wedding took place in Schuylkill County, Pennsylvania, and it was no doubt a grand affair. A jubilant celebration was held with many family members in attendance, including Lydia's brothers, Jacob and George.

Barely settled into married life, the newlywed couple was soon expecting their first child. A son, Benjamin, was born in 1874, but was lost to them in 1875, less than two years later. A second son, Oliver Charles, was born December 13, 1875, bringing a spark of Christmas joy and a measure of comfort for the grieving parents. The couple's only daughter, Laura Louisa, was born in March of 1878. Lydia and Robert were living in Rush Township, Dauphin County, Pennsylvania, when Abel Robert was born in 1880. Robert was working as a coal miner, probably at the Brookside Colliery in Tower City, where he had been employed for many years. Lydia's parents, Michael and Magdalena, were living next door.

Of course, their lives had not been without tragedy. Two of Robert's older brothers served in the Civil War. Alexander F. Thompson served three enlistments and survived to be a prominent attorney and state senator, but William W. Thompson died in 1862 to disease while serving in the Union Army. Robert's sister Elizabeth died while serving as a nurse during the war and a half-brother, Charles, was lost to a mining accident.

An even more personal tragedy struck in October of 1883, when Lydia and her infant son both passed. Little Franklin Henry was only eight weeks old and Lydia was barely over the age of 27, but age was not a discriminating factor. Without the benefit of hospital care, many new mothers died from complications of deliveries. Puerperal fever, a postpartum infection also known as childbed fever, was a very real threat.

During her short life on this earth, Lydia was very well loved. Reverend Arthur Oakes presided with a comforting sermon, as many friends and family gathered close to aid Robert in his time of grief. As Robert was greatly respected, the funeral was the largest in the history of the town. The church overflowed with mourners, and the procession to the cemetery was long. Lydia and Franklin were buried together in Greenwood Cemetery at Tower City, Schuylkill County, Pennsylvania on October 14, 1883.

Valley Echo, Tower City, PA, October 20, 1883 wrote: Last Sunday Tower City witnessed a very sad, affecting and unusual scene in the funeral of Mrs. Robert Thompson and her youngest child. Mrs. Thompson was the daughter of M. and M. Goodman of Clarks Valley. She was a young-woman being but twenty-seven years, eight months and eleven days old on the day of her death. The age of her child, Franklin Henry, was eight weeks. It was the largest Sunday funeral in the history of our town, and was under the supervision of the Sons of America, of which order Mr. Thompson is a member. After a short service at the home, a very large concourse of sympathetic friends joined in the mournful procession to the church, which was crowded to the utmost capacity, hundreds being unable to gain admission. Anxious to hear, they thronged the doorway and windows, and with breathless attention, listened to a sermon by the Rev. Arthur Oakes. After the sermon in the church, the services were continued in the cemetery, where, amid weeping relatives and sorrowing friends, mother and son, side by side, were lowered in the same grave.

> They rest in peace, waiting the resurrection morn, when
> The sainted mother shall wake and in her lap
> Clasp her dear babe, partner of her grave,
> And heritor with her of heaven; a flower
> Washed by the blood of Jesus, from the stain
> Of native guilt, even in its early bud.

Even with the support of family and friends, Robert took Lydia's death hard and became very ill. At the time, Robert was a member of the Patriotic Order Sons of America, probably at Washington Post 54 in Tower City. It was a fraternal group whose main goals were to support the public school system and to encourage patriotism and respect for the nation's heritage and Constitution. It was also their purpose to support fellow "brothers" in their hour of need. The group assisted with Lydia's funeral and stood by Robert, which greatly helped in his recovery.

Robert eventually regained his strength and began to rebuild his life. Rising to prominence in the area, Robert had taken a three-year position in the township government as a supervisor, which may have also included duties as a tax collector. He was fortunate enough to find love again with Mary Margaret Moser Uhler, a widow. The two would soon marry and have at least two children together. Their daughter, Agnes Ellen Lenora, was born in September 1888 in Tower City and baptized shortly thereafter. It is possible that they had another daughter named Lillie, but this may have simply been a nickname used by Agnes.

Lillie married twice and had several children. She is buried in Greenwood Cemetery with her second husband, Charles Haubenstine. A son, Allen Herbert, was born in January 1891, in Tower City. He served in WWI and was a great source of pride for the family. He died in 1962 and is buried in Greenwood Cemetery along with other Thompson family members.

As if the loss of loved ones through illness and disease were not enough, fate would deal yet another blow to Robert. As he was returning from his job as Porter Township supervisor, his normally docile horse was spooked by a bicycle and bolted. Robert was thrown from his carriage and he sustained a severely broken leg that required hospital care. Had he landed on the other side of the road, he may have been thrown down a steep embankment and killed. It was a narrow escape from death.

Mortal peril would soon strike again. Robert had already lost a son to diphtheria when he himself was struck down by another terrible disease. While just as common and deadly a malady, typhoid fever was often transmitted through contaminated food or drinking water. It would claim Robert on October 10, 1907, one day after the 24th anniversary of Lydia's death. His burial took place in Greenwood Cemetery at Tower City on Sunday, October 13, 1907. With autumn leaves falling like the tears of those bereaved, Robert was finally at rest with his wife and children.

Schuylkill County, Pennsylvania: Volume 2 By J.H. Beers and Co, care of Jim Thompson, wrote: Robert, the son of Alexander Thompson, was born at York Farm, and died in 1909. During the greater part of his life he was engaged at mine work, being employed for many years at the Brookside colliery, at Tower City. He served three years as supervisor of Porter Township, and was looked upon as a citizen of substantial character, deservedly respected by all who knew him. His wife, Lydia Goodman, died in 1883, and they are buried in the Greenwood cemetery near Tower City. They were the parents of four children: Oliver; Laura Louise, who is the wife of Charles McGough, of Frankford, Pa.; Abel, living in Porter Township; and Benjamin, who died young. Robert Thompson, who buried his wife and youngest child last week, is very sick. Robert Thompson of Sheridan lost a two-year-old boy of diphtheritic croup. Interment took place on Thursday in Tower City Cemetery. Child by the second wife. Supervisor Robert Thompson is adding a portico to his house in Sheridan. Robert Thompson, of Sheridan, one of the Supervisors of Porter Township, met with an accident while returning home from his day's work on Tuesday, which might have cost him his life. He escaped, however, with a broken leg which will keep him confined to the house for several months to come. On the day of the accident, Mr. Thompson had a force of men at work near Keffers. It was his custom, when working any distance from home, to ride to and from work in a carriage. The horse, of which he is the owner, is kind and gentle and fearless of all things except bicycles. While coming down the State road on the evening of the accident he stopped to converse with a party whom he met. While thus engaged a bicycle and rider came along which frightened the horse who made a plunge, throwing Mr. Thompson out of the buggy to the upper side of the road. Had he fallen on the lower side, he probably would have been thrown down the embankment which might have resulted fatally. After the accident he was taken to his home where Dr. Phillips reduced the fracture which was found to be a bad one, right below the kneecap of the right leg. The injured man is unfortunate in having his legs broken. This is the third or fourth time he has had to suffer from similar injuries. He was taken to the Pottsville hospital on Wednesday afternoon.

Several of Robert and Lydia's children were still living when Robert passed on. Oliver, who was born in Rush Township, rose to prominence in the community of Tower City. There he became the prosperous owner of the Mansion Hotel. He married Blanche Charlesworth, who was born in 1883 and who would die at age 32 in 1915. Laura Louisa would marry Charles McGough around 1903, and the couple would have several wonderful children. Appreciating the value of family, Laura remained close to her half-brother, Allen, for many years.

Abel Robert would marry Augusta Mae "Gussie" Hensel on June 15, 1904. Robert and Lydia would have a short but happy life together. They had five children, four of whom lived to adulthood to carry on the Thompson family legacy, Abel Robert Thompson was the direct ancestor of the Thompson line.

http://www.findagrave.com/cgibin/fg.cgi?page=gr&GRid=113035911

writes: Robert's brother Alexander F was the son of Alexander and Isabella (Pennman) Thompson, in 1860 he was a laborer and miner living in Porter Township, Schuylkill County. He stood 5' 11" tall and had brown hair and gray eyes. A Civil War veteran, he enlisted in Pottsville, Schuylkill County, on August 2, 1862 (with great audacity claiming to be twenty-one years of age), mustered into federal service at Harrisburg August 10 as a private with Co. F, 129th Pennsylvania Infantry, and honorably discharged with his company May 18, 1863. During the Gettysburg crisis of July 1863, he enrolled as a corporal with Co. E, 39th Pennsylvania Emergency Militia, and honorably discharged with his company August 2, 1863. He last enlisted in Pottsville January 23, 1864, mustered into federal service at Philadelphia February 21 as a private with Co. G, 7th Pennsylvania Cavalry (80th Pa), promoted to corporal July 1, 1865, and honorably discharged with his company August 23, 1865. After the war, he worked in the mines where he earned the tuition to pay for a four-year education at Freeburg Academy. He later read for the law in Harrisburg and was admitted to the bar in 1877. He married Elizabeth A. "Lizzie" Halk October 24, 1872, in Lykens, Dauphin County, and fathered William Claude (b. 1873) and Warren Ray (b. @1876). He served a term as state representative and two more in the state senate. He was a member of Tower City's Thompson Post No. 174, G.A.R., and later of Lykens Post No. 232. Hon. Alexander Thompson, eldest surviving son of Alexander Thompson, has been a very prominent man in his district, a member of the Dauphin county bar and at one time a member of the State Senate. During the Civil war he served" in the Union army. His home is at Lykens, Dauphin County, and he is also very well known in Schuylkill County. Since 1912 he has been blind, having lost his sight in an explosion on his farm at Lykens.

Robert Bruce Thompson was counted in the census in 1850 in Norwegian, Schuylkill County, Pennsylvania. He was counted in the census in 1860 in Porter, Schuylkill County, Pennsylvania. He was counted in the census in 1870 in Norwegian, Schuylkill County, Pennsylvania (w/father). He was employed as a Laborer in 1870. He was employed as a Coal miner in 1880. He lived in Rush, Dauphin County, Pennsylvania in 1880. He was counted in the census in 1880 in Rush, Dauphin County, Pennsylvania. He was employed as a Township Supervisor from 1899-1901 in Porter Township, Schuylkill County, Pennsylvania. He lived in Pottsville, Schuylkill County, Pennsylvania in 1900 (Pottsville Hospital, 500 Washington St.). He was employed as a Supervisor in 1900. He was counted in the census in 1900 in Pottsville, Schuylkill County, Pennsylvania. He was employed as a Tax collector about 1900. His funeral took place in 1907 in Tower City, Schuylkill County, Pennsylvania (John [F] Dreisingacer). He was employed as a Business in 1907. He was buried on October 13, 1907 in Tower City, Schuylkill County, Pennsylvania (Greenwood Cemetery). His cause of death was Typhoid fever w/contaminated water. He was named after Robert Thompson, his grandfather. He was affiliated with the Methodist religion. Member: (Members Sons of America)

Lydia Ann Goodman was baptized on February 20, 1856 in Pennsylvania. She was counted in the census in 1860 in Rush Township, Dauphin County, Pennsylvania (unlisted w/father, possibly married). She was counted in the census in 1870 in Rush, Dauphin County, Pennsylvania. She was employed as a Keeping house in 1880. She was counted in the census in 1880 in Rush, Dauphin County, Pennsylvania. She was buried on October 14, 1883 in Tower City, Schuylkill County, Pennsylvania (Greenwood Cemetery). She was affiliated with the Methodist religion. She signed her will (Intestate). Her cause of death was Complications of pregnancy.

HOWARD A.C. HENSEL
& CLARA M. UPDEGROVE

In the summer of 1858, Andrew Guise Hensel and Catherine Workman Hensel welcomed their fourth son and named him Howard Andrew Carson Hensel, using an atypical four names. Howard's name certainly celebrated his father and grandfather, both named Andrew. The Carson name was meaningful, as it was used by two of Howard's brothers when naming their sons. Howard's parents and his two older brothers, Joseph and Ira, welcomed the new addition with joy and excitement to their home in Wiconisco, Pennsylvania. The eldest son, John Henry William, died as an infant, as was sadly common at the time.

The Reverend William Yose presided over Howard's baptism, and the neighbors and nearby cousins came to welcome the new baby. With three boys born within four years of one another, it was a busy household that would continue to grow. Over the next eight years, four daughters were added to the family: Catherine, Lillian, Clarissa, and Emma filled out a family of eight children.

In 1870, their father, Andrew, worked as a plasterer, helping to keep the ever increasing number of miners in the region housed. In 1877, mother, Catherine, passed away, leaving the younger members of the family without a mother as they came of age. Howard was eighteen at that time and had likely already been working to help support the family. In 1880, he was still at home working as a laborer, helping his father to support his sisters while also saving for his own future.

In the same year that the Hensels welcomed their youngest daughter, the Updegrove family announced the birth of their second daughter, Clara Matilda, one day after Thanksgiving, on November 30, 1866, in Lower Ranch Creek. That December, she was baptized by Reverend Brady and introduced to the community. Her big sister, Anna, about two years old, was particularly proud. Her parents, Daniel Updegrove, a laborer and miner who was originally from Wiconisco, and Sarah Culp, from nearby Union County, would have two more children— William and Nora—in the following years.

Having likely met through one of Howard's co-workers, Howard and Clara took to each other quickly and were married after a brief courtship on his 26th birthday—September 2, 1884—surrounded by family and friends in Wiconisco. Howard's sisters, who were near to Clara's age, were buzzing with excitement for the event. His older brothers came to offer congratulations and advice. Naturally, Clara's sisters, Anna and Nora, were heavily involved in dressing and beautifying the bride.

While the white dress had been popularized by Queen Victoria, middle- and working-class brides often chose more practical colors. Clara wore a dark brown and cream-colored dress with neat, modest embroidery and a high neck. This would be her best dress for formal occasions in the coming years. Similarly, Howard's new suit, tailored in dark brown to complement his wife's dress, would serve as his best attire for some time after the ceremony. A joyous wedding was held that Tuesday morning, followed by a wedding breakfast that gave time for congratulations and greetings. The young couple's neighbors wished them luck and fertility, and indeed Howard and Clara were blessed with both.

Clara was seventeen years old when she was married, and not long after her eighteenth birthday, on February 16, 1885, she gave birth to their first child, Augusta Mae, who would be known as "Gussie." The next year brought a son, Arthur. Then came two girls, Helen and Lillian, in 1888 and 1889, respectively. By 1890, Howard had four children to care for, and he had taken up coal mining, perhaps for higher wages than he could earn elsewhere as a laborer at that time. The family continued to grow as Elmer joined them in 1891, and both Myrtle and Clara were born in 1895. A third boy, Victor was born in 1897. The year 1899 brought a daughter, Virginia, into the fold.

Howard and Clara were literate, able to read and write, and were one of only two families of this generation to own a home by 1900, rather than rent—Thomas and Mary Batdorf being the other family. The Batdorfs were the sole family to own the home outright, as the Hensels were carrying a mortgage. By 1910, the Hensels owned their home clear and free.

At the turn of the century, Howard and Clara had nine children, all less than fifteen years of age. To help make ends meet, the eldest son, Arthur, was chipping in as a day laborer and coal miner at the age of thirteen. The family stepped into the next century boldly, bringing in a final son, Howard, and a final daughter, Edna, in 1902 and 1905. Eleven children made for a home more boisterous and busy than either parent had been brought up in, though only the younger six required much care. By the time Edna was born, the eldest five were old enough to take on jobs and responsibilities in the house to ease the burden on their parents.

At some point, Howard got out of the mines and into working with lumber. Perhaps the frequency of mining accidents, such as the 1892 explosion at nearby York Farm Colliery that killed fifteen men, or the periodic unrest over working conditions, or those poor conditions themselves, persuaded him to find a new line of work. By 1910, Howard had moved up to the position of engineer at a planing mill producing finished lumber, and his son Elmer was working at the same place as a carpenter. These jobs were less prone to disruptions in work than coal mining and were better paying as well. Having settled into a steady career as a skilled worker, Howard could look to the next decade with optimism.

By 1915, Howard had become a pillar of the community. Most of his eleven children were grown and beginning their own families, and he had reached the dignity that often comes to a man in his mid-fifties as his gray hair start to show. Similarly, Clara had grown from a blushing teenage bride to a loving grandmother as she approached 50, still youthful but with more pronounced laugh lines.

Howard took an active role in the local chapter of the Patriotic Order Sons of America, Washington Camp, encouraging patriotism and supporting public education. In those years of rapid immigration to America, such groups sought to help newcomers embrace their new home. He also accepted a position as deacon for one of the several Methodist parishes in the area, taking part in the spiritual education of his friends and neighbors.

Howard had a calling to save his brothers not only through Sunday services but also through practical action for workplace safety. In the 1920s,

Howard branched out to firefighting—first in the coal mines, and later for Bestock Underwear Mills in Tower City, Pennsylvania. In both the mining and the textile industries, fire remained a constant danger. Having a long history of coal mining, Schuylkill County also had a rich history of volunteer firefighting companies to match, including more than 130 organizations over the years.

During the 1920s, Fords buzzed on the streets of the cities to the east and new electric refrigerators hummed in homes while fires roared in Appalachian coal country. The booming postwar economy had prompted the mining industry to expand, digging more and deeper mines and exposing larger than ever numbers of miners to various risks. Poorly ventilated mines were the primary cause as 597 Pennsylvania coal miners died in coal dust explosions during that decade— a larger toll than in the 1910s or 1930s.

Larger mines required more non-mining work for safety measures such as ventilation. Consequently, the then-growing union movement continually struggled with the industry over safety provisions, making workers' health a primary concern. It stands to reason that as the nation turned its attention to industrial safety, local community leaders such as Howard were involved with hands-on implementation of important reforms that were needed in these increasingly mechanized workplaces.

In addition to prospering in the postwar economy, the Hensel family had been fortunate when it came to war. Both Howard and Clara's fathers had been mustered during the Civil War, and both returned home safely. Similarly, their luck held out when the States got involved in the First World War. The Hensels' immediate family did not suffer losses, but they undoubtedly were affected by the tragedies that befell their neighbors and friends during the war. They planted their Victory Garden, conserved their resources, and lent aid to their neighbors whose boys went off to war.

Rather, it was the following decade that would trouble the Hensels. Howard and Clara remained engaged as leaders within their community and family until Clara fell ill with cancer in the winter of her 59th year. She would not see her sixtieth birthday, succumbing on March 28, 1926. She was laid to rest in Greenwood Cemetery, Tower City, Schuylkill County, Pennsylvania, on the last day of March. Howard—and indeed the entire family— tried their best to adjust to life without the dear wife of 41 years and mother of eleven children.

In the way that many lasting marriages end, Howard did not linger long before joining his wife in the afterlife the next year. The cause of death was determined to be arteriosclerosis, but perhaps loneliness was what really ailed his heart when he passed on June 6, 1927, at 68 years of age. On June 9, he was interred alongside his wife in Greenwood Cemetery.

The next generation of the Hensel family would have to weather the difficult years of depression and war that would soon follow without the guidance of their dear parents. While times were often challenging, the family would persevere. At this point, Gussie was a widow, having lost her husband, Abel Robert Thompson, in 1918. She was caring for her younger children and earning money as a seamstress. She likely took over as matron of the family, being the eldest of her generation. Including Gussie's family of five children, Howard and Clara had a total of nineteen grandchildren. Daughter Gussie Hensel was the direct ancestor of the Thompson line.

Howard Andrew Carson Hensel was baptized about 1858 in Dauphin County, Pennsylvania (Rev. Wm Yose). He was counted in the census in 1860 in Porter, Schuylkill County, Pennsylvania. He was counted in the census in

1870 in Wiconisco, Dauphin County, Pennsylvania. He was employed as a Laborer in 1880. He was counted in the census in 1880 in Wiconisco, Dauphin County, Pennsylvania. He was employed as a Coal miner in 1900. He was counted in the census in 1900 in Tower City, Schuylkill County, Pennsylvania. He was employed as an Engineer, at a Mill in 1910. He was counted in the census in 1910 in Tower City, Schuylkill County, Pennsylvania. He lived in Tower City, Schuylkill County, Pennsylvania from 1910-1920 (Wiconisco Ave.). He was employed as a Deacon, Methodist Church about 1915. He was employed as a Fireman, Coal mine in 1920. He was counted in the census in 1920 in Tower City, Schuylkill County, Pennsylvania. He was employed as a Fireman, Bestock Underwear Mills in 1927 in Tower City, Pennsylvania. He lived in Tower City, Schuylkill County, Pennsylvania in 1927 (Hand and Wiconisco Aves.). His funeral took place in 1927 in Tower City, Schuylkill County, Pennsylvania (Duane Snyder, 304 E Grand Ave.). He signed his will on June 6, 1927 in Schuylkill County, Pennsylvania (No 1, Vol 28, page 412). He was buried on June 9, 1927 in Tower City, Schuylkill County, Pennsylvania (Greenwood Cemetery). He signed his will on June 20, 1927 in Schuylkill County, Pennsylvania (No 15, page 286). He was named after Father Andrew Hensel and local renowned John Carson, founder of Carsonville, PA. Member: (Member Patriotic Order of Sons of America) He was affiliated with the Methodist religion. His cause of death was Arteriosclerosis. Howard Personality Analysis: He had a lot of pride. Strong self-esteem. Imaginative.

There's a high probability that Howard's Pennybacker ancestors and Clara Opdengraef ancestors knew each other both in Crefeld, Germany and Germantown. Six generations later the two descendants would marry! Howard Personality Analysis II: Howard was a man who was easily enthused. He had a quick mind and it was easy for him to become interested in a subject quickly, only to drop it when something more interesting came along. He had an impulse towards beauty in all its forms and had a love of sensual pleasure. Howard was a great conversationalist and had the ability to talk openly about a subject and yet remain secretive about it. He would hold court over the subject that he was secretive about in such a way as to convince other people that he was right and close the case so to speak. Such was his charisma and his story telling ability that his account would be accepted as the final version and he would succeed in averting attention away from the more truthful and from his perspective, uncomfortable account of particular events. At the time of writing this signature Howard tired easily but had the mental energy and spirit to summon enough determination such that he could regain his strength and finish the task at hand. Although his interests and eagerness may not have necessarily stayed the course, his practical sense and fear of losing face would give him the extra energy needed. Howard had a bit of a love affair with the past. On the positive front he had a brilliant memory and a love of history but once he locked his thoughts into a historical event it was difficult for him to let it go; he could not forget painful events nor forgive people very easily. Not only was Howard a collector of memories but also artistic objects or indeed anything that he found to be beautiful. Howard was a charming fellow who could easily sway individuals into seeing things his way, however he could also quite easily convince himself. It was a difficult task for him to gain an accurate perspective on himself and account for his own weaknesses. Howard was a bit of a dreamer who benefitted greatly from the company of sensible individuals as they grounded him in reality. Howard was an original character. He was a warm man, susceptible to sensual distraction and was always ready to face new situations. His world was very much comprised of his relations to people. His social milieu was no doubt a colorful scene replete with constant conversation, humor and artistic observation.

Clara Matilda Updegrove was baptized in December 1866 in Schuylkill County, Pennsylvania (Rev. Brady). She was counted in the census in 1870 in Williamstown, Dauphin County, Pennsylvania. She was counted in the census in 1880 in Williamstown, Dauphin County, Pennsylvania. She was counted in the census in 1900 in Tower City, Schuylkill County, Pennsylvania. She was counted in the census in 1910 in Tower City, Schuylkill County, Pennsylvania. She was counted in the census in 1920 in Tower City, Schuylkill County, Pennsylvania. Her funeral took place in 1926 in Tower City, Schuylkill County, Pennsylvania (Duane Snyder, 304 E Grand Ave.). She was employed as a Housewife in 1926. She was buried on March 31, 1926 in Tower City, Schuylkill County, Pennsylvania (Greenwood Cemetery). She signed her will (Intestate). She was affiliated with the Methodist < Lutheran religion. Her cause of death was Metastatic carcinoma of medial atrium and left chest w/carcinoma breast.

THOMAS E. BATDORF
& MARY L. PETERS

When Thomas Batdorf, named for his uncle Thomas Batdorf, was born to Peter Batdorf and Elizabeth Welker Batdorf in the Big Run, Dauphin County, Pennsylvania in 1851; the United States of America was only seventy-five years old and Dauphin County was only sixty-five years old. Travel was by stagecoach, Conestoga wagon, canal, and ferry. Roads were dirt and, in the spring, nearly impassable mud, including the main road that connected Millersburg, Big Run, Lykens, and Elizabethville, and is Route 209 today. Thomas, according to the 1900 census return, was literate, able to read and write.

The anthracite coal industry, which would dominate the economy in later years, was in its infancy in 1851, the coal having been discovered in 1825 and first shipped out of the area in 1834 to Millersburg by the Lykens Valley Railroad and Coal Company. At Millersburg, it was loaded on a Susquehanna River pole boat ferry. The railroad, which used horse power on a flat strip rail, was the fourth in the United States and the first in Dauphin County. Derailments were frequent and the 16-mile trip could take two days. Shipments stopped in 1845 when the railroad broke down until 1848 when the Wiconisco Canal was built and the railroad was improved with a T-rail. The coal was shipped as bulk ore until 1848 when the first coal breaker was built in Lykens.

With the coal industry just emerging in 1851 when Thomas was born, Dauphin County was virtually all rural and the economy depended on farming, hunting, fishing, and logging. Though much of the forests had been clear-cut for farms, buildings, heat, and lumber, perhaps 60 percent was still deeply wooded and home to pheasants, turkeys, deer, bear, and possibly even wolves and elk, though they were declining in Pennsylvania. The streams and lakes teemed with shad, salmon, and perch.

By December 6, 1874, when Thomas married Mary Peters, much had changed. Thousands more acres had been clear-cut, roads improved, and passenger train service established. Berrysburg, Elizabethville, and Lykens were officially incorporated as boroughs.

As Thomas had been, Mary was born in Dauphin County. Her father was Samuel Peters, who had been born in Union County, and she was named after her mother, Mary Swartz, who had been born in Mifflin, a township in Juniata County, the next county to the northeast of Dauphin County. Mary was the last of Samuel and Mary's seven children. Preceding her were John, Emma, Jonathan, Matthew, Matilda, and Jane. As of 1900, Mary is the only ancestor of this generation who could not read or write.

Though Pennsylvania's 1790 state constitution had mandated free public primary education, few children in the Lykens/Elizabethville area went to school beyond the equivalent of seventh grade. Note that Mary was only sixteen when she married Thomas. Thomas also came from a large family, being the tenth of eleven children of Peter and Mary Louise. Thomas's older siblings were Esther, Jonas, Elizabeth, Susan, John, Sarah, Peter, Anna, and Rebecca, and he was followed by his sister Louisa.

After Thomas and Mary married, they settled in Elizabethville, where it is likely he was working in the mines, as the 1880 census shows his occupation as a laborer and the 1890 census shows him working as a miner. "Miner" was not a general term for mine workers, but rather a specific job that required certification. The 1910 census shows him as a retired laborer.

The 1870 census shows that four years before he married he was a blacksmith apprentice in Berrysburg to Henry Wise, twenty-four, who had a wife, Sarah, and a one-year old son, Charles. Thomas was a religious man. He was baptized in the German Reformed St. Peter's Church in Lykens and buried St. John's Evangelical Lutheran Cemetery in Loyalton when he died in 1916.

It is known that at least twice he attended the Pennsylvania Evangelical Conference in Berrysburg. In 1904 he attended with his wife and daughter Mary Ellen. In 1906 he attended with his wife, son Adam and daughter Frances. As of 1900, Thomas and Mary—as well as contemporaries Howard and Clara Hensel—were the only two families of this generation to own, rather than rent, a house. The Batdorfs were the sole family to own the home outright, as the Hensel had a mortgage. However, by 1910, the Batdorfs were back to renting, having sold their first home.

Thomas died at the age of sixty-five of heart and kidney disease. Mary survived Thomas by eight years, dying in 1924 of a cerebral hemorrhage. Mary Louisa Peters was buried on August 6, 1924, in St. John's Cemetery, Loyalton, from the Buffington Funeral Home. Before she married Thomas, she was counted in the census in 1860 and 1870 with her family in Mifflin and Washington Townships, Dauphin County.

In 1880, 1890, 1900, and 1910 she was counted in Washington Township and Elizabethville with her husband. After his death, and four years before her death, she was counted in the census in 1920, still in Elizabethville, working as a housekeeper. Thomas and his siblings lived through famous historical events, including the violent United Mine Workers Strike of 1902—the only strike in which a sitting president, Theodore Roosevelt, intervened—and the Civil War.

Elizabethville was an important rail center during the Civil War. Men from the surrounding towns boarded trains there for Harrisburg to be mustered into the army. Among them was John Batdorf. Thomas, perhaps inspired by his older brother, though he was only fourteen in 1865 the last year of the war, lied about his age and enlisted. Unlike the five-foot-tall woman he would one day marry, Thomas was tall for his age, close to six feet. It was easy for the enlistment officers to believe he was eighteen, which was the age of enlistment. The Army did not require proof of age but nearly as soon as Thomas joined, the war was over.

While Thomas Batdorf, a man of family faith and country, and Mary Peters came from large families, their families were modest compared to the family they would create. They were the parents of seventeen children, born between the years of 1875 and 1899, a large family even by eighteenth century standards. Five of their children died in childhood, of those that lived into adulthood, their seventh child, James, is the direct ancestor of the Thompson line.

Thomas Edward Batdorf was baptized on October 12, 1851 in Loyalton, Dauphin County, Pennsylvania (St. Peters (Hoffmans) Reformed). He was counted in the census in 1860 in Lykens, Dauphin County, Pennsylvania. He was educated at School in 1860. He served in the military about 1865 in Dauphin County, Pennsylvania (Civil War, Private, Age may be prohibited). He was counted in the census in 1870 in Berrysburg, Dauphin County, Pennsylvania (Wise). He was employed as an Apprentice to Blacksmith in 1870. He was counted in the census in 1880 in Washington, Dauphin County,

Pennsylvania. He was employed as a Laborer in 1880. He was employed as a Coal miner in 1900. He was counted in the census in 1900 in Washington, Dauphin County, Pennsylvania. He was employed as a Retired laborer in 1910. He lived in Elizabethville, Dauphin County, Pennsylvania in 1910 (W. Main St.). He was counted in the census in 1910 in Elizabethville, Dauphin County, Pennsylvania. His funeral took place in 1916 in Elizabethville, Dauphin County, Pennsylvania (Buffington Funeral Home). He was employed as a Laborer in 1916. He was buried on August 16, 1916 in Loyalton, Dauphin County, Pennsylvania (St. Johns (Oakdale) Cemetery). His height was 6 foot. He was affiliated with the Reformed religion. He was named after Thomas Batdorf, uncle. His cause of death was mitral insufficiency and Bright's disease (i.e., chronic inflammation of kidneys).

Mary Louisa Peters was counted in the census in 1860 in Mifflin, Dauphin County, Pennsylvania. She was counted in the census in 1870 in Lykens, Dauphin County, Pennsylvania (unlisted). She was employed as a Keeping house in 1880. She was counted in the census in 1880 in Washington, Dauphin County, Pennsylvania. She was counted in the census in 1900 in Washington, Dauphin County, Pennsylvania. She was counted in the census in 1910 in Elizabethville, Dauphin County, Pennsylvania. She was counted in the census in 1920 in Elizabethville, Dauphin County, Pennsylvania. She lived in Elizabethville, Dauphin County, Pennsylvania in 1920 (Main St.). She was employed as a Housekeeper in 1924. Her funeral took place in 1924 in Elizabethville, Dauphin County, Pennsylvania (Buffington Funeral Home). She was buried on August 6, 1924 in Loyalton, Dauphin County, Pennsylvania (St. Johns (Oakdale) Cemetery). Her cause of death was cerebral hemorrhage. She signed her will (Intestate). She was affiliated with the Reformed < Lutheran religion. Her height was 4 foot, 12inches. She was named after Mary Ann Swartz, mother.

JOHN H. WERT
& ADELINE ROW

John Henry Wert was born in Dalmatia, Northumberland County, Pennsylvania, in 1855, the third of the eventual ten children of David M. Wert and Catherine Shoop. David was a farm laborer, born on All Fool's Day in 1829, in Powell's Valley, Dauphin County to Jacob Wert. John's mother, Catherine, born on February 24, 1830, in Northumberland County, was the daughter of John Shoop and Sarah Wertz. John was named for his grandfather, John Shoop.

John and older siblings Elizabeth and Anna were born in Northumberland County. His younger siblings, Mary, Melinda, Amelia, Daniel, and Isaac, were born after the family moved to adjacent Dauphin County, which was more prosperous than Northumberland.

John was working as a blacksmith in Washington Township, Dauphin County, when he met his wife, Adeline Row. A New Year's baby, Adeline was born in Dauphin County near Lykens borough on January 2, 1860. Her father was Daniel Row and her mother was Susan Frantz. Daniel was the son of John William Rowe and Barbara Rudy. He was born on July 10, 1813, in Dauphin County. Susan Frantz was born March 23, 1819, in Dauphin County. She was the daughter of Adam Frantz and Susan Gieseman.

Adeline was the youngest of seven siblings, following Sarah, Angelina, Adam, Susan, Amelia, and Leah. By 1870, the family had broken up. Adeline was living with her aunt, Susan Ely. Her father, Daniel, died on the final day of July in 1871, when Adeline was eleven. John and Adeline, according to the 1900 census return, were literate, able to read and write.

John and Adeline married in 1878. She was eighteen, he was twenty-three. They wed in the "Church of the Hill," St. John's Lutheran Church. Built of stone on a hill overlooking the Lykens Valley in 1872, it replaced a log church built in 1802. The parish roots dated back to 1773 when the Reverend J. Enderline, a pioneer missionary, came to Lykens Valley.

John and Adeline settled in Washington Township, Dauphin County. By 1900, John had given up blacksmithing. The trade was in decline with the rise of factories, the development of the casting process, and less demand for horses in agriculture and transport. He became a freelance day laborer. That meant he was not on regular payroll of a farm or mine, but hired himself out on a daily basis where labor was needed. Since work was not steady, he needed help supporting his family. Adeline helped out running a farm on their property in Washington Township in the 1910s. At this time, the Werts, as well as the Hensels, were the only two families of this generation to own a home clear and free.

In 1879 they had a daughter, Caroline Wert. They eventually had five more children. Harriet was born in 1881. Another child, about whom little is known, was born in 1883. Florence was born on March 6, 1886. Beulah was born on New Year's Eve in 1889. Finally, Margaret was born in 1904.

John was a big man for the day at six-foot and a hard and willing worker. He coveted a union job with one of the coal companies. But in May 1902, United Mine Workers president John Mitchell organized an anthracite workers strike. In November of that year, U.S. President Teddy Roosevelt, fearing a shortage of coal for the winter, threatened to send in federal troops to take over the mines. Only then did the sides agree to end the strike.

After the strike, the coal companies refused to let replacement workers go and over half the men who went on strike in Lykens Valley were not called back. That didn't help John. But the growth of the anthracite industry did help. The growth of the coal industry, and the Dauphin economy, was jumped-started by the Civil War. John and Adeline's home in Washington Township was only 80 miles from the Mason-Dixon Line and 60 miles from Gettysburg. Thus, Dauphin County, as a breadbasket and coal producer, was important to the Union. Pennsylvania supplied 80 percent of the Union Army's iron, all of its anthracite coal, and much of its textiles and food, with Dauphin a large contributor.

After the Civil War an enormous demand for anthracite and technological advances in mining during the industrial revolution fueled exponential growth in the industry. America's entry into World War I created even more demand. The anthracite industry peaked in 1917, when one hundred eighty thousand workers harvested one hundred million tons of coal throughout the anthracite region of Eastern Pennsylvania.

John was one of those workers. He was hired by the Susquehanna Colliery in Lykens in the 1910s. This is evident because in the 1910 census he was a "day laborer" and in 1920 he was a "laborer–coal mine." John was still working for the Susquehanna Colliery in 1922, when a modern electric plant was built to provide electricity to all the local collieries. The $2 million plant burned "coal dirt," or culm, the by-product of coal processing.

John was 67 and still working for Susquehanna in October of 1924, when he was crushed by rolling logs while cutting timber for mine tunnels. He was taken to the Harrisburg Hospital where he died. Cause of death was a hemorrhage and shock from fractured ribs and other injuries. He outlived Adeline by three years. She was fifty-nine when she died of natural causes in 1921. John and Adeline were waked at the Buffington Funeral Home in Elizabethville and buried in St. John's Cemetery.

Though mine work was dangerous and workers were paid less than their value, the pay for a union mine worker in the 1910s and early twenties was better than the average worker's salary in other industries. In the decades before their deaths, John and Adeline may have had some extra income from his job and her farm. Their daughter Beulah, who was ten in 1900, lived with them. As they lived in rural Washington Township they likely had fun taking Beulah to family and church picnics, fairs, moving pictures, and baseball games in the boroughs around the township. They lived on State Road, which was macadam by the 1910s and provided easy access to Elizabethville and Lykens.

In these towns, Adeline could shop at general merchandise and confectionary stores. At the market she could find butter at twenty cents per pound, eggs at eighteen cents per dozen, and dressed chickens at ten cents per pound. As she ran a small farm she may have been a buyer or seller. John might visit taverns, billiard halls, and cigar stores. If they needed to visit the state capital, Harrisburg, twenty miles to the south, they could leave from the train station in Elizabethville—an important troop depot in the Civil War.

Built in 1875, the station is still standing today. Also in the towns in the 1880s and 1890s banks were established, rudimentary telephone service began, water companies were organized, and fire departments were formed. Electric lights and moving pictures came in 1909, though these conveniences arrived much later in the townships. They must have seemed like amazing technologies to John and Adeline, who had grown up before electricity, plumbing, and paved roads.

As they traveled among the towns, John and Adeline may have been even more amazed to see a flying machine in the sky. In April of 1913, Walter Johnson of New York flew from Millersburg to Wisconisco in thirteen minutes.

Fair going was a pastime. The biggest was seven miles from Lykens in Gratz, which boasted a first-class horse track. At baseball games, John and Adeline might well have watched family members play in the Twin County League. It is known that in 1921, the center fielder, named Wert, set a league record for stolen bases, and a player named Row batted .326 and was third in the league in runs. As mentioned, John and Adeline had at least enough schooling to be literate, as reading newspapers was a popular pastime.

The towns all had local papers at one time or another and people also read the Harrisburg Patriot, which chronicled daily life in its town columns. Folks might read that "a coat of paint greatly improved Adam Row's house in Lykens" or "Carrie Wert of Millersburg visited her parents, John, and wife for several days." "Carrie" was a nickname for daughter Caroline.

In addition to his fierce work ethic, John was a devoted family man. In 1920, a grandson, John Schoffer, age seven, lived with him and Adeline. John and Adeline's youngest daughter, Beulah, is the direct ancestor of the Thompson line. After she married James "Edward" Batdorf, they and her parents lived on adjacent farms at 46 and 47 State Road in Washington Township.

John Henry Wert was counted in the census in 1860 in Lower Mahanoy, Northumberland County, Pennsylvania. He was counted in the census in 1870 in Lykens, Dauphin County, Pennsylvania. He was counted in the census in 1880 in Washington, Dauphin County, Pennsylvania. He was employed as a Blacksmith in 1880. He was employed as a Day laborer in 1900. He was counted in the census in 1900 in Washington, Dauphin County, Pennsylvania. He was employed as a Laborer, [illegible] in 1910. He was counted in the census in 1910 in Washington, Dauphin County, Pennsylvania (enumerated twice). He was employed as a Laborer in 1920. He lived in Washington, Dauphin County, Pennsylvania in 1920 (State Road 199). He was counted in the census in 1920 in Washington, Dauphin County, Pennsylvania. He signed his will in 1924 in Dauphin County, Pennsylvania (N-Z, 1785-1937, File 264). His funeral took place in 1924 in Elizabethville, Dauphin County, Pennsylvania (Buffington Funeral Home). He was employed as a Timber laborer, Susquehanna Colliery Co in 1924 in Dauphin County, Pennsylvania. He was buried on November 2, 1924 in Berrysburg, Dauphin County, Pennsylvania (St. Johns (Hill) Lutheran). His estate was probated between November 19, 1924-1938 in Washington Township, Dauphin County, Pennsylvania. His cause of death was hemorrhage and shock from fractured ribs and other abdominal injuries from rolling timber. He was named after Uncle Henry Wert and grandfather John Shoop. He was affiliated with the Lutheran religion. His height was 6 foot.

Adeline Row was counted in the census in 1860 in Washington, Dauphin County, Pennsylvania. She was baptized on March 11, 1860 in Berrysburg, Dauphin County, Pennsylvania (St. Johns (Hill) Lutheran). She was counted in the census in 1870 in Wiconisco, Dauphin County, Pennsylvania. She was educated at School in 1870. She was counted in the census in 1880 in Washington, Dauphin County, Pennsylvania. She was employed as a Keeping house in 1880. She was counted in the census in 1900 in Washington, Dauphin County, Pennsylvania. She was listed as "Owned farm" about 1900. She was counted in the census in 1910 in Washington, Dauphin County, Pennsylvania. She was counted in the census in 1920 in Washington, Dauphin County, Pennsylvania. She was employed as a Housewife in 1921. She lived in Lykens, Dauphin County, Pennsylvania in 1921. Her funeral took place in 1921 in Elizabethville, Dauphin County, Pennsylvania (Buffington Funeral Home). She was buried on March 10, 1921 in Berrysburg, Dauphin County, Pennsylvania (St. Johns (Hill) Lutheran). Her height was 5 foot, 5 inches. She signed her will (Intestate). Her cause of death was Sero-fibrinous pleurisy w/myocarditis. She was affiliated with the Lutheran religion.

J. FREDERICK DUNCAN
& CATHERINE MCCLOUD

Johannes Friedrich Dankert—later anglicized to Frederick Duncan—was raised in Prussia during the confessional Lutheran migration to the New World, being born April of 1836 in Hohenkirchen, the son of William Gehrhart Heinrich Dankert and Maria Carolina Henriette Kelling of. Frederick was the youngest of six children, living in a time that was extremely difficult for a young man to live with the religious unrest and economic turmoil of that day.

Approximately 5,000 to 7,000 Orthodox Lutherans emigrated to the U.S. for religious reasons over a ten-year span starting in 1839, when the King of Prussia Frederick William III merged the two main religions, Lutheran and Reformed churches. Crop failure and poor economic conditions were other reasons listed for the mass exodus of Prussia/Germany between 1830 and 1920. Over 700,000 people left the country during that time for America and London.

The 1840s and 1850s, particularly in Frederick's birth area, was a period of great upheaval. A Grand Ducal regulation governs over the Mecklenburg-Schwerin process for issuing passports to emigrants. Revolution throughout Europe including Mecklenberg. A Grand Ducal regulation in the territory of Mecklenburg-Schwerin, permitting emigration. The "Freienwalder Schiedsspruch" permits the Constitutional hereditary settlement to be reinstated.

Beginning of mass emigration to America. Political, social and economic ills caused the great emigration wave end of the, from 1853 to 1908 nearly 120,000 people migrated from Mecklenburg. Adopted Ordinance on the acquisition and loss of property of Mecklenburg citizens. Country Regulation on emigration to non-European countries.

Possibly spurred on by letters from friends or family who had already emigrated, Frederick made his voyage to the U.S. around the age of 26; most likely entering through New York, where a vast majority of German immigrants entered. The lure of land for as low as $1.25 an acre—due to the Homestead Act of 1862—may have brought him westward to Pennsylvania.

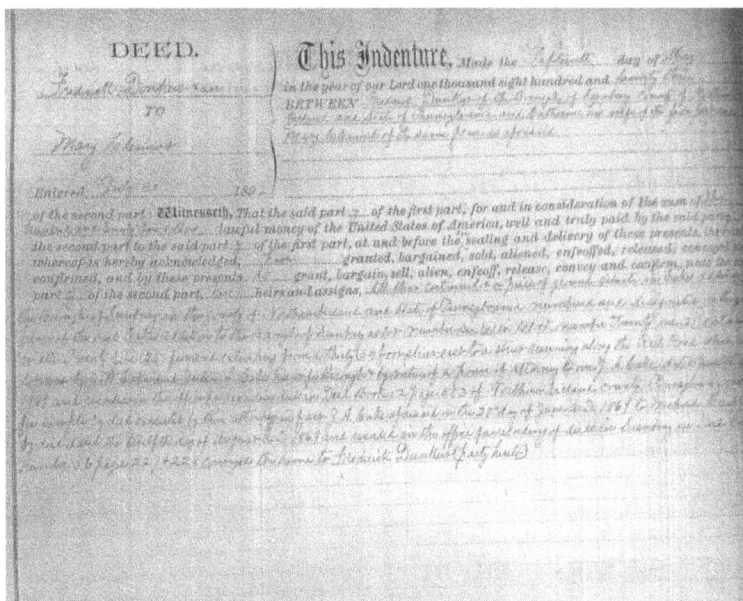

He settled in Sunbury, Pennsylvania, a predominantly Scottish area. As time went by, Frederick's last name was ultimately recorded as Duncan. The change may have been made by the local clerks not knowing how to spell his name or maybe wishing to make a more Anglicized spelling of the Prussian name. Fredrick may have changed his name himself to better fit in with the local population. However, Fredrick kept the latter spelling throughout the rest of his life. All of his children were born with the surname of Duncan.

Sunbury is located near where the north and west branches of the Susquehanna River came together. The town became a port on the Pennsylvania Canal and was a major railroad center. The area boomed with the development of local coalmines and various industries such as textile mills. It is possible that Frederick was working in one of these industries when he met the love of his life, Catherine McCloud. The couple married in 1870.

Catherine McCloud was born and raised in Pennsylvania, as were same as her parents, David McCloud and Mary Sarvis. Catherine was born in Hallowing Run and lived all of her life in Northumberland County. Eventually her parents, along with their nine children, Joseph, Sarah, Mary Ann, Catherine, Daniel, Frederick, Jeremiah, Judith and William moved to Sunbury the county seat of Northumberland County. Catherine was twenty-one when she married Frederick and he was 31.

According to the 1880 census return, Catherine was illiterate but by 1900 she was able to read and write. Frederick, born in Germany, was not literate in English, having lived a short time in America. He and Mary Batdorf were the only two illiterate ancestors of this generation. Frederick and Catherine had six children Melinda, Sarah, William, Gertrude, Hannah Lilly and Charles. They continued to live in Sunbury through their married life, with their children attending local school.

Sunbury had five dominant religions: Lutheran, Reformed, Baptist, Presbyterian, and Catholic. Fredrick was most likely Lutheran. Catherine may have been Lutheran, but probably converted from one of the other religions when she married Fredrick. Whatever the case may be, all the children were baptized in Zion Evangelical Lutheran Church. Built in 1791, the church is one of the earliest Lutheran churches in America.

In addition to raising their children, both parents worked outside the home. When the couple married, Catherine worked as a housekeeper, possibly at the City Hotel, in Sunbury—where Thomas Edison installed the first successful three-wire electrical lighting system in the U.S. on July 4, 1883.

Sadly, they only had twelve years of marriage. Fredrick died in 1882—the same year Charley was born. At the time of his passing, their oldest daughter, Melinda, was only eleven. In the culture of the time, the oldest son would take on the role of the father in this situation, but William was only seven years old at the time of his father's passing.

It must have been very hard for Catherine having so many young children to care for. At the time, there was no welfare system to help a young mother raising six children on her own. Being the strong and determined woman that she was, Catherine would not take handouts from the neighbors or the church. She sought out employment with higher wages working as domestic help and later as a day laborer, possibly in the textile mills.

Catherine worked hard to support her children before her death in 1903 of dropsy, which today is called edema of the kidney. Her condition was complicated by heart disease. Her legacy of hard work and love undoubtedly held on for generations as the young mother who raised her six children alone and kept her family tightly knit. Most of her children lived out their lives in Sunbury.

Catherine rested knowing that she had raised all of her children to adulthood. Surely one of her last big pleasures was seeing her oldest son, William, marry and carry on the Duncan name. Frederick and Catherine's third child, William, was the direct ancestor of the Thompson line.

John Frederick Duncan Dankert was baptized on May 1, 1836 in Hohenkirchen, Prussia (Nordwestmecklenburg, Mecklenburg-Vorpommern, Germany). He immigrated to Germany to USA on May 12, 1857 (ship Humboldt). He was counted in the census in 1860. He owned $500 in 1870. He was counted in the census in 1870 in Sunbury, Northumberland County, Pennsylvania. He was employed as a Laborer from

1870-1880. He lived in Sunbury, Northumberland County, Pennsylvania in 1880 (Short St.). He was counted in the census in 1880 in Sunbury, Northumberland County, Pennsylvania. He lived in Pennsylvania in 1880 (Short St.). He was buried in 1882 in Sunbury, Northumberland County, Pennsylvania (Old Cemetery Sunbury). He signed his will (Intestate). He was affiliated with the Evangelical Lutheran religion.

Catherine McCloud was born on March 5, 1849 in Pennsylvania. She was counted in the census in 1850 in Lower Augusta, Northumberland County, Pennsylvania. She was counted in the census in 1860 in Sunbury, Northumberland County, Pennsylvania. She was counted in the census in 1870 in Augusta, Northumberland County, Pennsylvania. She was employed as a Servant about 1870. She was employed as a Keeping house in 1880. She was counted in the census in 1880 in Sunbury, Northumberland County, Pennsylvania. She was employed as a Day laborer in 1900. She lived in Pennsylvania in 1900 (927 Railroad Ave.). She was counted in the census in 1900 in Sunbury, Northumberland County, Pennsylvania. She lived in Sunbury, Northumberland County, Pennsylvania in 1900 (927 Railroad Ave.). She lived in Pennsylvania in 1903 (1014 R.R. Ave.). She lived in Sunbury, Northumberland County, Pennsylvania in 1903 (1014 R.R. Ave.). She was buried on January 6, 1903 in Sunbury, Northumberland County, Pennsylvania (Old Sunbury Cemetery). She signed her will (Intestate). Her cause of death was Dropsy (i.e., Edema of kidney) w/heart disease. She was affiliated with the Evangelical Lutheran religion.

JOSEPH P. LAYMAN
& REBECCA J. OVERLANDER

Just before the outbreak of the American Civil War, on January 8, 1859, Joseph Pierce Layman was born to Michael Layman and Elmira Elizabeth Raymond in Airville, York County, Pennsylvania. He was the seventh of nine siblings: Jacob, Sarah, Uriah, Mary, Elmira, Charles, Lillian, and Theodore.

A short buggy ride away in Chanceford, York County, Pennsylvania, Rebecca Jane Overlander was born to Jacob Warner Oberlander and Sarah Ann Gipe in October of the same year. She was the fifth of eleven siblings: Luther, Sarah, Edward, Adeline, Caroline, Samuel, Margaret, Emaline, Barbara, and Jacob. Joseph and Rebecca, according to the 1900 census return, were literate, able to read and write.

Pennsylvanians were strong sympathizers with the Union during the Civil War, sending more than 36,000 men to the battlefields for the North. Joseph's father was one  of the many who fought to end slavery and reunite the United States of America. York County sent five companies: Worth Infantry, York Rifles, Marion Rifles, Hanover Infantry, and the York Volunteers to fight for the cause. The 87th Regiment was composed of almost entirely York County men. Joseph's father may have been in one of these regiments.

Joseph and Rebecca may have been too young to understand the full impact of the war, both being very young when the war started. Joseph was aware only that his father was no longer around and may have developed separation anxiety.

They may have been standing along the roadside, wondering what all the commotion was about as their parents and siblings cheered the troops passing through their respective towns. They must have felt the resentment of the Confederate occupation of the City of York in 1863 from their family members. By the time the nearby Battle of Gettysburg and the smaller scrimmages that lead up to it were fought in 1865, they were old enough to feel the ground shake from the cannon explosions and see the hasty movements of troops going to and coming from battle. This must have struck fear and confusion in their young minds.

Nevertheless, they grew up; Joseph probably tending to his parents' dairy cows and crops, which was the main agriculture of the day in most of the rural areas of York County. Airville was a small rural community that had its population counted in the Lower Chanceford census, along with Peach Bottom and Fawn townships.

Rebecca, on the other hand, lived in nearby Chanceford, a larger town where possibly Joseph and his parents sold their milk, butter, and produce. As time went by, Rebecca caught the eye of Joseph, maybe at a town social or dance, or maybe they met when he was delivering his family's products to her mother. We really don't know how they met, but we do know that they were married in 1877 in Chanceford.

Joseph and Rebecca had fourteen children: Lillian, Charlotte "Lottie"—who became the Thompson family matriarch—Earl, Nelson, Charles, Daniel,

Chester, Theodore, Joseph, Mabel, Margaret, Ralph, Leroy, and Martha. Shortly after they were married, Joseph and Rebecca moved to Brogueville, York County, Pennsylvania, where Lottie was born. Another move took the family to Columbia, Lancaster County, Pennsylvania possibly for Joseph's job with the railroad. He was a brakeman and then later an engineer. The promotion to engineer could have been the reason the family moved to Sunbury, Northumberland County, Pennsylvania. Rebecca was a homemaker throughout their marriage.

As a side note, Joseph's brother Charles Layman married Margaret "Maggie" McKinley, a cousin of President McKinley. They connection is shown here:

1) John McKinley and Margaret
...2) David McKinley and Anna Rose
......3) William McKinley
.........4) Stephen McKinley and Jane
............5) William McKinley and Margaret
...............6) Margaret J McKinley and Charles Layman
......3) James McKinley
.........4) William McKinley and Nancy Allison
............5) William McKinley (President of USA)

As of 1910, Rebecca was renting a home in Sunbury but Joseph was absent from the census, either in Pennsylvania or Illinois. The 1920 census reported Joseph and Rebecca were living in Chicago, Illinois with their youngest children Lee and Martha. Lee, listed as the head of the house, was 24 at the time and working as a bookkeeper and Martha was twenty-one working as a telephone operator. Joseph, 64, and no longer worked for the railroad, instead working in the storeroom of a packinghouse.

Why did the Laymans relocate to Chicago? Possibly, since Joseph suffered from heart disease, a move to Chicago would include more specialized medicine of the day. Joseph's many years working as an engineer, he undoubtedly made numerous runs to Chicago and would have been familiar with the area. There is potential that Joseph either remarried or lived with a woman named Mary, which is possibly why he is not with Rebecca in 1910.

While in Chicago, Rebecca was harkened back to Pennsylvania to assist their son Nelson who had contracted pneumonia. Unfortunately, Rebecca also caught the relentless disease and passed away in 1921 of lobar pneumonia at the Hazelton State Hospital in Pennsylvania. This scenario is unlikely given pneumonia is an acute illness, coming on suddenly, usually when a person's immune system is weak.

Joseph passed away three years later in 1924 and was buried in Chicago. His cause of death was listed as valvular heart disease and chronic nephritis and cystitis. Joseph and Rebecca's second child, Lottie, was the direct ancestor of the Thompson line.

Joseph Pierce Layman was counted in the census in 1860 in Lower Chanceford, York County, Pennsylvania. He was counted in the census in 1870 in Lower Chanceford, York County, Pennsylvania. He was educated at School in 1870. He was counted in the census in 1880. He was employed as a Brakeman, Railroad in 1900. He was counted in the census in 1900 in Sunbury, Northumberland County, Pennsylvania (Laynon). He lived in Pennsylvania in 1900 (209 3rd St.). He lived in Sunbury, Northumberland

County, Pennsylvania in 1900 (209 3rd St.). He was counted in the census in 1910. He was employed as an Engineer about 1910. He lived in Chicago, Cook, Illinois in 1920 (Blackstone Avenue). He was counted in the census in 1920 in Chicago, Cook County, Illinois. He was employed as a Store room, Packing House in 1920. He lived in Chicago, Cook County, Illinois in

1924. He lived in Chicago, Cook County, Illinois in 1924 (908 W 70th St.). He lived in Chicago, Cook County, Illinois in 1924 (908 W 70th St.). He was employed as an Engineer, Stationary and Locomotive in 1924. He lived in Chicago, Cook County, Illinois in 1924. He was buried on February 22, 1924 in Chicago, Cook County, Illinois (Evergreen Cemetery, Lot SG 157, Part #6). His funeral took place on February 22, 1924 in Chicago, Cook County, Illinois (JJ Sullivan). He was affiliated with the Methodist religion. His cause of death was Valvular heart disease (aortic) w/chronic nephritis and cystitis.

Rebecca Jane Overlander was counted in the census in 1860 in Chanceford, York County, Pennsylvania (listed as Margaret). She was educated at School in 1870. She was counted in the census in 1870 in Chanceford, York County, Pennsylvania (Rebeck). She was counted in the census in 1880. She was employed as a Homemaker about 1885. She was counted in the census in 1900 in Sunbury, Northumberland County, Pennsylvania. She lived in Sunbury, Northumberland County, Pennsylvania in 1910 (517 Chestnut St.). She was counted in the census in 1910 in Sunbury, Northumberland County, Pennsylvania (Laymer). She lived in Pennsylvania in 1910 (517 Chestnut St.). She was counted in the census in 1920 in Chicago, Cook County, Illinois. She lived in Weatherly, Carbon County, Pennsylvania in 1921 (son Nelson's). She lived in Weatherly, Carbon County, Pennsylvania in 1921 (son Nelson's). She was buried on November 23, 1921 in Sunbury, Northumberland County, Pennsylvania (Pomfret Manor Cemetery, Plot 130B). Her cause of death was Pneumonia, Labor. She signed her will (Intestate). She was affiliated with the Methodist < Lutheran religion. Her cause of death was Rebecca came home from Chicago to help her ailing son Nelson Layman, she caught pneumonia from him and passed away at Hazelton Hospital in 1921.

JAMES M. ANDERSON
& LUCETTA GAUGLER

James Anderson and Lucetta Gaugler were born eight months apart in the village of Chapman, Pennsylvania, which lies on the west bank of the Susquehanna. In the year of their births, 1854, Chapman lay in Union County, but the part of Union County in which they were born would be separated and renamed Snyder County the year after their birth.

Both of their families had deep roots in Union County, Pennsylvania: of their four parents, all but one was born in Union County. That parent, James's mother, Catherine Bordner, had been born in neighboring Northumberland County right across the river.

Born in April of 1854, James was the seventh child of Elijah Anderson and Catherine Bordner Anderson. His older six siblings were Samuel Benjamin, Mary Pamela, Susan, Sarah Adeline, Josephine, and Emma Jane. After James came two sisters, Evaline Edith and Catherine.

Lucetta was born not far away and only eight months later on Christmas Day. She was named after her mother's sister, Aunt Lucetta. Years later, Lucetta's granddaughter Mamie Lucetta Anderson would, in turn, be named after her. Lucetta's parents were Abraham Gaugler and Kesiah Kelly Gaugler. Like James, she was the seventh child of her family, but her family was even larger, comprised of fifteen children. After bearing a son, a daughter, a son, a daughter, and a son, Kesiah Gaugler went on to give birth to ten daughters in a row. Preceding Lucetta were John, Adeline, George, Emaline, James, and Elizabeth Jane. After Lucetta came Isabelle, daughter K. J., Sarah, Minerva, Alice, Caroline, and Ella. According to the census returns, James and Lucetta were literate, able to read and write.

The birth names of James's and Lucetta's parents suggest that both of them represented the various ethnic strains of early Pennsylvania—its early German population mixed with somewhat later waves of English and Irish immigrants. Anderson is clearly an English name, as Kelly is an Irish name. But both James and Lucetta each also had a parent whose ancestors were part of Pennsylvania's strong German heritage. Bordner, James's mother's maiden name is most likely a variant of the Middle Low German name "Bartner." Gaugler, Lucetta's father's name, stems from South German or Swiss German, with a distant original meaning being "jester" or "entertainer."

In such a small community, the Anderson and Gaugler families were sure to have known each other. James and Lucetta might have been childhood friends. Pennsylvania's 1790 State Constitution had mandated free public primary education. We can well imagine James and Lucetta sitting in the same classroom in a one-room school house, learning their ABCs and numbers, and walking home together after school.

Their childhood friendship gradually blossomed, as they grew older, into friendship, affection, love, and a desire to spend their lives together. Or, did uniting in marriage just seem the logical next step for 19-yearolds whose families had been acquainted for their entire lives?

Marriage in rural America in the 19th century had a somewhat different meaning than it does today. Married couples are expected to care for one another, but in the 19th century the institution of marriage was built upon a religious, legal, and social framework, and marriage was considered to be much more of an economic relationship. With none of the labor-saving devices we take for granted today, division of labor between a man and a woman was essential. It was nearly impossible for a person to live alone.

By the time they were nineteen years old, James and Lucetta had known each other for at least thirteen years. At the very least, their marriage was based on long acquaintance and some degree of affection. Quite possibly, this acquaintance had grown into love. As was typical for married couples of that era, James and Lucetta began a family. Their oldest was Charles, followed in 1880 by William. Then came two more sons, Theodore and Thomas. After four boys in a row, Amy Josephine became the Andersons' first girl. She was joined next by another sister, Catherine.

James and Lucetta continued to reside in Chapman and the adjacent Port Trevorton until James's death in 1899. James was working as a laborer in 1880. There were a number of industries in which a strong, tireless man could find employment. Local mines yielded huge amounts of coal, and laborers were required both at the mines and at the Pennsylvania Canal port that had been dredged in the Susquehanna River at Port Trevorton, giving it the name of "Port." James might also have worked in the lumber industry, which was still in the process of removing the white pine, Eastern hemlock, and hardwood forests that had once covered 90% of the land area of Pennsylvania.

James might have worked in agriculture, too, since farming was, and still is, an important element of the local economy. In the late 19th century, Snyder County farmers specialized in wheat as a cash crop and corn for livestock feed, dairy cattle, and hogs. In addition, rye was a common crop used in the distilling industry. Other industries that were prominent—and in which James could have worked at one time or another—included tanning, barrel making, gunsmithing, and furniture manufacture.

James could also have worked on Pennsylvania's canal system. In Pennsylvania, a vast network of canals—with locks where necessary—had been dug in order to transport floating logs as well as barges for carrying coal, agricultural products, and passengers. In James's prime working years, some canals were still being dug and they all needed constant maintenance. The total length of Pennsylvania's network of canals eventually exceeded 1,200 miles.

By the year of James's and Lucetta's birth, however, railroads had begun displacing canals, and work for the Pennsylvania Railroad was an important source of employment for residents of Snyder County. James Anderson could have found steady work in any of these industries. Certainly, with a wife and six children, he needed to stay employed.

Though James was the seventh child of his parents, upon his mother Catherine's death in 1893 it fell on him to serve as administrator of probate. Unfortunately, there seems to have been disagreement among the Anderson siblings, with legal documents filed protesting James's administration.

In 1899, at the age of forty-five, James died in Port Trevorton, Pennsylvania. The cause of death was lip and throat cancer. At the end of the 19th century, surgical removal of cancerous tissue was the only available

treatment, but it is unlikely that a workingman in rural Pennsylvania would have had access to any kind of surgery. It is likely that his death was prolonged and painful.

Within a year of James's death, Lucetta moved to Sunbury—a larger town about a dozen miles up the Susquehanna River from Port Trevorton. Her oldest son, Charles, was no longer living with his mother, but Lucetta's household still included William, Theodore, Thomas, Amy, and Kate. Life for a widow with five children would have been difficult, but Lucetta could depend upon her older children to work and contribute money to the family's finances. William, the oldest son remaining at home, was employed as a woodworker.

Ten years later, in 1910, Lucetta was left with only one child, Katie, and they rented a home in Sunbury. In 1916, at the age of sixty-one, still living in Sunbury, Lucetta passed away as a result of heart disease. She was buried at St. Johns United Methodist Church, Port Trevorton, where her husband James had been buried seventeen years earlier. James and Lucetta's second son, William, born in 1880, was the direct ancestor of the Thompson line.

James M Anderson was counted in the census in 1860 in Chapman, Snyder County, Pennsylvania. He was counted in the census in 1870 in Chapman, Snyder County, Pennsylvania. He was educated at School in 1870. He was counted in the census in 1880 in Chapman, Snyder County, Pennsylvania. He was employed as a Laborer in 1880. He signed his will about 1893 (James protested the administration of Mother Catherine's probate). He was buried in 1899 in Port Trevorton, Snyder County, Pennsylvania (St. Johns (Mt. Zion) United Methodist). His cause of death was Lip and throat cancer. He was affiliated with the Methodist religion.

Lucetta Gaugler was counted in the census in 1860 in Chapman, Snyder County, Pennsylvania. She was educated at School in 1860. She was counted in the census in 1870 in Union County, Snyder County, Pennsylvania. She was counted in the census in 1880 in Chapman, Snyder County, Pennsylvania. She was employed as a Keeping house in 1880. She was employed as a Day laborer in 1900. She lived in Pennsylvania in 1900 (200 Front St.). She lived in Sunbury, Northumberland County, Pennsylvania in 1900 (200 Front St.). She was counted in the census in 1900 in Sunbury, Northumberland County, Pennsylvania. She was counted in the census in 1910 in Sunbury, Northumberland County, Pennsylvania. She lived in Sunbury, Northumberland County, Pennsylvania in 1910 (1068 Miller St.). She lived in Pennsylvania in 1910 (1068 Miller St.). Her funeral took place in 1916 in Pennsylvania (Shipman). She lived in Sunbury, Northumberland County, Pennsylvania in 1916 (1046 Miller St.). She lived in Pennsylvania in 1916 (1046 Miller St.). Her funeral took place in 1916 in Sunbury, Northumberland County, Pennsylvania (Shipman). She was buried on November 10, 1916 in Port Trevorton, Snyder County, Pennsylvania (St. Johns (Mt. Zion) United Methodist). Her cause of death was acute dilatation of heart w/myocarditis. She signed her will (Intestate). She was named after Lucetta Kelly, aunt. S She was affiliated with the Methodist religion.

JAMES P. KEEFER
& EMMA L. LIVEZLEY

James Pollock Keefer was born in 1859 in Sunbury, Northumberland County, Pennsylvania. James spent his childhood and teen years living in Sunbury and in the next township to the north, Upper Augusta.

James's parents, Michael A. Keefer and Margaret Matilda Bucher, were lifelong residents of Northumberland County. James was raised in a typical 19thcentury family, the sixth of seven children. Margaret was James's oldest sibling, followed by Mary, Anna Elizabeth, Alice, and Charles. Then came James followed by his sister Emma J. Keefer. According to the 1880 census return, James and Emma were literate, able to read and write. In 1900 James' father Michael, James' daughter Emma and the remaining Keefer family members were able to read and write.

By the time he was twenty-one, James had briefly moved to Pottsville, about 40 miles to the east in Schuylkill County. In Pottsville, he met Emma Louisa Livezly, who was four years his junior. They were married around 1880, when James was twenty-one and Emma was seventeen.

Emma, the daughter of George Culin Livezly and Anna Maria Kent, was born in Pottsville in November 1863, during the very first November Thanksgiving, recently proclaimed by President Lincoln. Emma was baptized within the month and

her birth family was even larger than James's; she was the fifth of eight. George and Anna's first child was John Lawrence. Emma never knew her second brother— George was born in 1857 and died at about one year of age. Then came Emma's two older sisters, Georgeann and Eleanor Loretta. After Emma came George Culin, James, and Annzella.

When James met and married Emma, he was working as a cigar maker in Pottsville. Cigars were almost a necessity for men in those days, and cigar making was a widespread industry including both home manufacture and larger factories. In New York City in 1880, there were more than 1,000 separate cigar making firms. Tobacco leaf was prepared by workers called "strippers," who carefully removed the heavy stems from the leaves. Then the cigar maker would wrap the leaf in a wrapper, demonstrating the level of his craftsmanship by making a perfectly rolled cigar and minimizing waste. Cigar making was not a pleasant occupation. Tobacco stems and powdered leaves sent thick clouds of dust into the air, and cigar makers spent long hours hunched over their work surfaces.

James and Emma soon moved to Ashland, a small borough twelve miles northwest of Pottsville. Ashland had about 4,000 residents by 1882, the year of Emma Keefer's birth. Set in an environment of dense forest, in the previous two decades it had become a prominent coal-mining town. It is probable that James relocated the family to Ashland in order to work in the mining industry.

It was in Ashland that their child, Emma Louisa Keefer, given her mother's name certainly as a tribute, was born. Mother Emma died just four days after the birth of their first and only child. Mother Emma was buried in the Pottsville Cemetery in Ashland, Pennsylvania. Emma was confirmed, married, became pregnant, delivered her child and died all within a one-year period. She was only eighteen when she passed.

By 1892, James had moved their family to James's hometown, Sunbury. James joined the National Guard serving in the 12th Pennsylvania Regiment, Company E, and worked as a brakeman in the Sunbury railroad yards.

A railroad brakeman was an essential member of a railroad train's crew—he was responsible for applying the brakes to slow the train. Brake levers might be either inside or outside the train cars, and brakemen often had to climb to the top of moving trains to operate the brakes from the roof. In addition, brakemen might be responsible for setting couplings between cars and managing the switches that sent trains from one rail to another. With any of those duties, serious injuries and deaths were not uncommon.

It was in that dangerous occupation that James lost his life. He was only 33, and when he was buried in Penn's Sunbury Cemetery and he left behind daughter Emma, Railroading was known as an incredibly dangerous occupation. In fact, seven years after James' death, President Harrison said to Congress, "It is a reproach to our civilization that any class of American workmen should, in the pursuit of a necessary and useful vocation, be subjected to a peril of life and limb as great as that of a soldier in time of war." The Federal Employers Liability Act, which passed in 1908, directly addressed railroads' responsibility for deaths such as James's.

However, in 1892, railroads took no responsibility for the widows and families of workers killed on the job, and daughter Emma was left on her own, eventually relocating to the home of her paternal grandparents Michael and Margaret Keefer, in Sunbury, Pennsylvania. James and Emma's eldest daughter, Emma, was the direct ancestor of the Thompson line.

James Pollock Keefer was counted in the census in 1860 in Upper Augusta, Northumberland County, Pennsylvania. He was counted in the census in 1870 in Pennsylvania. He was employed as a Cigar maker in 1880. He lived in Ashland, Schuylkill County, Pennsylvania in 1880 (Center St.). He lived in Ashland, Schuylkill County, Pennsylvania in 1880 (West Centre Road). He lived in Ashland, Schuylkill County, Pennsylvania in 1880 (201 Centre St.). He was counted in the census in 1880 in Ashland, Schuylkill County, Pennsylvania (Maurer). He was buried in 1892 in Sunbury, Northumberland County, Pennsylvania (Penns (Lower) Sunbury Cemetery, Lot D222). He served in the military in 1892 in Pennsylvania (National Guard, 12th Pennsylvania Reg, Co E). He was employed as a Brakeman, Railroad in 1892. His cause of death was Railroad accident, injuries rec'd in an accident at the Sunbury railroad yards. He was affiliated with the Methodist religion.

Emma Louise Livezly was baptized in December 1863 in Schuylkill County, Pennsylvania. She was counted in the census in 1870 in Ashland, Schuylkill County, Pennsylvania. She lived in Ashland, Schuylkill County, Pennsylvania in 1880 (170 Walnut St). She was counted in the census in 1880 in Ashland, Schuylkill County, Pennsylvania. She was buried in 1882 in Pottsville, Schuylkill County, Pennsylvania (Christ Cemetery). She was affiliated with the Christ United Lutheran Church religion in 1882 in Ashland, Schuylkill County, Pennsylvania. She signed her will (Intestate). She was employed as a Homemaker. She was affiliated with the Methodist < Lutheran religion.

ALFRED MASON
& HANNAH (?) MASON

Alfred Mason, son of Moses Mason, was born between 1825-1830 in Georgia, USA. He died between 1880-1900 in Washington Co, Georgia, USA. He married Hannah about 1846 in Georgia. Hannah was born in 1829 in Georgia, USA. She died between 1900-1910 in Washington Co, Georgia, USA.

Alfred Mason was employed as a Farming in 1870. He was counted in the census in 1870 in Cato, Washington, Georgia, USA. He was counted in the census in 1880 in Cato, Washington, Georgia, USA. He was employed as a Farmer in 1880.

Hannah was counted in the census in 1870 in Cato, Washington, Georgia, USA. She was employed as a Keeping house between 1870-1880. She was counted in the census in 1880 in Cato, Washington, Georgia, USA. She was counted in the census in 1900 in Cato, Washington, Georgia, USA.

Hannah and Alfred Mason had the following children:

i.   Edward "Ned" Mason was born in 1847 in Washington County, Georgia, USA.

ii.   Noah Mason was born in 1848 in Georgia.

iii.   Thomas Mason was born in 1853 in Georgia. He married Pheobe Walker on May 2, 1874. She was born in 1852 in Georgia.

iv.   James Mason was born about 1855 in Georgia.

v.   Linda Mason was born in 1856 in Georgia. She married Daniel Middleton in 1878. He was born about 1855 in Georgia.

vi.   Andrew Mason was born in 1857 in Georgia. He married Ellen

Walker on June 22, 1871. She was born in 1850.

vii.   Jacob "Jake" Mason was born in 1859 in Georgia. He married Ellen Adams on November 18, 1876. She was born in 1859 in Georgia.

viii.   George Mason was born in 1861 in Georgia. He married Charlotte Andrews on May 27, 1882.

ix.   Jefferson D Mason was born in 1862 in Georgia. He married Carrie Moffett in 1894.

x.   Josephine Mason was born in 1864 in Georgia. She married King Reeves.

xi.   Alfred Mason was born in 1868 in Georgia. He married Harriet Cumming on November 25, 1886.

xii.   Cleveland Mason was born in 1870 in Georgia.

GEORGE BROWN
& MAY A. (?) BROWN

George Brown, son of Samuel and Ranie (Rhinor) Brown, was born about 1822 in Georgia, USA. He died between 1870-1880 in Georgia, USA. He married May A about 1851 in Georgia. May was born about 1836 in Georgia, USA. She died between 1870-1880 in Georgia, USA.

George Brown was employed as a Farmer in 1870. He was counted in the census in 1870 in Davisboro, Washington County, Georgia, USA. He was counted in the census in 1880.

May was employed as a Keeping house in 1870. She was counted in the census in 1870 in Davisboro, Washington County, Georgia, USA. She was counted in the census in 1880.

May and George Brown had the following children:

i.   Ranie Brown was born in December 1852 in Washington County, Georgia, USA.

ii.   Rachel Brown was born in 1854 in Georgia.

iii.   Samuel Brown was born in 1856 in Georgia.

iv.   Simon Brown was born in 1857 in Georgia.

v.   Mary Brown was born in 1861 in Georgia.

vi.   Remus Brown was born in 1863 in Georgia.

MASON SHATEEN
& SALLIE MORGAN

Mason Shatteen was born about 1835 in Georgia, USA. He died between 1880-1900 in Georgia. He married Sallie Morgan about 1861 in Georgia. Sallie Morgan, daughter of Thomas Morgan, was born in March 1847 in Davisboro, Washington County, Georgia, USA. She died on November 10, 1927 in Savannah, Chatham County, Georgia, USA.

Mason Shatteen was counted in the census in 1870. He was employed as a Farmer in 1880. He was counted in the census in 1880 in Davisboro, Washington County, Georgia, USA.

Sallie Morgan was counted in the census in 1870. She was counted in the census in 1880 in Davisboro, Washington County, Georgia, USA. She was employed as a K house in 1880. She was employed as a Servant in 1900 in Farm laborer. She was counted in the census in 1900 in Davisboro, Washington County, Georgia, USA. She was counted in the census in 1910 in Militia Dt 85, Jefferson County, Georgia, USA. She lived in Church St., Savannah, Chatham County, Georgia, USA in 1920. She was counted in the census in 1920 in Savannah, Chatham County, Georgia, USA. She lived in 440 Eagle St., Savannah, Chatham County, Georgia, USA in 1927. She was employed as a Domestic in 1927. She was buried on November 13, 1927 in Laurel Grove Cemetery, Savannah, Chatham County, Georgia, USA. Her funeral took place on November 13, 1927 in McKelsey-Powell County, 712 W Broad St., Savannah, Chatham County, Georgia, USA. Her cause of death was Chronic myocarditis.

Sallie Morgan and Mason Shatteen had the following children:

i.   Linnie Shatteen was born in 1862 in Georgia.

ii.   Anne "Annie" M Shatteen was born about 1862 in Washington County, Georgia, USA.

iii.   James Shatteen was born in 1866 in Georgia. He married Lulu. She was born in 1872 in Georgia. He married Susan Hall on December 27, 1889.

iv.   Lillian "Lillie" Shatteen was born in 1868 in Georgia. She died about 1870.

SAMUEL J. FORSYTHE
& AMELIA DEANE

Samuel James Forsythe, son of Nelson Forsythe and Elizabeth Hampton, was born about 1850 in West Indies (Eng). He married Amelia Deane about 1880 in West Indies (Eng). Amelia Deane was born about 1860 in West Indies (Eng).

Amelia Deane and Samuel James Forsythe had the following children:

i.   Percy Campbell Forsythe was born in January 1882 in Bahamas, West Indies (Eng).

ii.   Harriet "Hattie" Forsythe was born in 1883 in West Indies (Eng).

iii.   Frederick Forsythe was born in 1884 in West Indies (Eng).

iv.   Theodore Forsythe was born in 1886 in West Indies (Eng). He married Stella. She was born in 1885 in VA.

JOSEPH WASHINGTON
& MARY ROBINSON

Joseph "Joe" Washington, son of Joseph Washington and Tenia, was born about 1867 in Daufuskie, Beaufort County, South Carolina, USA. He died on November 30, 1922 in Beaufort, Beaufort County, South Carolina, USA. He married Mary Robinson about 1900. Mary Robinson, daughter of Robert Robinson and Hester was born in May 1870 in Hilton Head, Beaufort County, South Carolina, USA. She died on April 29, 1939 in Savannah, Chatham County, Georgia, USA.

Joseph "Joe" Washington was counted in the census in 1870. He was counted in the census in 1880 in St. Helena Island, Beaufort County, South Carolina, USA. He was educated at school in 1880. He was employed as a Works on farm in 1880. He was counted in the census in 1900 in Beaufort, Beaufort County, South Carolina, USA. He was employed as a Day laborer in 1900. He was counted in the census in 1910 in Beaufort, Beaufort County, South Carolina, USA. He was counted in the census in 1920 in Beaufort, Beaufort County, South Carolina, USA. He was employed as a Farm laborer in 1922. He was buried on December 1, 1922 in Gray's Hill, Beaufort County, South Carolina, USA. His cause of death was Pneumonia.

Mary Robinson was counted in the census in 1880 in Hilton Head, Beaufort County, South Carolina, USA. She was counted in the census in 1900 in Beaufort, Beaufort County, South Carolina, USA. She was employed as a Proprietor (Boarding house) in 1910. She lived in 3 E. Broad, Savannah, Chatham County, Georgia, USA in 1910. She was counted in the census in 1910 in Savannah, Chatham County, Georgia, USA. She lived in 321 Bay St., Savannah, Chatham County, Georgia, USA in 1920. She was employed as a Proprietor (Lunch room) in 1920. She was counted in the census in 1920 in Savannah, Chatham County, Georgia, USA. She lived in 120 Randolph St., Savannah, Georgia, USA in 1930. She was counted in the census in 1930 in Savannah, Chatham County, Georgia, USA. She lived in 120 Reynolds St., Savannah, Chatham County, Georgia, USA in 1930. She was employed as a Cook (Boarding house) in 1930. She was buried on May 1, 1939 in Laurel Grove South Cemetery, Savannah, Chatham County, Georgia, USA.

Mary Robinson and Joseph "Joe" Washington had the following children:

i.   Albert Ernest Robinson Washington was born in 1896 in South Carolina.

ii.   Nina Washington was born on October 31, 1908 in Daufuskie, Beaufort County, South Carolina, USA.

iii.   Charles H Robinson Washington was born in 1909 in Georgia.

DUNCAN C. CURRY
& ELIZABETH ALSTON

Duncan C Curry, son of Fortune and Mary Curry, was born in May 1869 in Beaufort Co, South Carolina, USA. He died on June 3, 1914 in Savannah, Chatham County, Georgia, USA. He married Elizabeth "Bessie" Alston about 1890 in Georgia. Elizabeth "Bessie" Alston, daughter of Benjamin "Ben" Alston and Lucretia. was born in December 1870 in Beaufort Co, South Carolina, USA. She died on October 14, 1948 in Chatham County, Georgia, USA.

Duncan C Curry was counted in the census in 1870 in St Peters, Beaufort County, South Carolina, USA. He was counted in the census in 1880 in Lawnton, Hampton County, South Carolina, USA. He lived in Indian Ln, 3d E. of canal, Savannah, Chatham County, Georgia, USA in 1890. He was employed as a RR Laborer in 1900. He was counted in the census in 1900 in 1st Militia, Chatham County, Georgia, USA. He lived in 619 W Lumber St., Savannah, Chatham County, Georgia, USA in 1909. He was employed as a Laborer (On wharf) in 1910. He lived in 610 Oglethorpe Ave, Savannah, Georgia, USA in 1910. He was counted in the census in 1910 in Savannah, Chatham County, Georgia, USA. He lived in 610 W. Williams St., Savannah, Chatham County, Georgia, USA in 1914. He was employed as a Laborer in 1914. He was buried in June 1914 in Laurel Grove Cemetery, Savannah, Chatham County, Georgia, USA. His cause of death was Cerebral congestion and hemorrhage.

Elizabeth "Bessie" Alston was counted in the census in 1880 in Lawnton, Hampton County, South Carolina, USA. She was counted in the census in 1900 in 1st Militia, Chatham County, Georgia, USA. She was counted in the census in 1910 in Savannah, Chatham County, Georgia, USA. She was counted in the census in 1920 in Savannah, Chatham County, Georgia, USA. She lived in 6 Dermon? St., Savannah, Chatham County, Georgia, USA in 1926. She was counted in the census in 1930. She was counted in the census in 1940 in Washington, Wilkes, Georgia. She was buried in 1948 in Laurel Grove Cemetery (South).

Elizabeth "Bessie" Alston and Duncan C Curry had the following children:

i.   William "Willie" Curry was born in 1892 in Georgia. He married Nellie. She was born in 1894 in Georgia.

ii.   Elizabeth "Bessie" Curry was born in 1894 in Georgia.

iii.   Ira Curry was born in 1895 in Georgia.

iv.   Hilda Curry was born in 1899 in Georgia.

v.   Rosa Louise Curry was born about 1899 in Savannah, Chatham County, Georgia, USA. She died in 1922 in Savannah, Chatham County, Georgia, USA.

vi.   Leola Curry was born in 1902 in Georgia.

vii.   Solomon Curry was born in 1904 in Georgia. He married Anne. She was born in 1907.

viii.   Edmonia Curry was born in 1906 in Georgia.

ix.   Frederick "Freddie" Curry was born on February 22, 1907 in Savannah, Chatham County, Georgia, USA.

ix.   Frampton Curry was born in 1909 in Georgia.

x.   Charles "Charlie" Curry was born on February 8, 1912 in Georgia. He died in April 1967 in Savannah, Chatham County, Georgia, USA.

JOSEPH BROWN
& NANCY FRAZIER

Joseph "Joe" Brown, son of Joseph "Joe" Brown and Lena Glover, was born on July 5, 1890 in Allendale, Barnwell (Allendale) County, South Carolina, USA. He died on December 23, 1942 in Chatham Co, Georgia, USA. He married Nancy Frazier about 1910 in Barnwell Co, South Carolina, USA. Nancy Frazier, daughter of Samuel "Sam" Frazier and Eva Thompson, was born in October 1886 in Barnwell County, South Carolina, USA. She died on March 11, 1950 in Chatham Co, Georgia, USA.

Joseph "Joe" Brown was counted in the census in 1900 in Allendale, Barnwell (Allendale), South Carolina, USA. He lived in Bill Exley farm, South Carolina, USA in 1908. He was counted in the census in 1910 in Allendale, Barnwell (Allendale), South Carolina, USA. He was employed as a Farm Labor (?) in 1910. He was employed as a Sawmill work (EF Woodward, Appleton, South Carolina, USA) in 1912. He was employed as a Farm Labor (Working out) in 1920. He lived in Johnson Landry Rd., Allendale County, South Carolina, USA in 1920. He was counted in the census in 1920 in Allendale, Allendale County, South Carolina, USA. He lived in 142 Lathrop (Oglethorpe) Ave., Savannah, Georgia, USA in 1930. He was counted in the census in 1930 in District 8, Chatham County, Georgia, USA. He was employed as a Laborer (Barnell? Factory) in 1930. He was counted in the census in 1940 in Chatham County, Georgia, USA. He was buried on April 3, 1951 in Laurel Grove South, Savannah. He had a medical condition of Medium height, medium weight.

Nancy Frazier was employed as a Farm Laborer in 1900. She was counted in the census in 1900 in Bull Pond, Barnwell County, South Carolina, USA. She was employed as a Farmer (Parents) in 1910. She was counted in the census in 1910 in Allendale, Barnwell (Allendale), South Carolina, USA. She was employed as a Farm Labor (Working out) in 1920. She was counted in the census in 1920 in Allendale, Allendale County, South Carolina, USA. She was counted in the census in 1930 in District 8, Chatham County, Georgia, USA. She was counted in the census in 1940 in Chatham County, Georgia, USA.

Nancy Frazier and Joseph "Joe" Brown had the following children:

i.   Elizabeth Brown was born between June 6-11 1911 in Allendale, Barnwell (Allendale), South Carolina, USA.

ii.   Josephine Brown was born in 1915 in South Carolina.

iii.   Christopher Columbus Brown was born in 1916 in South Carolina.

iv.   Benjamin Brown was born in 1919 in South Carolina.

v.   Dorothy Mae Brown was born about 1920 in South Carolina. She married Miller.

vi.   Ellis Brown was born about 1920 in South Carolina.

vii.   Lillian "Lillie" Brown was born about 1920 in South Carolina.

viii. Ella Lee Brown was born on October 27, 1921 in South Carolina. She died on December 8, 1999 in Atlanta, Fulton County, Georgia, USA. She married Gould.

ix.   Adam Brown was born in 1924 in South Carolina.

x.   Eva Mae Brown was born on May 14, 1924 in South Carolina. She died on April 7, 1988 in Savannah, Chatham County, Georgia, USA. She married Grant.

IRENEO ROMANO
& FELICE VITALE

Ireneo Romano, son of Giuseppe Romano and Angela di Simone, was born on 2 December 1820 in St. Agata, Palermo, Sicily, Italy and died in Sicily, Italy. Ireneo married Felice Vitale about 1857 in Sicily, Italy, daughter of Erasmo Vitale and Maria Viviano. Felice was born on 16 November 1828 in St. Agata, Palermo, Sicily, Italy and died in Sicily, Italy.

The known children of Ireneo and Felice Vitale are Pietro Giuseppe Romano was born between 18 July 1858 and 1861 in Alia, Palermo, Sicily, Italy, and died after 1920, probably in Sicily, Italy and Carlo Romano.

Ireneo Becomes an Orphan. Giuseppe Romano dies on 25 August 1823; his death is recorded in Santa Cristina parish, Palermo, Sicily. Angela Di Simone dies on 25 January 1825; her death is recorded in the parish of Brancaccio, an early Palermo suburb.

At age 5, Ireneo Romano finds himself an orphan. It seems most likely that he was taken in by family – grandparents or an aunt of uncle, but no details are known.

The young Sicilian had been lulled almost into a slumber by the warmth of the morning sun and the movement of the carreto. He was snapped into alertness when his cousin muttered a curse and jerked the little cart to a halt. Glancing up, he saw that a man had run out of the alleyway and almost into the path of the mule. Now he watched him run into the dockyard and attempt to hide among the cargo waiting to be loaded onto the ship. A moment later, four campieri charged out of the alley and followed the man into the yard. All four men were armed with heavy cudgels and long knives;

one carried a pike. The watcher thought that he recognized at least one of them as Don Niccolosi's man.

For a few minutes, the running man made a game effort of it as he dodged about trying to keep casks and bales between him and the campieri. The outcome was never in doubt, of course, and the only question in the young man's mind as he watched from the cart was whether the man would be merely beaten within an inch or his life or killed outright. The answer came quickly and the man lay bleeding on the ground. One of the campieri retrieved a bag from the felled man and the four walked back toward the cart and the alley from which they had come. As they passed the cart, one of the campieri hoisted the recovered sack and said "He stole oranges."

As the men disappeared down the alley, his cousin started the mule on its way. The young man on the cart said nothing, but he glanced once more at the man on the ground. At most, the sack; could have held 10 or 12 oranges. Just one of Don Niccolosi's trees would produce hundreds of oranges each year and for a dozen, the man had been killed – or at least nearly so. He shook himself as if to clear his head. That was foolish thinking. The first lesson to take from this was that the man was a great fool to risk his life for so little potential gain. The second lesson was that he would take care not to cross Don Niccolosi.

In 1825, King Ferdinand dies and his son, Francis succeeds him. Just five years later, King Francis dies and is succeeded by his son, Ferdinand II. During all of this, very little changes for the Sicilians. Soon the hostilities toward the King's government resume and so do the executions. The overwhelming suppression has an effect; there is little open rebellion, and little organization among the Sicilian rebels.

Cholera! The Cholera epidemic that has been terrorizing Europe is loose in Sicily and people are dropping faster than they can be carried away. The young man did not know what to do or how to act. He found it hard to fear an unseen threat, but very easy to fear the sight of carts full of the dead being moved down the city streets. But now Uncle Paolo had decided it was time to flee. Now they were preparing to flee.

"Dress in rough clothes, work clothes," his uncle ordered. "The damned superstitious peasants have gone insane. They think that the epidemic is some evil worked on them by the government and the rich. They have been killing the government workers sent to aid them and Antonino to me that they had even stoned the Sisters of Charity while they were visiting the sick and dying. He says that even wearing a decent coat will earn you an attack"

The carts are quickly loaded and they take to the road. They are going to a cousin's house in Alia a small town in the mountains southeast of Palermo. Uncle hopes that the cooler climate and fewer people will give them a better chance of escaping the cholera.

Six weeks later, it is clear that the flight to the mountains has not worked; nearly half of the population of Alia has died. The young man has worked with the men of Alia to bury the victims of the epidemic. At the height of the deaths, they had no time for ceremony or individual graves. More than 300 of the cholera victims went into a mass grave. It is a memory that will stay with him forever.

Before the end of the year, it is estimated that about 25% of the population of Sicily has died.

The revolt against the government that started with the peasant reaction to the cholera has turned into a full political movement and the authorities in Naples and their Austrian allies have suppressed the movement with a ferocious vengeance. Even the most trivial suspicion of liberalism is enough to get a man imprisoned, flogged and tortured.

For the first time ever, the major Palermo and Messina come together in their disdain and in their conspiracy's against the king. In a September 1847, a peasant rising in Reggio Calabria spread across the strait to Messina, stimulating even more unrest in Sicily.

Despite everything, life goes on apace. Children grow into men and women, old people die. The seasons pass with crops planted and harvested. The ships come and go at Palermo. It is a time of relative peace, but through it all, the Sicilians continue to chafe under the Bourbon rule.

In Palermo on January 9, 1848, a veteran of the 1820 revolution named Francesco Bagnasco released a pamphlet that called for an uprising on the King's birthday. Sicily took him up on it with a passion. The radicals, who initiated the rising, were seeking autonomy and constitutional government. The peasants and urban poor thought little of constitutionalism. They would fight for more basic reasons; they would fight for land and work.

The streets of Palermo started to fill almost immediately in response to the call to arms and by the twelfth, the birthday of King Ferdinand, they were packed. The revolution was on.

Buoyed by the initial success of the Sicilians, Neapolitans rebels also took up arms. Pressure from both sides influenced the King to buy himself time by granting Sicilian demands – he reinstated Sicily's constitution and reconvened a Sicilian parliament. For about a year, Sicily reveled in new-found freedom.

But with the help of loyalists in Naples, by the end of the year the King quelled his threat at home and turned his attention on the Sicilian rebels. As usual, it was

Palermo that had been the instigator and it was Palermo that bore the brunt of his retribution. Rather than confront the rebels in the tortuous streets of the hostile city, the army decided to bombard Palermo from the fortress of Castellamare. The bombardment laid waste to much of the City. The people tried to surrender, but the King ignored them. The bombardment continued for two days after the rebels surrendered. That week, the King earned the name that would follow him through history – King Bomba.

When it was all over, the young Sicilian walked through his neighborhood, hardly recognizing the familiar old streets. Too much. This was just too much. Maybe it was time to leave Palermo and join his cousins inland.

First light was just breaking as he harnessed the donkey to the old carreto. As he worked, he quickly studied the little cart with a practiced eye, checking the wheels and the key joints. The carreto was old, but still sturdy – he had put on new wheels just last year. And if this year brought a good harvest, he would have the fading side paintings restored. The paintings were of the famous scene where St. Agata saved her town from the lava flow of one of Mount Etna's more or less regular eruptions by laying her sacred scarf in the path of the lava. Getting the paintings restored would be appropriate this year. The constant pillar of smoke in the east told him that the ancient volcano was showing its anger once again.

His inspection complete, the man loaded a little packet of food and his water bottle into the cart along with a few tools before leading the donkey out into street. The clangs and thumps drifting to him through fresh morning air told him that the village of Alia was stirring, but a quick glance around revealed no one else on the street. That was okay with him; he enjoyed being the first one out. There would be less dust on the road to the fields. He mounted the cart and twitched the reins to start the donkey down the road toward his new fields.

Like the peasant farmers who actually worked his lands, he and his family lived in town, while most of his fields lay some miles away in the little valleys. He liked living in the city and when he went to the fields, he usually enjoyed the long, slow morning ride. A man could think out here, accompanied only by his own thoughts and the occasional song of a goldfinch from the fields that he passed. And today he had much to think about. He needed to start the Inquilini to work on the 200 acres at the top of the valley

As he cleared the first turn in the road, he saw that he was not the first out after all; there was a small group of laborers walking down the road ahead of him. As he got closer, he saw that he did not know them. Had they been his men, he probably would have offered them a ride. Since they were not, he nodded to them and continued alone. It never occurred to him to offer them a ride and it never occurred to the men to expect the offer of one. After all, he was a Borgesi and they were Contadinas and among the three general classes of farmer in Sicily at the end of the 18th and throughout the 19th century, the Borgesi were at the top and the Contadini were at the bottom.

Borgesi like him were the middlemen; they leased large sections of land from the absentee land owners, rented plots of it to tenant farmers, and farmed the remainder themselves. On the land they held to themselves, they tended to be managers who only very rarely actually worked the land. The Contadini, on the other hand, were the wage-earning field workers on the farms of Sicily. In the common vernacular, the differences between the farming classes were often reduced to the "caps", the workers, and the "hats", the bosses.

The Borgesi smiled to himself, knowing that he had been lucky. It had by no means been assured that he would succeed in his role when he had first moved from his job as a sort of junior merchant in the family business to active management of the land. He had missed the activity of the city at first, but he was happy being the middleman now. By being stingy with his earnings and with a small inheritance from his father and his uncle, he had been able expand his holdings.

These little two wheeled wagons were the standard form of transportation for working to middle class Sicilians well into the early 1900s. Families with more money might have two carts, a carreto del lavoro (work cart) and a carreto del gara (for parades and ceremonies such as wedding and religious festivals).

Peasant farmers who worked the land, but never owned it, lived in towns that were often many miles from the fields that they worked. During busy parts of the season, it was common for them to build straw shelters where they would sleep during the work week before returning to their homes on the weekend.

His current leases were mostly in almonds and in olives and carobs. He would love to have wheat fields, but none of his leaseholds were big enough to make wheat profitable.

But now his cousin was after him to go partners on some new lands that were nearer to Lercara than to Alia. There was even some talk of taking mineral rights on the land and mining the sulfur themselves. And if that didn't work out, he felt pretty sure that he could contract more land in that area when it became available. His family was prospering – and a good thing, too, with a new son in the house. If things continued to go well, it would be another good year.

JACOB H. WITTLE
& M. CATHERINE "KATE" KYLE

Jacob Harvey Wittle, son of John Wittle and Anna Hummer, was born on December 23, 1830 in Lancaster County, Pennsylvania, USA. He died on March 14, 1879 in Grantville, Dauphin County, Pennsylvania, USA. He married Mary Catherine "Kate" Kyle on March 13, 1857 in Lititz, Lancaster County, Pennsylvania, USA. Mary Catherine "Kate" Kyle, daughter of William Kyle and Mary "Mollie" Juliana Whitmoyer, was born on December 31, 1835 in Lancaster County, Pennsylvania, USA. She died on November 23, 1907 in Harrisburg, Dauphin County, Pennsylvania, USA.

Jacob Harvey Wittle was counted in the census in 1830 in father (Warwick, Lancaster County, Pennsylvania, USA). He was counted in the census in 1840 in Not listed. He was counted in the census in 1850 in Penn, Lancaster County, Pennsylvania, USA(Harman). He was employed as a Laborer between 1850-1870. He was counted in the census in 1860 in Lower Paxton, Dauphin County, Pennsylvania, USA. He served in the military between August 23, 1864-June 21, 1865 (Civil War, Private, 201st Reg Pennsylvania, USA Inf, Co C (Harrisburg, Capt. George W. Fenn). He was counted in the census in 1870 in Lower Paxton, Dauphin County, Pennsylvania, USA. He was buried in March 1879 in Shoops Burial Grds, near Harrisburg, Dauphin County, Pennsylvania, USA. He was buried in March 1879 in East Harrisburg Cemetery, Harrisburg, Dauphin County, Pennsylvania, USA. He died on March 13, 1879 in Grantville, Dauphin County, Pennsylvania, USA. His cause of death was Heart disease.

Mary Catherine "Kate" Kyle was counted in the census in 1840 in father (Lancaster, Lancaster County, Pennsylvania, USA). She was counted in the census in 1850 in Penn, Lancaster County, Pennsylvania, USA(Brubaker). She was counted in the census in 1860 in Lower Paxton, Dauphin County, Pennsylvania, USA. She was employed as a Servant about 1860. She was employed as a Keeping house in 1870. She was counted in the census in 1870 in Lower Paxton, Dauphin County, Pennsylvania, USA. She was counted in the census in 1880. She lived in 1329 Bartine, Harrisburg, Pennsylvania, USA about 1882. She lived in 1304 N Front St., Harrisburg, Dauphin County, Pennsylvania, USA between 1887-1890. She lived in 117 Broad, Harrisburg, Dauphin County, Pennsylvania, USA between 1887-1900. She lived in 1336 Penn, Harrisburg, Dauphin County, Pennsylvania, USA between 1887-1900. She was employed as a Domestic between 1887-1900. Pension: September 9, 1887 in Pennsylvania, USA She was counted in the census in 1900 in Harrisburg, Dauphin County, Pennsylvania, USA(Catherine). She lived in 1520 Susquehanna St., Harrisburg, Dauphin County, Pennsylvania, USA in 1907. She was employed as a Housewife in 1907. Her funeral took place in 1907 in Hawkins Funeral, 3 Cumberland St., Harrisburg, Dauphin County, Pennsylvania, USA. She was buried on November 26, 1907 in East Harrisburg Cemetery, Harrisburg, Dauphin County, Pennsylvania, USA. Her cause of death was Heart disease.

Mary Catherine "Kate" Kyle and Jacob Harvey Wittle had the following children:

i.   Mary Ellen Wittle was born in 1859 in Harrisburg, Dauphin County, Pennsylvania, USA. She married Charles J DeHaven. He was born in 1863 in Pennsylvania, USA.

ii.   James M Wittle was born in 1861 in Pennsylvania, USA.

iii.   Sarah Alice Wittle was born in 1862 in Pennsylvania, USA.

iv.   Frances "Fannie" Matilda Wittle was born in 1865 in Pennsylvania, USA. She married William Stuckey. He was born in 1865 in Pennsylvania, USA.

v.   John Elmer Wittle was born on August 10, 1866 in Harrisburg, Dauphin County, Pennsylvania, USA.

vi.   Harvey Jacob Wittle was born in 1868 in Pennsylvania, USA. He married Emma Louise Sweigard. She was born in 1873 in Pennsylvania, USA.

vii.   Adam Wittle was born in 1869 in Pennsylvania, USA.

viii.   Catherine "Kate" Minerva Wittle was born in 1870 in Pennsylvania, USA. She married William C Wenrick. He was born in 1870 in Pennsylvania, USA.

ix.   Amy Jane Wittle was born in 1871 in Pennsylvania, USA.

x.   Jonas Edwin Wittle was born in 1872 in Pennsylvania, USA.

xi.   Harriet Elizabeth Wittle was born in 1874 in Pennsylvania, USA. She married Matthew F Wenrick. He was born in 1876 in Pennsylvania, USA.

xii.   George Joseph Wittle was born in 1876 in Dauphin County, Pennsylvania, USA. He died in 1930. He married Mary Jane "Jennie" Connor. She was born in 1875 in Pennsylvania, USA. She died in 1949.

xiii.   Hilda May Wittle was born in 1879 in Harrisburg, Dauphin County, Pennsylvania, USA.

HENRY MINNICK
& LUCY A. SHEETS

Henry Minick, son of John Minick and Elizabeth "Lizzie" Yaeger, was born on February 28, 1842 in Dauphin County, Pennsylvania, USA. He died on February 28, 1907 in Harrisburg, Dauphin County, Pennsylvania, USA. He married Lucy Ann Sheets about 1862 in Dauphin County, Pennsylvania, USA.

Lucy Ann Sheets, daughter of George W Sheets and Mary Elizabeth McKim, was born in September 1842 in Dauphin County, Pennsylvania, USA. She died on September 13, 1924 in Harrisburg State Hospital, Harrisburg, Dauphin County, Pennsylvania, USA.

Henry Minick was counted in the census in 1850. He was employed as a App. carpenter in 1860. He was counted in the census in 1860 in 22 ward, Philadelphia County, Pennsylvania, USA (John Hergershimer). He was educated at School in 1860. He served in the military on July 31, 1862 (Civil War, private 127th Reg Pennsylvania, USA, Co F (Harrisburg, Capt. William W Jennings). He was employed as a Carpenter between 1864-1865. He lived in Harrisburg, Dauphin County, Pennsylvania, USA between 1864-1865. He served in the military between February 3, 1864-August 30, 1865 (Civil War, Private, 55th Reg Pennsylvania, USA Inf, Co G (Harrisburg, Capt. Isaac Waterbury). He was employed as a Works on R. Road in 1870. He was counted in the census in 1870 in Harrisburg Ward 6, Dauphin County, Pennsylvania, USA. He was employed as a Laborer (Railroad) in 1880. He was counted in the census in 1880 in Harrisburg, Dauphin County, Pennsylvania, USA. He lived in 121 Sayford Ave., Harrisburg, Dauphin

County, Pennsylvania, USA between 1880-1900. He signed his will on January 16, 1895 in Harrisburg, Dauphin County, Pennsylvania, USA. He was counted in the census in 1900 in wife as head (Harrisburg, Dauphin County, Pennsylvania, USA). His funeral took place in 1907 in Hawkins Funeral, 3 Cumberland St., Harrisburg, Dauphin County, Pennsylvania, USA. He was employed as a Car Repairman in 1907. He was buried on March 3, 1907 in Harrisburg Cemetery, Harrisburg, Dauphin County, Pennsylvania, USA. His estate was probated on March 4, 1907 in Harrisburg, Dauphin County, Pennsylvania, USA. He had a medical condition of Hair black, Complexion fair, Eyes dark. His cause of death was Pulmonary tuberculosis w/carcinoma of tongue. His height was 5 ' 9 ".

Lucy Ann Sheets was educated at School in 1850. She was counted in the census in 1850 in Jefferson, Dauphin County, Pennsylvania, USA. She was counted in the census in 1860 in Harrisburg, Dauphin County, Pennsylvania, USA(Seibtone). She was employed as a Domestic in 1860. She was counted in the census in 1870 in Harrisburg, Dauphin County, Pennsylvania, USA. She was employed as a Keeping house between 1870-1880. She was counted in the census in 1880 in Harrisburg, Dauphin County, Pennsylvania, USA. She was counted in the census in 1900 in Harrisburg, Dauphin County, Pennsylvania, USA. Pension: March 6, 1907 in Pennsylvania, USA She was counted in the census in 1910 in Harrisburg, Dauphin County, Pennsylvania, USA. She was counted in the census in 1920 in Harrisburg, Dauphin County, Pennsylvania, USA. She lived in 121 Sayford St., Harrisburg, Dauphin County, Pennsylvania, USA in 1920. Her funeral took place in 1924 in Hawkins Funeral, Harrisburg, Dauphin County, Pennsylvania, USA. She was buried on September 16, 1924 in Harrisburg

Cemetery, Harrisburg, Dauphin County, Pennsylvania, USA. Her cause of death was Mitral insufficiency.

Lucy Ann Sheets and Henry Minick had the following children:

i.   William N Minnich was born in 1863 in Pennsylvania, USA.

ii.   Frances Minnich was born in 1868 in Pennsylvania, USA. She died in 1872.

iii.   Harry R Minnich was born in 1870 in Pennsylvania, USA. He married Bertha Pilkey. She was born in 1870 in Pennsylvania, USA.

iv. Mary Elizabeth Minnich was born on March 13, 1873 in Harrisburg, Dauphin County, Pennsylvania, USA.

v.   Irvin E Minnich was born in 1874 in Pennsylvania, USA. He married Edith. She was born in 1878 in MD.

vi.   Lawrence D Minnich was born in 1876 in Pennsylvania, USA. He married Mabel H. She was born in 1878 in Pennsylvania, USA.

vii.   Elmer E Minnich was born in 1880 in Pennsylvania, USA. He married Caroline "Carrie" L Heiser. She was born in 1882.

JACOB F. STEWART
& MATILDA A. MCKINSEY

Jacob Franklin Stewart, son of Louis Luther Stewart and Martha Elizabeth Smith, was born on August 26, 1869 in Cumberland County, Pennsylvania, USA. He died on April 13, 1950 in County Home, Carlisle, Cumberland County, Pennsylvania, USA. He married Matilda "Tillie" A McKinsey in 1894 in Cumberland County, Pennsylvania, USA.

Matilda "Tillie" A McKinsey, daughter of James McKinsey and Susan Fry, was born in July 1873 in West Fairview, Cumberland County, Pennsylvania, USA. She died on September 15, 1938 in East Pennsboro, Cumberland County, Pennsylvania, USA.

Jacob Franklin Stewart was counted in the census in 1870 in East Pennsboro, Cumberland County, Pennsylvania, USA. He was counted in the census in 1880 in East Pennsboro, Cumberland County, Pennsylvania, USA. He was employed as a Lab [Laborer] in 1898. He lived in Wormleysburg, Cumberland County, Pennsylvania, USA in 1898. He was employed as a Day laborer in 1900. He was counted in the census in 1900 in East Pennsboro, Cumberland County, Pennsylvania, USA. He was ordained in 1910 in Laborer (odd jobs). He was counted in the census in 1910 in East Pennsboro, Cumberland County, Pennsylvania, USA. He was employed as a Riverman in 1918. He lived in Wormleysburg, Cumberland County, Pennsylvania, USA in 1918. He was counted in the census in 1920. He was counted in the census in 1930. He lived in N. 3rd St., Wormleysburg, Cumberland County, Pennsylvania, USA in 1950. He was employed as a Retired (Coal Barges) in 1950. He was buried on April 15, 1950 in St. Johns Cemetery, Hampden Tp.,

Cumberland County, Pennsylvania, USA. His funeral took place on April 15, 1950 in C.M. Musselman, Lemoyne, Cumberland County, Pennsylvania, USA. His cause of death was Acute myocardial failure, Chr. myo. fibrocarditis, CRVD, Senility.

Matilda "Tillie" A McKinsey was counted in the census in 1880 in East Pennsboro, Cumberland County, Pennsylvania, USA. She lived in Wormleysburg, Cumberland County, Pennsylvania, USA in 1898. She was counted in the census in 1900 in East Pennsboro, Cumberland County, Pennsylvania, USA. She was counted in the census in 1910 in East Pennsboro, Cumberland County, Pennsylvania, USA. She was employed as a Housekeeping between 1918-1938. She was counted in the census in 1920. She was counted in the census in 1930 in Wormleysburg, Cumberland County, Pennsylvania, USA. She lived in South Enola, Cumberland County, Pennsylvania, USA in 1938. Her funeral took place in 1938 in A.C. Scherich, West Fairview, Cumberland County, Pennsylvania, USA. She was buried on September 17, 1938 in Zion (Brick) Lutheran, Enola, Cumberland County, Pennsylvania, USA (listed Montzear). Her cause of death was Arteriosclerosis chronic myocarditis, chronic nephritis w/abscesses of both hip.

Matilda "Tillie" A McKinsey and Jacob Franklin Stewart had the following children:

i.   Lydia E Stewart was born in 1895 in Pennsylvania, USA. She married Irvin E Berkheimer. He was born about 1900.

ii.   Harriet "Hattie" Stewart I was born in 1896 in Pennsylvania, USA.

iii. John "Johnny" Martin Louis Stewart was born on July 18, 1898 in Home, Wormleysburg, Cumberland County, Pennsylvania, USA.

iv.   May A Stewart was born in 1904 in Pennsylvania, USA.

v.   Lillian Gertrude Stewart was born in 1906 in Pennsylvania, USA. She died in 1998. She married Norman A Kelly. He was born in 1912. She married Earl Spong.

ROBERT C. SHOVER
& ELIZABETH A. SHANNON

Robert Charles Shover, son of John E Shover and Margaret "Maggie" Tabitha Piper, was born on May 1, 1878 in Cumberland Co, Pennsylvania, USA. He died on May 4, 1933 in Harrisburg, Dauphin County, Pennsylvania, USA. He married Elizabeth "Bessie" A Shannon on January 21, 1899 in Harrisburg, Dauphin County, Pennsylvania, USA.

Elizabeth "Bessie" A Shannon, daughter of Cyrus W Shannon and Mary "Mollie" Jane Swoveland, was born on April 30, 1883 in Cumberland Co, Pennsylvania, USA. She died on January 21, 1928 in Harrisburg, Dauphin County, Pennsylvania, USA.

Robert Charles Shover was counted in the census in 1880 in Shippensburg, Cumberland, Pennsylvania, USA. He was employed as a Railroader in 1899. He lived in Harrisburg, Dauphin County, Pennsylvania, USA in 1899. He was counted in the census in 1900 in Shippensburg, Cumberland, Pennsylvania, USA. He was employed as an Assistant (Undertaker) in 1910. He lived in 1302 North 2nd St., Harrisburg, Dauphin County, Pennsylvania, USA in 1910. He was counted in the census in 1910 in Harrisburg, Dauphin County, Pennsylvania, USA(Smith). He was employed as a Brakeman (Cumberland Valley Railroad) in 1918. He lived in Front St., Shiremanstown, Cumberland County, Pennsylvania, USA in 1918. He lived in Plantation Bridge Road, Cumberland County, Pennsylvania, USA in 1920 (State Highway). He was employed as a Farm hand in 1920. He was counted in the census in 1920 in Silver Spring, Cumberland County, Pennsylvania, USA. He lived in 716 N 19th, Harrisburg, Dauphin County, Pennsylvania,

USA in 1930. He was counted in the census in 1930 in Harrisburg, Dauphin County, Pennsylvania, USA. He was employed as a Storekeeper (Stock room) in 1930. He was employed as a Clk (Highway garage) in 1930. He was employed as a Watchman (Comm. of Pennsylvania, USA) in 1933. His funeral took place in 1933 in Charles C. Baker, Harrisburg, Dauphin County, Pennsylvania, USA. He was buried on May 8, 1933 in Rolling Green Cemetery, Camp Hill, Cumberland County, Pennsylvania, USA. His cause of death was Acute cardiac dilatation w/mitral stenosis, aortic regurgitation.

Elizabeth "Bessie" A Shannon was employed as a Housework in 1899. She lived in Lees x Roads, Cumberland County, Pennsylvania, USA in 1899. She was counted in the census in 1900. She was buried on January 24, 1928 in Newfurtt Cemetery, Dauphin County, Pennsylvania. Her cause of death was Carcinoma of liver.

Elizabeth "Bessie" A Shannon and Robert Charles Shover had the following children:

i.   Charles L Shover was born about 1897 in Pennsylvania, USA.

ii. Catherine Ann "Kathleen Annie" Shover was born on August 6, 1902 in Harrisburg, Dauphin County, Pennsylvania, USA.

iii.   ? Shover was born in Pennsylvania, USA.

iv.   ? Shover was born in Pennsylvania, USA.

CARLO ACRI
& ROSALIE (?) ACRI

Charles (Carlo) Acri was born about 1840 in Italy. He died after 1875 in Italy. He married Rosalie (Rosalia) about 1860 in Cosenza, Calabria, Italy. Rosalie (Rosalia) was born about 1840 in Italy. She died after 1875 in Italy. Rosalie (Rosalia) was employed as a Homemaker.

Rosalie (Rosalia) and Charles (Carlo) Acri had the following children:

i. Frank (Francesco) Acri was born in April 1866 in Castiglione, Cosenza, Calabria, Italy.

ii. Salvatore Acri was born in 1874 in Italy.

MICHEL CURCIO
& ROSARIO (?) CURCIO

Michael (Michele) Curcio was born about 1840 in Castiglione Cosentino, Cosenza, Calabria, Italy. He died after 1891 in Pennsylvania, USA. He married Rosario about 1860 in Italy. Rosario was born about 1840 in Italy. She died about 1930 in Pennsylvania.

Michael (Michele) Curcio was employed as a Vineyard owner about 1865. He immigrated between 1874-1891. He lived in Etna, Allegheny County, Pennsylvania, USA in 1891.

Rosario and Michael (Michele) Curcio had the following children:

i.   Anthony (Antonio) Curcio was born in 1860 in Italy.

iii.   ii. Theresa (Teresa) Curcio was born on July 22, 1874 in Italy.

iv.   Joseph (Guiseppe) Curcio was born in 1878 in Italy.

v.   ? Curcio.

vi.   ? Curcio.

vii.   ? Curcio.

PASQUALE BARBUSCIO
& CARMINA C. BUGLIO

Pascal (Pasquale) Barbuscio, son of Gaetano Barbuscio and Ursula (Orsola) Marsico, was born on September 23, 1839 in Castiglione, Cosenza, Calabria, Italy. He died between 1900-1910 in Pennsylvania, USA. He married Carmine Catherine (Carmina Catarina) Buglio on May 13, 1863 in Castiglione, Cosenza, Calabria, Italy.

Carmine Catherine (Carmina Catarina) Buglio, daughter of Carmine Mario "Francis" Buglio and Josephine (Giuseppina) Magnelli, was born on April 19, 1843 in Castiglione, Cosenza, Calabria, Italy. She died between 1900-1910 in Pennsylvania, USA.

Pascal (Pasquale) Barbuscio lived in Via Nanca, Castiglione, Cosenza, Italy in 1880. He immigrated on November 12, 1894 (Italy to USA (ship Augusta Victoria). He was counted in the census in 1900 in Hazel, Luzerne County, Pennsylvania, USA. He was employed as a Day laborer in 1900.

Carmine Catherine (Carmina Catarina) Buglio immigrated on November 12, 1894 (Italy to New York, NY (ship Augusta Victoria). She was christened in 1900 in Hazel, Luzerne County, Pennsylvania, USA. She was employed as a Homemaker.

Carmine Catherine (Carmina Catarina) Buglio and Pascal (Pasquale) Barbuscio had the following children:

i.   Francis Barbuscio was born in 1864 in Italy.

ii.   Gaetano Barbuscio was born in 1865 in Italy. He married Maria Angela Lanza. She was born in 1871 in Italy.

iii.   Divinia Barbuscio was born in 1866 in Italy.

iv.   Ursula Barbuscio was born about 1869 in Italy. She died in 1869.

v.   Maria Barbuscio was born in 1875 in Italy. She died in 1877.

vi.   Maria Grazia Barbuscio was born in 1877 in Italy. She married Francis Magaro. He was born in 1870 in Italy.

viii. Raymond Frank (Raimondo Francesco) Barbush

vii. Salvatore Barbuscio was born in 1879 in Italy.

ix.   Ernest Rocco Barbuscio was born in 1883 in Italy.

PIETRO DESTEPHANO
& ORSOLA SAMMARCO

Peter (Pietro) DeStephano, son of Joseph (Giuseppe) Mario Santo DeStephano and Rose (Rosa) Martino, was born about 1861 in Castiglione, Cosenza, Calabria, Italy. He died after 1887 in Italy. He married Ursula (Orsola) Sammarco about 1885 in Italy.

Ursula (Orsola) Sammarco, daughter of Nicholas (Nicolo) Casper Sammarco and Maria Acri, was born in 1865 in Castiglione, Cosenza, Calabria, Italy. She died after 1887 in Italy.

Ursula (Orsola) Sammarco and Peter (Pietro) DeStephano had the following child:

i.   Maria "Sadie" Assunta DeStephano was born on May 8, 1887 in Castiglione, Cosenza, Calabria, Italy.

CHAPTER 6
Generation Six

More precious than our children are the children of our children
—Egyptian Proverb

Our Sixth Generation includes our 3G-gransparents, of the early 1880's.

Alexander Thompson's Scottish home

ALEXANDER THOMPSON
& ISABELLE S. PENMAN

A chill October wind mixed salt air with ash from the smokestacks of Edinburgh and carried it up to the farmlands south of the city as the Thompson family gathered to wait for a seventh child to join the clan. Robert Thompson, born June 1771 in Edgehead, and Janet Russell Thompson, born April 1791 in Borthwick, then married for sixteen years, named the boy Alexander upon his birth on October 22, 1805.

Alexander was born in Sauchenside Farm, Cranston, Midlothian, Scotland, and was baptized two weeks later on November third. The older siblings, Christina, Robert, William, Mary, George, and John, ages twelve to one year, quickly took to the new arrival. His sisters, in particular, were expected to help their mother with the younger children. Two younger brothers, John and James, would follow, filling out the family with seven brothers and two sisters.

Edinburgh was growing rapidly in the early nineteenth century, becoming a hub for lawyers and other professionals, and gobbling up nearby land to accommodate its growth. Scottish culture was having its heyday, generating a wealth of philosophy and literature, such as Sir Walter Scott's works of historical fiction. At this time Scotland's capital was known as the "Modern Athens," a place where people of modest birth were afforded the opportunity of rising to wealth and prominence. But the prosperity was not universal, and

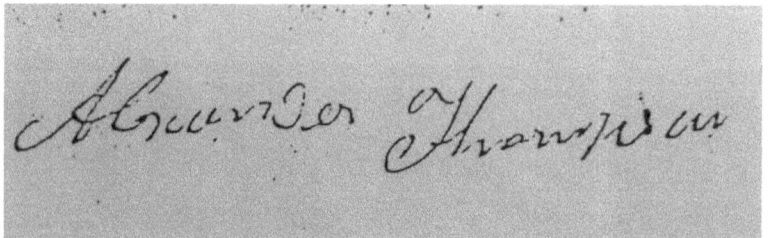

many poorer Scots sought their fortunes overseas, especially in the growing republic on the far side of the Atlantic.

Alexander Thompson was one of those Scots who found his prospects bleak in his homeland. Despite a quickly growing economy, the population was growing even faster, and competition for work was fierce in 1820s Scotland. As the fifth son in a large family, Alexander could only count on his family to do so much. So he did what many young Scots in his position were doing at the time— he got on a boat headed for America.

As was and remains typical of immigrants the world over, Alexander did not take this great journey alone. On the boat with him were his older brother George, George's wife Catherine Penman Thompson, and her younger siblings James, Isabelle, and Robert Penman, aged fifteen, eleven, and two years, respectively. The Nimrod landed in New York on July 9, 1827. Having just come of age twenty-one years old, Alexander was excited to get a chance in the "land of opportunity."

That opportunity came after a relatively short westward journey, in Middleport, Pennsylvania, where Alexander found work as a teamster, driving wagons loaded with machinery, timber, and other heavy goods. The Appalachian country northwest of Philadelphia was being developed for its ample natural resources, which were needed for the expanding coastal cities. Over the next few years, Alexander became part of the community in Schuylkill County—home to many other recent immigrants—and he obtained his naturalization papers on July 31, 1834. Having become a citizen and having saved scrupulously, Alexander was

ready to put down roots and start a family. He bought some land to farm and set his sights on finding a wife.

He didn't have to look very far, as he had already known the girl who would be his wife for several years at least: his sister-in-law's younger sister, Isabelle Stoddart Penman. Isabelle was born on May 9, 1816, in Newbattle, Scotland, the daughter of David Penman, born December 1775 in Gladsmuir and Elizabeth Stoddart, born about 1780. Isabelle, named for her ancestor Isabelle Wilson Brown, joined an already large family with elder siblings Miriam, John, Margaret, Catherine, Elizabeth, Anne, and James. She was eventually joined by two younger brothers, Alexander and Robert, who were four and eight years younger, respectively. Both the Thompsons and Penmans were educated. Alexander is listed as literate in the 1870 census.

There are sixteen couples in this generation, ten of which were fully literate, including the Thompson, Goodmans, Hensels, Batdorfs, Werts, McClouds, Oberlanders, Gauglers, Keefers and Livezlys. The Andersons and the Laymans of this generation, were slightly literate, where one adult was literate and one was not. Two families, the Peters and Rows, were completely illiterate. The Updegrove family became literate as adults and the Dankerts were Germans, the only couple of this generation not in America.

The Penman family was large and industrious, but they unfortunately lost their father at age 51 in 1826, which likely persuaded Catherine Penman Thompson to take her younger siblings with her from Scotland to America. With only one grown son, getting by with so many mouths to feed would have been difficult, so Catherine was doing her widowed mother a great service in taking some of the younger ones into her care. Eventually, their mother would join them in America, and she ended her days in Pottsville, Schuylkill County, Pennsylvania, in 1849.

When the Thompsons and Penmans set off to America, Isabelle was only eleven years old. However, since their journey, Isabelle had grown into a woman and Alexander had taken notice. The pair had a lot in common, from their nationality to common relatives. Also, Isabelle was the eighth child in a family of ten, circumstances quite similar to Alexander's upbringing. Upon her reaching eighteen years, the two were betrothed.

The Thompsons and Penmans celebrated New Year's Day 1835 with a wedding in Pottsville, Schuylkill County, Pennsylvania. Isabelle wore a dark green dress with a matching cape, suitable to the cold weather, and Alexander sported a brown coat with tails and green vest. The ceremony was held that morning at George and Catherine Thompson's home, and the new marriage was announced at the Presbyterian congregation the following Sunday.

Over the next fifteen years, Isabelle bore ten children. The first four were boys: George, Robert, who died as a child, David, and William. Two girls followed: Elizabeth and Janet; Alexander F. and Robert Bruce came next; and last, Isabelle and James filled out the household. Motherhood was rewarding in many respects for Isabelle, but it was also a risky affair considering the state of medicine at the time. Not long after James' birth, a house that had been full of children's laughter was quieted by the passing of their mother just after Thanksgiving on April 18, 1851, in Pottsville, Schuylkill County. Thanksgiving was traditional celebrated on April 13 until 1862. Isabelle was buried the next day in the York Farm Burial Grounds.

During his years with Isabelle, Alexander worked the land at York Farm in Schuylkill County, and the children grew and learned to work the land as well. While clearing a field on the farm, Alexander discovered veins of anthracite coal. He began selling the coal, which could be easily collected

258

from the surface. Anthracite coal was prized for its high burning temperature and less foul smoke than that produced by bituminous or "soft" coal. Later, this land would become the York Farm Colliery, one of the area's major coal mines.

Following Isabelle's death, the family got an infusion of new energy as Alexander married for a second time. Mary Bast, born in 1833, was not much older than the boys, George being only two years her junior. She was the daughter of Isaac Bast and Catharine Kline. The Bast family had eight children: the eldest son, Benneville; five daughters: Floranda, Rose, Mary, Catharine, and Sarah; and two younger sons: Jacob and Charles.

Despite Mary's youth, she was willing and able to take on the challenge of filling in as mother for Alexander's ten children, ages two to eighteen. What's more, she was also ready to mother her own children. That same year, Mary gave birth to the first of another large brood: a boy she named Isaac in honor of her father. The next year brought George—not to be confused with his half-brother George, the eldest of the family. Continuing the family's penchant to reuse names, the next two daughters were christened Isabelle and Mary. The pro creation continued as seven more boys were born: John, Andrew, Charles, Abraham, Winfield, William, and Elmer. A final daughter was named Rebecca.

The year after Alexander took Mary as his wife, the Thompsons left York Farm and bought a 110-acre farm in Porter Township, a then-undeveloped section of Schuylkill County. Alexander would later sell plots of this land, which would become the town of Sheridan in 1869. Alexander built a gristmill in 1857, then known as Thompson's mill. The mill was later sold to Grimm and Womer, and then to the Reading Company. The 1850s were prosperous for the Thompsons, as the family's property valuation nearly tripled during that decade, from $2,000 to more than $5,230. The 1870 census taker failed to record the family's property value but it can be estimated at $13,700. To put that amount in perspective, $13,700 of assets in 1870 calculates to over $250,000 in the present day. Compared to the other quite underprivileged contemporaries of this generation, the Thompson family was the only one that one may consider slightly well-to-do. Of all the sixteen families of this generation, twelve were below poverty, two—the Laymans and Oberlanders—were upper lower class, and two—The Gauglers and the Thompsons—were middle class.

While Alexander continued the development of his land, the Civil War broke out and three of his sons were called upon to serve in the Union Army. The family's devotion to the Union can also be seen in Alexander's registration as a Republican, and in the names of the younger sons, Abraham L. and William U.S.G., honoring presidents Lincoln and Grant during their terms in office. While those boys were much too young to serve, the older boys, David, William, and Alexander F., enlisted. William Thompson died at Frederick, Maryland, during his service in 1862. The eldest daughter, Elizabeth, also perished during the war while working as a nurse. David and Alexander F. would return intact from the fighting. Alexander F. served for three enlistments, and he would rise to prominence in the community after working his way through law school, becoming a lawyer and state senator.

During the 1860s and 1870s, Alexander continued to expand his business interests. In addition to his farm and mill, around 1860 he took a position as a superintendent overseeing various properties for Potts and

Company, which had established the Potts Colliery just over the county line in Columbia County in 1857. Coal companies often owned most, if not all, of the buildings in the new towns that sprung up around their mines, and having a local person of import oversee their properties would have been helpful.

In 1861, Alexander became the owner of a general store. Between 1865 and 1871, he took contract jobs for mines in the area, apparently buying properties and selling them to coal mining companies—in partnership with his father-in-law—as Bast and Thompson. Thus, Alexander Thompson continued to strive with the same earnestness and character that had earned him a place of distinction in his new home until his retirement in 1871.

Schuylkill County, Pennsylvania, By J.H. Beers and Co, Beers wrote: Alexander Thompson was a native of Scotland, and came to this country during his young manhood. The rest of his life was spent in Schuylkill county, Pa., where he was widely and favorably known during his active, useful career. He first settled at Middleport, where he was engaged in hauling machinery, timber, etc., and later lived at the York Farm, near Pottsville, which he bought, cultivating that tract for many years. He also had small drifts opened on the property and sold coal to the public, this being the first coal taken from the workings later developed into the famous York Farm colliery. After a long residence there he removed to Porter Township, in 1854, being one of the early settlers in this section, where he bought a farm of no acres, from which he subsequently sold a number of building lots for the town of Sharadin [Sheridan], which was laid out in 1869. This was his home until his death, which occurred Dec. 4, 1873; he is buried in the Greenwood cemetery in Porter Township. Besides farming, Mr. Thompson also engaged in milling in Porter Township, building a gristmill upon his tract which was known in his day as Thompson's mill. It was sold to Grimm and Womer, and later to the Reading Company, the present owners of the land. Mr. Thompson was a man of intelligence and strong character, and in his day was one of the most influential men in this section. By his first marriage, to Isabella Pennman, Mr. Thompson had nine children: George was killed at York Farm; David P., deceased, was a soldier in the Civil war; Elizabeth, deceased, was the wife of Hiram Kimmel; Janette married Benjamin Houtz; William died while serving in the Civil war; Alexander is living at Lykens, Pa.; Robert is deceased; Isabella is the widow of George Powell; James is living in West Virginia. For his second wife Mr. Thompson married Mary Bast, daughter of Isaac Bast, and by this union there was also a large family: Isaac B.; George, who is now living in Alaska; Mary, wife of Daniel Stout; John, residing at Sharadin, Pa.; Andrew, a resident of Michigan; Charles, deceased; Abraham, deceased; Winfield S., of Michigan; William U. S. G., deceased; Elmer E., of Sharadin; and Rebecca M., wife of Hoplin Evans, living on the old Thompson homestead in Porter Township.

Having homesteaded twice, married twice, fathered twenty-one children, and started several successful business ventures, Alexander Thompson no doubt inspired a great many of his friends and neighbors. But he, too, was mortal, and his vigor finally left him at the age of 68. He died on

December 4, 1873, in Tower City, Schuylkill County, Pennsylvania, and was laid to rest in Greenwood Cemetery underneath an impressive monument.

His son Charles would join him there in 1878. His wife Mary, his junior by 28 years, lived a long life and was finally laid to rest with her husband in 1910 at the age of 76. Alexander Thompson's legacy would continue well beyond his lifespan, shaping the community through his multitudinous progeny and the various commercial interests he had a hand in starting. His son Robert Bruce Thompson was a direct ancestor of the Thompson family line.

Alexander Personality Analysis: Like to acquire material things. The upper sample shows a losing of control, he probably had trouble following orders and could be quite stubborn. Highly sensitive, easily hurt about his appearance. Jealousy stroke appears here too. Very talkative. Good manual dexterity. Could take things apart, analyze and put back together. Was intuitive. Emotionally outgoing.

Alexander Personality Analysis 2: Alexander Thompson was an outwardly cheerful man; when he felt comfortable and at ease he was both talkative and charming. Although it was a difficult state for Alexander to hold due to restrictions related to his energy levels when the circumstances were right he could be highly animated, interested and observed. It was difficult for Alexander to think in a focused way for long periods of time, rather like his productivity and energy his thinking patterns would be constructed from short bursts. Likewise, it was difficult for him to find and settle into a single occupation in life. Although his thinking style did not make it possible for him to delve into any one subject matter in depth it did give him great intuition as he was able to think easily in impressions. Alexander was a restless man and his erratic energy made him indecisive. He was a genuine man though and really wore his heart on his sleeve. His overenthusiastic reactions would sometimes perplex those around him and he would have unusual insights and creative observations that would be interesting to some and eccentric to others. There were times I am sure where he would miss the main (consensual) point of a topic because of too much attention to detail. Alexander had a very original mind that was both curious and active. He was inquisitive up to the point of not just having passing interests but to where he actually had some very inventive ideas. Such was the pace of his thinking that it was difficult for him to rest his mind to the point where he could actually create cohesive records of his ideas. It was difficult for Alexander to deal with the stresses of life particularly those that related to competition. Being in a position where he had to compete was not an easy aspect of life for him to face (although he had competitive tendencies). He would over play, in his mind, qualities and faults of other people. As a consequence, his reactions could be quite defensive; rather than compete he would become easily offended and create a formal, conservative stance towards his competition. Sometimes he would be overly critical and act above it all, other times he would simply move on to another realm of activity. The great paradox of Alexander's life was that he was capable of intense emotions such that his internal emotional landscape changed constantly, however, it was very difficult for him to change his actual way of thinking and life in order to have a stronger emotional hold on himself. Instead, he found adventure and pleasure in changing his occupation and physical location. By the time he passed away given his restless nature he would have been delighted to have had seen so much of the world in so many different roles. Progression from 1836 to 1870: The way that the writing has progressed over the years is in line with the natural aging process; it is more irregular meaning that there is less organization in Alexander's mind. It is more angular and less rhythmic reflecting a grouchier and less flowing, harmonious life. Crucially there is less pressure reflecting a state of less energy. There is also a definite split in the surname in the second signature. Perhaps this is just one of because of an ink spill or other mark in that particular rendition. If it is a genuine mark on the paper made by Alexander himself then perhaps there was some sort of rift in the family which Alexander may have over-reacted or reacted badly to.

Alexander Thompson was baptized on November 3, 1805 in Cranston, Midlothian, Scotland. He lived in Middleport, Schuylkill County, Pennsylvania about 1827. He immigrated to Scotland to New York, New York on July 9, 1827 (ship Nimrod). He lived in Pottsville, Schuylkill County, Pennsylvania after 1828 (York Farm Burial Grounds). He was counted in the census in 1830 in Norwegian, Schuylkill County, Pennsylvania (w/mother-in-law). He was naturalized on July 31, 1834 in Schuylkill County, Pennsylvania. He was counted in the census in 1840 in Norwegian, Schuylkill County, Pennsylvania. He was employed as a Farming in 1850. He owned $2000 in 1850. He was counted in the census in 1850 in Norwegian, Schuylkill County, Pennsylvania. He was employed as a Laid out town of Sheridan, Pennsylvania in 1854. He lived in Porter, Schuylkill County, Pennsylvania in 1854. He was counted in the census in 1860 in Porter, Schuylkill County, Pennsylvania. He owned $5000 + $230 in 1860. He was employed as a Farmer in 1860. He was employed as a Superintendent, Potts and Co about 1860. He was employed as an Owner, General store from 1861-1873. He was employed as a Contract work, Mines from 1865-1871. He was counted in the census in 1870 in Norwegian, Schuylkill County, Pennsylvania. He was employed as a Laborer in 1870. He signed his will about 1872 in Schuylkill County, Pennsylvania (Book 4, page 142). He was buried in December 1873 in Tower City, Schuylkill County, Pennsylvania (Greenwood Cemetery). He signed his will on December 3, 1873 in Porter Township, Schuylkill County, Pennsylvania (Estate Files, 1874, Moyer, George-Wild). His estate was probated on December 17, 1873 in Porter Township, Schuylkill County, Pennsylvania. His estate was probated on January 25, 1912 in Porter Township, Schuylkill County, Pennsylvania (after Mary Thompson's death). He was employed as a Teamster. He owned est. $13,700. He was employed as a Colliery owner. He lived in Sheridan, Porter Township, Schuylkill County, Pennsylvania (Alexander Thompson

Homestead). He was affiliated with the Methodist religion. Political Party: (Republican)

Isabelle Stoddart Penman immigrated in 1828. She was counted in the census in 1830 in Norwegian, Schuylkill County, Pennsylvania (w/mother). She was counted in the census in 1840 in Norwegian, Schuylkill County, Pennsylvania (w/husband). She was employed as a Homemaker about 1840. She was counted in the census in 1850 in Norwegian, Schuylkill County, Pennsylvania. She was buried on April 19, 1851 in Pottsville, Schuylkill County, Pennsylvania (Presbyterian Cemetery, York Farm Burial Grounds). She signed her will (Intestate). She was affiliated with the Presbyterian religion. She was named after Great-grandmother Isabelle Wilson.

MICHAEL GOODMAN
& M. MAGDALENA BROWN

On a hot summer day, near the steaming banks of the Susquehanna River, John George Gutman and his wife, Susan Brown, welcomed a son. The Goodman and the Brown families, originally Gutman and Braun, were of Germanic backgrounds. Michael Goodman, born on June 10, 1806, in Lower Mahanoy, Northumberland County, Pennsylvania, was the youngest of four, having elder brothers, Benjamin and Daniel, and a sister. At the age of two, perhaps in anticipation of coming hard times and the death of his father George, Michael was taken to live with his grandfather in Berks County, Pennsylvania. The Goodman children would soon be sorrowed by the loss of their mother, Susan, a few years later.

Michael stayed with his grandfather until he was eighteen, when he moved to a farm south of Clarks Valley Road in Dauphin County, Pennsylvania, where he would live out his days. In the next year or so, he was confirmed in the Lutheran congregation at the old log church-school in Schuylkill County, Pennsylvania.

At the age of twenty-four, Michael married Mary Barbara Ramp, who was born about 1805. The couple would bear six children between 1835 and 1846. William, the eldest, would take over the farm and care for his father in his old age. William was followed by two sisters, Susan and Magdalena, then a brother, John. Two more girls, Sarah, known as Sallie; and Catherine, were the last children from this union.

In the 1830s and 1840s, Pennsylvania was the young republic's bread basket. With a climate similar to much of Europe, settlers were able to bring the bulk of their farming knowledge to use in this region, growing fruits and grains from Europe, as well as adopting native plants and techniques. Pennsylvania farmers produced grains, meats, and dairy products, as well as manufactured products such as leather and flaxseed oil. In 1840, more than 77 percent of the 4.8 million employed persons in Pennsylvania were occupied in agriculture.

Mary Barbara unfortunately passed in 1846, likely due to complications from Catherine's birth. After some fifteen years of marriage, Michael—being in his early forties—was now a very eligible widower with many good years left in him. Soon the area matchmakers set to work finding a wife to once again make the farmstead a home.

A woman from the area—who was also older than the usual marrying age—proved to be a suitable match. Mary Magdalena Brown, daughter of Peter Brown and Anna Maria Carl, was a decade Michael's junior, being born in 1816 in Rush, Dauphin County, Pennsylvania. Anna Maria is believed to be from the George Carl family and these families also originally hailed from Germany. Following the custom that her family had brought from Europe, she went by Magdalena. She was the fifth of eight children, having elder siblings John, Peter, William, and Anna. Her younger siblings were Philip, Rebecca, and Elizabeth. They were grandchildren to Peter Braun, who fought for the British during the Revolution and, interestingly after the War, secured a job working for George Washington. Michael Goodman and Magdalena Brown were married about 1848 in Schuylkill

County, Pennsylvania. The 1870 census listed both Michael and Magdalena as literate.

There are sixteen couples in this generation, ten of which were fully literate, including the Thompson, Goodmans, Hensels, Batdorfs, Werts, McClouds, Oberlanders, Gauglers, Keefers and Livezlys. The Andersons and the Laymans of this generation, were slightly literate, where one adult was literate and one was not. Two families, the Peters and Rows, were completely illiterate. The Updegrove family became literate as adults and the Dankerts were Germans, the only couple of this generation not in America.

Michael and Magdalena had four children. Anna was born later in the same year they were married and two boys, Jacob and George, were to follow. Amid the joys of a new set of births, another tragedy befell the family as Catherine, the youngest child from Michael's first marriage, passed away about 1855, only about nine years old. The family was completed with the birth of Lydia, the last child, in 1856.

During this period, Michael took to working as a carpenter. Since by the 1850s his older sons were teenagers and thus able to take over a large part of the farm work, the head of the household was free to pursue a new craft. Between farming and carpentry, the Goodman family did well in the tumultuous years from 1850 to 1870, increasing their net worth from $1,000 to more than $2,200—more than $40,000 in modern equivalents.

The Goodman farm endured changing times and adapted accordingly. In the middle of the century, railroads were spreading into new regions of the rapidly expanding nation. The railroads brought access to the vast prairies of the Midwest and the Great Plains, and to ever-increasing supplies of grains and meat. The farmers of the east had to adapt to these changing markets.

Wheat production was being replaced with milk, butter, hay, potatoes, poultry, eggs, and other products that were needed in the fast-growing urban populations of Philadelphia and Baltimore. This period also saw the early stages of mechanization on farms, as binders and harvesters changed the Northern farm economy and the cotton gin revolutionized the South.

These changes contributed to the growing rift between the regions, eventually exploding into the Civil War. It is likely that John, the second son, enlisted in 1861 at the age of twenty. John was fortunate to return home, marry, and have a family. It appears that this branch of the Goodman family was not fated to grieve for a lost son, as many of their neighbors and relatives were.

After many prosperous years, the 1880s brought the ravages of age to the Goodman family. Michael and Magdalena had enjoyed 36 years together, but again Michael found himself outliving a wife. At the age of 68, Magdalena died on December 17, 1884 in Tower City, Schuylkill, Pennsylvania. She was laid to rest at Zion Public Square Lutheran Cemetery, Tower City, Schuylkill County, Pennsylvania. Michael would not be alone after his second wife's passing; he spent his golden years living on the farm—which had become his son William's livelihood—surrounded by his many children and grandchildren.

Michael was a church-goer. The Evangelical Church, a predecessor to the modern United Methodist Church, suffered a division in 1894. Nearly a third of the denomination split off and formed the United Evangelical Church, while the remainder was known as the

Evangelical Association. United Evangelical members were generally more progressive, favoring the use of English language rather than the traditional German, greater local control, and less authoritarian leadership.

The schism was largely about personalities and culture rather than about theology, but it was serious nonetheless. "In some congregations, the controversy divided families, led to verbal and physical attacks, and ended in court battles over the church property. Eventually, or as some have said, 'when enough funerals had taken place,' the factions reunited in 1922 to form the Evangelical Church." Since the secular courts sided with the Evangelical Association regarding ownership of church property, many United Evangelical congregations were starting from the ground up in the 1890's, and thus Michael's leadership in his congregation was likely needed and much appreciated.

In what would be his final summer, Michael Goodman hosted a great gathering of his family on Sunday, August 19, at the farmstead. "The family dinner was spread in bountiful manner under the ancient cherry tree, and a happy feast was enjoyed by all present, numbering 43 persons of the Goodman freundschaft. At the planting of that cherry tree, great grandfather Michael Goodman, who was 94 years of age in June, did not think of such a gathering under its branches, and as the venerable father offered thanks at the dinner table, he expressed the desire that they would all meet at the festal board of Heaven."

Clearly Michael was anticipating the inevitable: he died two days after Christmas in 1900, in Rush, Dauphin County, Pennsylvania. The Tower City, Porter Township Centennial wrote: Michael Goodman was born June 10, 1806, and came to this valley as a young man and was confirmed in the old log church-school in July 1825, according to the old church records. He married Mary Magdalena Brown, a granddaughter of the original Peter Braun. Michael purchased the farm south of the Clark's Valley Road just east of the Dauphin County line and lived there until his death on December 27, 1900, at the grand age of ninety-four. His wife died December 17, 1884, and both are buried in the cemetery in the public square. In his later years, he gave his farm to his son William, who was born November 20, 1835, and died January 30, 1907. He married Christina Hand, a daughter of John Hand, Jr., and they had the following children: Catherine, who first married Lincoln Rhoads and on his death married Herman Niehenke; Ernaline, who married Elwood Showers; Mary, wife of Isaac Thompson; John; Lydia, married Nathan A. Reightler; George; Fayetta, married William Achenbach; Frank; Ellen, wife of William Novinger; and David. John Goodman married Hannah Houtz and their children were Harry II, Charles E., Golda, and Grace. Harry married Sadie P. Warfield and their child was Helen; Evelyn, married Frank Rosade; Lillian P.; John; Stuart; and Virginia, married J. Robert Hunsicker. Among the children of Ernaline Goodman Showers and her husband were Albert; Charles; Roy; Beulah, married George Schrope; Verna, married Robert Fegley. The children of Charles Showers were Lester; Helen; Anne, married Norman Unger; Violet; and Lawrence. A very pleasant and enjoyable affair was the reunion of the Goodman family, on Sunday, August 19, at the residence of Mr. and Mrs. William Goodman, in Clarks Valley, which is also the birthplace of Mr. Goodman. The following were present: Mrs. Isaac Thompson and children, Paul, Russel and Leona, Sheridan; Mr. and Mrs. Elwood Showers and children, Charles, Beulah, Raymond, Emma, Verna, and Albert, Tower City; Mr. and Mrs. David Goodman and children, Clarence and Elva, Orwin; Mrs. John Goodman and children, Harry, Charles, and Golda, Orwin; Mrs. Wm. Achenbach and children, Harry, Roy, and Frank of Philadelphia; Mrs. Catherine Rhoads and children, Charles, Oscar, Ira, Millie, and Lloyd, Sheridan; Mr. and Mrs. Nathan Rightler and children, Emily and Willie, Tower City; Frank Goodman and son George, Orwin; George Goodman, Clarks Valley; Mr. and Mrs. Wm. Novinger and daughter, Hattie; Tower City. Artist Rowland of Williamstown photographed the group under an old cherry tree planted scores of years ago by great grandfather Michael Goodman, who was also in attendance. The family dinner was spread in bountiful manner under the ancient cherry tree, and a happy feast was enjoyed by all present, numbering 43 persons. At the planting of that cherry tree, great grandfather Michael Goodman, who was 94 years of age in June, did not think of such a gathering under its branches, and as the venerable father offered thanks at the dinner table, he expressed the desire that they would all meet at the festal board of Heaven. May his desires be granted. As the hour arrived for the happy parties to return to their respective homes, all seemed to realize that in the changing scenes of time, another such a gathering might never occur in this world. After 60 years of earthly pilgrimage, Mr. and Mrs. Wm. Goodman were favored by a kind providence in the gathering of all their sons and daughters, with thirty of the grandchildren. It was an occasion of great joy of retrospective glances over the journey of life, and happy anticipations of a reunion in the golden world of eternal deliverance.

> Scattered o'er various fields by Heaven,
> Through various pathways led,
> What happiness in peace to meet
> Around a common head!
> The pleasures of the past recall,
> And tell the tales again
> Its infant dreams, and childhood joys,
> And youth's delightful reign,
> To plan the schemes of future bliss;
> Rejoicing to confess,
> That He whose love hath blessed the past
> The future, too, will bless.

The West Schuylkill Herald would add at his passing: Michael Goodman, the oldest and best-known citizen of this valley, died at the home of his son, William, in Clarks Valley at three a.m. last Thursday morning. His death was due to old age. . . . The deceased was probably the oldest man in the valley, being 94 years, 6 months, and 17 days. He followed farming for a living and retained great vitality up until about a year ago. Up to that time he frequently walked from his home to Williamstown, a distance of four miles. For the past year, however, his health had been failing. He was only bedfast, however, a short time before death overtook him. Early in his life he connected with the Evangelical Church. When the split occurred, he chose the United Evangelical. It is said that for 72 years he was a member and took great delight in church work. The funeral was held Sunday morning. Services were conducted in the U. E. Church by the pastor, Reverend S. N. Dissinger, assisted by Reverend C E Hess of Williamstown. Interment was made in the cemetery in this place.

Michael Goodman would see the beginning of a new Century, and live to be the oldest of any male in this line, finally resting in Zion Public Square Lutheran Cemetery, Tower City, Schuylkill County, Pennsylvania. Michael Goodman's youngest daughter, Lydia Ann Goodman, would marry Robert Bruce Thompson, and their progeny would carry the Thompson name to the present generation.

Michael Goodman lived in Berks County, Pennsylvania in 1808. He was counted in the census in 1810 (w/grandfather). He was counted in the census in 1820 (w/grandfather). He lived in Dauphin County, Pennsylvania in 1824. He was confirmed in July 1825 in Schuylkill County, Pennsylvania. He was counted in the census in 1830 in Hanover (Rush), Dauphin County, Pennsylvania. He was counted in the census in 1840 in Lower Mahantango, Schuylkill County, Pennsylvania. He was employed as a Carpenter in 1850. He owned $1000 in 1850. He was counted in the census in 1850 in Rush, Dauphin County, Pennsylvania. He lived in Rush Township, Dauphin County, Pennsylvania from 1858-1875. He was counted in the census in 1860 in Rush, Dauphin County, Pennsylvania. He owned $1000 + $600 in 1860. He was employed as a Farmer from 1860-1880. He was counted in the census in 1870 in Rush, Dauphin County, Pennsylvania. He owned $2000 + $200 in 1870. He was counted in the census in 1880 in Rush, Dauphin County, Pennsylvania. He was employed as a Retired in 1900. He was counted in the census in 1900 in Rush, Dauphin County, Pennsylvania (w/son William Goodman). He was buried in 1900 in Tower City, Schuylkill County, Pennsylvania (Zion (Public Square) Lutheran Cemetery). He was employed as a Farmer in 1901. His estate was probated on January 11, 1901 in Rush Township, Dauphin County, Pennsylvania. He was affiliated with the Lutheran religion. His cause of death was Old age.

Mary Magdalena Brown was counted in the census in 1820 in Rush, Dauphin County, Pennsylvania (unlisted). She was counted in the census in 1830 in Rush, Dauphin County, Pennsylvania (w/father). She was counted in the census in 1840 in Rush, Dauphin County, Pennsylvania (w/father). She was counted in the census in 1850 in Rush, Dauphin County, Pennsylvania. She was counted in the census in 1860 in Rush, Dauphin County, Pennsylvania (listed as Margaret). She was counted in the census in 1870 in Rush, Dauphin County, Pennsylvania. She was listed as a Keeping house from 1870-1880. She was counted in the census in 1880 in Rush, Dauphin County, Pennsylvania. She was buried in 1884 in Tower City,

Schuylkill County, Pennsylvania (Zion (Public Square) Lutheran Cemetery). She signed her will (Intestate). She was affiliated with the Methodist > Lutheran religion. She was named after Maria, her mother

ANDREW G. HENSEL
& A. CATHERINE WORKMAN

Andrew Guise Hensel was born on February 18, 1831, at home in New Bloomfield, Perry County, Pennsylvania. New Bloomfield is in the central Pennsylvania countryside, west of the Susquehanna River, an area then being rapidly developed for farming and industry. Andrew's father was Andrew W. Hensel, a shoemaker, born in Littlestown, near Gettysburg, Adams County, Pennsylvania, and his mother was Mary Guise, born in Northampton County, Pennsylvania.

Both the Hensel and Guise families seems to be descended from French Huguenots—la Hentzelle and de Guise—that left France to Germany and ultimate America. Named was the fifth of six children, preceded by his brother John Adam, sister Anna, and brothers John and George. After Andrew came Michael Hensel, who would later become a reverend. Andrew was given his father's name, Andrew, and the middle name, Guise, to honor the maternal line.

The Hensel family had been shaped by significant military experience. Father Andrew served in the War of 1812 as a private. He was among the noncommissioned officers and privates from Captain John McMillan's company, Colonel Fenton's regiment, of the Pennsylvania Militia, who crossed the Niagara into Canada, and also served in Buffalo, New York.

The Hensels' military pedigree extended another generation back as well. Both of Andrew's grandfathers, John Casper Hensel and John Adam Guise, served in the American Revolution, in York County, Pennsylvania, under Captain Will, and in Northampton County, Pennsylvania, under Captain Drapper, respectively.

When Andrew went to work, he garnered early experience as a servant, but he soon took up the profession of plasterer, playing a part in the spread of housing that came along with the ongoing expansion of mining in Pennsylvania. The steady influx of miners to the region generated demand in his field, so Andrew was able to enjoy a stable income and confidence in his plans to start a family.

At twenty-two years of age, Andrew would marry Anna Catherine Workman—known as Catherine—on March 17, 1853, amid St. Patrick's Day festivities in Halifax, Dauphin County, Pennsylvania. Never mind that they were married in a Methodist Episcopal congregation. Since most of the early immigrants to America from Ireland were Protestants, the holiday had not yet taken on the Catholic associations that became common in the late 1800s into the twentieth century. Rather, the Americans of the young republic celebrated St. Patrick's Day primarily as an act of anti-colonial solidarity with the Irish in their struggle for freedom from English rule. Since the two families were situated close to one another, it was likely a well-attended wedding, filling the building with friends and relatives on a Thursday morning as the beginnings of spring were just becoming noticeable in the hilly Pennsylvania countryside. The 1870 census listed both Andrew and Catherine as literate.

There are sixteen couples in this generation, ten of which were fully literate, including the Thompson, Goodmans, Hensels, Batdorfs, Werts,

McClouds, Oberlanders, Gauglers, Keefers and Livezlys. The Andersons and the Laymans of this generation, were slightly literate, where one adult was literate and one was not. Two families, the Peters and Rows, were completely illiterate. The Updegrove family became literate as adults and the Dankerts were Germans, the only couple of this generation not in America.

Catherine, the daughter of Joseph Workman and Susan Romberger, was born in Old Lincoln, Dauphin County, Pennsylvania, on May 17, 1838. The Workman were presumably German Wuertmann in origin and the Rombergers hailed from both the Palatinate and Bavaria. Catherine was only fourteen years old on her wedding day. Since she was the youngest of nine children, it is likely that economic concerns contributed to her early marriage. This was a common fact of life for the families of the working class at the time. Her sisters, Susan, Nancy, Elizabeth, and Carolina, reassured and advised the girl as the wedding approached and throughout the marriage.

Catherine had helped her sisters with their children, so she was aware of the duties and troubles of raising children. And she also knew something of the joy that children brought to a home. Of course, her four older brothers, Jacob, John, Henry, and Joseph, were surely protective of their youngest sister, but the repute of the Hensel family—and the two families' shared military history—may have eased any concerns about the match. Joseph, Catherine's father, served in the War of 1812, and her grandfather Balthasar Romberger and great-grandfather Jacob Lehman both served in the American Revolution in Lancaster County, Pennsylvania.

Soon the Hensel family was growing. Their first son, John, was born in the year they married, but he did not survive infancy. Catherine's pain eased slowly as more sons came quickly. The next year brought Joseph, then Ira two years later, and Howard after another two years. The family's growth slowed as the Civil War broke out and Andrew left home to serve in the Union Army.

In September 1862, Andrew Guise Hensel was mustered into Company F of the 155th Regiment of the Pennsylvania Infantry at Harrisburg. This unit would be attached to the 2nd Brigade, 3rd Division, 5th Army Corps, Army of the Potomac immediately after reaching Washington, where they were held in reserve during the battle of Antietam. Though they did not fight, the soldiers suffered the elements in these early days of the war due to a lack of basic provisions such as tents and uniforms. A great deal of these needs eventually were donated to units in the Army of the Potomac from the soldiers' communities back home.

The 155th first fought at the battle of Fredericksburg that December, during which they suffered heavy losses in an unsuccessful series of charges. "Captain Lee Anshultz was mortally wounded, dying the following day, and the color-sergeant, and the entire color guard were shot down." They also witnessed defeat near Chancellorsville, holding defensive positions. The 155th was later assigned to the 2nd Brigade, 2nd Division of the 5th Corps. At the battle of Gettysburg, the 155th was instrumental in the taking of Little Round Top on the second day of fighting, which helped secure the Union Army's defenses. They held that position on the following day, witnessing the final rebel charge from their unchallenged defensive position, and later pursued the retreating enemy.

The battle at Gettysburg helped to shape the unit's identity and likely contributed to the wealth of documentation available on the subject. A succession of injuries leading to honorable discharges among the officers in the wake of that battle led to the promotion of Alfred L. Pearson to Colonel.

Pearson and other officers of the 2nd Brigade led these men in learning the tactics of the French Light Infantry and adopted variations of French-style uniforms to match their inspiration. They came to be known as the Zouave Brigade, which included several units of infantry from Pennsylvania and New York, however the trend was more widespread.

Units from nearly all of the states on both sides—and the District of Columbia—styled themselves as Zouaves. The Zouaves of the 155th wore a light blue jacket with yellow trimming and tombeaus, or stylized false pockets; baggy blue trousers; and a red sash with matching red fez. They certainly drew a stark contrast with the straight lines and dark blue of the typical Union Army uniform. Subsequently, the unit was attached to various other brigades up until May 1864, when the unit would be reorganized as the 191st Regiment of the Pennsylvania Infantry. Private Hensel was assigned to Company G.

Pearson's Zouaves fought in many other battles and suffered great hardship: in one battle having 83 men killed or wounded in just ten minutes. But they also saw success, and Pearson was promoted to Major General before the war had ended, which happened before their eyes as the white flag was raised just as the Zouaves were heading into the town of Appomattox Court House for another fight.

Victory meant an end to the bitter suffering this unit had witnessed. Over two years and nine months of service, the combined losses for the 155th and 191st Regiments were six officers, 248 enlisted men killed or mortally wounded, and 272 enlisted men lost to disease—not to mention the death and destruction suffered by Confederates and civilians as well. The unit was mustered out at Washington on June 2, 1865, and then welcomed home with a celebration in Pittsburgh, as many of the men had been recruited from that region.

The www.civilwararchive.com wrote: Andrew, named after his father Andrew Hensel, joined the191st Regiment Infantry. Organized in the field from Veterans and Recruits of the Pennsylvania Reserve Corps May 31. 1864. Attached to 3rd Brigade, 3rd Division, 5th Army Corps, Army of the Potomac, to August, 1864. 1st Brigade, 3rd Division, 5th Army Corps, to September, 1864. 3rd Brigade, 2nd Division, 5th Army Corps, to June, 1865. Service--Battles about Cold Harbor, Va., June 1-12, 1864. Bethesda Church June 1-3. White Oak Swamp Bridge June 13. Before Petersburg June 16-18. Siege of Petersburg June 16, 1864, to April 2, 1865. Weldon Railroad June 21-23, 1864. Mine Explosion, Petersburg, July 30 (Reserve).

Weldon Railroad August 18-21. Poplar Springs Church September 29-October 2. Boydton Plank Road, Hatcher's Run, October 27-28, Warren's Expedition to Weldon Railroad December 7-12. Dabney's Mills, Hatcher's Run, February 5-7, 1865. Appomattox Campaign March 28-April 9. Lewis Farm, near Gravelly Run, March 29. White Oak Road March 31. Five Forks April 1. Appomattox Court House April 9. Surrender of Lee and his army. March to Washington, D.C., May 1-12. Grand Review May 23. Mustered out June 28, 1865. Regiment lost during service 1 Officer and 40 Enlisted men killed and mortally wounded and 161 Enlisted men by disease. Total 202. 155th Regiment Infantry: Organized at Pittsburg and Harrisburg September 2-19. 1862. Moved to Washington, D.C., September 4. Attached to 2nd Brigade, 3rd Division, 5th Army Corps, Army Potomac, to May, 1863. 3rd Brigade, 2nd Division. 5th Army Corps, to March, 1864. 4th Brigade, 1st Division, 5th Army Corps, to April, 1864. 1st Brigade, 1st Division, 5th Army Corps, to June, 1864. 1st Brigade, 2nd Division, 5th Army Corps, June, 1864. 2nd Brigade. 2nd Division, 5th Army Corps, to July, 1865. 2nd Brigade, 1st Division, 5th Army Corps, to December. 1864. 3rd Brigade, 1st Division, 5th Army Corps, to June, 1865. Service--Moved to Sharpsburg, Md., and duty there until October 30, 1862. Movement to Falmouth, Va., October 30-November 19. Battle of Fredericksburg December 12-15. Burnside's 2nd Campaign, "Mud March," January 20-24, 1863. Duty at Falmouth, Va., until

April 27. Chancellorsville Campaign April 27-May 6. Battle of Chancellorsville May 1-5. Gettysburg (Pa.) Campaign June 11-July 24. Battle of Gettysburg July 1-3. Pursuit of Lee July 5-24. Duty on line of the Rappahannock and Rapidan until October. Bristoe Campaign October 9-22. Auburn October 13. Advance to line of the Rappahannock November 7-8. Rappahannock Station November 7. Mine Run Campaign November 26-December 2. Duty on Orange and Alexandria Railroad until April, 1864. Rapidan Campaign May 4-June 12. Battles of the Wilderness May 5-7; Laurel Hill May 8; Spottsylvania May 8-12; Spottsylvania Court House May 12-21. Assault on the Salient May 12. North Anna River May 23-26. On line of the Pamunkey May 26-28. Totopotomoy May 28-31. Cold Harbor June 1-12. Bethesda Church June 1-3. Before Petersburg June 16-18. Siege of Petersburg June 16, 1864, to April 2, 1865. Mine Explosion, Petersburg, July 30 (Reserve). Six Mile House, Weldon Railroad, August 18-21. Poplar Springs Church, Peeble's Farm, September 29-October 2. Boydton Plank Road, Hatcher's Run, October 27-28. Warren's Raid on Weldon Railroad December 7-12. Dabney's Mills, Hatcher's Run, February 5-7, 1865. Appomattox Campaign March 28-April 9. Junction Boydton and Quaker Roads and Lewis Farm, near Gravelly Run, March 29. White Oak Road March 31. Five Forks April 1. Appomattox Court House April 9. Surrender of Lee and his army. Moved to Washington, D.C., May 1-12. Grand Review May 23. Mustered out June 2, 1865. Regiment lost during service 5 Officers and 137 Enlisted men killed and mortally wounded and 1 Officer and 111 Enlisted men by disease. Total 254.

The war years were terrible, but also wondrous for Andrew Hensel as his wife, Catherine, gave him four daughters between 1862 and 1866: Anna Catherine, named after her mother, Lillian, Anna, and Emma. In the postwar years, the sons of the Hensel family went to work in various professions, and continued expansion in the mining industry fueled Andrew's career as a plasterer. Wages in his field appear to have been good enough to raise a large family, though Andrew never accumulated a great deal of wealth. His valuation of property was $373 in 1860 and only $340—about $6,000 today—in 1870. Certainly the War, his growing family and inconsistent work made progress difficult, and taking inflation into account, his property valued out much less than the previous decade.

The bustling Hensel household fell silent in grief as the children lost their mother to untimely death at only 38 years old. Anna Catherine Workman died on February 10, 1877, in Joliett, Schuylkill County, Pennsylvania. She was laid to rest in Calvary United Methodist, Wiconisco, Dauphin County, Pennsylvania. The daughters were still living at home, though at fifteen Lillie was capable of taking on many of her mother's household responsibilities. Howard, the youngest son—then eighteen years old—continued to live at home at least until 1880, working as a laborer to support the younger children.

Eventually Andrew found himself ready to move forward after losing his wife of nearly 24 years. The family would have a stepmother when Andrew married Grace Arrison, though this union produced no children.

In the coming years, Andrew took to working as a mason and also as a school teacher. At the turn of the century, he was living as a boarder, likely exchanging his knowledge and experience for room and board. In 1908, Andrew got ill, diagnosed with Bright's disease, a chronic inflammation of the kidneys. After a sickness of a few months he died at age 77 on December 14, 1908, in Wiconisco, Dauphin County, Pennsylvania. Two days later he was put to rest in Calvary United Methodist Cemetery, Wiconisco, Dauphin County, Pennsylvania. His headstone was adorned with a flag-holder star marked G.A.R. for the Grand Army of the Republic, honoring his service in the Union Army.

A veteran, a father of eight children and grandfather of many, Andrew Guise Hensel lived through great upheavals and the steady pressure of America's industrial development. Andrew's son Howard Andrew Carson Hensel was the direct ancestor of the Thompson line.

Andrew Guise Hensel was counted in the census in 1840 in Centre, Perry County, Pennsylvania (w/father). He was counted in the census in 1850 in Centre, Perry County, Pennsylvania. He was employed as a Plasterer from 1850-1900. He was employed as a Servant about 1850. He was employed as a Plasterer in 1853. He was counted in the census in 1860 in Porter, Schuylkill County, Pennsylvania (Hentzel). He owned $250 + $123 in 1860. He was employed as a Teacher in 1864. He lived in East Hanover, Dauphin County, Pennsylvania in 1864. He served in the military on August 28, 1864 in Harrisburg > Pittsburgh, Pennsylvania (Civil War, Private, 155th Regiment Infantry, Company F). He served in the military on June 2, 1865 in Pennsylvania, Organized in fields (Civil War, Private, 191st Regiment Infantry, Company G). He owned $340 in 1870. He was counted in the census in 1870 in Wiconisco, Dauphin County, Pennsylvania. He was counted in the census in 1880 in Wiconisco, Dauphin County, Pennsylvania. Political Party: 1894 in Wiconisco, Dauphin County, Pennsylvania (Republican Assessor) He was employed as a Township Assessor in 1895 in Wiconisco, Dauphin County, Pennsylvania. He was employed as a Boarder in 1900. He was counted in the census in 1900 in Wiconisco, Dauphin County, Pennsylvania (Weist-Heheel). His funeral took place in 1908 in Lykens, Dauphin County, Pennsylvania (John Reiff). He was employed as a Mason and School teacher in 1908. He was buried on December 16, 1908 in Wiconisco, Dauphin County, Pennsylvania (Calvary (Union) United Methodist). He was affiliated with the Methodist < Reformed religion. He was named after Andrew Hensel, father and Mary Guise, mother. His cause of death was Bright's disease (i.e., chronic inflammation of kidneys) w/old age.

Anna Catherine Workman was counted in the census in 1840 in Wiconisco, Dauphin County, Pennsylvania (unlisted). She was counted in the census in 1850 in Wiconisco, Dauphin County, Pennsylvania. She was counted in the census in 1860 in Porter, Schuylkill County, Pennsylvania. She was employed as a Keeping house in 1870. She was counted in the census in 1870 in Wiconisco, Dauphin County, Pennsylvania. She was buried in 1877 in Wiconisco, Dauphin County, Pennsylvania (Calvary (Union) United Methodist). Her estate was probated on May 24, 1878. She was affiliated with the Methodist religion.

DANIEL UPDEGROVE
& SARAH A. CULP

Life was hard in the anthracite coal fields of eastern Pennsylvania following the Panic of 1837. Layoffs, wage cuts, and persistently high unemployment afflicted the nation, dooming President Van Buren's re-election campaign. John M. Updegrove, a laborer from Berks County, Pennsylvania and his wife, Elizabeth Reisch were struggling to keep their growing family fed. The couple had been married for fourteen years when they welcomed their fifth child, Daniel, on June 28, 1839.

The Updegroves have a deep German history with one English line, the Benfields of London, and the Reisch line was of German stock. Daniel's siblings Jacob, Catherine, John, and Nancy were excited, but his parents' joy was tempered with worry. By that time, eldest Jacob was old enough to be allowed to work. Though still a child, this would only be a help if there were work to be had. Two more children, Solomon and Rebecca, would come along in the middle of the next decade.

The Updegrove children were afforded basic education, but like most children of the day they also went to work at a young age. As a young man, Daniel became a blacksmith's apprentice, but within a few years he started working as a coal miner. In the 1860s, the coal country of Pennsylvania was in full production, continuously expanding the mines and fueling the Union's war effort.

During the early days of the war, Daniel met and soon married Salome Ann Culp, a girl five years his junior, born on the final day of June 1844, in Union County, Pennsylvania. Her parents, Jacob Culp and Elizabeth

Schneck, had one son and five daughters. Culp is an anglicized versions of Kolb. The Culps and Schnecks were from Northumberland County—current day Union County—Pennsylvania and were of Germanic descent. Salome, commonly called Sarah, and her siblings lost their mother in 1861, while Daniel and Salome were courting. Jacob found his house emptying quickly, but still he was pleased to see his second youngest married at the age of eighteen. The eldest brother, Jonas, who was Daniel's age, respected Daniel and trusted him to care for his little sister. Elizabeth, Henrietta, and Esther advised their younger sibling about her coming role as a wife, and fourteen-year old Fielta seemed quite taken with Mr. Updegrove.

The handsome young man with sandy hair and grey eyes had actually charmed the entire family. On October 9, 1862, there was a wedding at the Culp house, attended by neighbors, friends, and family. The young couple would not have an easy start in their new life, however, as Daniel would soon be enlisted in the war effort.

Inspired by tales of his great-grandfather John Daniel Angst, who volunteered in Berks County and served under Captain Bretz in the American Revolution, several members of the Updegrove family would fight in the war, including Aaron Updegrove, Daniel Updegrove, Henry K. Updegrove, John Updegrove, and Solomon Updegrove. His ancestor Daniel Angst was also the inspiration of his name, Daniel.

Daniel and his brother Solomon signed up in July 1863, just after Independence Day, to fight for the Union. Enlisting in Harrisburg, the two were placed under Captain Edward Savage as privates in the 9th Cavalry, Company B, of the 92nd Regiment Pennsylvania Volunteers. This unit was known as the Lochiel Cavalry. This distinctively named unit's exploits were quite well known even during the war through the regular correspondence of Private George Unkle with the Daily Evening Express.

The unit saw extensive action in Kentucky and Tennessee, facing off against Confederate cavalry units that had given the Union army trouble in the early phases of the war. Accounts of the Lochiel Cavalry paint a heroic picture of determined men crossing rugged terrain "on half rations, food half cooked, and boots worn off their feet by tramping over the rocks to ease their own good horses, and trusting to Providence to keep down the wide and swift rivers that drain these wild mountains," as they set to destroy key railways and outmaneuver foes.

Standing 5 foot 5 inches, Private Daniel was built well for riding, light enough that his horse would not wear out too quickly. The Updegrove brothers served with honor, surviving many battles. Solomon was struck down in action at Waynesboro, Georgia, on December 4, 1864. This loss pained Daniel for the rest of his days. As a particularly strange coincidence, another Pennsylvania man, Solomon S. Updegrove, who served in the 18th Cavalry, 163rd Regiment, survived the war and went on to become a prominent citizen. This peculiarity likely added to Daniel's grief over his dead brother.

But the war was not yet over, and Daniel's suffering was not quite through. Not long after losing his brother, Daniel was captured and held as a prisoner of war for twenty-one days in Libby Prison, at Richmond, Virginia. This aged warehouse on the banks of the James River caused the death of many Union soldiers due to illness, exposure, and starvation. The windows were barred but not shut,

and the prison was so overcrowded that men covered every bit of floor as they attempted to sleep through their shivering. While some died quickly, others endured for months, even digging an underground tunnel and staging a successful escape.

In the largest prison escape of the war, 109 Union POWs made their way single-file through the tunnel. Discovery of the escape was delayed until morning, helping 59 of the inmates to escape safely under the command of Captain Tower and Colonel Davis. Two men drowned in the James River, and 48 were recaptured. Daniel was lucky to only stay there for three weeks before being released, likely when the Union Army overtook Richmond on April 3, 1865. On that day much of the city burned as Confederates attempted to destroy stockpiled goods and the nearly starved populace of the city rioted.

The civilwarindex.com wrote: Thirty-ninth Infantry. - Cols., John S. McCalmont, James T. Kirk, Adoniram J. Warner; Lieut.-Cols., James T. Kirk, Adoniram J. Warner, James B. Knox, Ira Ayer, Jr.; Majs., Harrison Allen, Sion B. Smith, Ira Ayer, Jr., C. Miller Over. This was the 10th reserve regiment and was composed of men from the western part of the state, who rendezvoused at Camp Wilkins, Pittsburg. It left camp on July 18, 1861, for Harrisburg, where it was mustered into the U. S. service on the 21st for a three years' term, and then moved to Washington. On Aug. 1 it was sent to Tennallytown, and after a short service at Great Falls was assigned to the 3d brigade. This brigade made its winter quarters at Langley; fought at Dranesville in December; was ordered to the Peninsula in the spring of 1862; took part in the battles of Mechanicsville, Gaines' mill, Glendale, the second Bull Run, South mountain, Antietam and Fredericksburg and won many laurels. After Fredericksburg the reserves were ordered to Washington to recuperate, and in June, 1863, side by side with its old comrades of the 3d brigade, the 39th fought at Gettysburg, afterward joining in the pursuit of the enemy. The regiment remained with the Army of the Potomac through the winter; took part in the Mine Run campaign; engaged at the Wilderness in May, 1864, and then fought at Spottsylvania, Totopotomoy, and Bethesda Church. Soon after the last named action the veterans and recruits were transferred to the 190th and 191st Pa. infantry and the regiment returned to Pittsburg, where it was mustered out on June 11, 1864.

Despite the suffering and uncertainty of the war, Daniel was able to make it home to his wife on occasion. They welcomed a daughter, Anna, in 1864. Another daughter, Clara Matilda, came two years later, followed by William Henry, who died as an infant in 1871, and Nora Jane, born in 1874. With only three surviving children, the Updegrove household was not large for the time, but it was full of activity.

Daniel returned to mining after the war and the family subsisted on this moderate livelihood. In 1860 he claimed $0 property and by 1870, $100—about $2,000 in today's standard. Although none of his contemporaries would be called well-off, certainly Daniel's family was the poorest and most underprivileged of the generations included. Of all the sixteen families of this generation, four families were extremely impoverished, the Updegroves, the Peters, the Rows and the McClouds. Both Daniel and Sarah had only a few years of schooling, having been pulled away from school to work in their youth. The 1870 census shows that they were able to read but not able to write.

There are sixteen couples in this generation, ten of which were fully literate, including the Thompson, Goodmans, Hensels, Batdorfs, Werts, McClouds, Oberlanders, Gauglers, Keefers and Livezlys. The Andersons and the Laymans of this generation, were slightly literate, where one adult was literate and one was not. Two families, the Peters and Rows, were completely illiterate.

The Updegrove family was the one and only family of this generation who became literate as adults, as ten years later in 1880, both Daniel and Sarah are able to read and write. Perhaps the intermittent unemployment due to accidents, labor disputes, and disruptions in the market that was characteristic of a coal miner's life—he had been unemployed for four months in 1880—afforded Daniel sufficient time for self-education.

Hard luck characterized much of Daniel's professional life. In 1887, Daniel lost a lawsuit over some 50 acres of property possessed by Mr. J. M. Blum—upon which much of the town of Williamstown was built—that had been previously owned by Daniel's father, John. John Updegrove had filed the same claim and lost in 1875, and Daniel was bringing the claim up again following his father's death. Residents of Williamstown were not overly worried, counting the case as a long shot, and indeed Updegrove's case was soon dismissed by the Pennsylvania Supreme Court. At 48 years old, Daniel's prospects for advancement were not bright. He had lost the case and there was little for him to do but continue as a miner.

The Brookside Colliery was one of the most productive coal mines in the world through much of the nineteenth century and into the twentieth century. It was under continual expansion at the tail end of the 1800s, with new slopes being sunk. One of the great challenges of engineering the expansion of mines was providing adequate ventilation. As the mine is expanded, the amount of airflow required to prevent coal dust from accumulating and igniting also increases. This expensive and time-consuming work was a bane of contention between management and labor, as demands for profits versus a safe working environment fueled labor activism.

This antagonistic relationship was often rekindled when such an accident would occur. One such tragedy came on May 23, 1899, claiming the life of Daniel Updegrove, who was suffocated by mine gas likely caused by an explosion. He was laid to rest a few days later, on May 28, just short of 60 years old, in Seyberts Lutheran Cemetery in Williamstown, Dauphin County, Pennsylvania.

Daniel would be survived by his wife, Sarah, and their three daughters. Daniel's military pension was a help to the family, but Sarah ended up taking work as a domestic servant to make ends meet. Sarah would live to watch the family grow and to help them carry on through hard times, including the growing pains of mechanization in the mines and the similarly mechanized Great War in Europe. Eventually, a recurrent case of carcinoma of the shoulder would bring her to rest at the age of 79. She was reunited with her husband on July 6, 1923, in Seyberts Lutheran Cemetery. Daniel and Sarah's descendants would proliferate in the new century, their daughter Clara Matilda being the direct ancestor of the Thompson line.

Daniel Updegrove was counted in the census in 1840 in Wiconisco, Dauphin County, Pennsylvania (w/father). He was educated at School in 1850. He was counted in the census in 1850 in Wiconisco, Dauphin County, Pennsylvania. He was counted in the census in 1860 in Brady, Lycoming County, Pennsylvania (w/Hullsizer family, near father's home in Clinton). He was employed as a Blacksmith apprentice in 1860. He served in the military on July 1, 1863 in Pennsylvania (Civil War, Private, 39th Regiment Infantry, Company H). He was employed as a Miner from 1864-1865. He lived in Dauphin County, Pennsylvania from 1864-1865. He served in the military about 1864 in Richmond, Virginia (Libby Prison, POW, 21 days). He served in the military about 1865 in Dauphin County, Pennsylvania (9th Calvary; Another Daniel Updegrove (husband of Elizabeth). He was counted in the census in 1870 in Williamstown, Dauphin County, Pennsylvania. He owned $100 in 1870. He was employed as a Laborer in mine in 1870. He was counted in the census in 1880 in Williamstown, Dauphin County, Pennsylvania. He was employed as a Laborer in 1880. He lived in in 1890.

He was employed as a Miner, Brookside Colliery in 1899. He was buried on May 28, 1899 in Williamstown, Dauphin County, Pennsylvania (Seyberts (Old) Lutheran). He was affiliated with the Lutheran religion. His height was 5 foot, 5 inches. He had a medical condition of Hair sandy, Complexion Light, Eyes gray. He was named after Great grandfather Daniel Angst. His cause of death was listed as suffocated by mine gas.

Salome "Sarah" Ann Culp was counted in the census in 1850 in West Buffalo, Union County, Pennsylvania. She was educated at School in 1850. She was counted in the census in 1860 in Buffalo, Union County, Pennsylvania. She was counted in the census in 1870 in Williamstown, Dauphin County, Pennsylvania. She was employed as a Keeping house from 1870-1880. She was counted in the census in 1880 in Williamstown, Dauphin County, Pennsylvania. Pension: May 1899 in Pennsylvania She was counted in the census in 1900. She lived in Pottsville St., Williams, Dauphin County, Pennsylvania in 1910. She was counted in the census in 1910 in Williamstown, Dauphin County, Pennsylvania (Shadel). She lived in Tower City, Schuylkill County, Pennsylvania in 1920 (25 West Grand Ave.). She was counted in the census in 1920 in Tower City, Schuylkill County, Pennsylvania (Weist). She was employed as a Domestic in 1923. Her funeral took place in 1923 in Williamstown, Dauphin County, Pennsylvania (Aaron Ralphsson). She was buried on July 6, 1923 in Williamstown, Dauphin County, Pennsylvania (Seyberts (Old) Lutheran). Her estate was probated April 1927 in Harrisburg, Dauphin County, Pennsylvania. She signed her will (Intestate). Her cause of death was due to carcinoma of shoulder recurrent. She was named after also nee Hoffman. S She was affiliated with the Lutheran religion.

PETER BATDORF
& ELIZABETH WELKER

In a sense, Peter Batdorf and his wife, Elizabeth Welker, were war babies. She was born on November 23 in 1812, four months after America declared war on Great Britain beginning the War of 1812. He was born January 20, 1814, eleven months before the treaty was signed ending the war. The war must have seemed distant to their families—the only Pennsylvania battle was at Lake Erie. News of the battle probably took a month to reach Dauphin County, Pennsylvania.

Peter and Elizabeth were born in Lykens Township, Dauphin County, at a time when America was less than forty years old. Both were namesakes, he named for his father and grandfather, both named Peter, and she for her mother, Maria Elizabeth Messerschmidt. Lykens is named for Andrew Lycans, as it was commonly spelled at the time. He settled on a tract of about two hundred acres on the Whiconescong Creek in 1755, near what is now Loyalton Borough. He cleared land and built houses for his family and a small group of subsequent settlers. Lycans lived in relative peace for no more than a year.

Then in 1756, during the French and Indian War, Lycans was driven from his home and eventually died while retreating from Indians. The Indians were allied with the French against the British and the colonists. The hostilities with the Indians ended in 1764, after which Lycan's widow returned to the old home.

By 1810, when Peter was born, the Indians had been driven to the west. Peter was the first of nine children of Jacob Peter Batdorf and Maria

Catherine Daniel. Sarah, John, Catherine, Thomas, Jonathan, Daniel, Jacob, and Elizabeth were Peter's young siblings. The elder Peter was born in 1793 and his wife Elizabeth was born in 1792, both of Germanic descent. Senior Peter and wife Elizabeth were born in adjacent Berks County. The couple settled in Lykens, merely fifty miles from where they hailed.

Elizabeth Welker was the fourth child of John Welker and Maria Elizabeth Messerschmidt, both natives of Dauphin County. John was born in 1783 of German-Swiss descent, and Maria Elizabeth arrived in 1780 from a heritage of Germany. John's father, Valentine, and Maria's grandfather Andrew Messerschmidt, were honorable American Revolutionary soldiers. Elizabeth followed siblings George, Rachel, and a daughter whose name is not known. Her younger siblings were William, David, Anna, Sarah, and Joseph.

Peter was nineteen and Elizabeth was twenty-one when they were married in 1831, most likely in St. Peter's Reformed Church in nearby Loyalton. Also known as the Hoffman Church, it was erected about 1771 by Anthony Hautzon on land donated by the Hoffman family, early settlers in Lykens Township. Peter was baptized there and both he and Elizabeth were buried there. They both died in Dauphin County—she in 1868, he in 1880.

In each census during their lifetimes, Peter and Elizabeth were counted in Lykens Township—not to be confused with Lykens Borough, which was settled within the township in 1832, but not incorporated until 1871. The township was incorporated in 1810 covering fifty square miles in northern Dauphin County. In 1839, it was divided to form Wisconisco Township. In the pre-Civil War nineteenth century, Lykens Township was a remote area of scattered farms in a stunning green valley teeming with wildlife and fishing creeks. The population density was less ten per square mile.

Peter and Elizabeth would live out their lives where they were born. It's not likely they ever traveled more than ten to twenty miles from their home. There was nothing unusual about that. Travel was by wagon over dirt roads that were little more than widened and packed Indian trails. Moving a large family would have been daunting. Besides where would Peter and Elizabeth go, and to do what?

The American economy took off after the War of 1812. The steam engine, patented in 1783 by James Watt, came into widespread use in factories and mills, especially in New England and major cities in the East. But the Industrial Revolution was slow in coming to remote and sparsely populated rural areas like the Lykens Valley. There were no factories in the Dauphin County in the early decades of the nineteenth century. The first known stationary steam engine, as opposed to those used in trains and the ferries at Millersburg and Harrisburg, was brought to Lykens in 1830, when the Lycans settlement consisted of no more than thirty log homes.

Because of these conditions, the Lykens Valley economy was only marginally monetary-based before the Civil War. Self-sufficiency and barter drove the citizens' lives. Peter was self-sufficient as a Yeoman. Though "Yeoman" is commonly thought of as a low naval rank in nineteenth-century America, it also meant a family farmer who owned a small plot of land. Elizabeth kept house and probably made clothes to be handed down for their eleven children, at least in the early years of their marriage. While the first store was opened in the Lykens settlement in 1832, it wasn't until after the Civil War that mercantiles offered factory-made clothes affordable to average folks like the Batdorfs.

Esther was the first born of Peter and Elizabeth's children, followed by Jonas, Elizabeth, Susan, John, Sarah, Peter, Anna, Rebecca, Thomas, and Louisa. The family was closer to average than large for the time period.

Peter was probably a Yeoman for the first a decade or so of their marriage. In the 1840s, as Dauphin became more connected by canals and rail, he may have farmed cash crops such as wheat. In 1825, coal was discovered on Short Mountain overlooking Lykens Valley. This was no ordinary coal, but anthracite of the first order—89 percent carbon. It was shipped crudely by wagon until 1832, when the Lykens Valley Railroad and Coal Company was created by an act of the legislature. The railroad created a need for coal mining laborers that grew exponentially when local breakers were built, the first being erected in Dauphin County in 1848 right in Lykens.

Steam engines would come into widespread use in Dauphin with the rise of the coal industry. They were used to drive pumps, fans and conveyers before the collieries made electricity. The breakers increased coal production for the Civil War effort, the growth of factories, and large-scale iron forges. The need for laborers could be met only one way—immigration. They came from Scotland, Ireland, Germany, and other parts of Europe, doubling the population of Dauphin County in the mid-nineteenth century. Though the anthracite mines were notorious for accidents and worker exploitation, the coal greatly enhanced the Dauphin economy and sped technological advances.

Peter was literate, Elizabeth's ability was probably basic, and in 1870 Peter's second wife is listed as illiterate. There are sixteen couples in this generation, ten of which were fully literate, including the Thompson, Goodmans, Hensels, Batdorfs, Werts, McClouds, Oberlanders, Gauglers, Keefers and Livezlys. The Andersons and the Laymans of this generation,

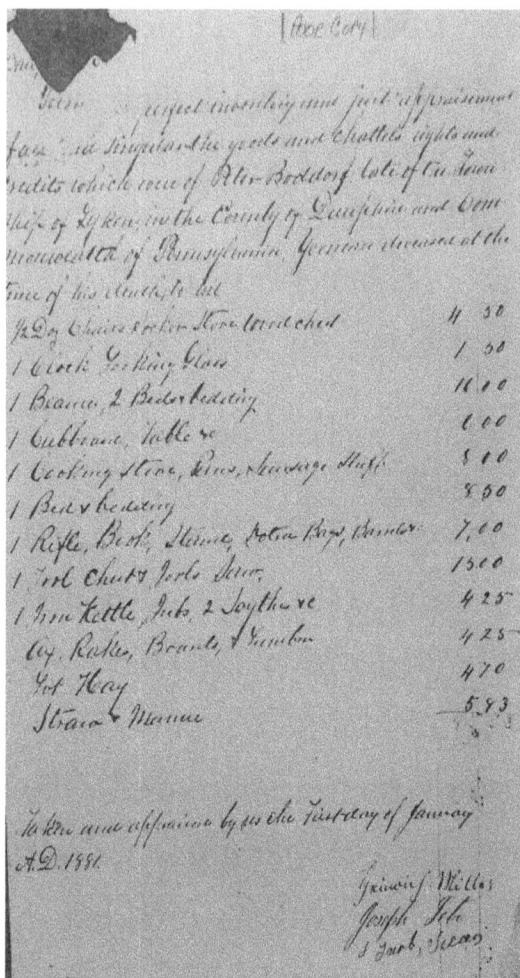

were slightly literate, where one adult was literate and one was not. Two families, the Peters and Rows, were completely illiterate. The Updegrove family became literate as adults and the Dankerts were Germans, the only couple of this generation not in America.

Peter entered his fifties during the Civil War. He was too old to be drafted, but took advantage of the ancillary jobs created by burgeoning coal industry and the war. Peter worked as a carpenter from 1850 to 1870. He may have been building log homes and churches for immigrant families. He might also have helped build furniture, canal locks, or railroads ties. The family property value increased steadily from 1850 to 1870, from $500 to $1150 to $1400, equating to about $25,000 in today value.

After Elizabeth died in 1868, Peter married Magdalena "Mollie" Lettich. His marriage to Mollie, and his advancing age, may have prompted Peter to go back to farming. He may have been aided by organizations of farmers, such as the Grange, that fought to improve the conditions for yeomen. The Pennsylvania Grange was organized in 1873. When Peter and Mollie married they were beyond childbearing years, but Peter and Elizabeth's second youngest, Thomas, was the direct ancestor of the Thompson line.

Peter Batdorf was baptized on February 27, 1814 in Loyalton, Dauphin County, Pennsylvania (St. Peters (Hoffman) Reformed). He was counted in the census in 1820 in Lykens, Dauphin County, Pennsylvania (w/father). He was counted in the census in 1830 in Lykens, Dauphin County, Pennsylvania (w/father). He was counted in the census in 1840 in Lykens, Dauphin County, Pennsylvania. He was employed as a Yeoman about 1840. He was counted in the census in 1850 in Lykens, Dauphin County, Pennsylvania. He owned $500 in 1850. He was employed as a Carpenter from 1850-1870. He lived in Wiconisco, Dauphin County, Pennsylvania in 1858. He owned $900 + $250 in 1860. He was counted in the census in 1860 in Lykens, Dauphin County, Pennsylvania. He owned $1000 + $400 in 1870. He was counted in the census in 1870 in Lykens, Dauphin County, Pennsylvania. He was employed as a Farmer in 1880. He was buried in 1880 in Loyalton, Dauphin County, Pennsylvania (St. Peters (Hoffman) Reformed). He was counted in the census in 1880 in Lykens, Dauphin County, Pennsylvania. His estate was probated on January 4, 1881 in Dauphin County, Pennsylvania. He signed his will (Intestate, Inventory at Dauphin County). He was named after Jacob Peter Batdorf, father. He was affiliated with the Reformed < Lutheran religion.

Elizabeth Welker was counted in the census in 1820 in Lykens, Dauphin County, Pennsylvania (w/father). She was counted in the census in 1830 in Lykens, Dauphin County, Pennsylvania (w/father). She was counted in the census in 1840 in Lykens, Dauphin County, Pennsylvania (w/husband). She was employed as a Homemaker about 1840. She was counted in the census in 1850 in Lykens, Dauphin County, Pennsylvania. Her estate was probated about 1854 (Elizabeth was not mentioned in father's will). She was counted in the census in 1860 in Lykens, Dauphin County, Pennsylvania. She was buried in 1868 in Loyalton, Dauphin County, Pennsylvania (St. Peters (Hoffman) Reformed). She signed her will (Intestate). She was affiliated with the Reformed religion. She was named after Maria Elizabeth Messerschmidt, her mother.

SAMUEL PETERS
& MARY A. SWARTZ

How remote was Union County, Pennsylvania, when Samuel Peters was born there in 1821? In 1821, the Pennsylvania Canal system hadn't yet reached Union. A railroad connection was forty-plus years away. Fewer than fifty years earlier, the area was on the frontier of European settlement. The County had been formed in 1813 when land west of the Susquehanna River was separated from Northumberland County. It was divided into Union and Snyder counties in 1855. Samuel was the first born of five children of Leonard Peters and Susan Enders. Both of the families are of presumably German ancestry. Samuel was followed by brother John, and a sisters Margaret and Barbara.

Samuel's father, Leonard, was born in Dauphin County in 1787 and lived in Dauphin County, Pennsylvania where he met and married Susan. As with most of the early settlers of Dauphin County, Leonard likely migrated there for work or to acquire land, which was being allotted by application.

When Samuel grew up he did not go to school, as there weren't any in the Buffalo area. In 1834, the state legislature passed a bill mandating counties to create common, or public, schools. Afraid of the cost, most of which had to be met at the local level, Union County created a committee of fifteen men to draft a resolution objecting to the bill. It passed in Union Township 154 to 12 in 1840. Countywide the vote was 1,620 to 267. As soon as Samuel was old enough—eight or so—he most likely worked for his father on the family's subsistence farm.

When he was thirteen in 1834, a "black" frost hit the Buffalo Valley on May 31 and June 1. It was so cold that whole orchards of apples, pears, and cherries were killed. Bears looking for food came down from the mountains to feed on green corn and scores were killed by farmers. Birds survived and thrived, as caterpillars were prodigious.

Samuel went out on his own when he married Mary Ann Swartz, who had been born in nearby Juniata County in 1821 to Peter and Maria Christina Swartz. Juniata County was formed on March 2, 1831, from parts of Mifflin County. Peter Swartz, was a native Pennsylvanian, born in 1774, and Maria Christina in 1771. Research seems to dictate these two families were also of German heritage.

Samuel and Mary Ann were married about 1842, when both were in their early twenties. They may have been married at the Lutheran and Reformed Church that was dedicated in Buffalo Township in 1839. In the 1840 census, Samuel was living with his mother and Mary Ann was living with her father in Union Township, Union County. By 1850, they were counted together in the census in Union County with three children; the oldest, John, was six. They had six more children: Emma, Jonathan, Matthew, Matilda, and twins Jane and Mary Louisa, who were born in 1858.

There are sixteen couples in this generation, ten of which were fully literate, including the Thompson, Goodmans, Hensels, Batdorfs, Werts, McClouds, Oberlanders, Gauglers, Keefers and Livezlys. The Andersons and the Laymans of this generation, were slightly literate, where one adult was literate and one was not. Two families, the Peters represented here and Rows, were completely illiterate. The Updegrove family became literate as adults and the Dankerts were Germans, the only couple of this generation not in America.

There were merely 242 families in Union Township in 1850 and a total population of 1,436. Nearly every family had its own home. There were 235 dwellings in the township. There was one merchant and two clerks at the township's only mercantile business. There was one inn and one physician. Three men were employed as lime burners. There were a smattering of blacksmiths and wheelwrights, but eighty-five percent of the men worked as farmers or laborers, Samuel among them.

In the mid-nineteenth century, there was plenty of labor to be done in Central Pennsylvania. Forested land had to be cleared for the building of settlements, roads, rail beds, gristmills, dams, and canals. Much of the money for such projects came from lotteries. The Union Canal lottery was conducted in 1826. Sometime in the 1850s Samuel and Mary Ann moved east to Mifflin Township in Dauphin County, where Peters was a common surname. Peters Mountain runs for thirty miles in central Dauphin County.

Dauphin was further east and closer to the roads and rail lines to Philadelphia, York, and Harrisburg than Union. Dauphin had been settled earlier and was more progressive, more populated, more developed and richer than Union. For example, Dauphin had a good school system, with nine one-room schoolhouses, as early as 1830. It is likely Samuel and Mary moved for better work opportunities for Samuel, but the existence of good schools may also have been a lure. Perhaps Mary, who could not read and write, wanted better for her children. It is known that Jonathan and Tillie, at least, went to school in Dauphin.

In 1860, Samuel was still working as a laborer at a time when there was even more work available. The anthracite coal industry was heating up in Dauphin County. Though it is believed Samuel never worked directly for a coal company, the industry created peripheral work. Better road and railroads were needed for the industry. Homes, churches, and schools were needed in the boroughs for the immigrant mineworkers. Samuel could have worked as a laborer for farmers, road builders, carpenters, or stonemasons.

The farmers also benefited from the better roads and railroads as they moved from subsistence farming to the commercial farming of food for cities. Philadelphia was having a growth spurt of its own, and could not feed itself. Dauphin County provided commercial quantities of wheat, corn, linseed oil, rye, and whiskey. The Civil War build-up—which began when Lincoln was re-elected President in November—and the war itself also increased economic activity and work.

The Peters family had no property value in 1850, and $150 by 1860. This is the equivalent of about $3,500. After Samuel passed, Mary was head of household in 1870 with a property value of only $100. Of all the sixteen families of this generation, four families were extremely impoverished, the Updegroves, the Peters, the Rows and the McClouds. There seems to be a chance Samuel fought and died in the Civil War, as we find no record of him after 1861. There was a Samuel Peters who was a soldier from the area, but it has not been proven to be our Samuel.

During the war, Samuel went to Perry County, a small county that bordered Dauphin at the Susquehanna north of Harrisburg in the Millersburg area. It's not known what Samuel was doing in Perry County. What is known is that he died there in before 1865 and that before he left Dauphin he and Mary had one last child, Mary Louisa. Perry wasn't far from Samuel's home in Dauphin by rail or from where he grew up in Union by ferry. He was only 44 was buried in Perry County.

Mary Ann outlived Samuel by thirty-two years. After his death she moved to the Lykens area and worked as a housekeeper. In the 1880s she retired and moved in with her daughter, Jane, and her husband Alfred Row in Washington Township, Dauphin County. She was seventy-five when she died in 1897 of heart disease. She was buried in St. Johns Oakdale Cemetery, Loyalton. Samuel and May left a legacy— family. Their caboose Mary, one of the twins they had in their late thirties, turned out to be the direct line to the Thompson family.

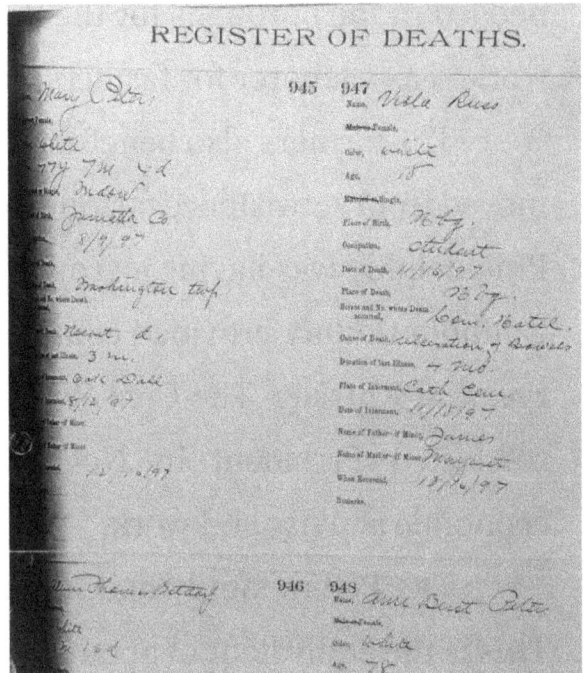

Samuel Peters was counted in the census in 1830 in Buffalo, Union County, Pennsylvania (w/father). He was counted in the census in 1840 in Buffalo, Union County, Pennsylvania (w/grandfather Peters). He was employed as a Laborer in 1850. He owned $0 in 1850. He was counted in the census in 1850 in Union, Union (Snyder) County, Pennsylvania. He lived in Washington, Dauphin County, Pennsylvania in 1858 (Uniontown (Pillow). He was counted in the census in 1860 in Mifflin, Dauphin County, Pennsylvania. He was employed as a Laborer in 1860. He owned $150 in 1860. He was buried circa 1865 in Perry County, Pennsylvania. He served in the military (Research should be done into Samuel's possible Civil War service and resulting death.).

Mary Ann Swartz was counted in the census in 1820 in McAllistertown (MacAllisterville), Greenwood, Mifflin (Juniata) County, Pennsylvania (w/father). She was counted in the census in 1830 in Greenwood, Juniata County, Pennsylvania (w/father). She was counted in the census in 1840 in Greenwood, Juniata County, Pennsylvania (w/father). She was counted in the census in 1850 in Union, Union County, Pennsylvania. She was counted in the census in 1860 in Mifflin, Dauphin County, Pennsylvania. She lived in Lykens Township, Dauphin County, Pennsylvania in 1862 (Near Specktown and Mountain Road). She was employed as a Keeping house in 1870. She owned $100 in 1870. She was counted in the census in 1870 in Lykens,

Dauphin County, Pennsylvania. She lived in Lykens, Dauphin County, Pennsylvania in 1875 (State Road 199). She was counted in the census in 1880 in Washington, Dauphin County, Pennsylvania (w/Row). She was employed as a Retired house keeper in 1880. She was buried on August 12, 1897 in Loyalton, Dauphin County, Pennsylvania (St. Johns (Oakdale) Cemetery; There are unmarked stones for this family near large tree). Her cause of death was Heart disease. She signed her will (Intestate). She was affiliated with the Lutheran religion. She was named after Mother Maria.

DAVID M. WERT
& CATHERINE SHOOP

David Wert was the son of parents who bucked the odds. His father, Jacob Wert, and mother, Sarah Elizabeth Faber, both native Pennsylvanians, were born in 1804 and 1807, respectively, when the average life expectancy was forty-five years. Jacob lived to eighty-four and Sarah lived to ninety-five. Jacob's grandfather John Miller and Sarah's two grandfathers, John Faber and Jonas Rudy, all fought for American Independence. The Werts were of German ancestry and the Rudy of German-Swiss roots.

Though not as long-lived as his parents, David did live to seventy-one, a longer-than-average lifespan in the nineteenth century. During his life, David worked as a laborer, was married twice, and fathered fourteen children. But it was one of the ten children he had with his first wife, Catherine Shoop, who is of most interest here.

David was born in Powells Valley, Dauphin County, Pennsylvania, on All Fool's Day of 1829. David was the oldest of nine siblings, followed by Elizabeth, Catherine, Sarah, John, Adam, Peter, Matthew, and Martha. He died two years before his mother on December 9, 1900, in Dayton, Dauphin County, Pennsylvania, of lung congestion. He was buried from the Calvary United Methodist, or Union, Church in Wiconisco, Dauphin County. Wisconisco was laid out in 1848. The church was erected in 1854.

David married Catherine Shoop about 1849 in Dauphin County. He was twenty and she was nineteen. Catherine was the daughter of John Shoop and Sarah Wertz, both of distant German ancestry. John's grandfather John George Schupp and Sarah's grandfather Michael Garman helped defend our freedoms, soldiering during the American Revolution. Catherine was born on February 24, 1830, in Northumberland County, which borders Dauphin to the north. Catherine was baptized on March 6, 1830, in the Stone Valley Reformed Lutheran Church, named for her maternal grandmother Catherine Garman Wertz. The church was established in the 1770s. She was the second oldest of four girls. Her older sister was Anna Shoop and her younger sisters were Anna Maria, Elizabeth, and Salome.

David and Catherine probably met at a church function or through relatives. In any case, they didn't live far apart. Catherine was counted in the census in 1830 and 1840 with her father in Lower Mahanoy, Northumberland County, which was about ten to fifteen miles from Halifax, Dauphin County, where David was counted in the census in 1830 and 1840 with his family.

Both David and Catherine were literate. There are sixteen couples in this generation, ten of which were fully literate, including the Thompson, Goodmans, Hensels, Batdorfs, Werts, McClouds, Oberlanders, Gauglers, Keefers and Livezlys. The Andersons and the Laymans of this generation, were slightly literate, where one adult was literate and one was not. Two families, the Peters and Rows, were completely illiterate. The Updegrove family became literate as adults and the Dankerts were Germans, the only couple of this generation not in America.

After they married, David and Catherine moved to Upper Paxton, Dauphin County, which was right between their families' homes in Halifax and Lower Mahanoy. They most likely moved for work, though being equidistant from their families was a plus. Upper Paxton was bordered by Mahantango Mountain to the north, Berry Mountain to the south, and the Susquehanna River to the west. The nearest town, Millersburg, was an important ferry town on the river. The area was rich with timber, streams, and wildlife.

As a laborer, David might have worked building roads, laying rail, and digging canals, though more likely as a farmer. They lived in Upper Paxton in the early 1850s, but in the late 1850s, they moved to her home area of Lower Mahanoy, Northumberland County. David was not drafted during the Civil War—though he was well within age, being thirty—but he was married with four children under age six, and that may have been a factor for his exclusion.

Perhaps prompted by Catherine's father's death in 1859, David and Catherine moved again to the Lykens area of Washington Township in Dauphin County, where they were counted in the census of 1870. By then they had all of their ten children: Elizabeth, Anna, John Henry, Mary, Melinda, Martha, Catherine, Amelia, Daniel, and Isaac. David likely worked as a farm laborer for one of their neighbors. There was plenty of work—the area was booming economically with the growth of the anthracite coal industry.

Immigrants were moving to the area to work the mines and they had to be fed, clothed, and housed. Also, commercial farming was growing as families moved into the cities following the Civil War, where they were more likely to buy food than to grow it. This was the beginning of a trend that would accelerate with the Industrial Revolution.

Recreation in the Dauphin area in the eighteenth century revolved around family, church, neighborhoods, organizations such as the Grange, and work. Families gathered at holidays, churches held socials, neighbors got together to build barns and Granges, and workplaces threw picnics with games for kids and adults. The Wert family claimed merely $100 in property in 1850 and 1860, but with a slightly prosperous 1860s, it increased to $1400 by 1870. This is about $26,000 in today's money.

Catherine died on June 8, 1872. She was buried from St. Peters Reformed Lutheran Church, also known as the Hoffman Church, in Loyalton, Dauphin County, near Lykens. After Catherine's death, David moved by himself to Union Township, Berks County, where he was counted in the 1880 census as a boarder of Winfred Allison, a widower with three young children.

Son John, then fifteen, went to live with Jacob and Elizabeth Seiler in Jackson Township, Northumberland County. His sisters Martha and Catherine lived with families in the Lykens area as maids or servants. By 1900, David and second wife, Elizabeth Bellis, moved back to Washington Township, Dauphin County.

The many place names mentioned above might leave the impression that the families traveled widely in the eighteenth century, but they didn't. Powells Valley, Stone Valley, Upper Paxton, Lower Mahanoy, Lykens, Washington Township, Jackson Township, Wisconisco, Halifax, and the counties of Dauphin, Northumberland, and Union are all within five to twenty-five miles of each other and the larger Lykens Valley area.

The climate was moderate with plenty of rain. All the areas had similar landscapes of lush valleys and rolling mountains of hardwood trees—such as oak, chestnut, hickory, and beech—and softer woods like white pine. But these landscapes changed during David's lifetime. When Europeans first explored the area, trees covered more than 90 percent of Dauphin County's 400,000 acres. But steel plows and axles allowed European settlers to quickly clear large areas of forest for subsistence farming. There were probably one thousand subsistence farms in Dauphin County by 1860.

In the later part of the century, clear-cutting to lay out towns and facilitate mining destroyed large swaths of forest. By the 1850s, Pennsylvania was the nation's largest supplier of lumber and other wood products such as wood alcohol and tannic acid from hemlock, used to process hides. By 1900, the year David died, Dauphin had lost more than 60 percent of its forests. Rain washed soil from the clear-cut areas into streams, and forest fires burned through the dead stumps, dry branches, scrub brush, and saplings, ruining fish and wildlife habitat.

The Europeans saw the forests as dollar signs and as an impediment to development. Little attention was paid to the negative effects of clear-cutting until the Pennsylvania Commission of Forestry was founded in 1901. After World War I, many rural Pennsylvanians moved into the cities and abandoned farms were reforested.

David Wert was not one of those who moved to a city, though by 1890s— when he moved to Lykens—it was a well-developed area due to the economic spillover of the anthracite industry. David was still working as a laborer right up until his death in 1900. It was David's son John Henry who was the direct ancestor of the Thompson line.

David M Wert was counted in the census in 1830 in Halifax, Dauphin County, Pennsylvania (w/father). He was counted in the census in 1840 in Jackson, Dauphin County, Pennsylvania (w/father). He was counted in the census in 1850 in Upper Paxton, Dauphin County, Pennsylvania. He was employed as a Laborer in 1850. He owned $100 in 1850. He lived in Upper Paxton Township, Dauphin County, Pennsylvania in 1858 (Killinger, Central Township area). He was counted in the census in 1860 in Lower Mahanoy Northumberland County, Pennsylvania. He owned $100 in 1860. He lived in Washington, Dauphin County, Pennsylvania in 1864. He was employed as a Farmer in 1864. He was employed as a Laborer in 1870. He owned $1000 + $400 in 1870. He was counted in the census in 1870 in Lykens, Dauphin County, Pennsylvania. He was counted in the census in 1880. He was employed as a Laborer in 1900. He was counted in the census in 1900 in Washington, Dauphin County, Pennsylvania (West). He was buried on December 12, 1900 in Wiconisco, Dauphin County, Pennsylvania (Calvary United Methodist Cemetery w/second wife Elizabeth). He was affiliated with the Lutheran religion. His cause of death was Congestion of Lungs.

Catherine Shoop was counted in the census in 1830 in Lower Mahanoy, Northumberland County, Pennsylvania (w/father). She was baptized on March 6, 1830 in Dalmatia, Northumberland County, Pennsylvania (Zion (Stone Valley) Lutheran). She was counted in the census in 1840 in Lower Mahanoy, Northumberland County, Pennsylvania (w/father). She was counted in the census in 1850 in Upper Paxtang, Dauphin County, Pennsylvania. She was counted in the census in 1850 in Lower Mahanoy, Northumberland County, Pennsylvania (Catherine is in both her parent's and husband's household. Catherine Shoop and Catherine Baker must be designated clearly.). She was counted in the census in 1860 in Lower Mahanoy Northumberland County, Pennsylvania. She was employed as a Keeping house in 1870. She was counted in the census in 1870 in Lykens, Dauphin County, Pennsylvania. She was buried in 1872 in Loyalton, Dauphin County, Pennsylvania (St. Peters (Hoffman) Reformed). Her estate was probated on June 23, 1880 in Dauphin County, Pennsylvania.

She signed her will (Intestate). She was affiliated with the Lutheran/Reformed religion. She was named after Joanna Catherine Garman, her grandmother.

DANIEL ROW
& SUSAN FRANTZ

Daniel Row was born on July 10, 1813, in Dauphin County, Pennsylvania. Though the War of 1812, being fought at the time, had no impact in Dauphin County, numerous Dauphinites enlisted to ward of the United Kingdom threat, including his future father-in-law, Adam Frantz. The only Pennsylvania Battle was on Lake Erie, where Captain Perry defeated the British two months after Daniel was born.

Daniel was the third child of John William Rowe and Barbara Rudy. Adding to the service-front, Daniel's two grandfather, Francis Rowe and Jacob Rudy, fought for American Independence and a William Rowe did fight in the War of 1812, quite possibly Daniel's father. Daniel's older siblings were Wendell and Jacob. His younger siblings were Susan, John, Elizabeth, Sarah, and Joseph.

The Rowe and Rudy families were of German descent. Daniel lived to age fifty-eight. He died on the final day of July in 1871, in Dauphin County. Though that was a fairly long life for the time, he was outlived by both his parents. His father, John William, was born in June 1785 in Strasburg, Lancaster County, Pennsylvania, and lived to age ninety-two, dying in 1877 in Berrysburg, Dauphin County. Daniel's mother, Barbara, was born in April 1796 also in Strasburg. She died at age eighty-five on December 15, 1881, also in Berrysburg, Dauphin County.

Daniel's parents migrated to Dauphin from Strasburg, Pennsylvania soon after they married, probably around 1810. The Strasburg-Lancaster area was more developed than Dauphin County, which was an area of forests pockmarked by subsistence farms. It is likely Daniel and Susan moved for the adventure—a desire to strike out on their own and for land—perhaps urged on by relatives who were already in Dauphin.

It wasn't an easy journey. Though only 75 miles, the journey likely took a week to ten days by Conestoga wagon, stagecoach, or on foot or horseback. They may have been in a caravan of settlers traveling on dirt roads that were little more than widened Indian trails passing through the Blue, Second, and Peters Mountains. In any case, when Daniel was born, they were in Dauphin in the Halifax area. John was working as a farm laborer.

Daniel married Susan Frantz, a native of Dauphin County, in the late 1830s when she was in her late teens and he was twenty-five. This is evident because both were living with their parents in 1830 and they were together in 1840. Susan Frantz was born March 23, 1819 to a family of American Germans. She was named for her mother, Susan Giesemen, who was born in 1787 in Tulpehocken, Berks County. Her father, Adam Frantz, was born in 1780 in Lykens, Dauphin County. She was the third youngest of their eight children. Her older siblings were William, Jacob, Catherine, John, and Christina and her younger siblings were Sarah and Samuel.

There are sixteen couples in this generation, ten of which were fully literate, including the Thompson, Goodmans, Hensels, Batdorfs, Werts, McClouds, Oberlanders, Gauglers, Keefers and Livezlys. The Andersons and the Laymans of this generation, were slightly literate, where one adult was literate and one was not. Two families, the Peters and Rows of whom this narrative details, were completely illiterate. The Updegrove family became literate as adults and the Dankerts were Germans, the only couple of this generation not in America. However, the Rows did afford their children education benefits that were denied them, as their offspring could all read and write.

Unlike her husband's parents, Susan's parents died young. Her father was in his forties when died between 1825 and 1830 in Dauphin County. Her mother was forty-nine when she died in 1826. It was a fate that would also befall Susan. She died in 1861 at age forty-two, with four young girls—Susan, Amelia, Leah, and Adeline—still living at home. The girls were four of the seven children of Daniel and Susan. Their older siblings were Sarah, Angeline, and Adam, the lone son.

After Susan's death, the family scattered. In 1870, Daniel—who would die within a year—was living with Jacob Zerber in Berrysburg and still working as a laborer. Daughter Susan was eighteen and working as a cook in a boarding home near Berrysburg. Amelia was living with David Matter, a successful farmer in Washington Township. Leah was living with John Lebo, a butcher in Lykens. Adeline was just three doors away living with her aunt Susan Ely and attending school. Daniel never attended school and was illiterate, not an unusual circumstance for men of his generation who worked farms in rural Pennsylvania.

But Daniel had a descendant who was different: Daniel's nephew, Jonas Row was one of the most interesting members of the extended family. Jonas was a farmer, yes, but he attended school. Over the years, he was active in politics and was a supervisor of roads, a tax collector, and a justice of the peace. He was also a butcher and a merchant. Somehow he found time to be a deacon, trustee, and Sunday-school superintendent and teacher in the Lutheran Church. During the Civil War in 1863, Jonas enlisted in the Union Army at Harrisburg. Assigned to the One Hundred and Twenty-seventh Regiment, Pennsylvania volunteers, under Colonel Jennings and Captain

Bell, he participated in the battle of Gettysburg and was wounded in the knee. He was discharged after only three months' service. Though the wound left him lame him for life, it didn't stop him from re-enlisting in the fall of 1863. With Company F, Sixteenth Pennsylvania, he was at Petersburg for five days, where bravery in action got him promoted to the rank of Orderly to General Gregg. Jonas was at the surrender of General Lee, and was mustered out of service in 1865. After the war, he bought fifty-five acres and sunk $5,000 into developing a farm. He took a loss on that farm after using it as security for a loan for a friend. But again, he was not stopped from achieving his goals. He bought another eighty acres in Jefferson Township near Lykens and built a successful farm. Well-known and highly respected, he died in Schuylkill County at the age of eighty-two.

In 1871 Bright's disease, a chronic inflammation of kidneys, caused the demise of Daniel. For the first half of Daniel's life, the economy of the Lykens Valley area of Dauphin County was subsistence farming and the few peripheral businesses needed to support the farms, such as blacksmiths and lime burners, who burned limestone to create lime for fertilizer. There was very little commerce. Three things changed that in the second half of Daniel's life: the growth of the anthracite coal industry, the Civil War, and the emergence of the industrial revolution. Improved roads, the Pennsylvania canal system, and rail lines connected the area to the outside world. Timber, coal, and farm products became valuable commodities. Money replaced barter and banks were established in the towns such as Lykens, Berrysburg, and Elizabethville.

Daniel was always counted as a nonspecific laborer in the census reports during his adult life. Though he wasn't a union miner or railroader, it's not hard to imagine him doing any or all of the necessary down-to-earth labor the modernization of Dauphin County required. There was plenty of work for a man with a strong back and a shovel. The Row family was only valued at $240 in 1850 and even less in 1860, at $200, about $5,000 and by 1870 he was, as mentioned, living with his son-in-law Jacob, carrying no property value. Of all the sixteen families of this generation, four families were extremely impoverished, the Updegroves, the Peters, the Rows and the McClouds.

Daniel was buried from the St. John's Lutheran Church in Berrysburg, Dauphin County, just as his wife, Susan, had been ten years earlier. Also known as the "Church of the Hill," it was the same church where Daniel was baptized in 1813. It was also the same church where generations of the extended family were baptized, married, and buried. The "Church of the Hill" had been built of stone on a hill overlooking the Lykens Valley in 1872, replacing a log church built in 1802. The parish roots dated back to 1773, when the Reverend J. Enderline, a pioneer missionary, came to Lykens Valley. Daniel and Susan's youngest daughter, Adeline, was the direct line ancestor to the Thompson family.

Daniel Row was baptized on August 14, 1813 in Berrysburg, Dauphin County, Pennsylvania (St. Johns (Hill) Lutheran). He was counted in the

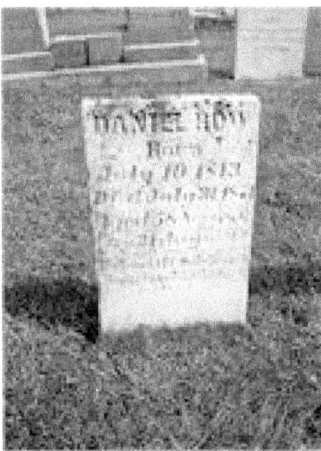

census in 1820 in Mifflin, Dauphin County, Pennsylvania (w/father). He was counted in the census in 1830 in Halifax, Dauphin County, Pennsylvania (w/father). He was counted in the census in 1840 in Wiconisco, Dauphin County, Pennsylvania. He owned $240 in 1850. He was counted in the census in 1850 in Washington, Dauphin County, Pennsylvania. He was employed as a Laborer from 1850-1870. He owned $200 in 1860. He was counted in the census in 1860 in Washington, Dauphin County, Pennsylvania. He owned $0 in 1870. He was counted in the census in 1870 in Wiconisco, Dauphin County, Pennsylvania. He was buried in July 1871 in Berrysburg, Dauphin

County, Pennsylvania (St. Johns (Hill) Lutheran). His estate was probated on August 28, 1871 in Dauphin County, Pennsylvania (1873 Orphans Court). He was affiliated with the Lutheran religion. His cause of death was Bright's disease (i.e., chronic inflammation of kidneys).

Susan Frantz was counted in the census in 1820 in Mifflin, Dauphin County, Pennsylvania (w/father). She was counted in the census in 1830 (w/family, both parents passed). She was counted in the census in 1840 in Wiconisco, Dauphin County, Pennsylvania (w/husband). She was counted in the census in 1850 in Washington, Dauphin County, Pennsylvania. She was counted in the census in 1860 in Washington, Dauphin County, Pennsylvania. She was buried in 1861 in Berrysburg, Dauphin County, Pennsylvania (St. Johns (Hill) Lutheran). She was affiliated with the Lutheran religion. She signed her will (Intestate). She was named after Susan Gieseman, her mother. She was employed as a Homemaker.

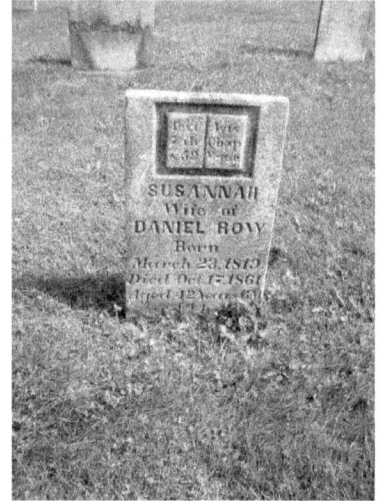

W. GEHRHART HEINRICH
& M.C. HENRIETTE KELLING

William Gehrhart Heinrich Dankert, son of John Peter George Dankert and Catharine Magdalena Westphals was born on December 13, 1797 in Gressow, Germany. He died about Abt. 1850 in Prussia. He married Maria Carolina Henriette Kelling, daughter of Nicholas Kelling and Anna Dorothy Koppelmann in 1817 in Germany. Maria Carolina Henriette Kelling, daughter of Nicholas Kelling and Anna Dorothy Koppelmann was born on July 27, 1794 in Hohenkirchen, Mecklenburg Schwerin, Germany.

She died on January 31, 1865 in Hohenkirchen, Mecklenburg-Schwerin, Germany. The Dankerts and Kellings and their ancestry resided in the Northern German area of Mecklenberg. Maria Carolina Henriette Kelling and William Gehrhart Heinrich Dankert had the following children: Friedrich Heinrich Dankert, Margaretha Sophia Dorothea Dankert, Carl Johan Rudolph Dankert, Maria Sophia Dorothea Dankert, Sophia Dorothea Magdelena Dankert and John Frederick Dankert.

Typically, this family would have farmed in a rural area. The family endured hardships of the time and era. In the 1790's there was a ban on emigration to America for the Mecklenburg-Schwerin locals. French looting and destruction began in the 1800's of Mecklenburg communities and the Napoleonic Confederation recruited locals to fight against the Russians.

Of the over 2,000 recruited less than 100 survived. In the 1810's the Confederation of the Rhine initiates, beginning of Liberation against Napoleon. The German Act permitted emigration to other states in the German Confederation. Congress of Vienna denotes Mecklenburg-Schwerin and Mecklenburg-Strelitz are grand duchies and members of the German Bundestag.

The abolition of serfdom in the 1820's in Mecklenburg-Schwerin, totaling 393,000 inhabitants. Negotiations began to regulate relations between landlords and peasants, that is, the farmers should be the owner, or leaseholder of the land they farm. By the 1840's a Grand Ducal regulation governs over the Mecklenburg-Schwerin process for issuing passports to emigrants. There are Revolutions throughout Europe including Mecklenberg.

The *Freienwalder Schiedsspruch* of the 1850's permits the Constitutional hereditary settlement to be reinstated. Beginning of mass emigration to America. Political, social and economic ills caused the great emigration wave end of the, from 1853 to 1908 nearly 120,000 people migrated from Mecklenburg. Adopted Ordinance on the acquisition and loss of property of Mecklenburg citizens. Country Regulation on emigration to non-European countries.

This brief time table shows the difficulties arising in Germany that lead to their son Frederick to go head-strong to America:

1790's Ban on emigration to America for the Mecklenburg-Schwerin locals.
1800's French looting and destruction of Mecklenburg communities. Napoleonic Confederation recruited locals to fight against the Russians. Of the over 2,000 recruited less than 100 survived.
1810's Confederation of the Rhine. Beginning of Liberation against Napoleon. The German Act permitted emigration to other states in the German Confederation. Congress of Vienna denotes Mecklenburg-Schwerin and Mecklenburg-Strelitz are grand duchies and members of the German Bundestag.
1820's The abolition of serfdom in Mecklenburg. Mecklenburg-Schwerin has 393,000 inhabitants. Negotiations began to regulate relations between landlords and peasants, that is, the farmers should be the owner, or leaseholder of the land they farm.
1840's A Grand Ducal regulation governs over the Mecklenburg-Schwerin process for issuing passports to emigrants. Revolution throughout Europe including Mecklenberg. A Grand Ducal regulation in the territory of Mecklenburg-Schwerin, permitting emigration.
1850's The "Freienwalder Schiedsspruch" permits the Constitutional hereditary settlement to be reinstated. Beginning of mass emigration to America. Political, social and economic ills caused the great emigration wave end of the, from 1853 to 1908 nearly 120,000 people migrated from Mecklenburg. Adopted Ordinance on the acquisition and loss of property of Mecklenburg citizens. Country Regulation on emigration to non-European countries.

In this generation, there are sixteen couples, ten of which were fully literate, including the Thompson, Goodmans, Hensels, Batdorfs, Werts, McClouds, Oberlanders, Gauglers, Keefers and Livezlys. The Andersons and the Laymans of this generation, were slightly literate, where one adult was literate and one was not. Two families, the Peters and Rows, were completely illiterate. The Updegrove family became literate as adults and the Dankerts were Germans, the only couple of this generation not in America. The assumption is that they were not literate in German.

Since this family was the only one not in America, we have no certain way of relating the financial circumstance of the Dankerts to the other families of this generation, but suffice it to say they were probably the least privileged and poorest of the group. Their son John Frederick Dankert left his homeland alone about 1865, immigrated to America and settled in Sunbury, Pennsylvania. As an American, Frederick became a Duncan and was the direct ancestor of the Thompson line.

William Gerard Heinrich Dankert was counted in the census in 1819 in Niendorf, Prussia (Nordwestmecklenburg, Mecklenburg-Vorpommern, Germany). He was affiliated with the Evangelical Lutheran religion.

Maria Carolina Henriette Kelling was counted in the census in 1819 in Niendorf, Prussia (Nordwestmecklenburg, Mecklenburg-Vorpommern, Germany). She was affiliated with the Evangelical Lutheran religion.

DAVID MCCLOUD
& MARY SARVIS

David McCloud was born around 1807 to David McCloud, probably in Northumberland County Pennsylvania, where he lived most of his life and married his wife Mary Sarvis, the probable daughter of Jacob and Elizabeth Sarvis. The McClouds and Sarvises were both presumable of Irish ancestry. The couple married sometime around 1835, when David was 28 and Mary was twenty years old.

The young couple married in Augusta, one of the seven original townships established in Northumberland. The seven townships created in 1772 were Augusta, Eagle, Buffalo, Penn's, Turbot, Wyoming, and Muncy. The townships were divided and subdivided, into new townships and counties, as the population of the area grew. Augusta was divided into Upper and Lower Augusta in 1846.

Augusta and Turbot are the only townships of the original seven that are still in Northumberland County. Sunbury remains the county seat. It is believed that David may have grown up in Augusta. One of the earlier censuses shows David living in Augusta with his parents, who were in their 70s or 80s. David was 23 at the time of this census.

Pennsylvanians of that time were extremely patriotic and had a well-organized militia and navy. They played a dominant role in the Revolutionary, 1812 and Civil wars. David was still young when the War of 1812 broke out, but as he grew up he surely heard stories of how Pennsylvanian General Jacob J. Brown successfully defended Sackets Bay from a British invasion in 1813; or how Oliver Hazard Perry won the Battle of Lake Erie with his fleet of ships built at Erie by native Pennsylvanian Daniel Dobbins.

Listening to these fire-ring stories from the older men may have inspired him to seek employment in the nautical industry as he grew up. During the early nineteenth century small steam boats and some sail boats were the main transportation for people and commodities such as coal from the Wyoming basin, located in northern Northumberland County, to other communities along the Susquehanna River. David may have worked on a boat or ferry in the county's extensive canal system at this time, or possibly as a laborer in one of the shipping yards along the Susquehanna River in Augusta.

The State of Pennsylvania spent a great deal of money constructing canal systems between Shamokin Dam, Sunbury, Northumberland, and adjacent points. Similar facilities were provided on the West Branch, and also on the division between Northumberland and Harrisburg.

During the prosperous days of the canal, Northumberland was an important point on the water highway. Two packet boats, the George Denison and Gertrude, were launched in 1835 for the express purpose of transporting people between Northumberland and Wilkes-Barre. Although, hundreds of thousands of dollars were collected in annual tolls, the State Public Works never made their money back on the canal systems.

Shortly after the couple married, the railroads made the canal systems almost obsolete. To avoid further expenses with maintenance and repairs, the State sold the main line between Philadelphia and Pittsburg to the Pennsylvania Railroad Company, and the West Branch division was sold to the Philadelphia and Erie Railroad Company. The North Branch division was sold to the Pennsylvania Canal Company and was used mainly to transport coal until later in the century.

As jobs on the canals became scarce, David may have gone to work for one of the railroad companies, active in Northumberland County. Another thought is that David may have worked in the abundant coal fields of the area. The first coal was marketed from the Shamokin coal basin, just across the Shamokin Creek from Augusta, in 1814. From then on Pennsylvania, particularly Northumberland County became a major resource for coal in the nineteenth century.

Both David and Mary were literate. There are sixteen couples in this generation, ten of which were fully literate, including the Thompson, Goodmans, Hensels, Batdorfs, Werts, McClouds, Oberlanders, Gauglers, Keefers and Livezlys. The Andersons and the Laymans of this generation, were slightly literate, where one adult was literate and one was not. Two families, the Peters and Rows, were completely illiterate. The Updegrove family became literate as adults and the Dankerts were Germans, the only couple of this generation not in America.

By 1840, the couple had two children: Joseph, born in 1836, and Sarah, born in 1839. The couple went on to have seven more children: Mary Ann, born in 1844; Catherine, born in 1847, who became the Matriarch of the Thompson family; Daniel, born in 1849; Frederick, born in 1852; Jeremiah, born in 1853; Judith, born in 1855, and William, born in 1856. The couple moved around the area frequently, possibly following the opening of new coal mines or the extensions of the railroad. Hollowing Run and Sunbury were two of the towns the family lived in, although, they kept returning to Augusta.

They were counted as residents of Augusta in the 1830 and 1840 census and as residents of Lower Augusta in the census from 1850 through 1880. The latter of these census records show real estate owned by the couple valued at $100 in 1850 and $140 in 1860—about $3,600 today. After David passed, Mary was able to increase the property value at $250 a decade later. Of all the sixteen families of this generation, four families were extremely impoverished, the Updegroves, the Peters, the Rows and the McClouds.

David passed away sometime before May 19, 1864. Mary was around 49 years old when David died. Their youngest children, Judith and William, were only around nine and eight. In the 1870 census, Jerry, Judith, and William were the only children still living with their mother. By this time, Catherine was already married and probably had all of her six children before her mother died, sometime between 1880 and 1890. David and Mary's fourth child, Catherine, was the direct ancestor of the Thompson line.

David McCloud was counted in the census in 1810 (w/father). He was counted in the census in 1820 (w/father). He was counted in the census in 1830 in Augusta, Northumberland County, Pennsylvania (w/father). He was counted in the census in 1840 in Augusta, Northumberland County, Pennsylvania. He was counted in the census in 1850 in Lower Augusta, Northumberland County, Pennsylvania (Daniel Mcleod). He owned $100 in 1850. He was employed as a Laborer from 1850-1860. He lived in Lower Augusta, Northumberland County, Pennsylvania in 1858 (Off Hallowing Run Road). He was counted in the census in 1860 in Lower Augusta, Northumberland County, Pennsylvania. He owned $100 + $40 in 1860. His estate was probated on May 19, 1864 in Lower Augusta, Northumberland County, Pennsylvania. He was named after David McCloud, his father. He was affiliated with the Evangelical Lutheran religion. He was employed as a Keeping house.

Mary Sarvis was counted in the census in 1820. She was counted in the census in 1830. She was counted in the census in 1840 in Augusta, Northumberland County, Pennsylvania (w/husband). She was counted in the census in 1850 in Lower Augusta, Northumberland County, Pennsylvania. She was counted in the census in 1860 in Lower Augusta,

Northumberland County, Pennsylvania. She was counted in the census in 1870 in Lower Augusta, Northumberland County, Pennsylvania. She owned $100 + $150 in 1870. She was employed as a Keeping house in 1880. She was counted in the census in 1880 in Lower Augusta, Northumberland County, Pennsylvania. She lived in Lower Augusta, Northumberland County, Pennsylvania about 1880 (Little Mahanoy area). She was buried in July 1900 in Sunbury, Northumberland County, Pennsylvania (Pomfret Manor Cemetery, Plot 816C). She signed her will (Intestate). She was affiliated with the Evangelical Lutheran religion.

MICHAEL L. LAYMAN
& ELMIRA E. RAYMOND

Michael Layman was born in Marietta, Lancaster County, Pennsylvania, on October 10, 1818. He was the oldest of eight children born to Michael Layman and Sarah Klein. His father was born in Centre County, and his mother in Lancaster County, both of German heritage. Michael, along with his brothers and sisters, Catherine, Christina, Elizabeth, George, Henry, Sophia, and David lived in Lancaster County for most of their lives. Michael was the third in a line of Michael Laymans, beginning with his grandfather who commonly went by Leyman.

Lancaster County was one of the seven original counties of Pennsylvania. Farming flourished in the rich carbonate soil with relatively little slope, moderate climate, and evenly distributed rainfall. Nearly two-thirds of the county was farmland then and still is today.

Marietta began as a small Indian trading post in the early 1700s. By the 1820s Marietta experienced a cultural and economic boom. The construction of the Pennsylvania Canal at Marietta attracted entrepreneurs and made it easier for farmers to sell their crops for higher prices in cities like Philadelphia and Baltimore, and even downstream to New Orleans. The flatboat was popular with farmers of that time to transport their crops. The boats were only twelve to sixteen feet wide but could be as long as 100 feet. Steamboats and the railroads soon offered a quicker and less hazardous means of getting their crops to market.

As a child, Michael probably worked the family farm. He no doubt accompanied his father on one or more of the journeys transporting their crops to market. Corn, wheat, hay, tobacco, and vegetables were the main cash crop of the area. Michael and his father could load up to 1,500 pounds of crops on their flatboat, which could garn around $5,000 in the larger cities. That would be around $80,000 by today's standards, certainly a good payoff for the year's wages. As time went on, Michael became enchanted by a young woman in Elizabethtown, about nine miles from Marietta.

Elmira Elizabeth Raymond, daughter of John Reiman and Barbara Elizabeth Rousch, was born January 17, 1824, in Maytown, York County, Pennsylvania. John and Elizabeth both had German ancestry, and Reiman was typically anglicized to Raymond. Elmira's grandfather John Henry Reiman was fought for American Independence in 1782. At some point between Elmira's birth and when she met Michael, the family moved the six miles from Maytown to Elizabethtown. It's possible that John was also a farmer and bought a farm in the predominantly farming community of Elizabethtown.

John and the elder Michael may have been business acquaintances, partnering in the flatboat to take their crops to market. This could explain how the young couple met. With their families in the same business, Michael and Elmira may have had ample time to fall in love. John and Elizabeth moved from Elizabethtown back to York County at some point, possibly to Lower Chanceford.

Perhaps as John and Elizabeth saw the love kindling in their daughter, they wanted to avoid a marriage because of the different faiths of the families; Elmira's family was Lutheran and Michael's family was Methodist. Or maybe it was the age difference with Michael being six years older than Elmira that spurred the move. But true love cannot be kept apart. Probably shortly after their move, John passed away in 1841 when Elmira was seventeen. Michael and Elmira surely kept in touch, writing love letters to each other. Michael was pledging his undying love and Elmira was torn between her love for Michael and not wanting to leave her mother alone.

As fate would have it, love always wins. The young couple was married on April 3, 1845, in Christ Lutheran Church in Elizabethtown with the approval of her mother. They most likely lived on the Layman family farm in Marietta after they wed. Elmira must have converted to the Methodist religion after her mother passed away—sometime after 1841—as she and Michael were both buried in the Bethel United Methodist Cemetery in Lower Chanceford.

Leaving her mother alone was undoubtedly a concern for Elmira. Two years after they married, Michael moved his young bride and their two children—Jacob, age one and Sarah, only a few months old—to Lower Chanceford so that Elmira could be closer to her mother. Michael and Elmira went on to have seven more children: Uriah, Mary, Elmira, Charles, Joseph—who is in the direct line of the Thompson family—Lillian, and Theodore.

An interesting point to note is that Charles married Margaret McKinley a cousin of William McKinley, the 25th President of the United States. McKinley served from March 4, 1897, until his assassination in September 1901, six months into his second term. He was the last veteran of the American Civil War to serve as president. McKinley was a national Republican leader; his signature

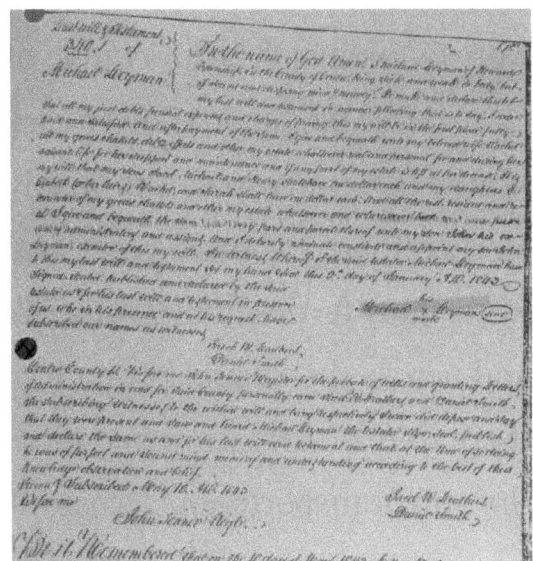

issue was high tariffs on imports as a formula for prosperity, as typified by his McKinley Tariff of 1890.

As the Republican candidate in the 1896 presidential election, he upheld the gold standard and promoted pluralism among ethnic groups. His campaign, designed by Mark Hanna, introduced new advertising-style campaign techniques that revolutionized campaign practices and beat back the crusading of his arch-rival, William Jennings Bryan. The 1896 election is often considered a realigning election that marked the beginning of the Progressive Era. Sadly, Sarah and Mary passed away while young, around 1950; possibly an accident took both young girls.

There are sixteen couples in this generation, ten of which were fully literate, including the Thompson, Goodmans, Hensels, Batdorfs, Werts, McClouds, Oberlanders, Gauglers, Keefers and Livezlys. The Andersons and the Laymans highlighted here of this generation, were slightly literate, where one adult was literate and one was not. Elmira could read and write but Michael could not. Two families, the Peters and Rows, were completely illiterate. The Updegrove family became literate as adults and the Dankerts were Germans, the only couple of this generation not in America.

After moving to Lower Chanceford, Michael went to work for the Tide Water Canal Company, probably working the weigh lock on the canal. He worked there for three years and then began working as a boatman. There were many ferries in that area. With Michael's experience taking goods down and across the Susquehanna River, he had no problem finding a job. Since there were no bridges across the Susquehanna River at that time, ferries were the only transportation across the river.

Boatmen would load people, goods, and supplies onto the flat bottomed ferry on one side and use poles to maneuver the ferry to the other side, where everything would be taken off and a new load put on for the trip back across the river. Boatmen were well paid, usually receiving a portion of the toll paid to the ferry company. There were usually hotels, restaurants, and taverns on each side of the river to refresh the weary travelers.

In 1855, a bridge was built across the river by the York Bridge Company. This was a very exciting time for the people who lived in York Furnace and the surrounding area. The Lancaster Examiner of November 20, 1855, celebrated the opening of the bridge. The paper said that the York County people of Fawn, Lower Chanceford, and Peach Bottom would no longer be cut off from commerce in the winter, when the Susquehanna and Tidewater canal was closed and roads were bad to York. Now they could easily get to Lancaster to do their buying and selling.

However, the excitement was short-lived. The bridge was opened in October 1855, but on April 5, 1856, the strongest windstorm known up to that time blew down the four spans across the eastern channel. They were carried downriver, but the contractors retrieved the timbers and started rebuilding. It was completed—some say to the last few planks—when, in early February of 1857, a severe ice flood destroyed it and took it away. The bridge was not rebuilt after that.

Unrest was brewing throughout the state that abolished slavery in 1780. But it wasn't until 1850 that the last slave in Pennsylvania was freed. The workings of the Underground Railroad were becoming less secretive. Michael surely heard about the Christiana Riots—where freed black men dared to rise up against white slave owners looking for a runaway—in Lancaster County in letters from home and in the Lancaster Examiner.

There was more and more opposition to slavery among the white religious population. Now there was news of the Southern states wanting to break away from the North because of the outcry to end slavery. Michael was surely not surprised when Fort Sumter thundered the call to war in 1861. Michael was one of the first to enlist in one of the five companies: Worth Infantry, York Rifles, Marion Rifles, Hanover Infantry, and the York Volunteers, organized in York County.

Michael must have had reservations about heading off to war and leaving his children and pregnant wife. Their last child, Theodore, was not born until 1862, yet he knew he had to fight this war for his children's sake. Reservations aside, knowing his own great-grandfather, John Jacob—and quite possible his grandfather, the original Michael—fought for the American Revolution, would help him push onward through these tough ordeals.

The family's personal property increased from $1,275 in 1860 to $5,500 in 1870, over $100,000 by today's standards. The Laymans, as well as the Oberlander family, were the two families of this generation, beginning with virtually nothing, succeeded through difficult and trying times.

History of York County, Pennsylvania. John Gibson, Historical Editor, Chicago: F. A. Battey Publishing Co., wrote: Michael Lyman son of Michael Lyman and Sarah Kline, was born in Lancaster County, PA in 1823. His father was born in Centre County, and his mother in Lancaster County, PA. Our subject remained in his native county until 1847, when he came to York County and entered the employ of the Tide Water Canal Company, and was located in Lower Chanceford Township. Here he continued to work for three years, and then began boating, which he continued until 1870, when he removed to York Furnace and engaged in the hotel business. He remained there until 1884, when he removed to Shank's Ferry and entered the hotel business. Mr. Lyman was married in 1845, to Miss Elmira Raymond, of Dauphin County, PA. They have seven children: Jacob, Uriah, Ella, Joseph, Charley, Lilly and Theodore. Mr. Lyman is a member of Lodge No. 125, of the Brotherhood of the Union. Related to William McKinley (January 29, 1843 - September 14, 1901) the 25th President of the United States.

It must have been a frightening time for his children—hearing of the battles and watching the soldiers as they went marching by their home on the way to war—knowing that their father was out there somewhere. Jacob, just barely 15, was now the man of the house, and most likely went out to get a job and support the family. It was a terrifying time for the young family, but they all pulled together until their father and husband came home.

Michael went back to work as a boatman on the ferries when the war was over. However, he longed for the feel of dirt in his hands again. Before long, he was living in York Furnace on a piece of land in a large home and crops in the field. As the children started to go out on their own, Michael and Elmira began to take in boarders.

Michael and Elmira were getting older and perhaps thought to get out of the farming business. They moved to Shanks Ferry around 1880 and went into the hotel business. Life was good for them until their youngest son, Theodore, died at the age of 25. Elmira passed away the following year in 1888 and Michael joined her four years later. Michael and Elmira's seventh child, Joseph, was the direct ancestor of the Thompson line.

Michael L Layman was counted in the census in 1820 (w/father). He was counted in the census in 1830 in Lancaster County, Pennsylvania (w/father). He was employed as a Farmer about 1835. He was counted in the census in 1840 in East Donegal, Lancaster County, Pennsylvania (w/father). He lived in York County, Pennsylvania in 1847. He was counted in the census in 1850 in Lower Chanceford, York County, Pennsylvania. He was employed as a Boatman from 1850-1860. He was counted in the census in 1860 in Lower Chanceford, York County, Pennsylvania. He owned $600 + $675 in 1860. He served in the military between 1861-1865 in Pennsylvania (Civil War, Private, US Army). He was employed as a Farmer in 1870. He was counted in the census in 1870 in Lower Chanceford, York County, Pennsylvania. He owned $3000 + $2500 in 1870. He was employed as a Lanlord [Landlord] in 1880. He was counted in the census in 1880 in Lower Chanceford, York County, Pennsylvania. He was buried in May 1892 in Lower Chanceford, York County, Pennsylvania (Bethel United Methodist). He was affiliated with the Methodist < Lutheran religion. He was named after Michael Leyman, his father. He was employed as a Shenk's Ferry. He was employed as a York Furnace.

Elmira Elizabeth Raymond was counted in the census in 1830 in Spring Garden, York County, Pennsylvania (w/father). She was counted in the census in 1840 in Spring Garden, York County, Pennsylvania. She was counted in the census in 1850 in Lower Chanceford, York County, Pennsylvania. She was counted in the census in 1860 in Lower Chanceford, York County, Pennsylvania. She was counted in the census in 1870 in Lower Chanceford, York County, Pennsylvania. She was employed as a Keeping house  from 1870-1880. She was counted in the census in 1880 in Lower Chanceford, York County, Pennsylvania. She was buried in November 1888 in Lower Chanceford, York County, Pennsylvania (Bethel United Methodist). She signed her will (Intestate). She was affiliated with the Methodist religion.

JACOB W. OBERLANDER
& SARAH A. WARNER

Jacob Warner Oberlander was born to a German farming family in 1819, in Chanceford, York County, Pennsylvania. He was the sixth of twelve children born to Michael Baugher Oberlander and Maria Catherine Warner. He was named for his paternal grandfather, Jacob Oberlander, a Lutheran farmer of York County and was donned Warner as a middle name to commemorate his notable maternal family, begun from John George Werner.

The Oberlander's farm was probably in the family for generations; possibly forged by Jacob's great-grandfather, Andrew Miller, from land given to him for his service in the Revolutionary War. He served in the York Pennsylvania Regiment.

The practice of awarding land as payment for military service had been a common practice in the North American British Empire. At the time of the Revolutionary War, Colonial governments—under the assumption that they would win—offered land to those who enlisted in the Colonial Army. The farm was undoubtedly very large in order to provide for Jacob's eleven brothers and sisters: Catherine, Daniel, Peter, Samuel, Sarah, Elizabeth, Mary, Susan, William, Michael, and Christian. It is quite possible that Jacob's grandparents, Jacob Oberlander and Susan Baugher, also lived on the farm along with other members of the family, as was the German custom of the time.

Most of the farms of that time were 100-plus acres. Jacob's great-grandfather probably started the clearing-out process of the land that continued with his grandfather and father. Jacob himself surely cut down trees and pulled out stumps to prepare a new field. It wasn't until the 1850s that settlers in the southern counties of Pennsylvania had more than fifty percent of their property improved.

Agriculture was the main occupation of Chanceford residents during this time. Wheat, rye, corn, orchard fruits, and tobacco were big cash crops that were taken to markets as far away as Baltimore and Philadelphia, and on to the coast for export to European counties.

Few of the farmers in this time were fully self-sufficient. Garden crops and services were traded locally to sustain their existence in the area. Some of the farmers formed "farming districts" and would pool their produce and resources—such as wagons or boats—to make the most of their trips to the distant markets.

Agriculture passed through several phases before moving into the Industrial Age during the second half of the century. At first the land was cleared, then the fresh soil was planted and replanted until it would no longer produce. Then came the discovery that lime would replenish the soil.

The Oberlanders probably built a lime-kiln and hauled large limestone shipments from the river to their kiln, where they would burn it before plowing it into the fields. Soon they found that it was cheaper to buy the lime at the river already burnt and haul it back to their farm. Liming gave way to other fertilizers such as manure, guano, super-phosphate of lime, and other types of soil additives.

The Industrial Age brought railroads, mills, ironworks, and distilleries. This gave the farmers local access to machinery that helped them produce more with less effort. Distilleries turned corn and wheat into liquor, which brought a higher price than the raw product. Mills turned wheat and rye into flour for easier shipping. There were two flouring mills in Chanceford, belonging to Samuel Warner and A. S. Warner, possibly members of Jacob's mother's family.

In his early twenties Jacob married Catherine Margaret Gipe, daughter of John Gipe and Elizabeth Durst, also undoubtable of German heritage. They had four children: John, Susan, Mary, and Elizabeth. Tragically, Catherine died shortly after Elizabeth's birth in 1854.

Shortly after her death, Jacob married Catherine's younger sister, Sarah Ann Gipe, on October 26, 1854. Sarah was around twenty years old when she married Jacob. The marriage was probably to provide care to Sarah's nephew and nieces, though possibly it was for love. Jacob and Sarah had their first child, Luther, in 1855 and they went on to have ten more children: Sarah, Edward, Adeline, Rebecca, Caroline, Samuel, Margaret, Emmaline, Barbara, and Jacob.

It's possible that Sarah's and Jacob's parents were friends. Keeping with the customs of his German ancestry he welcomed Sarah's mother into his home. Elizabeth is counted in the 1860 census along with Christian, Jacob's younger brother, as living with Jacob and Sarah. Elizabeth passed away in 1861.

There are sixteen couples in this generation, ten of which were fully literate, including the Thompson, Goodmans, Hensels, Batdorfs, Werts, McClouds, Oberlanders, Gauglers, Keefers and Livezlys. The Andersons and the Laymans of this generation, were slightly literate, where one adult was literate and one was not. Two families, the Peters and Rows, were completely illiterate. The Updegrove family became literate as adults and the Dankerts were Germans, the only couple of this generation not in America.

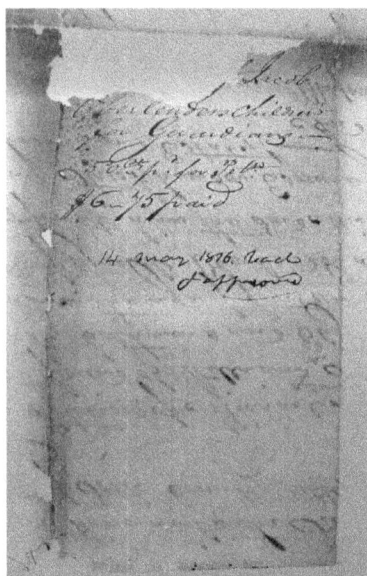

Sarah must have been a strong woman—she cared for her mother up to the end. Undoubtedly, she helped teach the children the workings of the family farm. It was common for the children and women to help with the everyday chores of the farm. She comforted their fears while they listened to the cannon fire of nearby battles during the Civil War. Possibly she was a member of one of the women's anti-slavery coalitions prominent prior to the war.

She probably worked alongside her husband during harvest time. She helped him increase the family's personal property from a minimal amount in 1850 to $4,640 in 1860 to finally $5,500 in 1870, over $100,000 by today's standards. The Oberlanders, as well as the Layman family, were the two families of this generation, beginning with virtually nothing, succeeded through difficult and trying times. Still Sarah took the time to nurture her children. Rebecca and the other children admired Sarah for her strength and loved her for her compassion.

Working the farm and raising fifteen children took its toll on Sarah though. Sarah passed away just before Christmas, 1874. Jacob raised the children by himself. Rebecca was just sixteen and her youngest brother was nine. Jacob lived about twenty-one more years, probably working the family farm with the help of his older children. The farming industry was changing—machinery was in common use on most farms. This probably gave him more time to clear off additional land. Jacob died just after Christmas, 1898. Jacob and Sarah's fifth child, Rebecca, was the direct ancestor of the Thompson line.

Jacob Warner Oberlander was counted in the census in 1820 (w/father). He was counted in the census in 1830 in Upper Chanceford, York County, Pennsylvania (w/father). He was counted in the census in 1840 in Upper Chanceford, York County, Pennsylvania (w/father). He owned $0 in 1850. He was counted in the census in 1850 in Chanceford, York County, Pennsylvania. He was employed as a Farmer from 1850-1880. He was counted in the census in 1860 in Chanceford, York County, Pennsylvania. He owned $4,000 + $640 in 1860. He was counted in the census in 1870 in Chanceford, York County, Pennsylvania. He owned $4,000 + $1,500 in 1870. He was counted in the census in 1880 in Chanceford, York County, Pennsylvania. He was buried in 1898 in New Bridgeville, York County, Pennsylvania (St. Lukes (Stahleys) Lutheran). He was affiliated with the Lutheran religion. He was named after Jacob Oberlander, his grandfather and Maria Catherine Warner, his mother.

Sarah "Sallie" Ann Gipe was counted in the census in 1840 in Chanceford, York County, Pennsylvania (w/father). She was counted in the census in 1850 in South ward York, York County, Pennsylvania (unlisted). She was counted in the census in 1860 in Chanceford, York County, Pennsylvania. She was employed as a Keeping house in 1870. She was counted in the census in 1870 in Chanceford, York County, Pennsylvania. She signed her will on November 25, 1874 in Chanceford, York County, Pennsylvania. She was buried in December 1874 in New Bridgeville, York County, Pennsylvania (St. Lukes (Stahleys) Lutheran). Her estate was probated on March 24, 1875 in Chanceford, York County, Pennsylvania (Book YY, page 192). She was affiliated with the Lutheran religion.

ELIJAH ANDERSON
& M. CATHERINE BORDNER

Elijah Anderson and Catherine Bordner were lifelong residents of Snyder and Northumberland counties in Pennsylvania. Their lives spanned the greater part of the nineteenth century and, except for Elijah's service in the Civil War, they rarely if ever felt the need to travel far from home.

Elijah was the son of William Anderson, of an Irish heritage, and Catherine Arnold, of a German background. Both William and Catherine had been born in Lancaster County, Pennsylvania and Catherine's grandfather, John George Herrold, was a Revolutionary War soldier. Their son Elijah was born in Chapman, Union County—which later split into multiple counties, including Elijah's birthplace in what would become Snyder County. He was baptized at one month old at Botshafts Lutheran Church in Union County. Elijah's grandfather, William Anderson, was a Revolutionary War soldier—a private in Lancaster's 6th Regiment, 4th Company, 6th Class.

Elijah was William and Catherine's fourth child. His older brothers were George, John, and Peter. After Elijah in 1820 came yet another brother, Samuel— the fifth boy in a row. Finally, Catherine presented the family with two girls, Elizabeth and Mary.

Catherine's parents, John Balthaser Bordner and Maria Magdalena Emerich, had been born in Berks County, southeast of Harrisburg, but by the time of Catherine's birth and baptism, the family had relocated to Lower Mahanoy, a rural township in Northumberland County just across the Susquehanna River from Chapman. The Bordner family was of German-Swiss heritage and the Emerichs were of German descent. Catherine's grandfather, Jacob Phillip Bortner, was also a Revolutionary War soldier—a private in Northumberland's militia.

Anderson, Catherine & Elijah c1890

Catherine was one of thirteen children born to the Bordner family over a span of twenty-one years. Preceding Catherine were five brothers in a row—John, Jacob, Jonathan, Philip, and Peter—and two sisters, Mary and Elizabeth. After Catherine in 1817, came Annabelle, Joseph, Louisa, Isaac, and George.

There are sixteen couples in this generation, ten of which were fully literate, including the Thompson, Goodmans, Hensels, Batdorfs, Werts, McClouds, Oberlanders, Gauglers, Keefers and Livezlys. The Andersons and the Laymans of this generation, were slightly literate, where one adult was literate and one was not. Elijah was literate but Catherine was not able to read or write. Two families, the Peters and Rows, were completely illiterate. The Updegrove family became literate as adults and the Dankerts were Germans, the only couple of this generation not in America.

Elijah and Catherine married in August 1843 in Lower Mahanoy. Elijah was twenty-three years old, and Catherine was twenty-six. Elijah and Catherine settled in Chapman, and keeping to the tradition of large families had nine children: Samuel, Mary, Susan, Sarah, Josephine, Emma, James, Evaline, and Catherine. Eventually, Elijah and Catherine passed away only a little more than a year apart—Elijah on October 18, 1892, in Port Trevorton, and Catherine on December 13, 1893, in Chapman. They were buried together at St. Johns United Methodist Church in Port Trevorton.

While Catherine was more than busy enough bearing and raising their large family, Elijah made his living as a tailor. Throughout the 19th century, clothing manufacture underwent profound changes. In the early part of this period, most clothing—except finely and expensively tailored garments for the wealthy—was hand-stitched by women at home. The first American factory for ready-made clothing was established in New York City in 1831. The patenting of the first practical sewing machine, in 1846, led to the establishment of a large-scale industry in ready-made clothing, depending for the most part on poorly paid women working in sweat-shop conditions.

It is unlikely that Elijah could have made a decent living by producing the sort of clothing that common people wore. He probably learned to custom-measure and hand-stitch expensive clothing for the more well-to-do citizens—both men and women—of his community. During one census, he is listed as a "retail merchant." This probably refers to some sort of shop in which Elijah tailored and sold the type of outer garments that most of his fellow Pennsylvanians could not afford.

Like so many men, the Civil War interrupted Elijah's life and career. In America's later wars, Elijah—at over 40 years of age and with nine children—would have been considered ineligible for service. In the Civil War, however, thousands of forty-year-old fathers found themselves in uniform.

The citizens of Pennsylvania played a huge role in the Civil War. More than 360,000 Pennsylvania men—more than from any other state except New York— served in the Union Army. Pennsylvania mustered 215 infantry regiments. In October 1862, Elijah became a private in the 172nd Regiment of the Pennsylvania Infantry, Company A, serving under Captain Mish T. Heinzelman.

The 172nd Pennsylvania was a "draft militia," a result of the Federal Militia Act of 1862 that was signed by President Lincoln in July 1862. The Union Army had previously been made up entirely of three-year volunteers, who were paid fairly substantial cash bounties upon enlisting. The Act of 1862 ordered the states to institute a draft of able-bodied men ages 18–45 to serve in draft militias for nine months.

"State line" sentiment was common in Pennsylvania. That is, Pennsylvanians were far more loyal to their state than they were to the United States. They eagerly joined emergency militias to defend Pennsylvania, but they often refused orders to cross the border, and they certainly were uninterested in following Federal orders to invade the South.

In mid-October, Pennsylvania began to draft men into draft militias. The imminent threat of being drafted—and therefore not receiving the cash bounties of volunteers—encouraged more than 200,000 men to volunteer for regular regiments. Another 80,000—including Elijah Anderson—were drafted into draft militia regiments. Most drafted regiments were sent on garrison duty far from action, but they freed up volunteer regiments for battle.

Elijah—like nearly all of his fellow draftees—was an inexperienced, barely trained soldier. The men of the 172nd received their brief training at Camp Curtin near Harrisburg. During the war, more than 300,000 soldiers moved through Camp Curtin, making it the largest army fort in either the Union or Confederate sides.

For most of its nine months of active service, the 172nd was assigned to garrison duty at Yorktown, Virginia. Toward the end of Elijah's nine-month tour of duty, however, he found himself on the move, on foot and by railroad. Elijah and the 172nd took part in the later stages of the Peninsula

Campaign in Virginia, the first large-scale Union offensive in the eastern theater of war. Then, joining the Army of the Potomac, the regiment took part in the pursuit of General Lee to Warrenton Junction, Virginia, from July 19th to 25th.

Fortunately, the 172nd was never in hot combat—the regiment lost thirteen men to disease, but none in battle. The regiment returned to Harrisburg and disbanded on August 1, 1863, one month after the Battle of Gettysburg, which had taken place just 80 miles south of the Anderson's home. It was no doubt with great relief that Catherine welcomed home her forty-three-year-old husband.

Elijah was surely pleased to resume his work as a tailor in place of his not-so-willing adventure as a soldier. The family's property value increased from nearly nothing to $100 by 1860 and $1,800 by 1870, equal to about $33,000 today. He had seen more of the world than he had ever expected to and there is no evidence in the record that he ever again traveled beyond a circle bounded by Chapman, Port Trevorton, and Lower Mahanoy. Elijah and Catherine's seventh child, James, was the direct ancestor of the Thompson line.

Elijah Anderson was baptized on February 15, 1820 in Chapman, Union (Snyder) County, Pennsylvania (Botshafts (Grubbs) Lutheran). He was counted in the census in 1830 in Chapman, Union (Snyder) County, Pennsylvania (w/mother). He was counted in the census in 1840 in Chapman, Union (Snyder) County, Pennsylvania (unlisted). He was counted in the census in 1850 in Chapman, Union (Snyder) County, Pennsylvania. He owned $0 in 1850. He was employed as a Tailor from 1850-1860. He was counted in the census in 1860 in Chapman, Snyder County, Pennsylvania. He owned $100 in 1860. He served in the military on July 8, 1861 in Harrisburg, Dauphin County, Pennsylvania (Civil War, Private, 172nd Reg Infantry, Company A, Capt. Mish T. Heinzelman). He was employed as a Ret. Merchant in 1870. He owned $1800 in 1870. He was counted in the census in 1870 in Chapman, Snyder County, Pennsylvania. He was counted in the census in 1880 in Danville, Montour County, Pennsylvania (Bolich). He was employed as a Tailor in 1880. He was buried in 1892 in Port Trevorton, Snyder County, Pennsylvania (St. Johns (Mt. Zion) United Methodist). He was affiliated with the Methodist < Lutheran religion.

Mary Catherine Bordner was baptized on December 24, 1817. She was counted in the census in 1820 (w/father). She was counted in the census in 1830 in Lower Mahanoy, Northumberland County, Pennsylvania (w/father). She was counted in the census in 1840 in Mahanoy, Northumberland County, Pennsylvania (w/father). She was counted in the census in 1850 in Chapman, Union (Snyder) County, Pennsylvania. She was counted in the census in 1860 in Chapman, Snyder County, Pennsylvania. She was counted in the census in 1870 in Chapman, Snyder County, Pennsylvania. She was employed as a Keeping house from 1870-1880. She was counted in the census in 1880 in Chapman, Snyder County, Pennsylvania. She was buried in 1893 in Port Trevorton, Snyder County, Pennsylvania (St. Johns (Mt. Zion) United Methodist). Her estate was probated on December 27, 1893 in Chapman Township, Snyder County, Pennsylvania. Her estate was probated in 1894 in Chapman Township, Snyder County, Pennsylvania. Her estate was probated on January 23, 1895 in Chapman Township, Snyder County, Pennsylvania. She was affiliated with the Methodist < Lutheran religion. S

NOTE: Research needed to verify this Civil War claim, seems the Elijah in service was born c1830, from Lower Mahanoy and unmarried in 1863. Elijah Anderson joined the 172nd Regiment Infantry: Organized at Harrisburg October 27 to November 29, 1862. Moved to Washington, D.C., December 2; thence to Newport News. Va., December 4, and to Yorktown, Va., December 12. Unassigned, Yorktown, Va., 4th. Corps, Dept. of Virginia, to April, 1863. West's Advance Brigade, 4th Corps, Dept. of Virginia, to June, 1863. 3rd Brigade, 1st Division, 4th Corps, to July, 1863. 1st Brigade, 3rd Division, 11th Corps, Army of the Potomac, to August, 1863. Service--Garrison duty at Yorktown, Va., until June, 1863. Dix's Peninsula Campaign June 27-July 7. Ordered to Washington, D.C., July 9. Join Army of the Potomac at Hagerstown, Md., July 14. Pursuit of Lee to Williamsport, Md. March to Warrenton Junction, Va., July 19-25, 1863. Ordered to Harrisburg, Pa., and mustered out August 1, 1863. Regiment lost during service 13 by disease. [http://www.civilwararchive.com/Unreghst/unpainf7.htm#172nd]

ABRAHAM GAUGLER
& KESIAH KELLY

Abraham Gaugler and Kesiah Kelly—his wife of 46 years—lived their entire lives in rural Snyder County, Pennsylvania. Census data through those years indicate residences in Chapman and Union townships and in unincorporated Port Trevor ton, all adjacent to one another on the west bank of the Susquehanna River.

Abraham was the sixth child of George Gaugler, born in Montgomery County, and Maria Magdalena who had been born in Northumberland County and whose maiden is unknown. Magdalena's family is presumed to be German as her husband George's was, Bavaria through-and-through. Abraham's older siblings were Maria, Sarah, Elizabeth, Christina, and John, and he was followed by George.

Kesiah's parents were William Kelly, born in Northumberland, now Snyder, County, and Elizabeth Shaffer also of Northumberland County. The Paternal Kelly clan was undoubtable Irish and the maternal Shaffer and Swartz families were of German stock. Kesiah was the oldest of ten, followed in order by Sophia, Mary, Uriah, Elizabeth, John James, John J., Caroline, Lucetta, and Hiram. Kesiah's grandfather, John Peter Shaffer, was a Revolutionary War soldier—a private in Berks County 6th Regiment, 5th Company.

Abraham was christened at the Botshaft's Lutheran Church in Chap man. In such a sparsely populated area, Abraham and Kesiah had likely known each other from early childhood. We can imagine them attending the same one-room schoolhouse to get the little bit of education they received—

reading, writing, very basic arithmetic—and whispering to each other during services at the local Lutheran Church.

Port Trevorton, around which the lives of Abraham and Kesiah revolved, was a tiny farming hub when they were children. Later, as coal mines were developed in the Zerbe Valley, the Trevorton and Susquehanna Railroad was built to bring coal to the town. It crossed the Susquehanna River on a long bridge from Herndon to Port Trevorton, and the canal basin that was built for off-loading the railcars gave the newly prospering town its appellation of "port." However, the railroad route from the mines to Port Trevorton was only in use for fifteen years, and when the bridge was removed in 1870 Port Trevorton rapidly slid back into its sleepy ways.

Abraham made his living not on the railroad or at the port, but as a farmer. Agriculture in the 19th century was a tedious backbreaking occupation. Horse drawn plows were used to break the soil and horse-drawn wagons brought produce to market.

In these years, Snyder County became more effectively connected to distant markets by Pennsylvania's growing canal and rail system. As a result, instead of subsistence farming, farmers were able to grow cash crops for markets throughout the nation and even in Europe.

The temperance movement had a substantial impact on Snyder County farmers. Growing rye for distilling into whiskey had been a profitable enterprise, especially after improved transportation facilitated getting whiskey to market. However, as the temperance movement decreased the demand for distilled products,

farmers in Snyder County shifted production away from rye grains and emphasized production of corn, wheat, pork, poultry, potatoes, and butter.

Even in a rural community such Snyder County the national nightmare of the Civil War had a profound effect. Thousands of young Pennsylvanians—lured by patriotism and by cash bounties—had volunteered for the Union Army. Eighty-thousand more—including men up to the age of forty-five—found themselves drafted by lottery into draft militias to serve for nine-month terms. In October 1862— the month of the draft lottery—Abraham was a forty-two-year-old father of eleven living children.

No matter how patriotic Abraham's sentiments may have been, it was probably with a great sigh of relief that he attended the public lottery and did not hear his name called. Instead, he remained at home on the farm growing foodstuffs to help feed the army and perhaps shifting some of his production into sheep, which were desperately needed to provide wool for uniforms.

Families in rural America in the 19th century were much larger than today's families, typically ranging from seven to twelve. In that time of rudimentary medical care and poorer nutrition and sanitation, parents expected that not all their children would live to adulthood. In rural areas in particular it was expected that surviving children would achieve their highest educational attainment at an early age and then go to work helping to support their families. As a result, families tended to have many children.

However, even in those times the family of Abraham Gaugler and Kesiah Kelly was exceptional. They had fifteen children, born over a span of twenty-two years. Kesiah's last child, Ella, was born when Kesiah was forty-seven years old. The family worked hard and amassed property value in 1860 of $3,100 and an exception increase to $13,340 by 1870, worth nearly $250,000 today. Of all the sixteen families of this generation, twelve were below poverty, two—the Laymans and Oberlanders—were upper lower class, and two—The Gauglers and the Thompsons—were middle class.

Abraham and Kesiah's children were John, Adeline, George, Emaline, James, Elizabeth, Lucetta, Isabelle, K. J., Sarah, Minerva, Alice, Anna, Caroline, and Ella. The Gauglers' fourth child, Emaline, was known as Ella. Born in 1848, she was married in her mid-teens and died at just sixteen years of age. Twenty-three years later, the Gauglers' named their fifteenth child Ella.

There are sixteen couples in this generation, ten of which were fully literate, including the Thompson, Goodmans, Hensels, Batdorfs, Werts, McClouds, Oberlanders, Gauglers, Keefers and Livezlys. The Andersons and the Laymans of this generation, were slightly literate, where one adult was literate and one was not. Two families, the Peters and Rows, were completely illiterate. The Updegrove family became literate as adults and the Dankerts were Germans, the only couple of this generation not in America.

We can wonder whether they looked back with sadness at Emaline who died so young and decided to name their latest—and last—child in memory of her long-deceased older sister. Another interesting thing to note about the Gauglers' children is the fact that three of their first five children were boys, but after that Kesiah gave birth to ten girls in a row.

When Abraham passed away at the grand age of eighty, as a result of apoplexy—paralysis due to stroke— and he had been a widower for fourteen years. Kesiah was buried at St. Johns United Methodist in Port Trevorton and in 1900 Abraham joined her. Abraham and Kesiah's seventh child, Lucetta, was the direct ancestor of the Thompson line.

Abraham Gaugler was baptized on August 1, 1820 in Port Trevorton, Union (Snyder) County, Pennsylvania (Botshafts (Grubbs) Lutheran). He was christened on August 13, 1826 in Chapman, Union (Snyder) County,

Pennsylvania (Botshafts (Grubbs) Lutheran). He was counted in the census in 1830 in Chapman, Union (Snyder) County, Pennsylvania (w/mother). He was counted in the census in 1840 (w/mother). He owned $0 in 1850. He was counted in the census in 1850 in Chapman, Union (Snyder) County, Pennsylvania. He was employed as a Farmer from 1850-1870. He was counted in the census in 1860 in Chapman, Snyder County, Pennsylvania. He owned $2600 + $500 in 1860. He lived in Chapman, Snyder County, Pennsylvania in 1864. He owned $12,000 + $1340 in 1870. He was counted

in the census in 1870 in Union, Snyder County, Pennsylvania. He was counted in the census in 1880 in Union, Snyder County, Pennsylvania. He was employed as a Laborer, Farm in 1880. He was counted in the census in 1900 in Union, Snyder County, Pennsylvania. He was employed as a Retired farmer in 1900. He was buried on August 26, 1900 in Port Trevorton, Snyder County, Pennsylvania (St. Johns (Mt. Zion) United Methodist). His cause of death was Apoplexy (i.e., paralysis due to stroke). He was affiliated with the Methodist < Lutheran religion.

Kesiah Josephine Kelly was counted in the census in 1830 in Chapman, Union (Snyder) County, Pennsylvania (w/father). She was counted in the census in 1840 in Chapman, Union (Snyder) County, Pennsylvania (w/father). She was counted in the census in 1850 in Chapman, Union (Snyder) County, Pennsylvania. She was counted in the census in 1860 in Chapman, Snyder County, Pennsylvania. She was counted in the census in 1870 in Union, Snyder County, Pennsylvania. She was employed as a Keeping house from 1870-1880. She was counted in the census in 1880 in Union, Snyder County, Pennsylvania. She was buried in May 1886 in Port Trevorton, Snyder County, Pennsylvania (St. Johns (Mt. Zion) United Methodist). She signed her will (Intestate). She was affiliated with the Methodist religion.

MICHAEL A. KEEFER
& M. MATILDA BUCHER

Michael A. Keefer and Margaret Matilda Bucher were born, married, raised their family, and passed away all within the radius of a very few miles. The town of Sunbury, in Northumberland County, Pennsylvania, was the focus for all the events of their lives. The farthest they seemed to have roamed was to Upper Augusta, the rural township adjacent to Sunbury.

Michael was born in 1815, the son of Daniel Keefer and Evaline "Eva" Arnold. Both of Michael's parents were born in Berks County—70 miles as the crow flies southeast of Sunbury—but they were married in Northumberland County and made their lifelong home there. Daniel and Eva were both of German stock.

Michael was the fifth child of eleven. First came Michael's three older sisters, Mary, Catherine, and Elizabeth. Michael and his twin brother, Samuel—the only boys in their entire family—were born next, to be followed by Anna, Juliana, Margaret, Matilda, Amelia, and Rosanna.

Margaret Matilda Bucher was born in 1827, when her husband-to-be, Michael Keefer, was just short of thirteen years old. For the first three decades of her life, she was commonly known as Matilda. During the nineteenth century, it was customary for the children of immigrant families from non-English-speaking parts of Europe to be called by their middle names. As the daughter of parents who were both of German extraction—with the surnames Bucher of Germany and Mantz of Switzerland—this custom would have applied to Matilda. Later, however, these people began to adopt the usage of immigrants from English-speaking nations and employ first names for everyday use. At this time, in around 1860, Matilda became more commonly Margaret.

Margaret's parents, John Henry Bucher and Elizabeth Mantz, were both native Pennsylvanians. Six siblings preceded Margaret: George, Harriet, Martin, Charles, Henry, and William. Two more, Mary and John, followed her.

Michael and Margaret lived a relatively commonplace life, rarely, if ever, venturing far from home. At forty-seven years old, Michael was too old—by two years—to be required to take part in the Civil War draft lottery of 1862. However, participating in the grand events of history was part of both their families' heritages. Two of Margaret's grandfathers and one great-grandfather had served in the Revolutionary War—John Conrad Bucher had fought at age 44, Henry W. Bucher had been a captain; and Nicholas Mantz, a private, had been listed as a prisoner of war. On Michael's side, his grandfather Peter Keefer had served in the 1st Pennsylvania Regiment.

There are sixteen couples in this generation, ten of which were fully literate, including the Thompson, Goodmans, Hensels, Batdorfs, Werts, McClouds, Oberlanders, Gauglers, Keefers and Livezlys. The Andersons and the Laymans of this generation, were slightly literate, where one adult was literate and one was not. Two families, the Peters and Rows, were completely illiterate. The Updegrove family became literate as adults and the Dankerts were Germans, the only couple of this generation not in America.

Michael and Margaret were the parents of seven children. Their first, Margaret, was born in 1845. She was followed by Mary, Anna, Alice, Charles, James—the Thompson direct ancestor—and, in 1860, Emma.

The first settlement at the site of Michael and Margaret's hometown, Sunbury, had been a multi-ethnic Native American village called Shamokin.

Early in the 18th century, Shamokin residents included Iroquois migrants from the north, Shawnee and Lenape retreating from the expanding white settlement of eastern Pennsylvania, and Native Americans from Virginia. In 1756, the British built Fort Augusta to provide protection for early British settlers in the Susquehanna Valley. The town of Sunbury was founded at the site in 1772, and it was in Sunbury that Michael and Margaret were born and lived their lives.

The censuses list Michael's occupation as "laborer," "farmer," and, in 1870, as "RR conductor." The primary industries of Northumberland County during Michael's lifetime were agriculture, timber, and coal mining. Timbering and coal mining required a steady supply of laborers so Michael may very well have spent some of his working life in those industries.

Farming had originally been a largely subsistence enterprise, but Pennsylvania's growing canal and rail systems had connected rural communities like Northumberland County to distant markets. During Michael's lifetime, cash crops included wheat, potatoes, corn, pork, and poultry. He listed "farmer" as his occupation in 1860.

The Pennsylvania Canal—the generic term for Pennsylvania's broad network of freight- and passenger-carrying rivers and canals—was under construction and use throughout the early part of the nineteenth century. A strong young man could easily have found work as a laborer in digging the canals, building locks, or working at docks where barges loaded cargoes of coal, fresh-cut timber, and agricultural products.

The Pennsylvania Railroad was founded in 1846 with main lines and spurs running between major cities, reaching into coal- and timber-producing regions, and eventually connecting with railroads and barge lines into other states. The new railroads opened up vast parts of Pennsylvania for the first time. As the Pittsburgh Daily Morning Post wrote in 1854, "There are people now living in Pittsburgh who have traveled diligently for a whole week to reach Philadelphia. The same persons can now go from our city to the eastern metropolis between sunrise and sunset of a summer's day, without fatigue, and without occasion for stopping to eat more than one meal."

Michael could have found heavy manual labor in the construction of rail lines, though when he was in his mid-fifties—no doubt exhausted by years of labor— he found less backbreaking work as a railroad conductor. This job would likely have taken him from one end of the state to the other. The Keefers were able to increase their property value from $0 to $1,320 to $2,000 from 1850 to 1870, equal to about current day $37,000.

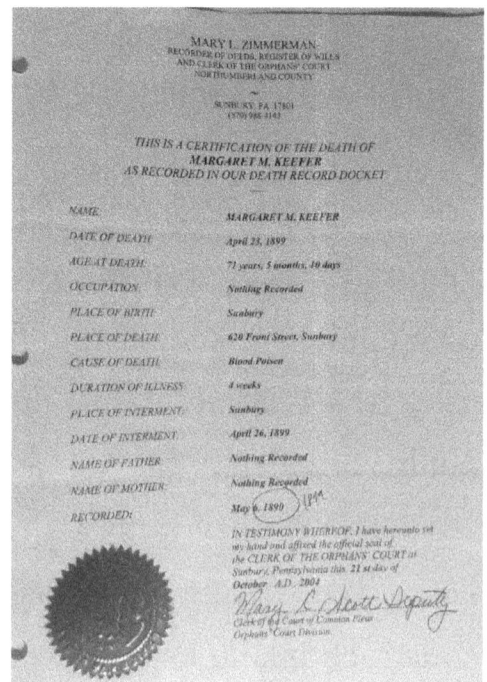

One of the great events of the Keefers' lifetime—whether they knew it or not— occurred in 1883 at the Sunbury City Hotel when the inventor Thomas Alva Edison installed the very first three-wire electric lighting system.

Margaret died at the age of seventy-two in 1899, and Michael followed her five years later at the grand age of eighty-nine. They were buried side by side in the Penn's Sunbury Cemetery. Michael's marker reads "Our Father.

M. A. Keefer. Died Feb. 25, 1904. Aged 79 Y. I. M. and 8 D." Michael and Margaret's sixth child, James, was the direct ancestor of the Thompson line.

Michael Personality Analysis: Michael was a man of enormous energy and stamina; he could work tirelessly for long hours. He could work constantly for weeks on end without having any rest days. Tenacity was something that came naturally to Michael, he learned to be organized and hardworking quickly; from an early age he had associated doing well (perhaps even just surviving) with being prepared, organized and knowing how to make things work. In the same way that he was a tenacious man in his working life, in his personal life he also found it difficult to let go of things. Michael would never forget anyone who had wronged him but also, he would always remember to return favors and pay debts. Michael was a lover of the good life; he had good taste and liked to be amused and put at ease. He may have had a quick temper however self-control always held him in check when it was required and even though his blood ran would run high on a consistent basis he never (or at least rarely) lost his cool. Michael was a memorable character; through his abundant energy and love of life he would have always left his mark wherever he went. As a result of his stoicism and ability to withhold his emotions there may have been occasions where Michael was misjudged by his peers; his reluctance to participate emotionally may have been misread as an attitude of ambivalence or even haughtiness. In actual fact it was just an attitude that he had learned in his early life; in Michael's mind good judgement came from reserve and observation. Michael was a determined and independent character who enjoyed time alone. He liked to have enough space and quiet time to think things through. For this reason, he may have been aloof and sometimes distant in his personal life, often glossing over the more uncomfortable details such that his life would have a greater chance of running smoothly. Michael was an intelligent man who had an effective personality. He carved out the personality he wanted from life and chose to be optimistic, clear thinking, stable, and congruent. As a result, he had cohesive ideas that were effective in real life. Michael's writing was strong and unrelenting and so was he. Whatever he attempted in his life, through the force of physical strength, cunning and sheer determination he made it work.

Michael Arnold Keefer was counted in the census in 1820 in Augusta, Northumberland County, Pennsylvania (w/father). He was christened on January 15, 1826. He was counted in the census in 1830 in Augusta, Northumberland County, Pennsylvania (w/father). He was counted in the census in 1840 in Augusta, Northumberland County, Pennsylvania (w/father). He was counted in the census in 1850 in Upper Augusta, Northumberland County, Pennsylvania. He was employed as a Laborer in 1850. He owned $0 in 1850. He lived in Upper Augusta, Northumberland County, Pennsylvania in 1858 (Mile Hill Road/Cold Run Road East). He lived in Upper Augusta, Northumberland County, Pennsylvania in 1858 (Mile Hill Road/Cold Run Road East). He was counted in the census in 1860 in Upper Augusta, Northumberland County, Pennsylvania. He was employed as a Farmer in 1860. He owned $900 + $420 in 1860. He served in the military between July 4-August 11, 1863 in Pennsylvania (Civil War, Private, 36th Regiment, Company F). He owned $1800 + $200 in 1870. He was employed as a Conductor, Railroad in 1870. He was counted in the census in 1870 in Sunbury, Northumberland County, Pennsylvania. He signed his will in 1874 (Excluded from father's will). He lived in Pennsylvania in 1880 (Front St.). He was employed as a Laborer in 1880. He lived in Sunbury, Northumberland County, Pennsylvania in 1880 (Front St.). He was counted in the census in 1880 in Sunbury, Northumberland County, Pennsylvania.

He lived in Sunbury, Northumberland County, Pennsylvania from 1892-1899 (Front St.). He lived in Pennsylvania from 1892-1899 (Front St.). He was counted in the census in 1900 in Sunbury, Northumberland County, Pennsylvania. He was employed as a Laborer in 1900. He was buried in 1904 in Sunbury, Northumberland County, Pennsylvania (Penns (Lower) Sunbury Cemetery). He lived in Pennsylvania in 1904 (1013 Penn St.). He was employed as a Laborer in 1904. He lived in Sunbury, Northumberland County, Pennsylvania in 1904 (1013 Penn St.). He was named after Uncle Michael Arnold. He was affiliated with the Methodist < Reformed religion. His cause of death was Pneumonia.

Margaret Matilda Bucher was counted in the census in 1830 in Augusta, Northumberland County, Pennsylvania (w/father). She was counted in the census in 1840 in Sunbury, Northumberland County, Pennsylvania (w/father). She was counted in the census in 1850 in Upper Augusta, Northumberland County, Pennsylvania. She was counted in the census in 1860 in Upper Augusta, Northumberland County, Pennsylvania. She was counted in the census in 1870 in Sunbury, Northumberland County, Pennsylvania. She was employed as a Keeping house in 1880. She was counted in the census in 1880 in Sunbury, Northumberland County, Pennsylvania. She lived in Pennsylvania in 1899 (620 Front St.). She lived in Sunbury, Northumberland County, Pennsylvania in 1899 (620 Front St.). She was buried on April 26, 1899 in Sunbury, Northumberland County, Pennsylvania (Penns (Lower) Sunbury Cemetery). She signed her will (Intestate). Her cause of death was blood poison (blood poisoning, i.e., bacterial infection). She was affiliated with the Methodist < Evangelical Lutheran religion.

"May each and every feather of its wings serve to write a Declaration of Independence for as many nations. - by Henry Bucher, brother of Matilda [Independence Day "The American Eagle Poetry, Sunbury American, Sunbury American, Sunbury, Pennsylvania, Saturday, July 12, 1845 - Page 2]

GEORGE C. LIVEZLY
& ANNA M. KENT

George Livezly left his influential Philadelphia family, changed the spelling of his surname, and settled in rural Schuylkill County, Pennsylvania. His wife, Anna Kent, traveled even farther—and in an even more adventurous manner— to reach her husband-to-be.

George was the seventh child of Jacob Livezey and Eleanor Culin. Jacob was from English stock and Eleanor's family was originally Swedish. George's grandfather, also named Jacob Livezey, fought for American Independence in 1777. George's elder siblings were Charles, John—who died very shortly after birth—John Culin—born the next year and named after his deceased brother—Sarah, James, and Mary. George was followed by Jacob. George's father was the son of yet another Jacob, a veteran of the Revolutionary War.

The original Livesay family emigrated from England to America, and was a well-known and controversial family in Philadelphia. George carries this surname along with George Culin, his maternal grandfather, a Presbyterian farmer form Kingsessing, Pennsylvania.

Sometime in the 1850s, when George was in his late twenties or early thirties, he decided to leave his family's home in Philadelphia—where they were prosperous and well regarded—and strike out for the hinterlands. The spelling of his name changed from "Livezey" to "Livezly." Although many surname variants were accidental or strictly due to clerk's individual spellings, this name change seems conscious and the 'l' is nearly in every spelling. Interestingly, however, it's only George Sr.'s family, not the case with any of his siblings, nephews or nieces, all who used Livezey or Livesay variants.

George made his way in the hatter's trade as he is listed in the censuses variously as a hatter, a hat dealer, and owner of a hat store. This would have been a thriving occupation as hats—from working men's caps to wealthy men's derbies and top hats—were an essential part of the male wardrobe in the middle of the 19th century.

As a dealer in hats—rather than as a craftsman who made them— George would have escaped the hatter's occupational hazard of mercury exposure. Hatters in Europe and America used mercuric nitrate to treat the fur of small animals for the manufacture of felt hats, which resulted in a chronic condition known as "hatters' shakes—leading to the popular expression "mad as a hatter". Though England banned the use of mercuric nitrate by 1900, American hat makers continued to use it until at least 1941.

Anna Maria Kent was born on Christmas Day in New Orleans, Louisiana, in 1839. Her parents George William Kent and Mary Jarvis, were of English descent. What is known is that Anna—while still a teenager—had been taken in by a Roman Catholic orphanage. This was often the destination for young girls whose mothers had died or whose parents were otherwise unable to care for them, and so this may have been young Anna's situation.

Anna was likely an Ursuline. The Ursuline Order had been established in New Orleans in 1727, caring for the sick and trying to convert the Native American inhabitants. The city was growing and the Ursulines were well established by 1840s, when Anna was still in New Orleans. The sisterhood apparently did not appeal to Anna, as she is soon listed as a "runaway nun."

Somehow she made her way to Ashland, Pennsylvania, living with the Taylor family, where she would eventually meet George Livezly. Southern

Pennsylvania had long been industrialized, but the area around Ashland remained mostly wilderness, broken only by a hotel that had been built on the main wagon road through the area.

However, Ashland lies in the anthracite coal region, and by 1846 miners were developing coal seams in the area. More people, including George and Anna, were attracted by the commercial activity, and by the mid-1850s, with 3,500 citizens, Ashland had a post office and a church. As a hat dealer, George would build his business and eventually open a store. Sometime around 1852, George and Anna married. Though they would move to New Jersey in later years, they remained in Ashland for four decades, raising their children there.

Their first child was a son, John. Next came George Jr., who lived only a year or so. After came three daughters: Georgeann, Eleanor, and Emma Louisa, followed by a second George Jr., James, and Anna. In the nineteenth century, it was extremely common to name a child after his grandfather. It was common for fathers to name their children—both boys and girls—after themselves.

George Livezly named their second child George Culin, after himself. When baby George died—as many babies did in those days— George named the next child, a girl, Georgeann, a combination of "George" and "Anna." But George apparently still wanted a son named after himself; and when—after two more daughters—Anna gave birth to a boy, George proudly named the boy "George Culin Livezly."

There are sixteen couples in this generation, ten of which were fully literate, including the Thompson, Goodmans, Hensels, Batdorfs, Werts, McClouds, Oberlanders, Gauglers, Keefers and Livezlys. The Andersons and the Laymans of this generation, were slightly literate, where one adult was literate and one was not. Two families, the Peters and Rows, were completely illiterate. The Updegrove family became literate as adults and the Dankerts were Germans, the only couple of this generation not in America.

Tragedy would befall the Livezly family, on multiple occasions. In addition to the first George Jr., infants Georgeann and James would pass in 1858 and John and Anna would only live to see their early teens, leaving the physical world around 1879. A final blow was sweet Emma, who newly married, died in 1882 due to complications of childbirth of her first child. The only surviving child after 1882 was the second George Jr. George Jr. would marry Nellie Birch and have four children, Emily, Charles, George and Morris. Neither Emily nor Morris would see their tenth birthdays and both Charles and George, while defending our country in France in World War I, would die in battle.

George was able to improve his family's property value from $0 in 1850 to $50 in 1860 to $1,500 on 1870, equivalent to about $28,000 in today's money. Although not tremendous, the Hat business was at least worthwhile enough to increase his value by thirty times during just one decade.

In 1880, George and Anna still lived in Ashland, but by 1890 they had moved to Cumberland County in far southern New Jersey, where they spent the about ten years living with their son George Jr. George Sr. passed away sometime between 1900 and 1910, presumably in New Jersey. Anna relocated to Warren, Massachusetts with son George Jr. and died August of 1910, being buried in Brattleboro, Connecticut, just across the border. George and Anna's fifth child, Emma, was the direct ancestor of the Thompson line.

George Culin Livezly was baptized on May 16, 1828 in Philadelphia, Philadelphia, Pennsylvania. He was counted in the census in 1830 (w/mother). He was counted in the census in 1840 (w/family, both parents passed). He was counted in the census in 1850 in Upper Delaware Ward, Philadelphia, Pennsylvania. He was employed as a Hatter from 1850-1865. He was counted in the census in 1860 in Pottsville, Schuylkill County, Pennsylvania. He owned $50 in 1860. He lived in Pottsville, Schuylkill County, Pennsylvania in 1864. He was counted in the census in 1870 in Ashland, Schuylkill County, Pennsylvania. He was employed as a Hat dealer in 1870. He owned 1500 in 1870. He lived in Ashland, Schuylkill County, Pennsylvania in 1880 (Walnut St.). He was counted in the census in 1880 in Ashland, Schuylkill County, Pennsylvania. He was employed as a Hat store in 1880. He lived in Ashland, Schuylkill County, Pennsylvania from 1880-1884. He lived in Cumberland County, New Jersey from 1891-1900. He was counted in the census in 1900 in Vineland, Cumberland County, New Jersey (Livetzly). He was buried about 1910 in Brattleboro, Windham County, Vermont (Prospect Hills Cemetery). He was named after George Culin, his grandfather. He was affiliated with the Methodist < Episcopal religion.

Anna Maria Kent was presumably a nunnery runaway as young teenager about 1845 in Louisiana. She was counted in the census in 1850 in Pottsville, Schuylkill County, Pennsylvania (Saylor [Taylor]). She was counted in the census in 1860 in Pottsville, Schuylkill County, Pennsylvania. She was employed as a Keeping house in 1870. She was counted in the census in 1870 in Ashland, Schuylkill County, Pennsylvania. She was counted in the census in 1880 in Ashland, Schuylkill County, Pennsylvania. She was employed as a Keeps house in 1880. She was counted in the census in 1900 in Vineland, Cumberland County, New Jersey. Her funeral took place in 1910 in Warren, Worcester County, Massachusetts. She was buried on August 17, 1910 in Brattleboro, Windham County, Vermont (Prospect Hills Cemetery). She was affiliated with the Methodist < Catholic religion. Her cause of death was Old age, exhaustion following accidental fall down stairs, fractured femur.

THOMAS MORGAN
& NANCY (?) MORGAN

Thomas Morgan, son of Tomlin Morgan, was born about 1820 in Davisboro, Washington County, Georgia, USA. He died after 1857 in Georgia. He married Nancy about 1840. Nancy was born about 1820 in Georgia.

Nancy and Thomas Morgan had the following child:

i.   Sallie Morgan was born in March 1847 in Davisboro, Washington County, Georgia, USA. She died on November 10, 1927 in Savannah, Chatham County, Georgia, USA. She married Mason Shatteen about 1861 in Georgia. He was born about 1835 in Georgia, USA. He died between 1880-1900 in Georgia.

NELSON FORSYTHE
& ELIZABETH HAMPTON

Nelson Forsythe was born about 1820 in Nassau, Bahamas, West Indies (Eng). He died after 1856. He married Elizabeth Hampton about 1850. Elizabeth Hampton was born about 1825 in West Indies (Eng). She died after 1856.

Elizabeth Hampton and Nelson Forsythe had the following child:

i.   Samuel James Forsythe was born about 1850 in West Indies (Eng). He married Amelia Deane about 1880 in West Indies (Eng). She was born about 1860 in West Indies (Eng).

JOSEPH WASHINGTON
& TENIA (?) WASHINGTON

Joseph Washington, son of Fortune and Saramah Washington, was born about 1830 in South Carolina, USA. He died between 1868-1880 in South Carolina, USA. He married Tenia about 1855 in South Carolina. Tenia was born about 1830 in South Carolina, USA. She died between 1880-1900 in South Carolina, USA.

Joseph Washington was counted in the census in 1870. He was counted in the census in 1880. Tenia was employed as a Farm labor in 1870. She was counted in the census in 1870. She was employed as a Keeps house in 1880. She was counted in the census in 1880 in St. Helena Island, Beaufort County, South Carolina, USA. She was counted in the census in 1900.

Tenia and Joseph Washington had the following children:

i.   Aaron Washington was born in 1860 in South Carolina.

ii.   Elizabeth "Betsy" Washington was born in 1864 in South Carolina.

iii.   Smart Washington was born in 1866 in South Carolina.

iv.   Joseph "Joe" Washington was born about 1867 in Daufuskie, Beaufort County, South Carolina, USA.

ROBERT ROBINSON
& HESTER (?) WASHINGTON

Robert Robinson, son Dinah, was born about 1831 in South Carolina. He died between 1885-1900 in South Carolina. He married Hester about 1854 in Beaufort Co, South Carolina, USA. Hester was born about 1840 in South Carolina, USA. She died between 1885-1900 in South Carolina.

Robert Robinson was counted in the census in 1870 in St. Lukes, Beaufort County, South Carolina, USA. He was employed as a Farmer between 1870-1880. He was counted in the census in 1880 in Hilton Head, Beaufort County, South Carolina, USA.

Hester was counted in the census in 1870 in St. Lukes, Beaufort County, South Carolina, USA. She was employed as a Keeping house in 1870. She was employed as a Farm laborer in 1880. She was counted in the census in 1880 in Hilton Head, Beaufort County, South Carolina, USA. She was counted in the census in 1900 in Edisto Island, Charleston County, South Carolina, USA.

Hester and Robert Robinson had the following children:

i.   Joseph Robinson was born in 1855 in South Carolina.

ii.   Emma Robinson was born in 1857 in South Carolina.

iii.   Elizabeth Robinson was born in 1863 in South Carolina.

iv.   Dolly Robinson was born in 1866 in South Carolina.

v.   Mary Robinson was born in May 1870 in Hilton Head, Beaufort County, South Carolina, USA.

vi.   Anna Robinson was born in 1873 in South Carolina.

vii.   Willis Robinson was born in 1875 in South Carolina.

viii.   John Robinson was born in 1876 in South Carolina.

FORTUNE CURRY
& MARY (?) CURRY

Fortune Curry was born about 1815 in South Carolina. He died between 1870-1880 in South Carolina. He married Mary about 1850 in South Carolina. Mary was born about 1820 in South Carolina, USA. She died between 1880-1900 in South Carolina.

Fortune Curry was employed as a Farm Laborer in 1870. He was counted in the census in 1870 in St Peters, Beaufort County, South Carolina, USA. Mary was employed as a Farm laborer in 1870. She was counted in the census in 1870 in St Peters, Beaufort County, South Carolina, USA. She was employed as a Farm laborer in 1880. She was counted in the census in 1880 in Lawnton, Hampton County, South Carolina, USA.

Mary and Fortune Curry had the following children:

i.   Emma Curry was born in 1854 in South Carolina.

ii.   Cyrus Curry was born in 1859 in South Carolina.

iii.   Duncan C Curry was born in May 1869 in Beaufort Co, South Carolina, USA.

BENJAMIN ALSTON
& LUCRETIA (?) ALSTON

Benjamin "Ben" Alston was born in August 1845 in South Carolina, USA. He died on August 15, 1918 in Savannah, Georgia, USA. He married Lucretia about 1863 in Beaufort Co, South Carolina, USA. Lucretia was born about 1840 in Georgia, USA. She died between 1880-1900 in South Carolina, USA.

Benjamin "Ben" Alston was counted in the census in 1870 in St. Peters, Beaufort County, South Carolina, USA. He was employed as a Farmer between 1870-1880. He was counted in the census in 1880 in Lawnton, Hampton, South Carolina, USA. He lived in Indian Ln, 3d E. of canal, Savannah, Chatham County, Georgia, USA in 1890. He was employed as a Farm laborer in 1900. He was counted in the census in 1900 in Militia Dt 8, Chatham, Georgia, USA. He was employed as a Farm laborer (Working out) in 1910. He was counted in the census in 1910 in Militia Dt 8, Chatham, Georgia, USA. He was buried in 1918 in Laurel Grove South Cemetery, Savannah, Chatham County, Georgia, USA. He was buried on August 16, 1918 in Savannah, Chatham County, Georgia, USA.

Lucretia was employed as a Farm labor in 1870. She was counted in the census in 1870 in St. Peters, Beaufort County, South Carolina, USA. She was employed as a Labor in 1880. She was counted in the census in 1880 in Lawnton, Hampton, South Carolina, USA.

Lucretia and Benjamin "Ben" Alston had the following children:

i.   Lucy Alston was born in 1865 in South Carolina.

ii.   Elizabeth "Bessie" Alston was born in December 1870 in Beaufort Co, South Carolina, USA.

iii.   Albert Alston was born in 1874 in South Carolina. He married Anna. She was born in 1883 in South Carolina.

iv.   Mary Alston was born in 1878 in South Carolina.

JOSEPH BROWN
& LENA GLOVER

Joseph "Joe" Brown, son of David Brown and Millie Hay, was born in September 1871 in South Carolina, USA. He died between 1910-1920 in Barnwell Co, South Carolina, USA. He married Lena Glover about 1889 in Barnwell Co, South Carolina, USA. Lena Glover, daughter of Joshua Glover and Lucia Harley, was born in January 1872 in Barnwell County, South Carolina, USA. She died between 1910-1920 in Barnwell County, South Carolina, USA.

Joseph "Joe" Brown was counted in the census in 1880 in Red Oak, Barnwell, South Carolina. He was employed as a Farmer in 1900. He was counted in the census in 1900 in Allendale, Barnwell (Allendale) County, South Carolina, USA. He was counted in the census in 1910 in Allendale, Barnwell (Allendale) County, South Carolina, USA. He was employed as a Farm Labor (General ?) in 1910.

Lena Glover was counted in the census in 1880 in Red Oak, Barnwell, South Carolina. She was employed as a Farm laborer in 1900. She was counted in the census in 1900 in Allendale, Barnwell (Allendale), South Carolina, USA. She was counted in the census in 1910 in Allendale, Barnwell (Allendale), South Carolina, USA. She was employed as a ? (Odd jobs) in 1910.

Lena Glover and Joseph "Joe" Brown had the following children:

i.   Linton Brown was born in 1889 in South Carolina.

ii.   Joseph "Joe" Brown was born on July 5, 1890 in Allendale, Barnwell (Allendale) County, South Carolina, USA.

iii.   William Brown was born in 1892 in South Carolina.

iv.   Richard Brown was born in 1896 in South Carolina.

SAMUEL FRAZIER
& EVA THOMPSON

Samuel "Sam" Frazier, son of Smart Frazier and Minda Jones, was born in July 1854 in Whitehall, Aiken, South Carolina, USA. He died on March 19, 1928 in Chatham County, Georgia, USA. He married Eva Thompson about 1879 in Barnwell Co, South Carolina, USA. Eva Thompson, daughter of Adam Thompson and Mary. was born in May 1860 in Allendale, Barnwell County, South Carolina, USA. She died on January 25, 1929 in Mutual Quarters, Mil. 8, Chatham County, Georgia, USA.

Samuel "Sam" Frazier was counted in the census in 1870 in Allendale, Barnwell (Allendale), South Carolina, USA. He was employed as a Farm laborer in 1870. He was counted in the census in 1880 in Allendale, Barnwell (Allendale), South Carolina, USA. He was employed as a Laborer in 1880. He was employed as a Farmer in 1900. He was counted in the census in 1900 in Bull Pond, Barnwell (Allendale), South Carolina, USA. He was employed as a Farmer (Private) in 1910. He was counted in the census in 1910 in Allendale, Barnwell (Allendale), South Carolina, USA. He was counted in the census in 1920 in Baldoc, Allendale County, South Carolina, USA. He was employed as a Farmer (General farm) in 1920. He lived in 16 Lathrop Ave., Mutual Quarters, Chatham County, Georgia, USA in 1928. He was buried on March 21, 1928 in Laurel Grove Cemetery, Savannah, Chatham County, Georgia, USA. His cause of death was Acute nephritis.

Eva Thompson was counted in the census in 1870 in Allendale, Barnwell County, South Carolina, USA. She was counted in the census in 1880 in Allendale, Barnwell (Allendale), South Carolina, USA. She was employed as a Laborer in 1880. She was counted in the census in 1900 in Bull Pond, Barnwell (Allendale), South Carolina, USA. She was employed as a Farm laborer in 1900. She was counted in the census in 1910 in Allendale, Barnwell (Allendale), South Carolina, USA. She was counted in the census in 1920 in Baldoc, Allendale Co County, South Carolina, USA. Her funeral took place in 1929 in ? Monroe Funeral Home, 611 W. Broad (now MLK Jr Blvd), Savannah, Chatham County, Georgia, USA. She was buried on January 27, 1929 in Laurel Grove Cemetery, Savannah, Chatham County, Georgia, USA. Her cause of death was Haemoplegia.

Eva Thompson and Samuel "Sam" Frazier had the following children:

i.   Whilhemina "Minnie" Frazier was born in 1881 in South Carolina. She married Gillison.

ii.   Samuel Frazier was born in 1882 in South Carolina.

iii.   Robert Frazier was born in 1884 in South Carolina. He married Julia. He married Nora. She was born in 1889.

iv.   Nancy Frazier was born in October 1886 in Barnwell County, South Carolina, USA.

v.   Benjamin Frazier was born in 1889 in South Carolina. He married Grace.

vi.   Mary "Mamie" Frazier was born in 1892 in South Carolina.

vii.   John W Frazier was born in 1893 in South Carolina.

viii.   Helen Frazier was born in 1896 in South Carolina.

ix. William "Willie" Frazier was born in 1898 in South Carolina. He married Whilhemina "Minnie". She was born in 1897.

x.   Susan Frazier was born in 1902 in South Carolina.

GIUSEPPE ROMANO
& ANGELA DI SIMONE

Giuseppe Romano, son of Antonio Romano and Maria, was born about 1780 in St. Agata, Palermo, Sicily and died on 25 August 1823 in St. Cristina, Palermo, Sicily. Another name for Giuseppe was Joseph Romano. Giuseppe married Angela di Simone, daughter of Antonio di Simone and Unknown, in Sicily in about 1815. Angela was born about 1792 in Italy and died on 20 January 1825 in Brancaccio, Palermo, Sicily, Italy.

The known child of Giuseppe Romano and Angela di Simone is Ireneo Romano was born on 2 December 1820 in St. Agata, Palermo, Sicily, Italy and died in Sicily, Italy.

The afternoon sun slanted down over the rooftops of nearby houses and here and there in Palermo small groups of men sat on the porticos, sipping coffee and talking business and politics. The major topic was the fact that the King and his sizeable retinue was returning to Naples. They had been a little worried over the potential ill effects of the presence of so many foreign troops. But the last four years had been easier than any of them had expected.

The King and family were rarely seen in Palermo. They had spent most of their time at the Chinese Villa which was built in a park at the foot of Mount Pellegrino, or at the Royal Hunting Lodge on his estate in the mountains near Corleone. And no one could complain about business; trade had been good with the increased visits from the English fleet. So now the conversation was about what might happen when the King returned to Naples. The pessimists said that business would slow. The realists said wait and see.

Just as surely as the summer brings the hot sirrocco blowing out of Africa, in Sicily the son follows the father into the family business. And it has been a good year for trade in Palermo. The Americans came seeking allies against the Barbary pirates. Sicily, who also lost ships and goods to the priates, joined the coalition, along with the Swedes, Maltese, Portuguese, and Moroccans to patrol the Mediterranean and interdict pirate actions. Not only did Palermo benefit from the better flow of trade goods, but they also made profits from supplying the fleets.

The young man stood near the warehouse door and watched as the ship unloaded soldiers and officers. It was an English ship, here, he had heard, to advise and support King Ferdinand in his argument with Napoleon. Apparently Napoleon had stopped playing and had sent his army south to conquer Naples and to install his brother on the throne.

Now, the English have once again rescued King Ferdinand and brought him to his palace in Sicily. Once again Ferdinand has brought his Neapolitan guards, along with a much larger band of ruffians. This time there is a much stronger contingent of the English Navy, too. After the initial excitement, life settles into a pace not much different than before.

God bless the English Navy! The King cannot survive without the support of the English and he knows it too well. The English Minister, Lord William Bentick, has used this fact to pressure the King into approving an English style Constitution for Sicily! There will be a representative Parliament, a real parliament, not that feudal facade of a parliamentary system that had existed in the past. Finally, Sicily's life and future will be in the hands of Sicilians!

Today, King Ferdinand personally opened the first session of the Sicilian Parliament. For the first time ever, Sicilians have a strong voice in their governance. There is much joy and celebration in Palermo.

The Austrians have defeated the French and have restored King Ferdinand to his throne in Naples. He has proclaimed himself king of the Kingdom of the Two Sicilies and has proclaimed that legislation and administration will be uniform throughout his Kingdom. He has destroyed the Sicilian constitution in all but name. Anger and frustration is everywhere in the streets of Palermo. The people want revolution, but for now cooler heads prevail. Diplomacy will get its chance.

Meanwhile, daily life goes on; young men court and marry, children grow, business gets done.

The military in Naples have revolted and forced the King to institute the Spanish Constitution of 1812. They have declared a united parliament for both Sicily and Naples, to be held in Naples. Sicily's parliament has rejected this outrageous proposition and has demanded that the King's union of the two kingdoms be repealed and that Sicily retain its right to its own parliament. The Neapolitans have refused. What now of Sicily's Constitution, Sicily's Parliament? Sicily has had representation for such a short time! But it has already grown precious and it will be retained! If doing so requires revolution, so be it.

At the end of July, Palermo declares Independence. Negotiations, small uprisings and skirmishes occur throughout August. At the end of August, 7,000 Neapolitan troops landed to enforce negotiations. One of the demands by the Army was that the Neapolitan forces occupy Palermo and that the Parliament be convened. The Parliament would then decide the question of independence. The Sicilian negotiators agree – but the people of Palermo do not.

The troops move on Palermo, but the people rise up against them fighting them in the streets. For days, the people seem to be winning. But on the 26th of September, the Neapolitans attack again, sacking and burning houses in the suburbs; murdering the inhabitants. The mob in Palermo retaliates by killing Neapolitan residents of Palermo and any who support them. That night, the Neapolitan fleet and the fortresses at Castellamare and Garita bombard the City with cannon fire as the troops capture the suburbs and began to slowly penetrate into the heart of Palermo. It is estimated that about 500 of the Neapolitans are killed that day and night – but about 4,000 Sicilians are killed. Within a few days, the populace is forced to surrender Palermo to the King's troops.

In the end, the revolution has been bitter and short with much destruction in the streets of Palermo. Hundreds of houses are destroyed along with businesses, libraries, and lives. And in the end nothing is gained. The Neapolitans want representative government for themselves, but not for Sicily. Their soldiers support the King against Sicily and there has been much bloodshed and destruction in the streets of Palermo. Hundreds have been arrested and executed. What a year for a son to be born.

Now the Neapolitans know how Sicily feels; their freedoms and Sicily's are all down the same hole. The Austrians have marched on Naples in support of King Ferdinand. All constitutions are abolished and the King is returned to absolute power. It is hard not to feel that the Neapolitans had it coming, but it is a black time for all.

The damage that the revolution had done to Palermo is slowly rebuilt. The carretas of Palermo take produce and goods to the port for shipping and receive other goods for delivery to the shops of Palermo and nearby towns. Business gets done, children grow, old people die; life goes on.

Politically, the concentration of power in the Kingdom of the Two Sicilies becomes even more concentrated in Naples. In Sicily, the anger of the people continues to fester and grows among the people. For the first time since in history the great city states of Sicily begin to join together in a national undertaking. A conspiracy begins to grow, a conspiracy against the King and the Neapolitans.

Spies tell the government in Naples about the plots; whenever there is a whisper that something may actually happen, the King's officers crush it with ruthless violence. In 1823, 3 men from Palermo and six from Messina are condemned and shot. Nine more are executed for a plot to poison bread and wine being delivered to the Austrian soldiers occupying the island.

JOHN WITTLE
& ANNA HUMMER

John Wittle, son of John Jacob Wittel and Anna Etler, was born on November 21, 1805 in Lancaster County, Pennsylvania, USA. He died on March 25, 1868 in Lancaster County, Pennsylvania, USA. He married Anna Hummer on November 11, 1828 in Brickerville, Lancaster County, Pennsylvania, USA.

Anna Hummer was born on January 20, 1802 in Pennsylvania, USA. She died on June 24, 1876 in Rapho, Lancaster County, Pennsylvania, USA.

John Wittle was counted in the census in 1810 in parents (w). He was counted in the census in 1820 in father (Warwick, Lancaster County, Pennsylvania, USA). He was counted in the census in 1830 in Warwick, Lancaster County, Pennsylvania, USA. He was counted in the census in 1840 in Warwick, Lancaster County, Pennsylvania, USA. He was affiliated with the Zion Evangelical Lutheran, Manheim, Pennsylvania, USA religion in 1841. He was employed as a Laborer in 1850. He was counted in the census in 1850 in Rapho, Lancaster County, Pennsylvania, USA. He was employed as a Day laborer in 1860. He was counted in the census in 1860 in Rapho, Lancaster County, Pennsylvania, USA. He was buried in 1868 in Private Mt. Pleasant Farm near Horst's Mill, Rapho, Lancaster County, Pennsylvania, USA. He was employed as a Shoemaker in 1869. His estate was probated in 1869 in Lancaster County, Pennsylvania, USA.

Anna Hummer was counted in the census in 1810. She was counted in the census in 1820. She was counted in the census in 1830 in Warwick, Lancaster County, Pennsylvania, USA. She was counted in the census in

1840 in Lancaster, Lancaster County, Pennsylvania, USA. She was counted in the census in 1850 in Rapho, Lancaster County, Pennsylvania, USA. She was counted in the census in 1860 in Rapho, Lancaster County, Pennsylvania, USA. She was counted in the census in 1870 in Rapho, Lancaster County, Pennsylvania, USA (son Cyrus Witble). She was buried in 1876. She was employed as a Homemaker.

Anna Hummer and John Wittle had the following children:

i.   Henry H Wittle was born in 1829 in Lancaster County, Pennsylvania, USA. He died in 1903. He married Barbara Heinaman. She was born in 1840 in Pennsylvania, USA.

ii.   Jacob Harvey Wittle was born on December 23, 1830 in Lancaster County, Pennsylvania, USA.

iii. Amy Wittle was born in 1833 in Pennsylvania, USA.

iv.   John Wittle was born in 1833 in Pennsylvania, USA. He died in 1862. He married Fianna Shaffer. She was born in 1840.

v.   Catherine "Kate" Wittle was born in 1835 in Pennsylvania, USA. She died in 1901. She married Henry Horst. He was born in 1829 in Pennsylvania, USA.

vi.   David H Wittle was born in 1837 in Pennsylvania, USA. He died in 1920. He married Barbara M Eschelman. She was born in 1847 in Pennsylvania, USA. She died in 1911.

vii. Mary Wittle was born in 1841 in Pennsylvania, USA. She died in 1896. She married Jacob Garber. He was born in 1838 in Pennsylvania, USA.

viii. Cyrus H Wittle was born in 1843 in Pennsylvania, USA. He died in 1916. He married Catherine Diffenderfer. She was born in 1849 in Pennsylvania, USA.

WILLIAM KYLE
& MARY J. WHITMOYER

William Kyle was born about 1795 in Pennsylvania, USA. He died between 1840-1850 in Lancaster County, Pennsylvania, USA. He married Mary "Mollie" Juliana Whitmoyer about 1825 in Lancaster,Pennsylvania, USA. Mary "Mollie" Juliana Whitmoyer was born about 1795 in Pennsylvania, USA. She died between 1840-1850 in Lancaster County, Pennsylvania, USA.

William Kyle was counted in the census in 1830 in Lampeter, Lancaster County, Pennsylvania, USA. He was counted in the census in 1840 in Lancaster, Lancaster County, Pennsylvania, USA.

Mary "Mollie" Juliana Whitmoyer was counted in the census in 1830 in husband (Lampeter, Lancaster County, Pennsylvania, USA). She was counted in the census in 1840 in husband (Lancaster, Lancaster County, Pennsylvania, USA).

Mary "Mollie" Juliana Whitmoyer and William Kyle had the following children:

i.   Jacob Kyle was born in 1827.

ii.   Henry Kyle was born in 1829. He married Anna. She was born in 1834 in Pennsylvania, USA.

iii.   Mary Catherine "Kate" Kyle was born on December 31, 1835 in Lancaster County, Pennsylvania, USA.

JOHN MINICK
& ELIZABETH YAEGER

John Minick was born about 1810 in Pennsylvania, USA. He died after 1842 in Pennsylvania, USA. He married Elizabeth "Lizzie" Yaeger about 1839 in Dauphin, Pennsylvania, USA. Elizabeth "Lizzie" Yaeger was born about 1810 in Pennsylvania, USA. She died after 1842 in Pennsylvania, USA.

John Minick was counted in the census in 1830. He was counted in the census in 1840 in Harrisburg, Dauphin County, Pennsylvania, USA. He was counted in the census in 1850. He was counted in the census in 1860. He was counted in the census in 1870. He lived in George Minnich Homestead, located in Warwick, Lancaster, Pennsylvania.

Elizabeth "Lizzie" Yaeger was counted in the census in 1830. She was counted in the census in 1840 in Harrisburg, Dauphin County, Pennsylvania, USA. She was counted in the census in 1850. She was counted in the census in 1860. She was counted in the census in 1870. Her cause of death was Dropsy.

Elizabeth "Lizzie" Yaeger and John Minick had the following children:

i.   Jeremiah Minick was born in 1836. He died in 1915.

ii.   Elizabeth Minick was born in 1841 in Pennsylvania, USA.

iii.   Mary Minick was born in 1841 in Pennsylvania, USA.

iv.   Henry Minick was born on February 28, 1842 in Dauphin County, Pennsylvania, USA.

GEORGE W. SHEETS
& MARY E. MCKIM

George W Sheets, son of John George Sheets and Mary "Polly" Forman, was born on February 15, 1812 in Susquehanna, Dauphin, Pennsylvania. He died on December 26, 1883 in Buffalo, Perry County, Pennsylvania, USA. He married Mary Elizabeth McKim between September-November 1835 in Dauphin County, Pennsylvania, USA. Mary Elizabeth McKim, daughter of James M McKim and Catherine Miller, was born on June 9, 1816 in Pennsylvania, USA. She died on November 10, 1887 in Dauphin County, Pennsylvania, USA.

George W Sheets was counted in the census in 1820 in Susquehanna, Dauphin County, Pennsylvania, USA. He lived in Relocated to Wayne Township, Dauphin County, Pennsylvania, USA about 1825. He was counted in the census in 1830 in parents (w). He was counted in the census in 1840 in Jackson, Dauphin County, Pennsylvania, USA. He was counted in the census in 1850 in Jefferson, Dauphin County, Pennsylvania, USA. He was employed as a Carpenter between 1850-1870. He was counted in the census in 1860 in Buffalo, Perry County, Pennsylvania, USA. He was counted in the census in 1870 in Buffalo, Perry County, Pennsylvania, USA. He was counted in the census in 1880 in Duncannon, Perry County, Pennsylvania, USA. He was buried in December 1883. His estate was probated between January 12-March 4, 1884 in Perry County, Pennsylvania, USA. His cause of death was Injuries received in a fall.

Mary Elizabeth McKim was counted in the census in 1820 in father (Carlisle, Cumberland County, Pennsylvania, USA). She was counted in the census in 1830 in father (Shippensburg, Cumberland County, Pennsylvania, USA). She immigrated before 1835. She was counted in the census in 1840 in parents (w). She was counted in the census in 1850 in Jefferson, Dauphin County, Pennsylvania, USA. She was counted in the census in 1860 in Jefferson, Dauphin County, Pennsylvania, USA. She was employed as a Keeping house in 1870. She was counted in the census in 1870 in Jefferson, Dauphin County, Pennsylvania, USA. She was counted in the census in 1880 in Ewington, Dauphin County, Pennsylvania, USA. She was buried in 1887 in St Pauls (Bowermans) Lutheran, Enterline, Dauphin County, Pennsylvania, USA. George W Sheets and Mary Elizabeth McKim were divorced about 1858 in Left wife Mary.

Mary Elizabeth McKim and George W Sheets had the following children:

i.   Joseph J Sheets was born in 1836 in Pennsylvania, USA. He married Catherine. She was born in 1839 in Pennsylvania, USA. He married Rebecca M. She was born in 1857 in Pennsylvania, USA.

ii.   Isaac Sheets was born in 1839 in Pennsylvania, USA. He married Frances "Fannie". She was born in 1842.

iii.   Sarah Ann Sheets was born in 1841 in Pennsylvania, USA.

iv.   Lucy Ann Sheets was born in September 1842 in Dauphin County, Pennsylvania, USA.

v.   Catherine "Kate" Sheets was born in 1843 in Pennsylvania, USA. She married John A Proudfoot. He was born in 1822 in Pennsylvania, USA.

vi.   Emmanuel Sheets was born in 1848 in Pennsylvania, USA. He married Elizabeth. She was born in 1848. She died in 1885.

vii.   William H Sheets was born in 1848 in Pennsylvania, USA. He married Mary M. She was born in 1854.

viii. Andrew Sheets was born in 1853 in Pennsylvania, USA. He married Jane. She was born in 1874 in Pennsylvania, USA.

ix. Helen A Sheets was born in 1853 in Pennsylvania, USA.

x. Agnes E Sheets was born in 1856 in Pennsylvania, USA.

xi. George Sheets was born in 1859 in Pennsylvania, USA.

LOUIS L. STEWART
& MARTHA E. SMITH

Louis Luther Stewart, son of Alexander Stewart, was born in May 1838 in Dauphin Co, Pennsylvania, USA. He died on December 18, 1876 in Cumberland County, Pennsylvania, USA. He married Martha Elizabeth Smith about 1860 in Cumberland, Pennsylvania, USA. Martha Elizabeth Smith, daughter of Daniel Smith, was born on December 14, 1840 in Lancaster County, Pennsylvania, USA. She died on January 8, 1926 in Wormleysburg, Cumberland County, Pennsylvania, USA.

Louis Luther Stewart was counted in the census in 1840 in Lower Swatara, Dauphin County, Pennsylvania, USA. He was educated at School in 1850. He was counted in the census in 1850 in Portsmouth (Middletown), Dauphin County, Pennsylvania, USA. He was counted in the census in 1860. He was employed as a Laborer in 1870. He was counted in the census in 1870 in East Pennsboro, Cumberland County, Pennsylvania, USA. He lived in Oysters Mill, Conodoquinet, Cumberland County, Pennsylvania, USA in 1876. He was buried in 1876 in Zion (Brick) Lutheran, Enola, Cumberland County, Pennsylvania, USA. He was buried about 1950 in He and his wife's remains and tombstone were moved from near Martin Stewart's old home to another cemetery. His height was 6 feet tall. His cause of death was Accidental shooting. He had a medical condition of Hair light, Complexion fair, Eyes blue, Lewis G Stewart, Civil War Veterans Card File, 1861-1866, Pennsylvania, USA State Archives, www.digitalarchives.state.pa.us.

Martha Elizabeth Smith was born on December 8, 1840 in

Pennsylvania, USA. She was counted in the census in 1850 in father (w). She was counted in the census in 1860 in Conoy, Lancaster County, Pennsylvania, USA(Haldeman). She was counted in the census in 1870 in East Pennsboro, Cumberland County, Pennsylvania, USA. She was employed as a Keeps house in 1870. She was counted in the census in 1880 in East Pennsboro, Cumberland County, Pennsylvania, USA. She was employed as a Servant in 1880. She was counted in the census in 1900 in East Pennsboro, Cumberland County, Pennsylvania, USA. She was employed as 'Own income' in 1910. She lived in North 2nd St. (West side), Wormleysburg, Cumberland County, Pennsylvania, USA in 1910. She was counted in the census in 1910 in daughter Emma (Wormleysburg, Cumberland County, Pennsylvania, USA). She was counted in the census in 1920 in East Pennsboro, Cumberland County, Pennsylvania, USA. She lived in 108 North 2nd St., Wormleysburg, Cumberland County, Pennsylvania, USA in 1920. She signed her will on April 3, 1925 in Wormleysburg, Cumberland County, Pennsylvania, USA. Her funeral took place in 1926 in C.M. Musselman, 324 Hummel Ave., Lemoyne, Cumberland County, Pennsylvania, USA. She was employed as a Housework in 1926. She was buried on January 12, 1926 in Zion (Brick) Lutheran, Enola, Cumberland County, Pennsylvania, USA. Her estate was probated on January 12, 1926 in Cumberland County, Pennsylvania, USA. Her cause of death was Uremic coma. She was buried in West Fairview Methodist Church, Pennsylvania, USA.

Martha Elizabeth Smith and Louis Luther Stewart had the following children:

i.   Mary Margaret Stewart was born in 1862 in Pennsylvania, USA.

ii.   John W Stewart was born in 1865 in Pennsylvania, USA. He married

Laura V. She was born in 1854 in Pennsylvania, USA.

iii.   Emma O Stewart was born in 1868 in Pennsylvania, USA. She married Guyer.

iv.   Jacob Franklin Stewart was born on August 26, 1869 in Cumberland County, Pennsylvania, USA.

v.   Martin B Stewart was born in 1875 in Pennsylvania, USA. He died in 1945. He married Lydia R McKinsey. She was born in 1880. She died in 1937.

vi.   Martha Stewart was born in 1875 in Pennsylvania, USA.

vii.   Louis L Stewart was born in 1876 in Pennsylvania, USA. He died in 1950. He married Mary Etta Surry. She was born in 1876 in Pennsylvania, USA.

viii.   ? Stewart was born in Pennsylvania, USA.

JAMES MCKINSEY
& SUSAN FRY

James McKinsey, son of Daniel McKinsey, was born in 1805 in Ireland. He died on May 20, 1883 in Enola, Cumberland County, Pennsylvania, USA. He married Susan Fry on December 25, 1851 in York County, Pennsylvania, USA. Susan Fry, daughter of Henry Fry, was born on November 13, 1826 in York County, Pennsylvania, USA. She died on October 15, 1909 in Enola, Cumberland County, Pennsylvania, USA.

James McKinsey was counted in the census in 1810 in parents (w). He was counted in the census in 1820 in parents (w). He was counted in the census in 1830 in parents (w). He was counted in the census in 1840 in Dickinson, Cumberland County, Pennsylvania, USA. He was counted in the census in 1850 in Lower Windsor, York County, Pennsylvania, USA. He was employed as a Laborer between 1850-1860. He was counted in the census in 1860 in Lower Windsor, York County, Pennsylvania, USA. He was employed as 'Works' in 1870. He was counted in the census in 1870 in East Pennsboro, Cumberland County, Pennsylvania, USA. He was counted in the census in 1880 in East Pennsboro, Cumberland County, Pennsylvania, USA. He was employed as a Laborer in 1880. He was buried in 1883 in Zion (Brick) Lutheran, Enola, Cumberland County, Pennsylvania, USA.

Susan Fry was counted in the census in 1830 in father (Windsor, York County, Pennsylvania, USA). She was counted in the census in 1840 in parents (w). She was counted in the census in 1850 in Windsor, York County, Pennsylvania, USA. She was counted in the census in 1860 in Lower Windsor, York County, Pennsylvania, USA. She was employed as a Keeps house in 1870. She was counted in the census in 1870 in East Pennsboro, Cumberland County, Pennsylvania, USA. She was counted in the census in 1880 in East Pennsboro, Cumberland County, Pennsylvania, USA. She was employed as a Keeping house in 1880. She was counted in the census in 1900. She was employed as a Housework in 1909. Her funeral took place in 1909 in C.M. Musselman, 324 Hummel Ave., Lemoyne, Cumberland County, Pennsylvania, USA. She lived in West Fairview, Cumberland County, Pennsylvania, USA in 1909. She was buried on October 18, 1909 in Zion (Brick) Lutheran, Enola, Cumberland County, Pennsylvania, USA. She was born in West Fairview, Cumberland County, Pennsylvania, USA. Her cause of death was Shock caused by being hit by railroad engine.

Susan Fry and James McKinsey had the following children:

i.   Thomas H McKinsey was born in 1854 in Pennsylvania, USA. He died in 1933. He married Leah A Hamilton. She was born in 1857 in Pennsylvania, USA. She died in 1917.

ii.   Charles McKinsey was born in 1861 in Pennsylvania, USA.

iii.   Emma L McKinsey was born in 1865 in Pennsylvania, USA. She married George William Geesey. He was born in 1852.

iv.   Barbara A McKinsey was born in 1869 in Pennsylvania, USA. She married James William Beck. He was born in 1859. She married Johnson.

v.   Matilda "Tillie" A McKinsey was born in July 1873 in West Fairview, Cumberland County, Pennsylvania, USA.

JOHN E. SHOVER
& MARGARET T. PIPER

John E Shover, son of Sebastian Shover and Anna "Annie" Elizabeth O'Donnell, was born on July 25, 1850 in Cumberland Co, Pennsylvania, USA. He died on March 20, 1917 in Harrisburg Hospital, Harrisburg, Dauphin County, Pennsylvania, USA. He married Margaret "Maggie" Tabitha Piper about 1873 in Cumberland County, Pennsylvania, USA. Margaret "Maggie" Tabitha Piper, daughter of George Piper and Agnes Harvey, was born in February 1851 in Amberson Valley, Franklin County, Pennsylvania, USA. She died on December 13, 1903 in Harrisburg, Dauphin County, Pennsylvania, USA.

John E Shover was counted in the census in 1860 in Dickinson, Cumberland County, Pennsylvania, USA. He was educated at School in 1860. He served in the military between 1863-1864 (Civil War, Private 1st Reg Pennsylvania, USA Inf, Co F (Harrisburg, Ramsey). He was counted in the census in 1870 in West Pennsboro, Cumberland County, Pennsylvania, USA. He was employed as a Works for CVCRR in 1880. He was counted in the census in 1880 in Shippensburg, Cumberland County, Pennsylvania, USA. Pension: May 20, 1899 in Pennsylvania, USA He served in the military on May 20, 1899 in Pension app. He lived in 1211 7th St., Harrisburg, Dauphin County, Pennsylvania, USA in 1900. He was counted in the census in 1900 in Harrisburg, Dauphin County, Pennsylvania, USA. He was counted in the census in 1910. He was employed as a Teamster in 1917. His funeral took place in 1917 in Hawkins Funeral, Harrisburg, Dauphin County, Pennsylvania, USA. He was buried on March 22, 1917 in East Harrisburg

Cemetery, Harrisburg, Dauphin County, Pennsylvania, USA. His cause of death was Concussion of the brain contributory cause kicked by a horse.

Margaret "Maggie" Tabitha Piper was counted in the census in 1860 in Fannett, Franklin County, Pennsylvania, USA. She was counted in the census in 1870 in Susquehanna, Dauphin County, Pennsylvania, USA. She was counted in the census in 1880 in Shippensburg, Cumberland County, Pennsylvania, USA. She was employed as a Keeping house in 1880. She was counted in the census in 1900 in Harrisburg, Dauphin County, Pennsylvania, USA. She lived in 114 Charles St., Harrisburg, Dauphin County, Pennsylvania, USA in 1903. She was buried on December 16, 1903 in East Harrisburg Cemetery, Harrisburg, Dauphin County, Pennsylvania, USA. Her cause of death was Paralysis.

Margaret "Maggie" Tabitha Piper and John E Shover had the following children:

i.   Mary A Shover was born in 1875 in Pennsylvania, USA.

ii.   Anna T Shover was born in 1876 in Pennsylvania, USA.

iii.   Robert Charles Shover was born on May 1, 1878 in Cumberland Co, Pennsylvania, USA.

iv.   Edna Shover was born in 1894 in Pennsylvania, USA.

CYRUS W. SHANNON
& MARY J. SWOVELAND

Cyrus W Shannon, son of James Shannon, was born in September 1848 in Southampton, Cumberland County, Pennsylvania, USA. He died on February 16, 1901 in Huckle Berry Land (Mainsville), Cumberland County, Pennsylvania, USA. He married Mary "Mollie" Jane Swoveland about 1870 in Cumberland County, Pennsylvania, USA.

Mary "Mollie" Jane Swoveland, daughter of Henry Swoveland and Rachel Wolf, was born in December 1848 in Franklin County, Pennsylvania, USA. She died on January 16, 1901 in Huckle Berry Land (Mainsville), Cumberland County, Pennsylvania, USA.

Cyrus W Shannon was born in February 1843 in Pennsylvania, USA. He was counted in the census in 1850. He was counted in the census in 1860 in South Hampton, Cumberland County, Pennsylvania, USA(Russell) (Living with John and Mary Russell). He served in the military between February 22, 1864-June 24, 1865 (Civil War, Private, 22nd Reg Pennsylvania, USA Cav, Co F (Chambersburg, Capt. Andrew J. Barr). He served in the military between June 24-October 31, 1865 (Civil War, Private, 3rd Reg MD Provisional Cav, Co G (Cumberland, MD). He was employed as a Day laborer in 1870. He was counted in the census in 1870 in South Hampton, Cumberland County, Pennsylvania, USA. He was counted in the census in 1880 in South Hampton, Cumberland County, Pennsylvania, USA (Sharmon). He was employed as a Laborer between 1880-1900. He lived in Southampton, Cumberland County, Pennsylvania, USA in 1890. Pension: January 22, 1891 in Pennsylvania, USA He served in the military on January

22, 1891 in Pension app. He was counted in the census in 1900 in South Hampton, Cumberland County, Pennsylvania, USA. He lived in Southampton, Cumberland County, Pennsylvania, USA about 1900. He was employed as a Retired in 1901. He died on February 2, 1901 in Southampton Township, Cumberland County, Pennsylvania, USA. He was buried on February 19, 1901 in Jacksonville Evangelical, Walnut Bottom, Cumberland County, Pennsylvania, USA (Gray Thorn). He signed his will on March 1, 1901 in Southampton Township, Cumberland County, Pennsylvania, USA. His estate was probated on March 8, 1901 in Southampton Township, Cumberland County, Pennsylvania, USA.

Mary "Mollie" Jane Swoveland was counted in the census in 1860. She was counted in the census in 1870 in South Hampton, Cumberland County, Pennsylvania, USA. She was employed as a Keeping house in 1870. She was employed as a Keeping house in 1880. She was counted in the census in 1880 in South Hampton, Cumberland County, Pennsylvania, USA. She was counted in the census in 1900 in South Hampton, Cumberland County, Pennsylvania, USA. She was employed as a House keeper between 1900-1901. She lived in Southampton, Cumberland County, Pennsylvania, USA about 1900. She was buried on January 18, 1901 in Jacksonville Evangelical, Walnut Bottom, Cumberland County, Pennsylvania, USA (Gray Thorn). Her cause of death was Heart trouble.

Mary "Mollie" Jane Swoveland and Cyrus W Shannon had the following children:

i.	Mary A Shannon was born in 1875 in Pennsylvania, USA. She married Louis W Smith.

ii.	John A Shannon was born about 1875 in Pennsylvania, USA. He married Anna. She was born in 1870 in Pennsylvania, USA. He married Mary

Anna Reath on June 28, 1915 in Cumberland County, Pennsylvania, USA. She was born in 1885 in Pennsylvania, USA.

iii.   Sarah Shannon was born in 1876 in Pennsylvania, USA. She married Joseph Kennedy Armstrong.

iv.   Elizabeth "Bessie" A Shannon was born on April 30, 1883 in Cumberland Co, Pennsylvania, USA.

GAETANO BARBUSCIO
& ORSOLA MARSICO

Gaetano Barbuscio, son of Joseph (Giuseppe) Barbuscio and Marianne (Marianna) Settino, was born about 1799 in Castiglione, Cosenza, Calabria, Italy. He died on September 20, 1862 in Castiglione, Cosenza, Calabria, Italy. He married Ursula (Orsola) Marsico on December 25, 1824 in Castiglione, Cosenza, Calabria, Italy.

Ursula (Orsola) Marsico, daughter of Joseph (Giuseppe) Marsico and Theresa (Teresa) Muto, was born about 1802 in Castiglione, Cosenza, Calabria, Italy. She died on March 24, 1862 in Castiglione, Cosenza, Calabria, Italy.

Ursula (Orsola) Marsico and Gaetano Barbuscio had the following children:

i.   Pascal (Pasquale) Barbuscio was born on September 23, 1839 in Castiglione, Cosenza, Calabria, Italy.

ii.   Joseph Barbuscio.

iii.   Peter Barbuscio was born in Italy.

CARMINE M. BUGLIO
& GIUSEPPINA MAGNELLI

Carmine Mario "Francis" Buglio, son of Casper Buglio and Catherine (Catarina) Preite, was born on February 6, 1811 in Castiglione, Cosenza, Calabria, Italy. He died on July 15, 1879 in Castiglione, Cosenza, Calabria, Italy. He married Josephine (Giuseppina) Magnelli on July 15, 1833 in Castiglione, Cosenza, Calabria, Italy.

Josephine (Giuseppina) Magnelli, daughter of Hyancinth Magnelli and Anna Marsico, was born on January 6, 1818 in Castiglione, Cosenza, Calabria, Italy. She died on July 25, 1856 in Castiglione, Cosenza, Calabria, Italy. Josephine (Giuseppina) Magnelli was employed as a Homemaker about 1840. She was buried in 1856.

Josephine (Giuseppina) Magnelli and Carmine Mario "Francis" Buglio had the following children:

i.   Rosa Buglio was born about 1834 in Italy.

ii.   Casper Buglio was born in 1838 in Italy. He died in 1839.

iii.   Casper Martino Buglio was born in 1840 in Italy. He died in 1842.

iv.   Carmine Catherine (Carmina Catarina) Buglio was born on April 19, 1843 in Castiglione, Cosenza, Calabria, Italy.

v.   Filomena Buglio was born in 1846 in Italy. She died in 1916 in Pennsylvania. She married Gaetano Magarao. He was born in 1844 in Italy.

vi.   Anthony Buglio was born in 1849 in Italy. He died in 1920. He married Filomena DeStephano. She was born in 1853 in Italy.

vii.   Casper Buglio was born in 1851 in Italy. He married Rosario Lio. She was born in 1860 in Italy.

GIUSEPPE M. DESTEPHANO
& ROSA MARTINO

Joseph (Giuseppe) Mario Santo DeStephano, son of Gabriel (Gabriele) DeStephano and Carmine (Carmina) Leone, was born about 1814 in Castiglione, Cosenza, Calabria, Italy. He died after 1861 in Italy. He married Rose (Rosa) Martino about 1850 in Italy.

Rose (Rosa) Martino, daughter of Joseph (Giuseppe) Martino and Josephine (Giuseppina) Carricato, was born about 1822 in Castiglione, Cosenza, Calabria, Italy. She died after 1861 in Italy.

Rose (Rosa) Martino and Joseph (Giuseppe) Mario Santo DeStephano had the following child:

i.   Peter (Pietro) DeStephano was born about 1861 in Castiglione, Cosenza, Calabria, Italy.

NICOLO C. SAMMARCO
& MARIA ACRI

Nicholas (Nicolo) Casper Sammarco, son of Peter (Pietro) Sammarco and Ursula (Orsola) Buglio, was born about 1833 in Castiglione, Cosenza, Calabria, Italy. He died after 1865 in Italy. He married Maria Acri about 1860 in Italy.

Maria Acri, daughter of Pascal (Pasquale) Acri and Marianne (Marianna) Maria Cairo, was born on November 22, 1834 in Castiglione, Cosenza, Calabria, Italy. She died on November 19, 1910 in Castiglione, Cosenza, Calabria, Italy.

Maria Acri and Nicholas (Nicolo) Casper Sammarco had the following child:

i.   Ursula (Orsola) Sammarco was born in 1865 in Castiglione, Cosenza, Calabria, Italy.

End of Generation 6, Remaining Generations are in:

COMPLETE FAMILY
HISTORY BIOGRAPHIES
- PART TWO -

PHOTOS

William, Charles, Katie & Amy Anderson

COMMONWEALTH OF PENNSYLVANIA • DEPARTMENT OF HEALTH • VITAL RECORDS
CERTIFICATE OF DEATH

033201

OF DECEDENT (First, Middle, Last): MAMIE LUCETTA DUNCAN

SEX: F
SOCIAL SECURITY NUMBER: 170 — 26 — 9870
DATE OF DEATH (Month, Day, Year): APR. 3, 1989

AGE (Birthday): 80 Yrs
DATE OF BIRTH: Apr. 11, 1908
BIRTHPLACE (City and State or Foreign Country): Jackson Twp. Snyder Co., Pa.
PLACE OF DEATH / HOSPITAL

WAS DECEDENT OF HISPANIC ORIGIN? No X
PLACE — White

COUNTY OF DEATH: MONTOUR
CITY, BORO, TWP OF DEATH: DERRY TWP. RD #2

WAS DECEDENT EVER IN U.S. ARMED FORCES? No X
DECEDENT'S EDUCATION: Elementary/Secondary 8

MARITAL STATUS: Widow
SURVIVING SPOUSE

DECEDENT'S USUAL OCCUPATION: Housewife
KIND OF BUSINESS/INDUSTRY

DECEDENT'S MAILING ADDRESS: RD #2 Box 574 Danville, Pa. 17821

DECEDENT'S ACTUAL RESIDENCE:
17a. State: PENNSYLVANIA
17b. County: MONTOUR
Did decedent live in a township? 17c. X Yes, decedent lived in: DERRY

FATHER'S NAME: William M. Anderson

MOTHER'S NAME (First, Middle, Maiden Surname): Emma L. Keefer

INFORMANT'S NAME: Mrs. Ethel Cameron
INFORMANT'S MAILING ADDRESS: RD2 Box 574, Danville, Pa. 17821

METHOD OF DISPOSITION: Burial X
DATE OF DISPOSITION: Apr. 5, 1989
PLACE OF DISPOSITION: Pomfret Manor Cemetery
LOCATION: Sunbury, Pa. 17801

NAME AND ADDRESS OF FACILITY: V. L. Seebold Funeral Home, Selinsgrove, Pa. 17870

SIGNATURE OF FUNERAL SERVICE LICENSEE
LICENSE NUMBER: FD-008585-L

WAS CASE REFERRED TO MEDICAL EXAMINER/CORONER? Yes X

TIME OF DEATH: 6:40 A
DATE PRONOUNCED DEAD: APR 3, 1989

PART I. CAUSE: CARCINOMA of Lung with Metastasis

MANNER OF DEATH: Natural X

WERE AUTOPSY FINDINGS AVAILABLE PRIOR TO COMPLETION OF CAUSE OF DEATH? No X

SIGNATURE AND TITLE OF CERTIFIER: James C. F. Rotenhaver MONTOUR Co. CORONER
DATE SIGNED: Apr. 3, 1989
NAME AND ADDRESS OF PERSON WHO COMPLETED CAUSE OF DEATH: James C. F. Rotenhaver R.D. #4, Box 240 Danville, Pa. 17821

DATE FILED: April 4, 1989

REGISTRAR'S SIGNATURE AND NUMBER: Maye L. Kelly   122

Mamie Anderson

James & Beulah Batdorf

Thomas batford's sister Elizabeth

Patricia, Retta, Bud, Mamie, Ethel, Irvin & Harry Duncan

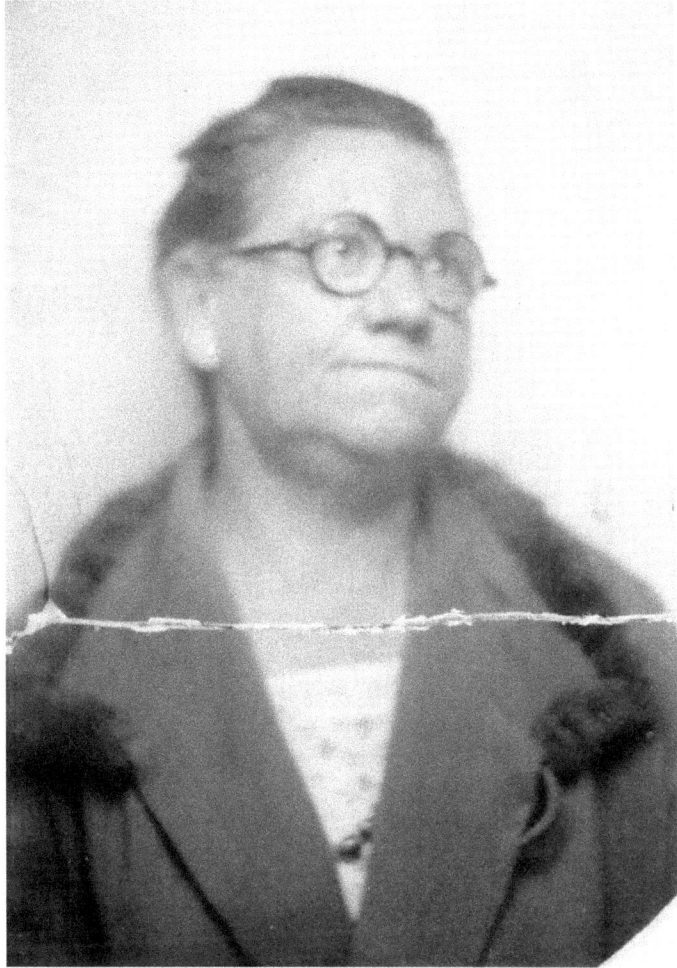

William Duncan's sister Melinda

Abel & Gussie Thompson's home

Harper Thompson

Robert Thompson's brother James and family

Abel Thompson

Gussie & Lydia Thompson

Thomas Livesay house

John & Adeline Wert

Magdalena Brown's niece, Mary Ann Miller

Emma Keefer

James Keefer

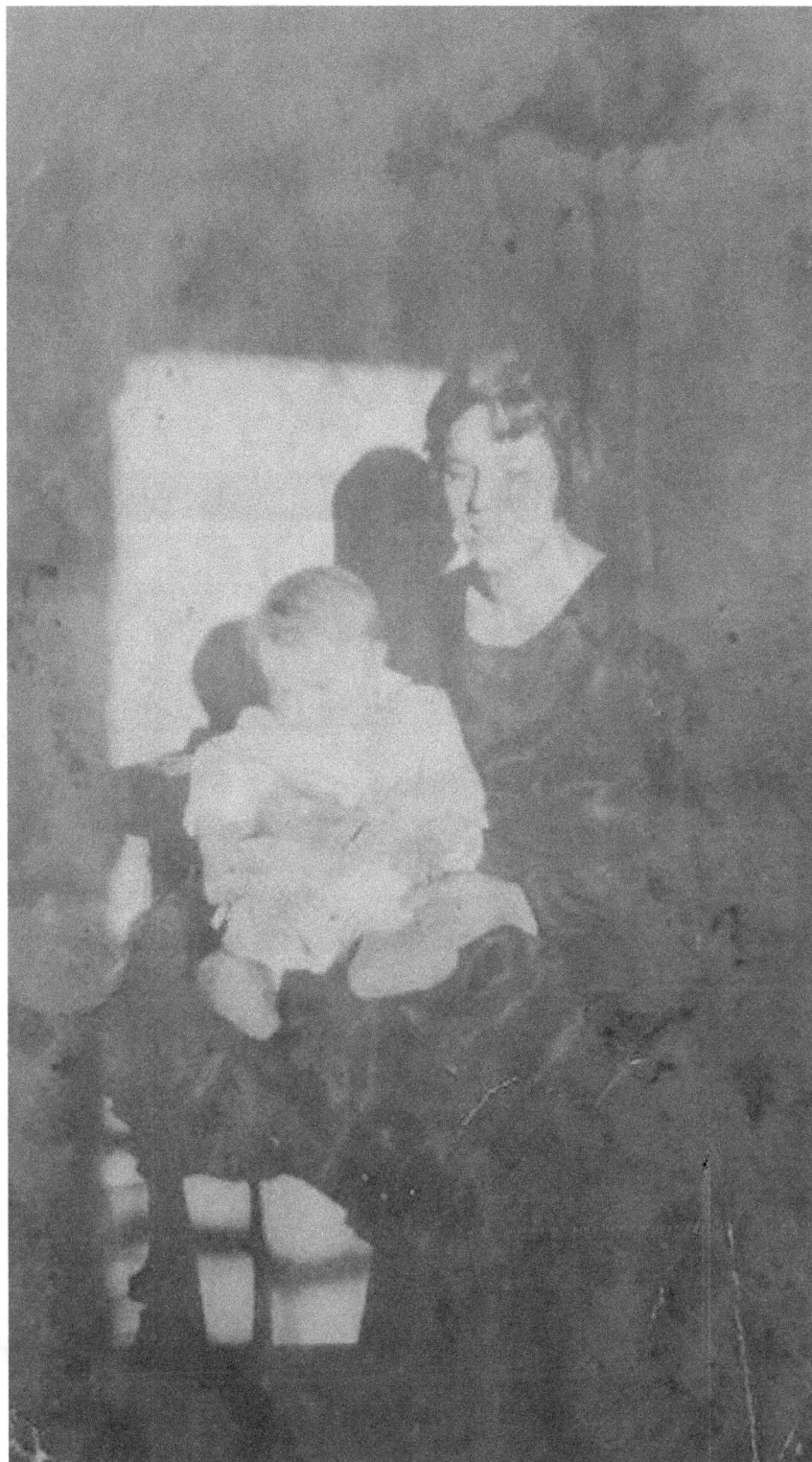

Emma Keefer and grandson Bud Duncan

Florence Malone, Bertha Johnston, Harry Matheny and David Malone
←

Mary Overlander Johnston

Mary Overlander Johnston, Sue McKeown, Bertha Johnston, Florence
←

Viola & Florence Johnston →

Mary Overlander Johnston
↑

Vi

Viola, Dorothy,
Florence, Ruth

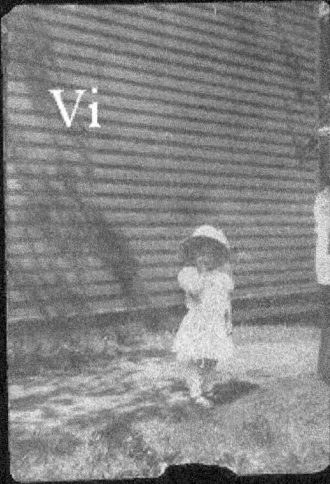

Bertha holding Florence, Edith
with Herbert Matheny, 1909

Florence &
Herbert 1912

Ruth B.,
Florence J.,
Tenevien K.

Harry W. Matheny

Lycurgas Johnston & Mary
Overlander Johnston

Michael Layman at York Furnace

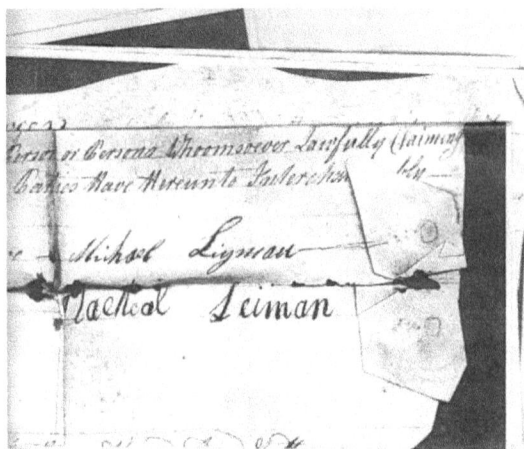

Michael & Rachel Layman

Anna Kent Livezly burial ground

Sarah Culp, Gussie Hensel, Clara Updegrove and child Harper Thompson

John and Esther Culp

Kesiah Kelly's brother Uriah

Kesiah Kelly's sister Caroline

CITATIONS

See the end of Volume 2 for the sources for our research. Thank you for your interest!

* 9 7 8 1 9 4 5 3 7 6 1 1 5 *